Responses in Responsibility

Flanders' architectural policy is lauded the world over. The *Architecture Yearbook* (now *Flanders Architectural Review*), at its launch in 1994, was one of the first instruments to highlight this achievement. This series of biennial publications is now a splendid tradition. The stories about architecture in Flanders are always keenly anticipated. And they are rich and polyphonic.

Subjects include approaches to heritage, climate-proofing our living environment, innovation and how we form a community. The stories also point to the social role of architects and their innovative insights and proposals on bioclimatic design, the reuse of existing buildings and how we live, work and relax.

Governments have always been committed clients in Flanders and Brussels. Our heritage bears witness to tradition and vision. Architectural quality is not just the result of superlative work by outstanding designers. It is also a choice on the clients' part. Public and private clients in Flanders have consistently proven themselves to be ambitious builders over the past two decades. They understand that quality architecture transcends the fulfilment of present-day needs. Clients want to contribute sustainably to long-term cohabitation.

Several examples of committed and ambitious commissioning can be found in this book. The creation of such opportunities is one of the key strengths of Flanders' current architectural policy. With it, we command international admiration and respect.

I am delighted that many buildings in this book have arisen through intensive collaborations between designers, clients and society. Several challenges we face together, such as reducing our ecological footprint, making our cities more intelligent and living more compactly with equal quality of life for all, have a spatial dimension.

This sixteenth edition of the *Flanders Architectural Review* not only showcases a marvellous array of exemplary projects, but also makes an appeal to us all. In this way, we can continue to collectively write Flanders' fascinating architectural story. A tale of which we can all be proud.

Jan Jambon

Minister-president of the Government of Flanders and Flemish Minister for Foreign Affairs, Culture, ICT and Facility Management

Responses in Responsibility

*Our times require a different,
less familiar type of thinking about responsibility.*[1]

Attempts to articulate architectural quality come and go, are often subjective and are always tethered to their time. This book is no different. Preparations began with the editorial board's call for submissions in June 2023. The editors' standpoint was clear from the outset. Anyone submitting a project had to also provide a critical insight into how it responded to social and environmental crises and how it navigated between regulations, ecological engagement, building conventions and economic constraints. The editors also emphasized their eagerness to hear about projects that question the typical relationships between clients, architects, builders, material suppliers, local residents and non-human organisms.

More than 300 projects were submitted in response to the call. The editorial board scrutinized and discussed them all. From the plans, photos and texts received, some 100 projects were selected for viewing. These were visited by at least two members of the editorial team, with many being seen by the entire board. This intensive process led to a multilayered and comprehensive overview of the projects. The visits not only yielded vital information about the programmes under consideration, but also contributed to the selection framework that the editorial team was actively constructing.

Carefulness

The project submissions all speak to the conditions in which architecture is created today. They are barometers of global, European and local evolutions. The scarcity of building materials and corresponding increase in costs, exacerbated by international conflicts, is keenly felt. Hybrid forms of living and working seem to have become more permanent in the post-pandemic world. This blurring of boundaries, both physical and mental, gives rise to new design briefs. Population growth in Flanders and Brussels, coupled with the need to preserve open areas, necessitates densification and the multifunctional use of space. These issues are not new, but their urgency is growing rapidly. Designers are exhorted to tackle them: to avoid encroaching on open terrain; to reduce impermeable paving; to work with circular, ethically sourced and energy-efficient materials from short production and transport chains; to support flora and fauna; to promote social inclusion; and to repair and improve historical, albeit problematic, buildings and spatial configurations. These are challenging and far-reaching tasks for architecture, all of which demand a multifaceted approach.

Carefulness was a recurrent attitude displayed by the designers and clients in the projects shortlisted by the editors. This carefulness extended to all users and parties involved, from establishing the project definition to obtaining planning permission and execution. The care that the editorial team experienced in the projects can be linked to the critical concept of caring architecture developed by feminist thinkers from the 1990s. At the highest level, caring architecture means taking responsibility for protecting our planet, a quality that makes itself felt in even the tiniest details. This translates into both caring for existing buildings, with an emphasis on respect and restoration, and caring for human and non-human users, now and in the future.[2]

A caring attitude also shines a spotlight on the 'shadow clients', a concept developed by environmental psychologist Adeola Enigbokan to embrace the parties who do not have a seat at the decision-making table.[3] Alongside the human, financial, material and ecological costs of a project, an expanded vision of caring also considers the democratic nature of decision-making processes. These broadened perspectives featured in the editorial team's discussions of the projects they viewed. Our deliberations went far beyond material outcomes to include usage and the mechanisms through which the programmes arose. We attempted to gauge the true social added value that the projects achieved.

Collaborative process

Within design offices, architecture workers with a diverse range of expertise drive projects forward together; when these are implemented, the input of professionals with a wealth of different specialisms is critical to achieving good results. Furthermore, the role of clients, future users and a midfield of government architects, quality advisory boards and municipal development firms is crucial. In architectural theory and criticism, there is a growing consciousness that architecture should be discussed as what it actually is, a collaborative project.

Indeed, the origins of many of the projects in this book lie with public and private clients who initiate construction schemes with devotion and a sense of responsibility. They are courageous and dare to do things differently. Some have been supported by engaged civil servants, quality advisory boards and municipal real-estate firms; others have acted out of an almost intuitive sense that market-driven solutions will not enable their project to contribute to a more inclusive, ecological and socially just society. In so doing, they far exceeded the bounds of traditional commissioning; their vision of responsibility also extended to animals and plants, vulnerable social groups and pre-existing spatial configurations. While we encountered many inspiring stories of exemplary clients whose projects went above and beyond their briefs to benefit society, our journeys along Flemish roads and through village centres revealed that, more often than not, things tend to go wrong rather than right. We found that the stakes are too high, and the interplay between client and architect too fragile, to tackle major challenges. Revitalizing the architectural community in Flanders, in terms of both raising awareness and supporting local authorities and clients, remains a difficult task.

Widening the lens also poses a challenge to how project authorship is elaborated in this book. It shifts the focus from the singular designer to a collaborative process. The focus on cooperation dramatically expands our conventional understanding of the architect's role. Indeed, designers perform multiple functions, often simultaneously. There are times when they act as policymakers (in full view or behind the scenes), and others when they become activists or botanists or when they steer participation schemes. Very often, they are directors of complex processes and mediate between divergent interests. Or they play the role of bridge builders: between experts in all manner of fields, users, clients' social and cultural ambitions, and regulatory frameworks. At other times, they are product developers, interior architects or specialists in sustainability and material science. In this multifocal perspective, architects navigate between these roles and their underlying responsibilities while actively creating a project. This requires considerable social and intellectual agility, which largely comes into play within a team context.

The shifting and multifaceted role of the architect is obviously consistent with the multilayered nature of architecture itself. As a result, the design can transcend false dilemmas. After all, many ambitions initially seem contradictory: circular construction while meeting the current building standards; affordable living versus preservation of the existing open space; appreciating the surviving heritage while creating climate-resilient buildings; and so on. The projects in this book prove that designers can excel at rethinking questions and reformulating problems. Good design can go beyond the complex interplay of forces. It is evident that architects have a unique role to play: they rise to the immense challenges of our time by creating concrete, experiential, meaningful and habitable living spaces. Within the framework of the project, they connect the large and abstract with the small and eminently tangible. Designing is not problem-solving, therefore, but synthesis: the capacity of design to transcend the sum of its parts.

The responsibility reveals itself in the responses

Architecture is never made in clear-cut conditions. The latter involve complex entanglements of social, economic, cultural, spatial and ecological factors. These have local manifestations, but are also part of larger force fields, which might be regional or even global. The published projects enter into a dialogue with these conditions. They offer a response but without stalling the discussion. The projects are a force for renewal, one that is expressed through the installation of new social and economic connections, the strengthening of cultural narratives, and for some – sadly, all too rarely still – the active fostering of ecological diversity. In this sense, they are regenerative.[4] The architectural response to the conditions reveals the responsibility shouldered by the architects. Donna Haraway used the concept of 'response-ability'[5] as an indicator of the ability to deal with today's ecological, ethical and social issues. This capacity to 'responsibly answer' always departs from the interdependence between people, and between humans and other living organisms. It comes with an openness and curiosity about the others and their needs, and dares to question everyday normative 'ways of doing'. The projects in this book all demonstrate the capacity to respond responsibly to the conditions of this era. The interleaving essays take a more detailed look at the subsidiary aspects of this capacity. The texts form pairs, each of which focuses on a specific theme.

Els Nulens and Petrus Kemme unfold several inspiring stories about the interplay between client and architect. Nulens illuminates how deep a client's engagement can be, and the enriching spatial, ecological and social impact that can be achieved when a client has the courage to colour outside the lines. Kemme was fascinated by special alliances between clients and architects on a compact, private scale. He sheds light on the social and cultural added value that these forms of 'small entrepreneurship' can generate, but also points out the limits of the model.

Carlo Menon sees the role of the architect shift from that of author, who fills a blank page, to editor, who works with existing material. The latter must embrace the complexity of the situation they find themselves in, just one player in a complicated power game. Menon shows that architecture has an innate ability to deal with the unexpected and the uncertain, and with commissions that are constantly evolving. Sofie De Caigny also regards this paradigm shift – from tabula rasa to a radical acceptance of what presents itself – as an interesting springboard for architects who seek a meaningful approach to current challenges. Like Menon, she sees qualities in projects that are established as iterative processes that are not time-bound but take time itself as a raw material. She advocates appreciation of restraint and subtlety.

Architecture is not only determined by external conditions but also by those within the professional field. These have been an explicit part of the social debate for the past two years. Spearheaded by a group of young architects on the one hand and a series of female voices in the professional field on the other, themes such as fair practices, gender balance and diversity have recently and emphatically taken centre stage in the architecture debate in Flanders and Belgium. Vjera Sleutel and Evelien Pieters have both written reflective essays on these subjects in which they critically analyse, respectively, the precarious position of young architects and the lack of diversity among members of the profession. For the first time, we also communicate the gender balance and the ages of the architectural workers in the firms whose projects are published in this book. These numbers provide an initial behind-the-scenes insight into the conditions in which architecture in Flanders and Brussels is made.

Klaske Havik and Saar Meganck were often struck by the power of the design thinking behind several of the projects they visited. Many offered incredibly relevant responses to urgent topical issues. Havik meticulously unravels, across three projects, how architecture can respond to the given social and spatial context by departing from the concepts of 'connecting', 'grounding' and 'improvising'. Meganck acknowledges the ways in which the careful treatment of people, materials, time, space and resources can steer a design. Through an analysis of specific projects, she argues that the greater the architect's engagement – with the commission, context and user –, the easier it will be for them to make good decisions when faced with tough choices. It is thanks to this involvement that these choices become generous.

Climate change and the shortage of housing are perennial fixtures of the public debate. Here too, the question arises as to how architects can deal with these issues. Petrus Kemme and Sofie De Caigny gathered a panel of experts for a multidimensional discussion about the housing crisis. They linked the outcomes of this debate to a number of striking residential construction projects visited during the compilation of this book. Dennis Pohl unravels architecture's ability to create a built environment that is climate-resilient. He sketches how in recent history, sustainability has all too often been reduced to measurable achievements within an object-based approach. Rooted in an analysis of several recently completed projects from Flanders and Brussels, he shows that this approach is too limiting and that true architectural sustainability goes much further.

The editorial board's discussions focused, from the outset, on the burning issues of today: democracy, the housing shortage, climate and ecology, and justice. The question was always, What is the architect's responsibility? Hülya Ertas concludes this book with an essay on the political significance of architecture and the accountability that lies therein. She advocates having the courage to make radical choices in favour of care, generosity and beauty.

This publication is a snapshot of the architecture in Flanders and Brussels. Thanks to how the book is compiled – a call for submissions, an analysis of 300 projects, followed by intensive site visits and discussions between editorial members from various disciplines –, its potential extends far beyond an inventory of good projects. Aware of this fact, the editors aspire for the book to also play a role in the further development of the professional field. It does this by making explicit the role it plays in the urgent quest for architectural relevance and responsibility vis-à-vis the current conditions. The editors thus embrace the meaning that Bruno Latour attached to objects with agency: we want this book to be an agent that speaks for 'the other', for all those who are overlooked in these kinds of publications.

The echo chamber of architecture is sorely lacking in diversity. Quality is typically determined and assessed from a one-sided viewpoint, namely by other architects and a select group of critics. As editors, we are aware of this fact. For this reason, we sought to transcend the image of the finished project and, in so doing, to consciously broaden the quality-defining echo chamber. This was achieved by listening, wherever possible, to the clients' voices. We also considered the democratic calibre of the projects, with respect to procedure, preparatory process, dialogue and intangible meanings. This is the lens through which we viewed the collaborative dimension and collective intelligence of each project. Of course, further steps can be taken in this vein by questioning a wider group of users about their experiences with the projects. We subsequently invited six photographers – Kimberley Dhollander, Farah Fervel, Delphine Mathy, Nick Moons, Illias Teirlinck and Laura Vleugels – to present, from an anthropological perspective, how life plays out in the selected buildings. In so doing, we act as circuit breakers on the control that architects exert over the visualization of their projects. To increase the contrast, the photographers' self-initiated shots are largely reproduced in black and white. The photographic content thus responds to the design of the book by atelier Haegeman Temmerman, which makes creative use of finite means, like the architecture within.

In words and images, we show that the projects in this book manoeuvre between systemic crises and practical everyday solutions. The projects illustrate how architecture has a role to play on both a small and large scale, and still more in the connection between these extremes. The editors do not focus on perfection as a sublime endpoint. We did choose projects that show what can be accomplished, despite all obstacles and imperfections. In this sense, they are all beacons of hope: their liveability proclaims that a rethinking of values is possible.

Sofie De Caigny and Dennis Pohl,
on behalf of the editorial board

1   Lydia Baan Hofman, 'Immanent Obligations of Response: Articulating Everyday Response-Abilities through Care', *Distinktion: Journal of Social Theory* (June 2023): 1–18.
2   Joan C. Tronto, 'Caring Architecture', in *Critical Care: Architecture for a Broken Planet*, ed. Fitz Angelika and Krasny Elke (Cambridge, MA and Vienna: MIT Press and AzW, 2019), 26–32.
3   Adeola Enigbokan, lecture, 6 February 2024 at Platform Architectuur en Feminisme. See www.paf.community/verslag/video-adeola-enigbokan-on-the-shadow-client-and-participatory-architecture-practices.
4   Sarah Ichiola and Michael Pawlyn, *Flourish: Design Paradigms for Our Planetary Emergency* (Charmouth: Triarchy Press, 2022).
5   Donna Haraway, *Staying with the Trouble: Making Kin in the Chthulucene* (Durham, NC: Duke University Press, 2016), 2.

ATAMA

PROJECT

Deelfabriek, Kortrijk

10

The former fire station in Kortrijk is a beacon in the city. The building is a model of modernist architecture. A low, rounded wing embraces the street corner and contrasts with the tower volume and stairwell, which mark the corner as an elegant, vertical element. The long horizontal windows stand out in the dark brick façades. The station was built in 1940 and listed as a monument in 2004.

The building has been repurposed as a meeting place where city, civic and neighbourhood initiatives meet in a 'Deelfabriek'. This 'sharing factory' was an existing city project, launched in 2017, that brought together various citizen initiatives while providing support to vulnerable families. The urban project is a model of the sharing economy. Soon after it was founded, however, the organization was already bursting at the seams and a move to the redeveloped fire station was prepared.

The large front hall is used as a central entrance and houses a social restaurant. Neighbourhood activities also take place here. The hall gives access to a new courtyard, which opens up the former stands of the fire engines. Some of those stands have been dismantled and transformed into outdoor rooms, bright and airy. The stands on the long wall of the courtyard have been converted into retail spaces for volunteer initiatives, each with its own entrance to the courtyard under a newly constructed gallery.

PROJECT **Deelfabriek**

situation plan 0 10 50

04

The design shows great architectural sensitivity. The team handled the existing building and the requirements of the users with particular care. They managed to strike a balance between making the most of the building's existing qualities, on the one hand, and a measured demolition and new additions, on the other. The front was soberly restored. The striking tower was fitted with a new work of light art that communicates with a series of other buildings in the city and pays tribute to the light architecture of the interwar period. Displayed above the entrances to the retail spaces in the courtyard are the names of the respective associations in illuminated letters which tie in with the curved light artwork in the tower. Around the new courtyard, the remaining fragments of the old fire station and the parapet above the colonnade are clad in polished metal strips that reflect their surroundings. These mirrored reflections are a source of confusion as much as of amusement.

05

PROJECT **ATAMA**

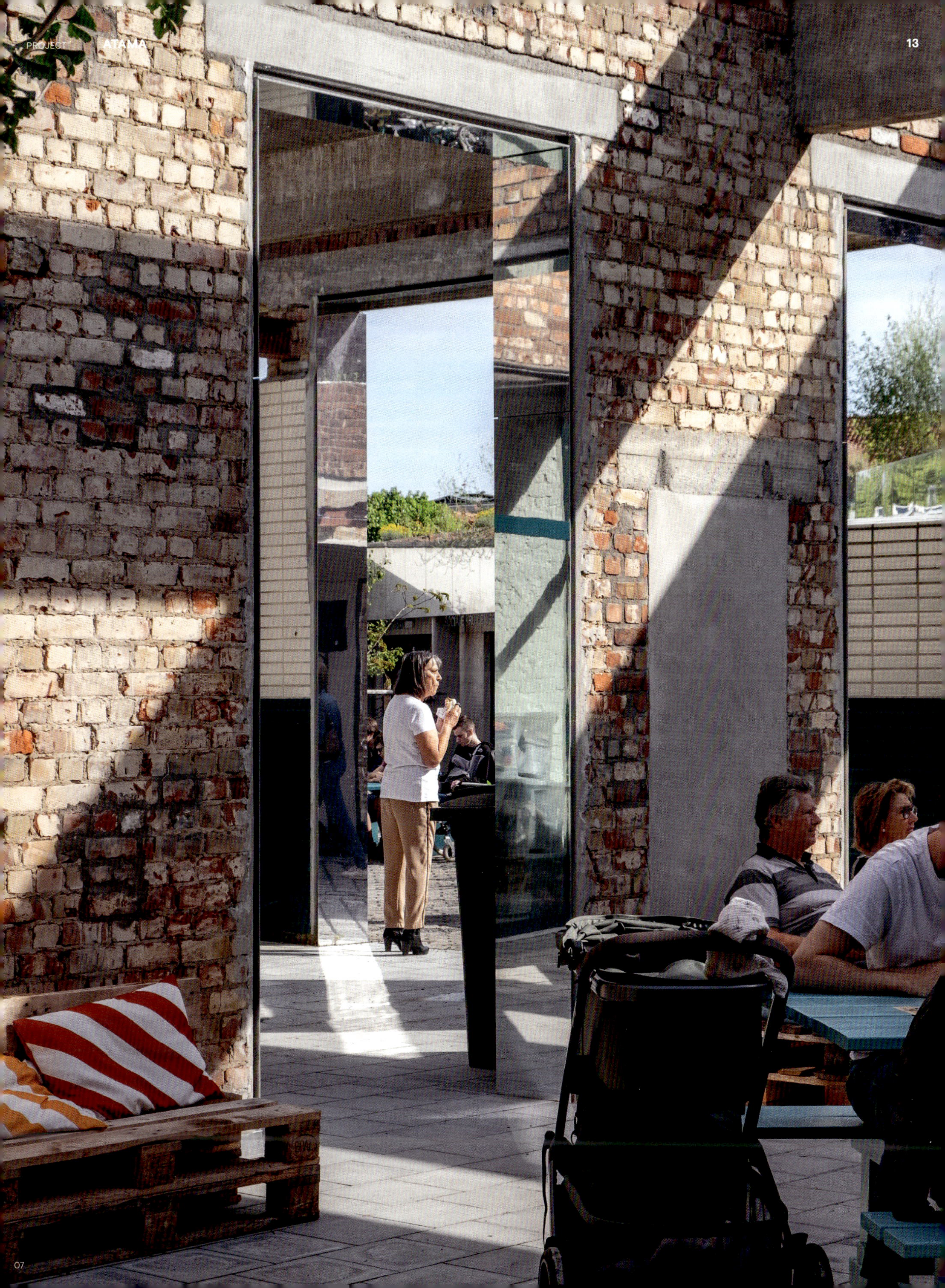

PROJECT **Deelfabriek** 14

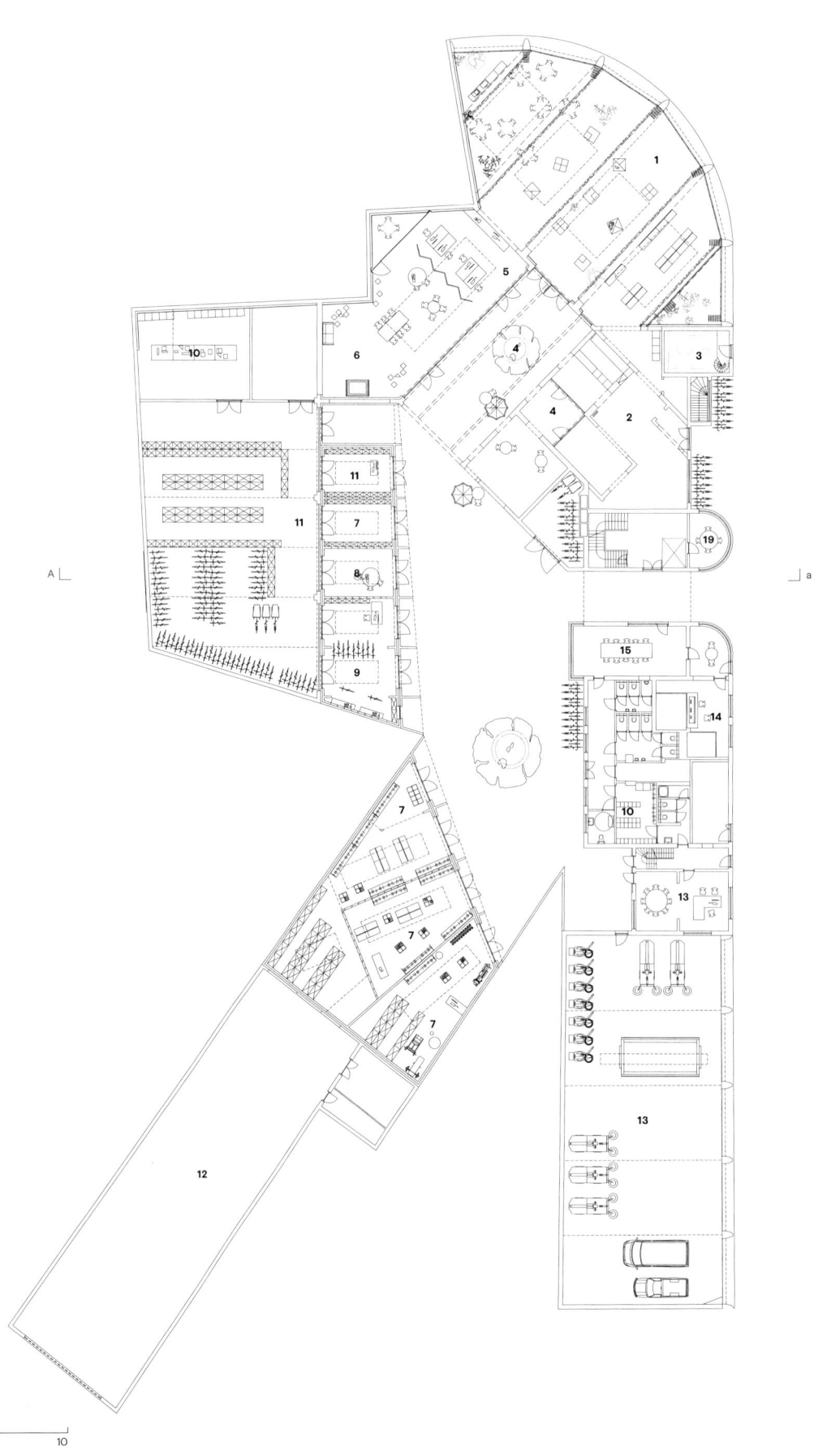

ground floor
1 market hall, **2** Swop & Go, **3** climbing tower, **4** garden room, **5** reception, **6** games library, **7** citizens' initiative, **8** instruments library, **9** bicycle kitchen, **10** collective workshop, **11** collective warehouse, **12** food distribution De Vaart, **13** Nette Stad, **14** audiobooks recording studio, **15** meeting room

PROJECT **Deelfabriek** 15

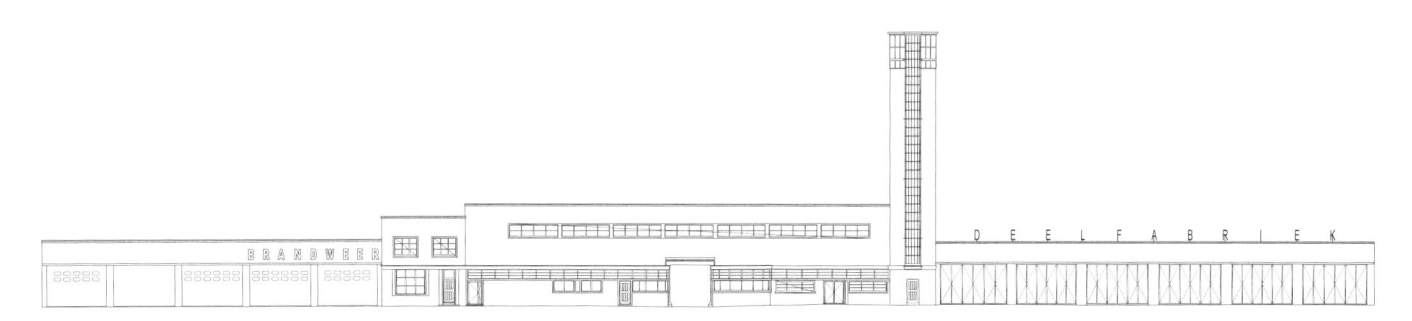

street façade

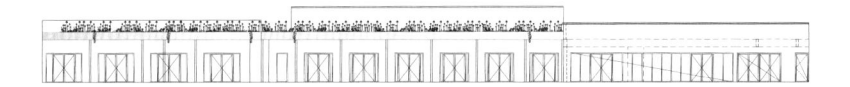

garden wall

section Aa 0 2 10

text
Els Nulens
photography
01, 06-08 © Farah Fervel
02-03, 05 © Stijn Bollaert
04 © Jelle Segers

project Deelfabriek **office** ATAMA **design team** Bram Aerts, Carolien Pasmans, Robin Cuvelier, Michiel Weekers, Sara Verstraete **website** www.atama.website **address** Rijkswachtstraat 5, 8500 Kortrijk **client** City of Kortrijk **awarded via** competition **design** June 2020 **completion** September 2023 **surface area** 3,300m² **volume** 26,500m³ **total building cost** €3,097,060 excl. VAT **total building cost per m²** €938 excl. VAT **main contractor** BOUW-TEC, Rekkem **art integration** Sandra E. Blatterer, Vienna (Austria) **stability studies** BDA Engineering, Wetteren **EPB and engineering studies** Studieburo De Klerck, Bruges **acoustics studies** Bureau De Fonseca, Waregem **safety coordination** Vecobo, Waregem

PROJECT   ATAMA

PROJECT **murmuur architecten**

PROJECT # De Ringelwikke primary school, Ronse

A newly established Steiner school stands on Ronse's border with Wallonia. The school wanted to embrace the rural surroundings of the Flemish Ardennes. The suitable location for this was found in a former disused inn on the road to Ellezelles. The extensive yard merges at the back into the relatively untouched hilly landscape.

murmuur designed the school within the U-shaped footprint of the inn to preserve and enhance its farmstead-like character (and to stay within the terms of the subsidies). Downstairs, the main building houses a gymnasium / refectory with kitchen, equipped to be used on occasion by third parties. Above that, classrooms stack up to the distinctive roof form. Deep-red wooden galleries on pastel-green steel columns make the classrooms accessible from outside. They connect to an external staircase that links all floors. In the wing, the administration is accessible between the inner courtyard, the side entrance and the yard behind the school. At the back, a multipurpose room has been 'raised', as it were – the end resting on the sanitary facilities – to create a gateway to the unpaved playground.

The architecture exudes the ethos of the school – 'Steiner goes rural' – from the structural level to that of detail. The building faces outwards, a framework within which pupils can move freely and be stimulated. For instance, the exterior circulation is robust enough to handle an excess of dirty boots, but refined in the way

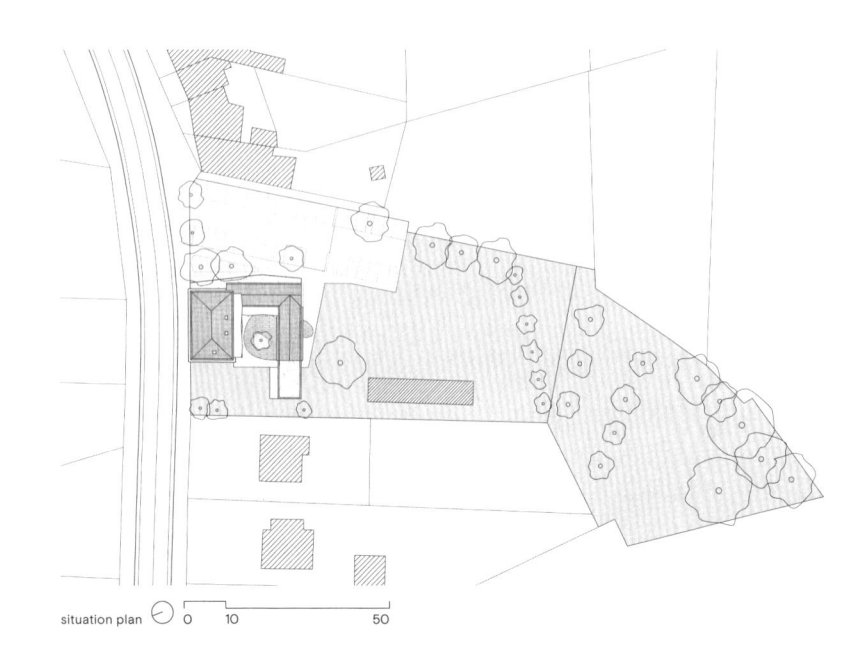

situation plan 0 10 50

PROJECT   **De Ringelwikke primary school**   19

the balustrade threads its way through the columns. The avoidance of straight lines is a deliberate motif, one which recurs in slightly curved ceilings and the Dutch truss. It is a nice place for children to grow up and develop in, as the huge demand also shows. The logical next step – to turn the school into a square-shaped farmstead – is already on the horizon, as soon as the necessary authorities and resources manage to keep up with the momentum of an ambitious school board.

PROJECT **murmuur architecten**

PROJECT **murmuur architecten**

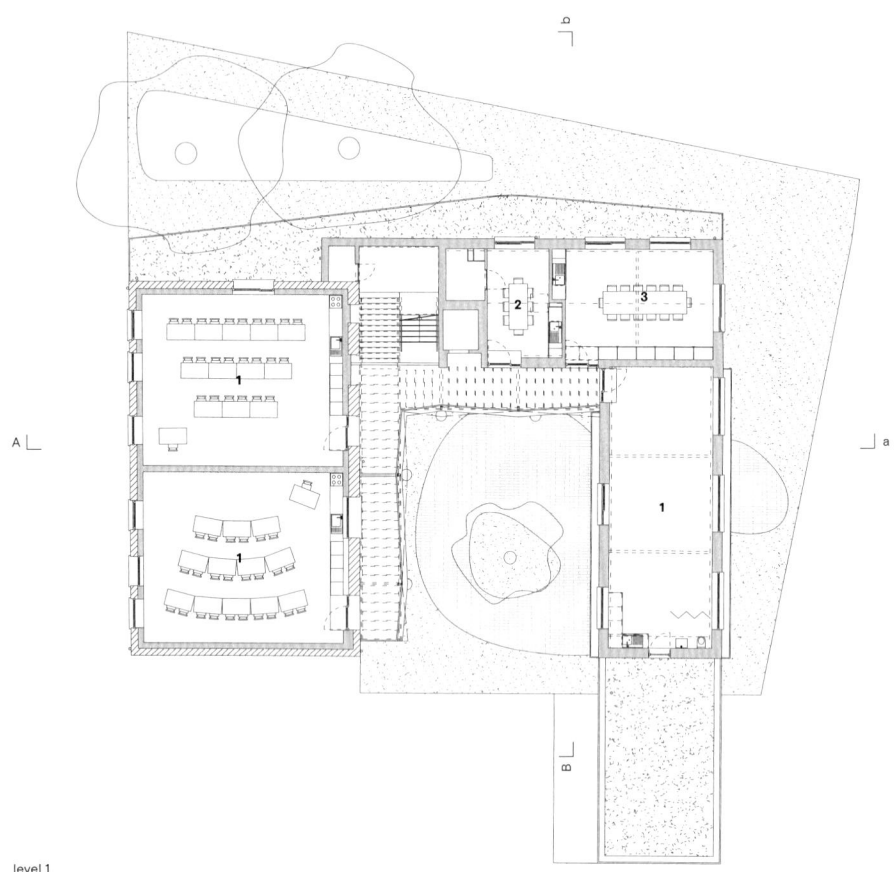

PROJECT **De Ringelwikke primary school** 22

level 1
1 classroom, **2** care space, **3** teachers' room

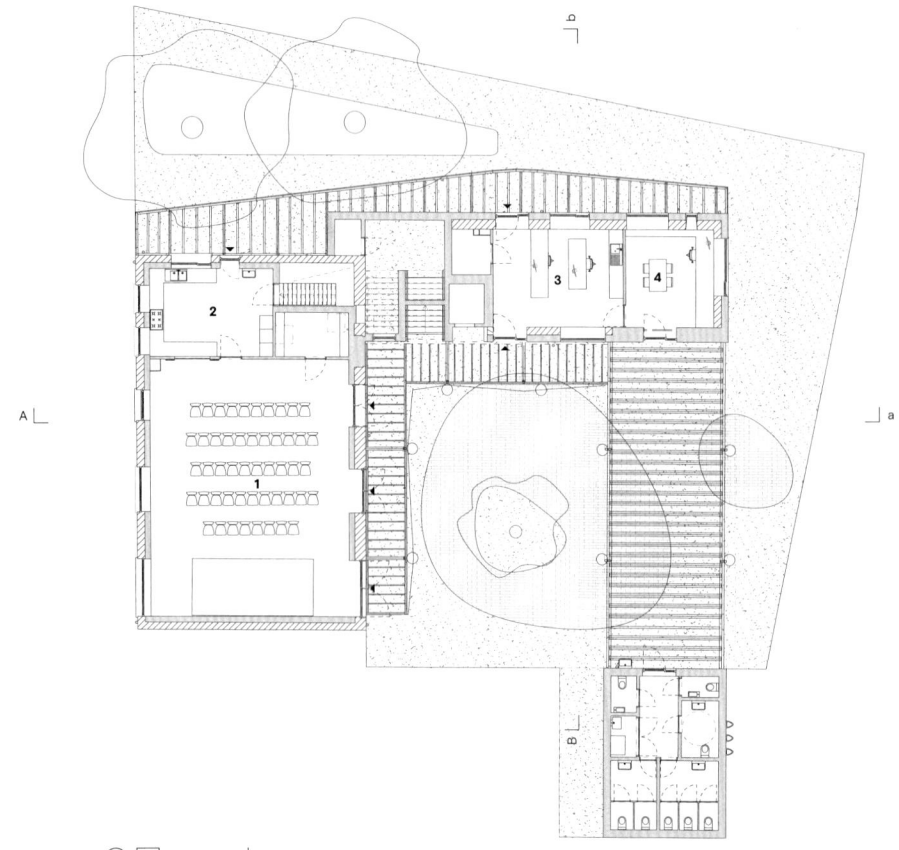

ground floor
1 multipurpose space, **2** kitchen, **3** reception and administration, **4** director's office

PROJECT **De Ringelwikke primary school** 23

section Aa

section Bb 0 1 5

text
Petrus Kemme
photography
01, 04-05, 07-09 © Laura Vleugels
02-03, 06 © Michiel De Cleene

project De Ringelwikke primary school **office** murmuur architecten
design team Loes Lonneville, Joana Martins, Pieter Vanderhoydonck **website** www.murmuur.eu
address Elzeelsesteenweg 647, 7890 Ronse **client** De Ringelwikke **design** December 2019
completion February 2023 **surface area** 2,456 m² **volume** 4,060 m³
total building cost €2,182,513 excl. VAT **total building cost per m²** €1,874 excl. VAT
main contractor Qubus, Aalter **stability studies** Stabimi, Zwalm **engineering studies** Thermiek, Leuven
EPB studies EMS, Deinze **safety coordination** VK-Robyn, Drongen

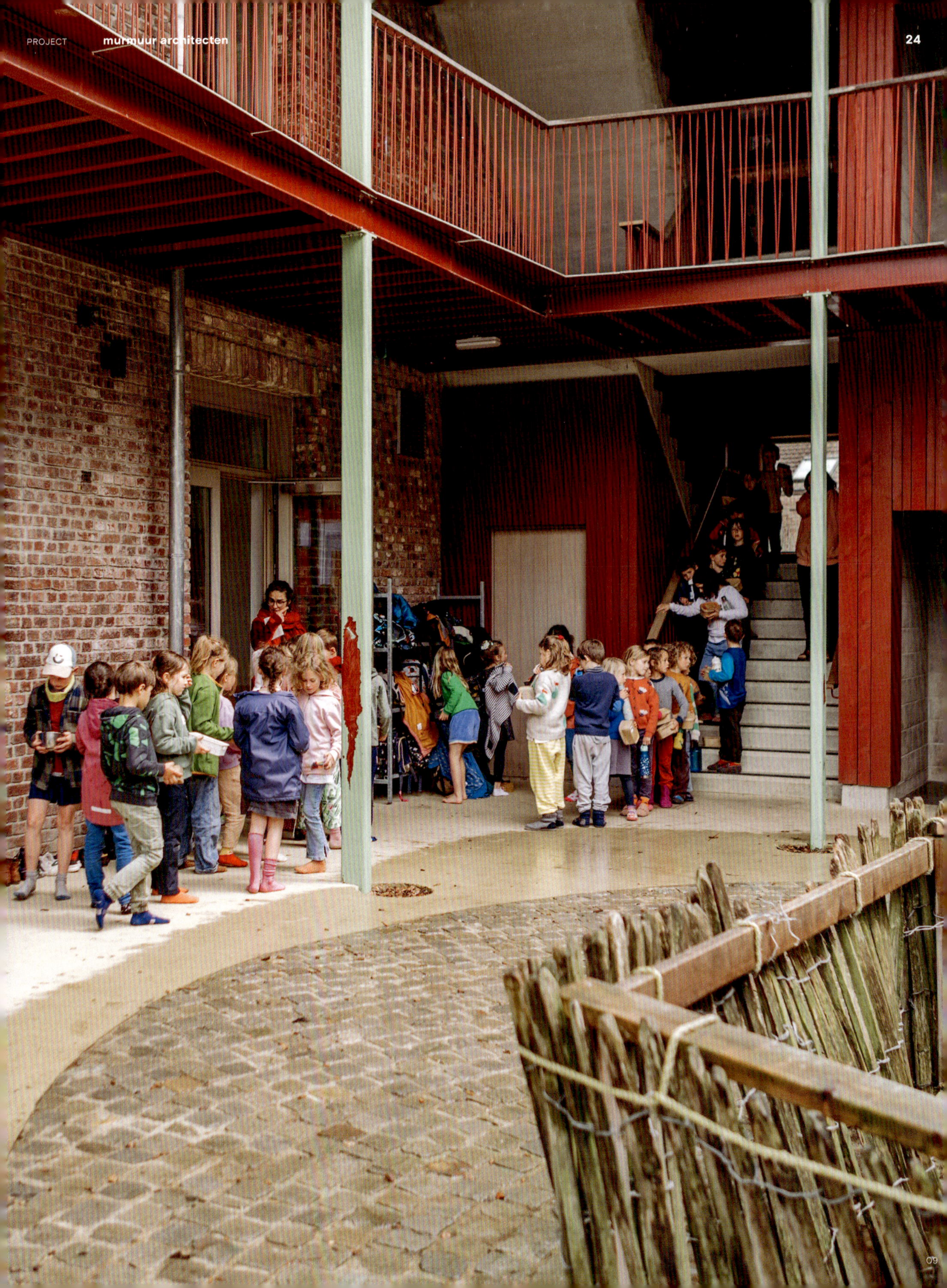

Socially Responsible and Fair Architecture

On the Importance of Social Commitment and Good Commissioning

Els Nulens

You cannot create high-quality architecture without tackling broader spatial and social issues. This is why our editorial team went looking for projects with distinct societal ambitions: projects that display an understanding and appreciation of the underlying spatial and ecological challenges, and that are based on groundbreaking processes but still acknowledge the importance of beauty. That desire to look at carefully designed, socially aware projects was voiced at our editorial board's very first meeting, and was then reflected in our call for submissions (see 'Editorial', p. 3).

At first sight, the submissions were perhaps not quite as explicitly radical as we had hoped. Still, we were able to visit projects whose approaches and attitudes I found highly commendable and that seem to chart an encouraging (new) path through the design landscape. These projects illustrate what an eye for design can lead to and, by extension, what designers are capable of. They bring new insights to the table and showcase a different and impassioned approach that is not only radically involved in society, but also radically committed to that involvement. They all led to architecture that is multilayered and does not stand alone. Architecture in which the eventual building is the material outcome of a thorough process, of carefully considered choices, explicit attention to the project's spatial context, and excellent work by real people.

A socially responsible approach

Spatial specifications and architecture have never been so complex. The reasons are manifold, including climate adaptation and sustainable energy, regulations, urbanization and spatial disarray, affordability and accessibility. Combined action is a prerequisite for the creation of spatial quality, beauty and fairness, but it can only be achieved when all parties join forces. Social responsibility is a key concept. Not just for policymakers, spatial planners, architects and other designers, but also users, neighbours and clients. Impassioned clients initiate carefully considered, holistic processes, which in turn create a more sustainable foundation for architecture.

Many of the selected projects displayed precisely this kind of enthusiasm and interaction – now in abundance, now almost imperceptibly. In all cases, however, both elements consistently proved crucial to the project. The trained eyes of designers and architects are also an essential part of a project's success. They can focus intently on specific details but simultaneously zoom outwards to seek answers to complex spatial puzzles. Through this process, apparent contradictions or impossibilities turn out to be reconcilable after all, and answers are often found beyond traditional frameworks and protocols imposed from outside. Architecture remains relevant today precisely because of this design-minded outlook and its quest for sustainable, innovative solutions.

In Aalbeke, a borough of Kortrijk, eighteen associations were rehoused in the existing community centre and the repurposed Church of St Cornelius. In 2016 urbain architectencollectief investigated ways of repurposing the church, in the context of the broader study assignment *Kerkenplan Kortrijk* (Church plan Kortrijk). Kortrijk's administrative department was simultaneously analysing the city's patrimony, with a view to rehoming Aalbeke's many local associations, which were scattered across the borough and sometimes occupied rather dilapidated premises. The analysis by the city authorities was already quite advanced, but mainly suggested keeping each

ESSAY   **Els Nulens**

ESSAY   **Els Nulens**

association in its current location, without any drastic operational changes. However, urbain immediately spotted a potential synergy between the church repurposing efforts and the patrimony study. The collective's designers managed to convince Kortrijk to pause the latter report and launch a new project instead, one that would merge the efforts to repurpose the church and rehouse Aalbeke's associations. When a call for tenders was announced, many firms responded, but urbain was the only one to submit nothing more than an approach rather than a specific spatial project. The collective had understood that solutions would only be successful if they were rooted in a conversation with the associations involved and that the best solutions would require getting them to think outside the box of their established locations and operations. Thus, urbain won the tender in February 2018 and this kick-started a consultative process within the city. With design research and architectural sketches in hand, the collective engaged in a dialogue with the associations as well as with the local church council and the authorities. The team managed to convince the local brass band, Harmonie van Aalbeke, to move to the community centre, for example, despite it having had its own venue and bar for as long as anyone could remember. When the band studied the drawings that highlighted the advantages of the prominent new location on the village's main square, it realized that the move could help it reach a new audience. Sharing a bar and sanitary facilities would also free up resources for things like improving the acoustics of the rehearsal space. Once the band was convinced of the benefits of a move, it participated in the rest of the process with a different attitude.

03

The old church was remodelled to accommodate a library, a rehearsal space for musicians and a meeting room, on top of a new liturgical space. The designers approached Aalbeke's local traditions with respect while demonstrating how to give them a new lease of life. The architecture collective not only redesigned and renovated the church, but also the community centre. It added an extension to improve accessibility and to give the village square an aesthetic facelift. The extension itself is rather humble – a nod to the historical worker's houses that once lined the square – but has a striking volume, and its large new windows frame the square in a contemporary way.

While process and leadership were of great importance in this project, the resulting architecture is anything but an afterthought. The architectural programme and spatial interventions go hand in hand, based on careful choices. Resources were spent to serve a functional purpose, but also to expressly create beauty. Nothing about the project to revamp the centre of Aalbeke was straightforward: every measure required hours of consultation, deliberation and piecing together. Somehow, however, magically the result appears entirely natural, as if the village had always looked this way.

project Church of St Cornelius and community centre **office** urbain architectencollectief **location** Aalbeke
see p. 37

As part of another project in Kortrijk, the city's listed fire station was repurposed and turned into a 'swap & share factory'. Lovingly restored, the former service building is now the new beating heart of the neighbourhood. The building adaptations were both modest and generous, sometimes even festive in their intent. The project's approach was tailored to the area and its economically vulnerable residents, who can now share and swap goods at the old fire station. Together with ATAMA, project manager Gudrun Verschueren approached the initiative with unwavering determination. The flexibility and spontaneity she exhibited throughout the trajectory are what make projects like this take off and fly. Through its dedicated public servant Verschueren, Kortrijk once again revealed itself to be a stellar client: one that embarks on an initiative with well-defined demands and then closely cooperates with the neighbourhood and the project's intended users. As in Aalbeke, Kortrijk's role as a client didn't end once the final brick was laid. The city authorities remain committed to the project, allowing the building to consistently achieve its underlying ambitions.

04

project Deelfabriek **office** ATAMA **location** Kortrijk see p. 9

In Schoten, meanwhile, the non-profit Anapneusis built a small-scale housing project for people who have experienced homelessness. Pol Hicguet was the driving force behind the scheme, a client who not only knows exactly what he wants but also inspires confidence. Bruno Spaas Architectuur was tasked with building the four studios. The client provided the firm with a (perhaps slightly too literal) definition of the project, which was based on the intended tenants' previous circumstances: they formerly occupied a run-down building on the same plot of land. The architect responded by suggesting a co-housing project instead, with four studios and a separate shared living space. The project is sparingly designed: there are no corridors in the house, and the external staircase and its landing, which lead to the three upper studios, are energy efficient. This allows the residents to interact but without it being an obligation. In this design, the client sees a translation of the residents' perceived needs: living together with just enough 'blank space', and in a compact layout.

Despite the project's budgetary constraints, the house was constructed in an ecologically intelligent way, because both client and architect were convinced that a 'healthy building' greatly improves the well-being of the residents. Circular materials such as chalk and hemp were used as insulation. The foundations contain shells to minimize the use of concrete, while the walls were plastered with clay. The entire building is heated with a heat pump, which is usually an expensive option. In this case, however, the client managed to renegotiate ▸

ESSAY **Els Nulens**

ESSAY **Els Nulens**

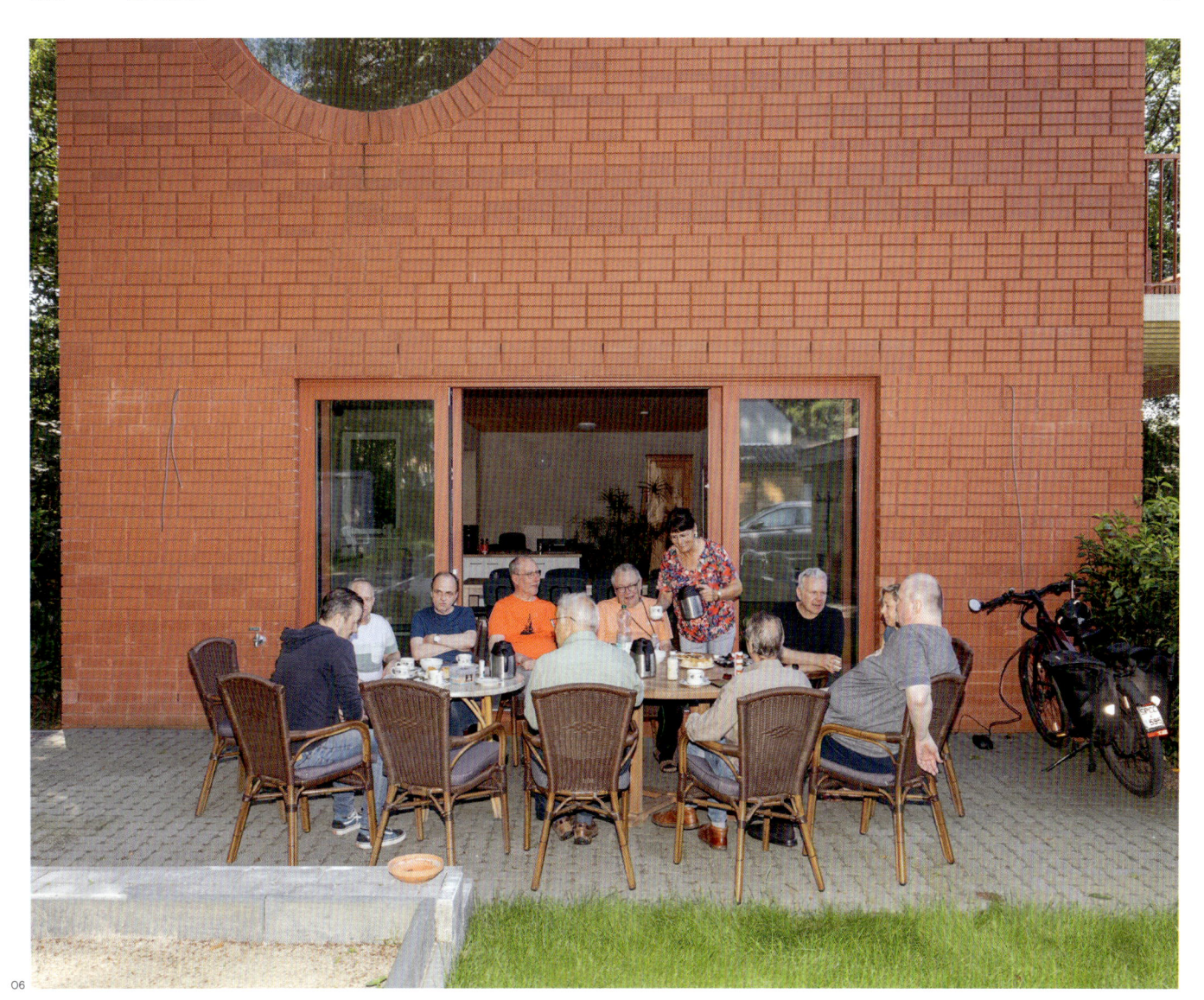

the cost with the pump manufacturer, who agreed to provide a (cheaper) test model. Seeing a modest non-profit achieve this level of ambition and quality is quite rare.

project Anapneusis community house
see p. 45
office Bruno Spaas Architectuur
location Schoten

Built on excellent commissioning

All the projects turned out to be rooted in excellent commissioning, whereby the process itself was given as much attention as the quality of the design. It may feel like good clientship has become something of a cliché these days, but its importance cannot be overemphasized. We repeatedly witnessed clients who not only express their commitment to society but also inspire and galvanize people. We were moved by their projects, which were fuelled by love, conscientiousness and social awareness. These are rare commodities in a society that seems increasingly driven by polarization and fear.

Michael De Herdt, head of the Ringelwikke school in Ronse, is a passionate individual and client. After many years spent teaching and working with troubled teens in Britain, he is convinced that education should lead the way rather than function as a corrective and that the school system can help to create a better world. Architecture has a role to play in this vision.

With the support of a group of parents and the school's teachers, De Herdt carefully drafted a project definition: after operating from container classrooms for three years, the school would be moved to a repurposed roadside inn in Ronse. The project was awarded to murmuur architecten, following a limited competition during which the applicants' approaches and draft spatial visions were assessed. The architect and client bonded over their shared belief that children deserve to spend their days in pleasant surroundings.

07

The inn's existing morphology was retained, but new facilities were built around the central courtyard. There is no circulation space in the building itself; instead, an open-air walkway connects the classrooms on the first and second floors. The client wanted to aim high – higher than the budget allowed, in fact, which forced the team to make choices. In close consultation with the client, the architect took some careful decisions. Some of the most eye-catching are the way every classroom has oak parquet flooring with underfloor heating; the fact that the façade and roof materials are pleasing to the eye and will age well; and the interesting contrast between the woven steel railing and solid brick building. All in all, the existing building was repurposed in a rational and well-balanced yet distinctive way.

project De Ringelwikke primary school
see p. 17
office murmuur architecten
location Ronse

A very different but equally thorough process lies at the heart of the M127 project in Antwerp, where the reuse of existing offices forms the basis of a renovated building. Marco Schoups' law firm was looking for a new home and advanced a series of ambitions that went far beyond 'a good office building'. As the client, Schoups wanted to strengthen the relationship between the building and the street. This led to the decision to recess the ground-floor façade, which created room for a surprisingly lofty gallery bordered by identical sculptural columns along the pavement. Moreover, by not designating an office function for the ground floor but instead seeking a manager for a coffee bar, an 'urban' pavement was created, where it is as pleasant to linger as it is to walk. Finally, the client also actively wanted to foster a close relationship with the neighbours. In careful dialogue with the church next door, a patch of open space was inserted between the two buildings. This sprinkling of greenery interrupts the street's solid line of façades. The church's storage and sanitary facilities were relocated, while its roof was turned into a shared solar-power farm. Rainwater is collected and used to flush both the church's new toilets and those of the law firm.

08

Perhaps the most distinctive feature of the project, however, is that it is a *Gesamtkunstwerk*, created not by a single designer but rather by a team of architects (the firms ono architectuur and Universal Design Studio), artist Philip Aguirre y Otegui, landscape architect Ludovic Devriendt, and the client, all of whom engaged in close dialogue with each other as they worked on the project during the pandemic (2020–21). Every actor was consulted about every decision, regardless of whether it fell within their discipline. The different players' curious but respectfully critical attitude towards each other resulted in a cross-pollination that left spatially observable traces. The multilayered nature of the project, its compilation of a unique colour palette, its blend of rough structures and refined finishings, and even the building's interaction with the pavement and the wider city all make for a convincing result.

project M127 office building with public plinth Ludovic Devriendt and Universal Design Studio
office ono architectuur with Philip Aguirre y Otegui, **location** Antwerp see p. 53

One notable aspect of all these projects is that their participatory nature does not pander to trends or obligations: it is a symbol of genuine communication and partnership. The M127 project team's dialogue with the neighbours truly focused on creating a better building – involving the neighbourhood was not a mechanism for speeding up the planning permission process. The fact that the pupils of the nearby music school hold their end-of-year concerts in the law firm's lobby, or that the church's priest agreed to let the adjacent lot be remodelled, all contributed to the project. The architects themselves mentioned that such an in-depth, multi-actor design trajectory is unusual for them, but felt it had led to a more interesting and refreshingly different result.

The same is true in Aalbeke: the associations may not have received exactly what they envisaged, but they were all meticulously consulted and involved. Engaging them in the process helped the team to understand what to prioritize, which in turn led to greater understanding and sped up the process. Because the associations are now the de facto users of the renovated community centre, their contributions will have a positive impact on the future use of the place and building. Participative cooperation between designers and clients, but also neighbours and users, truly bears fruit and helps to secure long-term commitment.

ESSAY Els Nulens

ESSAY   **Els Nulens**

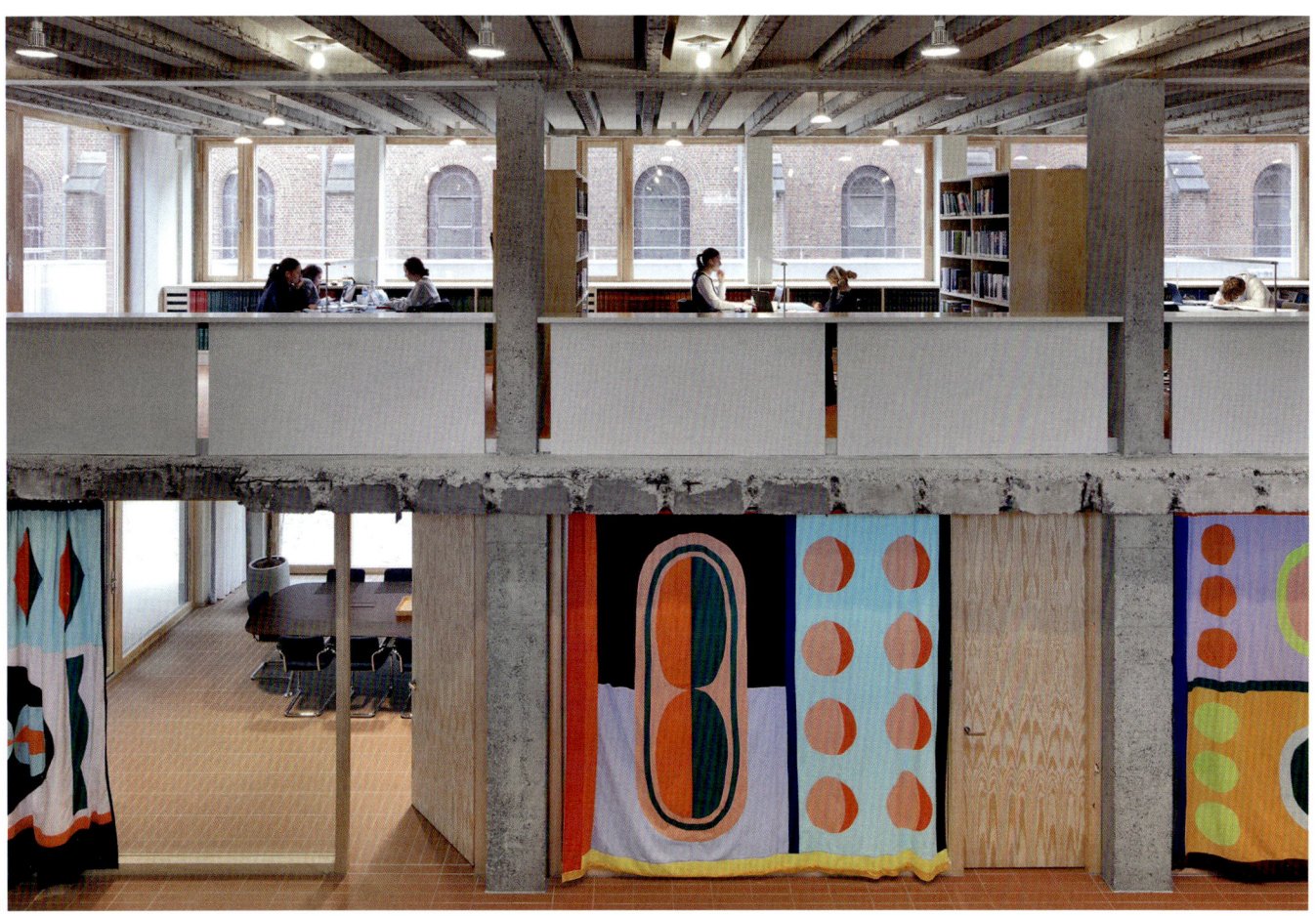

Architecture is a human effort. Underlying it are complex processes with fascinating and often highly interactive collaborations. These processes cannot always be planned, or even clearly traced in retrospect. Just like in any design project, there are moments of pure magic. Architectural processes are intricately intertwined with the innate chemistry of human relationships. One thing is clear: they benefit greatly from commitment and enthusiasm.

photography
01, 03, Church of St Cornelius and community centre, Aalbeke – urbain architectencollectief © Dennis De Smet
02, Church of St Cornelius and community centre, Aalbeke – urbain architectencollectief © Farah Fervel
04-05, Deelfabriek, Kortrijk – ATAMA © Farah Fervel
06, Anapneusis community house, Schoten – Bruno Spaas Architectuur © Nick Moons
07, 09, De Ringelwikke primary school, Ronse – murmuur architecten © Laura Vleugels
08, 10, M127 office building with public plinth, Antwerp – ono architectuur with Philip Aguirre y Otegui, Ludovic Devriendt and Universal Design Studio © Filip Dujardin

PROJECT **urbain architectencollectief**

37

01

PROJECT

Church of St Cornelius and community centre, Aalbeke

In the village of Aalbeke, a stone's throw from the city of Kortrijk, public functions and buildings have been rearranged in recent years according to a plan designed by urbain architectencollectief. The same firm had previously drawn up the study assignment *Kerkenplan Kortrijk*, a plan for the churches of Kortrijk. With this context in mind, the Church of St Cornelius, together with a community centre from the 1980s, formed the basis for a compact organization of public services, local associations and sparsely attended church services. Other public buildings, such as the old town hall, were sold off.

In the church, the designers reduced the space for services to a modest chapel in the former choir. The rest of the nave served as a joker in terms of floor plan and use of space. It made possible the connection between the chapel and the aisles, which are now home to classrooms for the music academy and a small village library. That multipurpose space is the expansion tank for each of the surrounding users. On its own, it can serve just as well for meetings and smaller events of local club life.

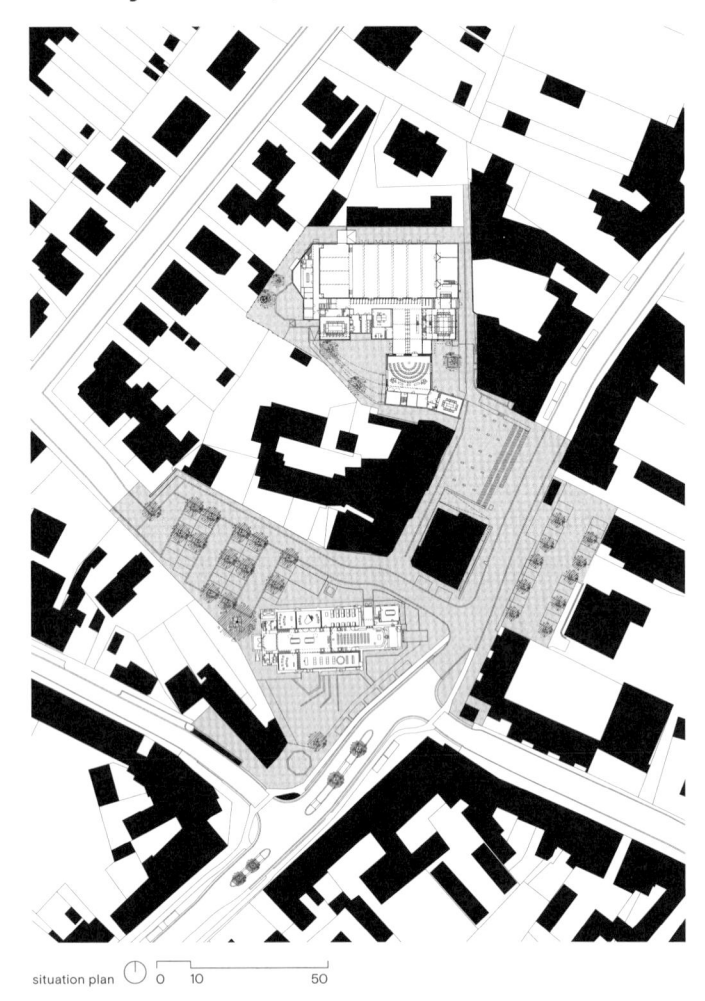

situation plan 0 10 50

PROJECT **Church of St Cornelius and community centre** 39

05

06

For larger events, the community centre, a hundred metres away, is a welcome legacy. Interventions in the main hall have been kept to a minimum. On the side of the village centre, a new extension, which replaces a number of terraced houses, gives the community centre a new appearance on Aalbekeplaats. The new construction embraced the scale and architectural language of the village, while concealing the imposing shell of the hall behind it. It also marks out a modest forecourt, which acts as a hinge between the village square, the foyer and the cafeteria of the existing building. The local brass band occupies the main space in the new building. In theory, their chairs and instruments can be put away in the storage room next to the rehearsal hall, so that this space too – in terms of size, somewhere between the big old hall and the multipurpose room in the church – can be shared with other users. In practice, it is clear that the band occupies a central position in village life. Their trophies adorn the space between two windows in the façade plane, which is actually meant to provide acoustic insulation.

PROJECT **urbain architectencollectief**

PROJECT   urbain architectencollectief

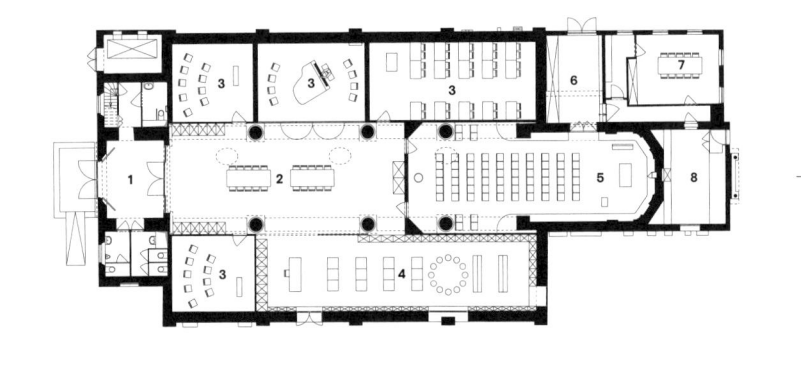

PROJECT   **Church of St Cornelius and community centre**   42

ground floor
1 entrance hall, 2 foyer, 3 music classrooms, 4 library, 5 liturgical room, 6 anteroom, 7 parish secretariat, 8 sacristy

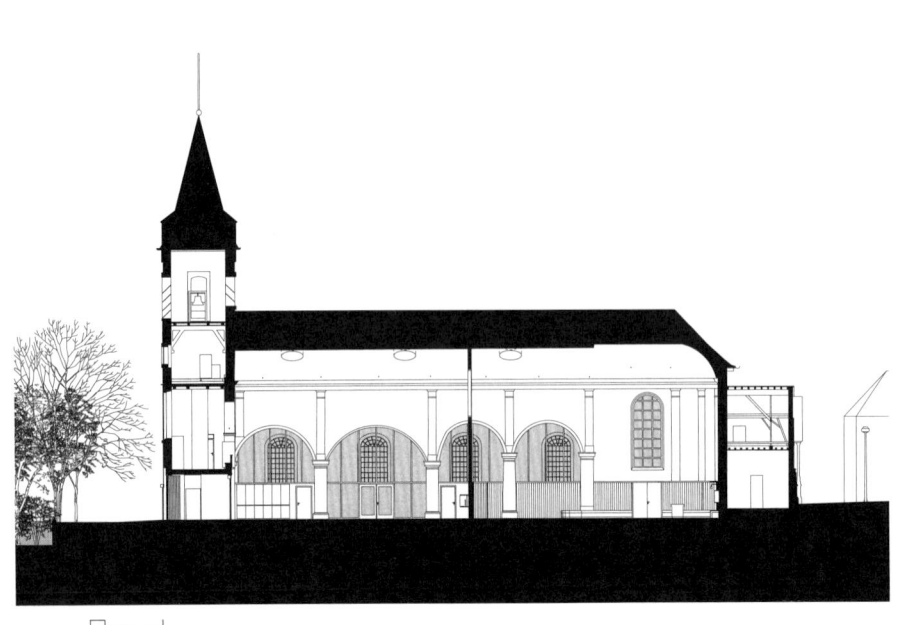

section Aa

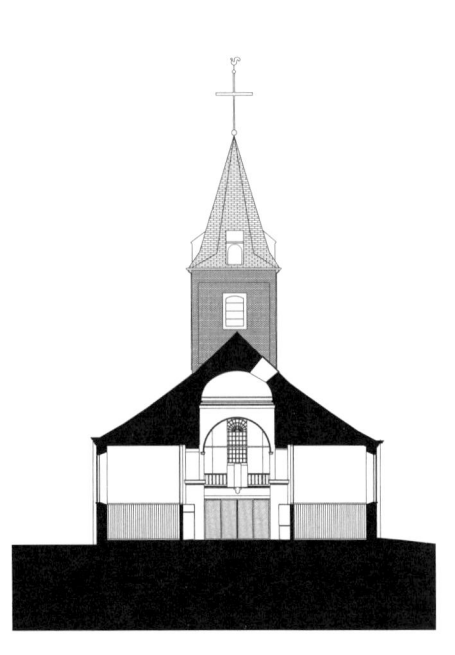

section Bb

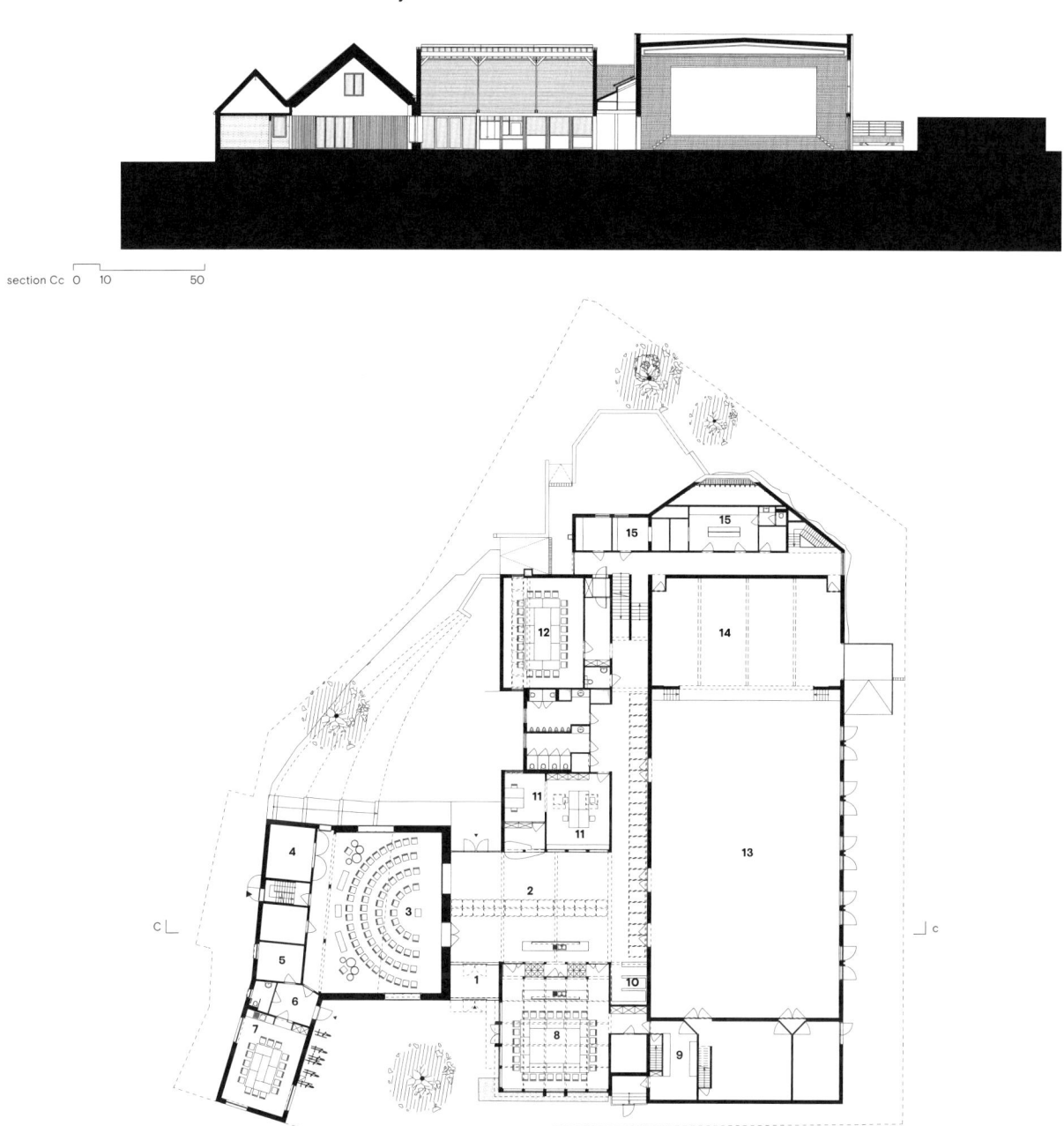

PROJECT   **Church of St Cornelius and community centre**   43

section Cc 0 10 50

ground floor 0 1 5

1 vestibule, **2** foyer, **3** music hall, **4** instrument storage, **5** office of local police officer, **6** entrance hall, **7** meeting room, **8** cafeteria, **9** kitchen, **10** cloakroom, **11** community centre office, **12** meeting room, **13** large hall, **14** permanent stage, **15** changing room

project Church of St Cornelius and community centre   **office** urbain architectencollectief
design team Dieter Delbaere, David Claus, David Niville, Eline Devos, Alexander De Mont, Sylvia Roelens, Thomas Balduyck   **website** www.urbain-ac.be
address (church) Aalbekeplaats 1A, 8511 Aalbeke (community centre) Krugerstraat 2, 8511 Aalbeke
client City of Kortrijk   **design** February 2018   **completion** (church) September 2022 (community centre) March 2023   **surface area** (church) 747 m² (community centre) 2,092 m²
volume (church) 6,680 m³ (community centre) 10,757 m³   **total building cost** (church) €2,000,000 excl. VAT (community centre) €1,520,000 excl. VAT   **total building cost per m²** (church) €2,677 excl. VAT (community centre) €726 excl. VAT **main contractor (structural work and finishing)** (church) Monument Vandekerckhove, Ingelmunster (community centre) Bouw & Renovatie, Rekkem
(HVAC) ASD, Roeselare   **(electricity)** Vandenberghe, Harelbeke
stability studies Sileghem & Partners, Zwevegem   **engineering studies** Tech3, Ghent
EPB studies Feys, Poperinge   **acoustics studies** Bureau De Fonseca, Grimbergen
landscape design urbain architectencollectief, Ghent   **safety coordination** Feys, Poperinge

text Petrus Kemme
photography
01, 07–09 © Farah Fervel
02–06 © Dennis De Smet

PROJECT   urbain architectencollectief

PROJECT Bruno Spaas Architectuur

PROJECT # Anapneusis community house, Schoten

The non-profit organization Anapneusis is a private association that takes care of former homeless people. In Schoten, it built a small-scale co-housing project, where people learn to live independently again after being homeless. Located at the end of a cul-de-sac near the E10 lake, the building replaces an existing home that, after a thorough investigation, could not be renovated efficiently.

The new construction houses four studios and a communal space. It is a compact volume with an external staircase and footbridge giving access to the three studios above.

The building was erected in a thoroughly sustainable way, which is quite ambitious and unusual for an organization that runs on donations and voluntary work and cannot rely on government subsidies. A timber frame, filled in with wood wool insulation and lime hemp, is finished on the inside with clay plaster. Clay and lime hemp score well in terms of both sound insulation and absorption, which, for vulnerable people in need of peace and quiet, offers an appropriate and sustainable solution. An additional advantage is that the materials provide natural moisture control

PROJECT **Anapneusis community house**

and air purification, requiring a minimum of techniques or ventilation systems.

The building looks like a single family home. Two setbacks in the façade articulate the three sequenced studios on the first floor and scale the volume. The careful detailing of the windows, the external gallery and the staircase create a sense of homeliness. At the same time, the building shows off a certain robustness. The use of red bricks and red roof tiles (which also integrate the solar panels), an asymmetrical ridge and the almost invisible edge of the roof give it a sculptural appearance. The generous windows in the end façade heighten the views of the recreational lake and its green surroundings. The last house in the street thus engages convincingly in dialogue with its recreational surroundings.

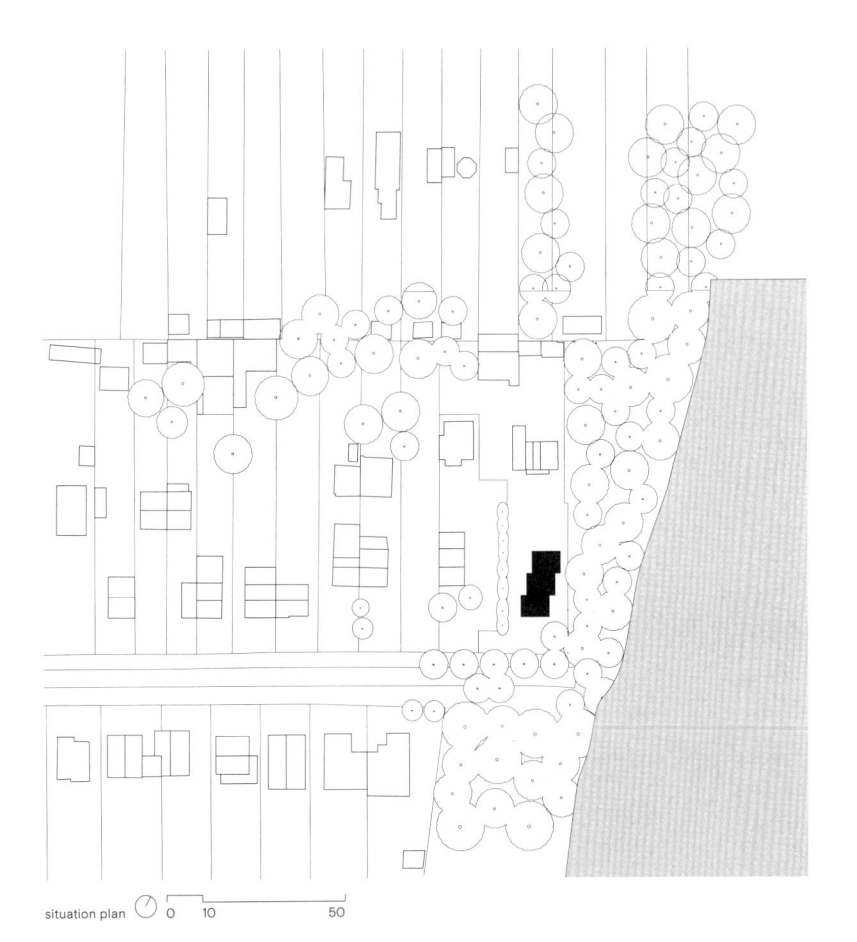

situation plan 0 10 50

PROJECT **Bruno Spaas Architectuur**

PROJECT **Bruno Spaas Architectuur**

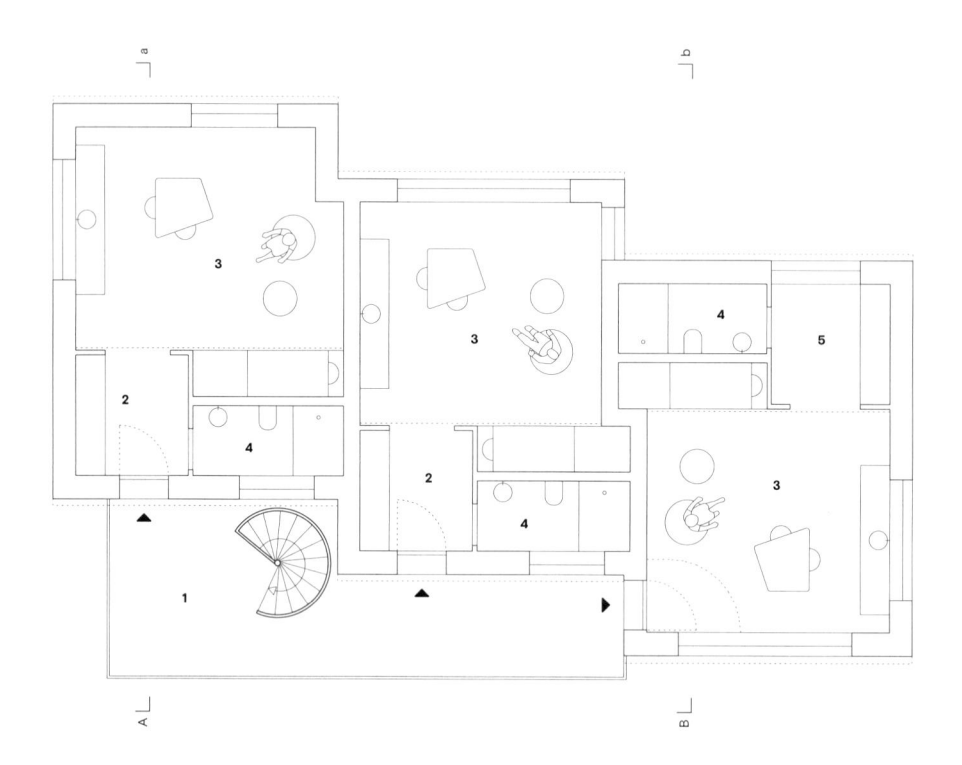

PROJECT **Anapneusis community house** 50

level 1
1 terrace, **2** entrance hall, **3** studio, **4** bathroom, **5** cloakroom

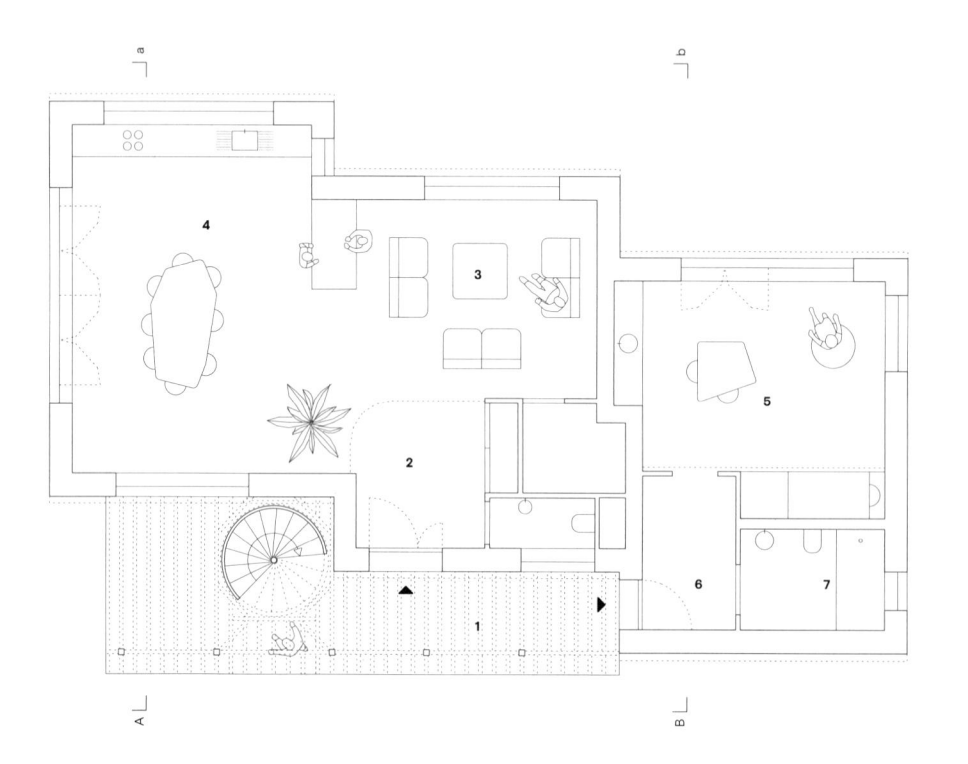

ground floor
1 covered outdoor area, **2** shared entrance hall, **3** shared living room, **4** shared kitchen-dining room, **5** studio, **6** entrance hall, **7** bathroom

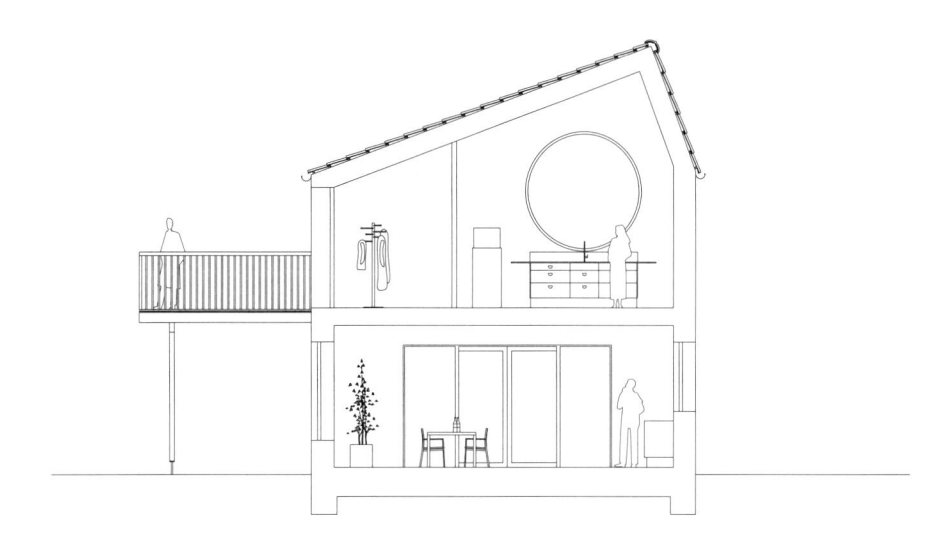

PROJECT   **Anapneusis community house**   51

section Aa

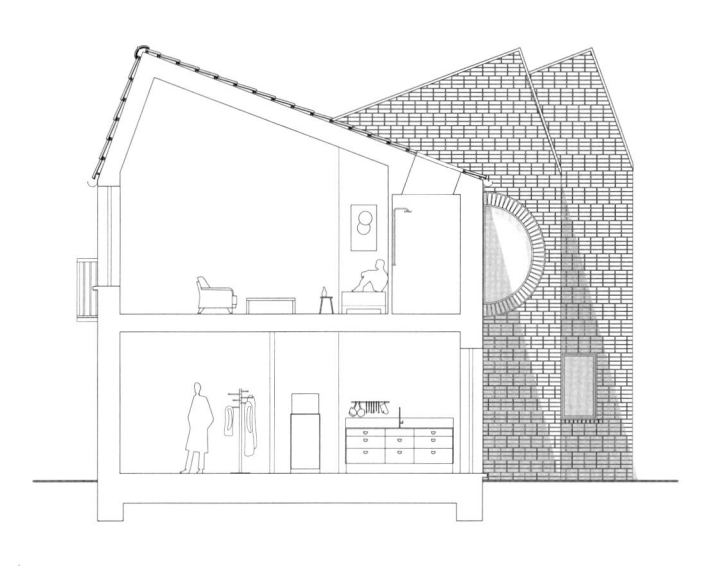

section Bb 0 1 5

text
Els Nulens
photography
01, 06–08 © Nick Moons
02–05 © Pieter Geerts

project Anapneusis community house   **office** Bruno Spaas Architectuur
design team Joni Nieuwenhuysen, Kelvin Obi, Bruno Spaas   **website** www.brunospaasarchitectuur.be
address Ruitersdreef 29, 2900 Schoten   **client** Anapneusis   **design** April 2019
completion April 2023   **surface area** 283 m²   **volume** NA   **total building cost** €475,000 excl. VAT
total building cost per m² €1,678 excl. VAT   **main contractor** Puur Bouwen, Balegem
EPB studies Bureau Van Den Broeck, Antwerp

PROJECT   **Bruno Spaas Architectuur**

PROJECT ono architectuur, Philip Aguirre y Otegui, Ludovic Devriendt, Universal Design Studio

PROJECT   **M127 office building with public plinth, Antwerp**   54

Wedged between the Church of the Holy Spirit and the music academy on the busy Mechelsesteenweg in Antwerp, an inward-looking office building from the 1960s has been converted into premises that fully engage with the neighbourhood. The law firm Schoups decided not only to establish its own office there, but also to make room for co-working spaces, a coffee bar with a terrace, a multipurpose atrium and a neighbourhood garden.

The design team consisting of ono architectuur, artist Philip Aguirre y Otegui, garden architect Ludovic Devriendt and Universal Design Studio stripped the building and left the concrete structure unfinished. They opened up two large voids: one for the atrium and the library above it, and one for the coffee bar with a lunch area above it. By setting back the façade in the plinth on the street side, space was created for a terrace near the coffee bar. Voluminous columns designed by Aguirre y Otegui add the necessary intimacy. The artist also created colourful curtains with which the meeting rooms around the atrium can be screened off and was jointly responsible for the choice of colours in the rest of the building. The façade, provisionally in simple red brick, is still awaiting an art finish.

Building and garden are both open to the neighbours. The music academy uses the atrium, with its grand piano, for recitals. It was also agreed

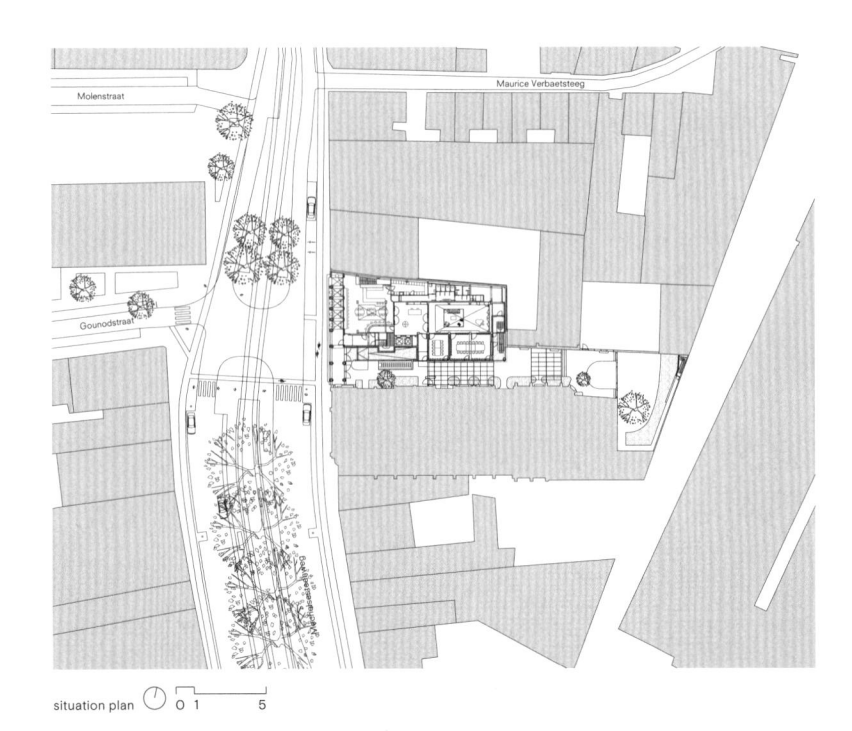

situation plan   0 1   5

PROJECT **M127 office building with public plinth**

with the church to demolish a series of storage areas to make room for the neighbourhood garden, which both the office building and church can access directly. Office and church jointly produce energy through solar panels on the church roofs and both also use rainwater collected in wells for the garden. Not only is the building in and of itself an achievement, at once robust and elegant, but it has also proved itself to be a wonderful neighbour. And that may be its biggest success.

PROJECT   **ono architectuur, Philip Aguirre y Otegui, Ludovic Devriendt, Universal Design Studio**   56

PROJECT　　ono architectuur, Philip Aguirre y Otegui, Ludovic Devriendt, Universal Design Studio

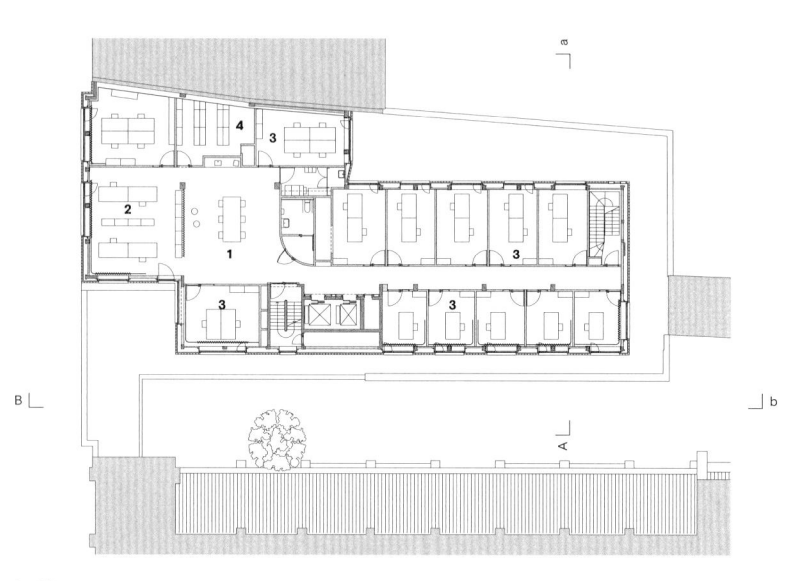

PROJECT   **M127 office building with public plinth**   58

level 3
1 relaxation room with kitchenette, **2** landscape office, **3** office space, **4** archive

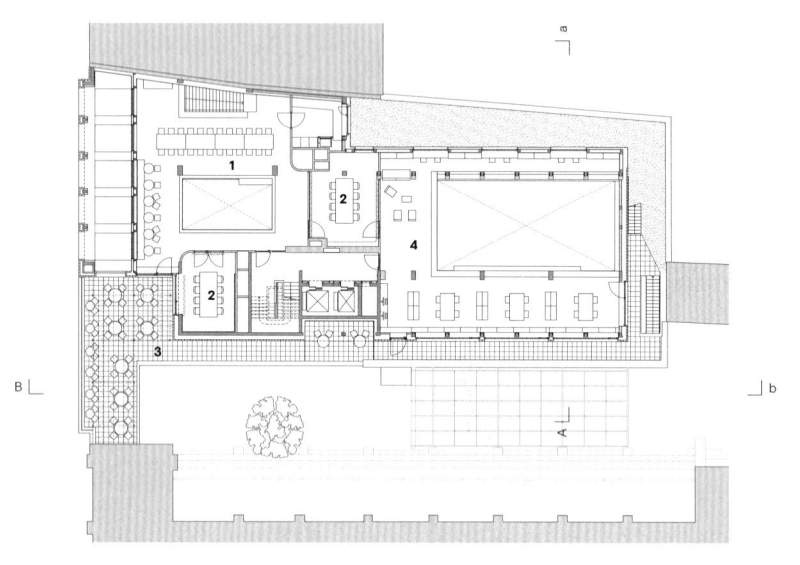

level 1
1 lunch room, **2** meeting room, **3** terrace, **4** library

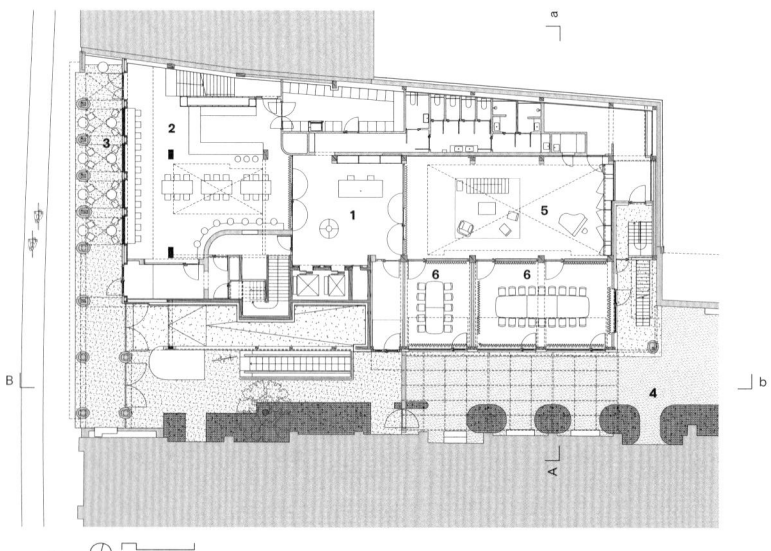

ground floor
1 reception, **2** catering room, **3** covered terrace, **4** community garden, **5** multipurpose hall, **6** meeting room

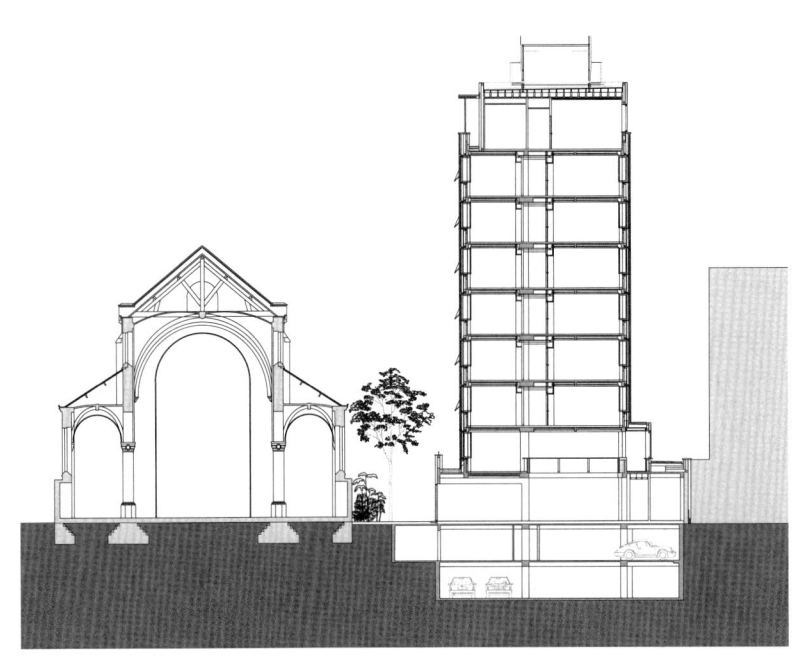

PROJECT **M127 office building with public plinth** 59

section Aa

section Bb 0 1 5

project M127 office building with public plinth **office** ono architectuur with Philip Aguirre y Otegui, Ludovic Devriendt and Universal Design Studio **design team** Gert Somers, Jonas Lindekens, Sara Verleye, Tom Beysen, Faber Martens, Selen Sürmeli, Kobe Gijbels, Benoit Stes, Lise Brusselmans, Ruben Kiewiet, Katrien Cammaert, Pieter Van Elst, David de Bruijn, Philip Aguirre y Otegui, Ludovic Devriendt, Paul Gulati, Satoshi Isono, Junko Yanagisawa, Maria Lucas, Lisl du Toit **website** www.ono-architectuur.be www.philipaguirre.be www.universaldesignstudio.com **address** Mechelsesteenweg 127-31, 2018 Antwerp **client** M127 **design** March 2020 **completion** July 2023 **surface area** 6,350 m² **volume** 19,050 m³ **total building cost** €8,950,000 excl. VAT **total building cost per m²** €1,409 excl. VAT **main contractor** Cordeel, Hoeselt **art integration** Philip Aguirre y Otegui, Antwerp **stability studies** Ney & Partners, Brussels **engineering studies** RCR, Herent **EPB and acoustics studies** Daidalos Peutz, Leuven **landscape design** Ludovic Devriendt, Antwerp **safety coordination** OCB, Kontich

text Evelien Pieters
photography
01, 07-09 © Illias Teirlinck
02-06 © Filip Dujardin

PROJECT   ono architectuur, Philip Aguirre y Otegui, Ludovic Devriendt, Universal Design Studio

ESSAY

Take and Give

The Intertwining of Architecture and Small Business as a Curse and a Blessing

Petrus Kemme

In this essay, we will stroll past recent small-scale architectural projects by entrepreneurs with public ambitions. The entrepreneurs and architects involved appear in shifting constellations, while their ambitions play different roles. En route, we will reflect on the way architecture and small-scale entrepreneurship are intertwined in the local (building) culture.

Corners and bricks

Crossing Tolpoort bridge, one enters the elongated market square that is the beating heart of Deinze. Just past the Church of Our Lady, a white corner building with five distinct floors comes into sight. Its smooth curves, particular window design and distinctive recessed balconies all hint at interwar architecture. Yet the snow-white walls and contemporary materials soon make us realize this must be a more recent building. A rather shameless exercise in art deco, in fact, and one that blends in perfectly in the mishmash of historical styles that is so typical of provincial cities in Flanders. An oxblood awning draws attention to the rounded ground-floor corner. It serves as the literal cherry atop the Letters & Co bookshop with coffee corner, designed by NERO.

  Inside, shop owners Chris and Lies greet their regular patrons by name. As self-proclaimed 'entrepreneurs who care' (no one ever ran an independent bookshop in the hope of getting rich!), they commissioned the building. Today, they both manage the property and live in the duplex flat on the top floor. The two flats below were sold at a premium – unavoidably, given the spiralling costs of construction in recent years. There has been a bookshop on this little corner for a number of years. In the past, however, the shop used to occupy a more humble, run-down building that was rented out by the neighbouring church. When the latter decided to sell, Chris and Lies seized the opportunity to not only buy the property, but also inject money into it. A financial but also personal decision to invest in the social and cultural fabric of their city.

  Commissioning a building seemed the best of both worlds. Used to getting things done, the entrepreneurial couple monitored the entire project and kept a critical, business-minded eye on proceedings. It was a once-in-a-lifetime project for the pair, like for most private clients. Their reputation was on the line, so they poured their hard-earned money and hours of their time into the project. The couple knew what they did and didn't want, and directly discussed their ideas with the architects. The architects in turn faced less of an 'administrative gap' than if they worked with a major project developer or the government. It also freed them from the responsibility to serve the public interest, which public projects tend to entail. Still, the building does have a social ambition, both in terms of its current use (including a modest contribution to the local housing market) and in terms of its architectural presence as it affects the entire look of the square.[1] It is strategically located on the intersection of the commercial Tolpoortstraat / market square axis and the cultural axis along the Leie river. This is an intersection Deinze has been investing in heavily in recent years.[2] If you didn't know that this corner had been home to Letters & Co for years, you would be forgiven for thinking the couple had engaged in a clever bit of speculation – because the combined residential-commercial property ingeniously responds to the recent redevelopment of the town centre. Well-natured opportunism, so to say.

[1] At the request of the city government and to secure planning permission, the architects decided on a setback top floor, to maintain the market square's unobstructed view on the church tower.

[2] Examples include the Academy of Fine Arts (WIT architecten, 2021), the city's administrative centre (Tony Fretton architects, 2016), the Leietheater (V+ and ATAMA, known as TRANS at the time, 2021), the redevelopment of the banks of the Leie and the market square (Marie-José Van Hee architecten and Robbrecht en Daem architecten, 2013), and Brielpoort bridge (Marie-José Van Hee architecten, 2021).

ESSAY   **Petrus Kemme**   62

ESSAY Petrus Kemme

project Letters & Co bookshop and group housing
design team Tim Marlier, Jelske De Swaef
client Chris Verhecken and Lies Scheerlinck
surface area 504 m² **volume** 1,400 m³
total building cost per m² €2,079,37 excl. VAT
stability studies Engitop, Deinze

office NERO **website** www.nero.be
address Markt 3, Emiel Clausplein 2, 9800 Deinze
design August 2020 **completion** May 2023
total building cost €1,048,000 excl. VAT
main contractor YVP, Deinze
EPB studies and safety coordination MijnEPB, Ghent

In Aalst, a similarly curved corner building serves as an even clearer example of a local entrepreneur responding to recent urban developments. Peper, which is best known locally for housing the Wally pizzeria on its ground floor, stands in the shadow of the relatively new city library, Utopia. The latter's recently constructed new wing makes up one side of a small, triangular square, along with a row of nineteenth-century workers' houses and the side wall of the former military Pupillenschool. The square feels a little 'tucked away', even though it is home to the library's main entrance and its café. This may be because the building is on the 'wrong' side of nearby arterial roads and shopping streets. At the end of the row of houses, an undeniably contemporary building, courtesy of Architecten De Bruyn, occupies the corner of Peperstraat.

  The corner building takes up largely the same amount of space as its unsalvageable predecessor, which had a similarly rounded front. Today, rounded windows accentuate the curve more than ever. Bricks of varying standard heights form a horizontally lined pattern on the façade, resulting in a visual dialogue with the masonry architecture of both the Pupillenschool and Utopia. Because the building's front harbours a cleverly covered parking spot (which just as easily accommodates a dining table), the street remains car-free, in line with local parking regulations. Window ledges that invite passers-by to sit down and rest make a smooth link between the urban outdoors and the restaurant's homely interior. Inside, a vertical open plan intersects the entire structure, from the restaurant up to an office space and the penthouse apartment. On the ground floor, the skylight accentuates the pizza oven's role as the hearth of the urban living room. The same bricks used in the building's façade set the tone inside, in line with the hip creed that 'unfinished equals finished'. As in Deinze, the building's architecture is a profound exercise in an eminently sellable style. The architectural message seems an instrumental part of the small enterprise's business plan.

  At dusk, Peper's rounded corners evoke Edward Hopper's painting *Nighthawks* (1942), in which a large curved window frames a lonely moment in the lives of three urbanites and a server at an all-night diner in New York. And while most corner establishments in provincial Flanders are livelier than the one in Hopper's scene, we are overcome by a sensation that is similar to the artist's magisterial evocation of alienation. Because while the rounded windows seem to invite the world into the pizzeria, there is still a clear distinction between inside and outside. The windows are a mirror, as it were, in which generosity and distance come eye to eye. There is nothing random about this roundedness: it is part of the stylish and smooth architectural language of the enterprising middle-class. It seduces some, while putting up thresholds for others. Because it is still mostly the safely established middle-class that adores the urban living-room architecture of small business owners. In fact, it would be an excellent subject for a *Flanders Architectural Review*.

project Corner building on Peperstraat **office** Architecten De Bruyn **website** www.architectendebruyn.be
address Peperstraat 32, 9300 Aalst **client** Kristof Cannoot **design** June 2022
completion December 2022 **surface area** 275 m² **volume** 1,060 m³
total building cost €600,000 excl. VAT **total building cost per m²** €2,180 excl. VAT

Houses and preservation

The shorthand between entrepreneur and architect becomes even easier to read when creatives themselves start building. Ghent's Brugse Poort neighbourhood is home to Household Practice, the brainchild of a former graphic designer and a social worker. The couple was able to purchase a walled-in inner area with thirteen lock-up garages. The garages were torn down to make way for a home for the young family, with an adjoining yoga studio (the graphic designer's new career). Along the way, they also decided to add a tiny coffee bar to the project.

It is no coincidence that the 'work volume' was built at the mouth of the alley, which is the only way to access the plot. It screens off the private area around the house but remains connected to it (or not) via a sliding door. Inspired by the clients' fondness for Californian architecture (Charles and Ray Eames in particular), the ensemble genuinely feels like a unified whole. The team at FELT architecture & design comes from the same socio-cultural middle-class in Ghent. The resulting architecture clearly demonstrates that architect and client spoke the same language. All parts of the project are carefully situated around a private garden. Their proportions, the lines of sight towards the surrounding buildings and the pathways between the living and working quarters are extremely precise and nuanced, while the materials and details are of high quality. Everything appears to be designed to perfection and harmoniously 'pronounced'.

The project's relationship with the surrounding neighbourhood, however, is less evident. The Brugse Poort was always one of the more socially marginalized parts of the city, but it has become increasingly gentrified in recent years. Especially in the area hemmed in by Rooigemlaan and the Bruges-Ghent Canal, many houses are in need of renovation or vacant; properties seem to simply be biding their time until they are snapped up by middle-class urbanites with good intentions and plenty of money in the bank. We are not questioning the clients intentions in any way. But given the neighbourhood in which they live, it feels important to note that their lot is roughly the same size as the plots of the four adjoining terraced houses combined. And the traditional residents of the Brugse Poort were perhaps not the target audience for a 'yoga studio-meets-coffee-bar' – an editor of the *Flanders Architectural Review*, on the other hand …

To be clear: the current situation is a marked improvement on the grotty cul-de-sac and run-down garages that previously stood on the site. But one cannot help but wonder whether the plot couldn't have been transformed in a way that would have been more meaningful for the neighbourhood. In 2023 Ghent adopted a new vision on urban blocks that actually comments on situations like this: 'Wherever possible, we want to reserve the inner areas of urban blocks for neighbourhood essentials: greenery and facilities … Inserting residential elements in inner areas has historically been an infrequent occurrence and is thus not advisable.'[3] While the new vision has no regulatory power, it is hard to imagine FELT's project being given the green light today, given this new policy framework. The threesome capitalized on a loophole in the city's policies at the time – like any resourceful entrepreneur, in other words. Thank goodness the project had at least some architectural and 'social' ambition (even though it mainly targets incoming middle-class urbanites), besides its residential and professional aims. Well-intended opportunism, so to say.

[3] 'Meer leefkwaliteit creëren in dichtbevolkte wijken', 18 April 2023, stad.gent/sites/default/files/media/documents/2023_NO_Bouwblokvisie_DEF_0.pdf, p. 20.

project Household practice Karel Verstraeten, Marie Lafosse, Michiel Hutsebaut
address Hamerstraat, 9000 Ghent
completion March 2022
total building cost €645,000 excl. VAT
main contractor Lab15, Ghent
EPB studies and safety coordination Vesting, Ghent
office FELT architecture & design
client private
surface area 340 m²
design team Jasper Stevens,
website www.felt.works
design October 2019
volume 1,115 m³
total building cost per m² €1,890 excl. VAT
stability studies Mouton, Ghent

On the next leg of our journey, we encounter the architect as client. This is precisely what happened in Antwerp's densely populated Borgerhout district, where local architects Oscar and An (import.export Architecture) snapped up a former Moroccan greengrocer's on Koxplein. They restructured the

ESSAY   **Petrus Kemme**   66

03

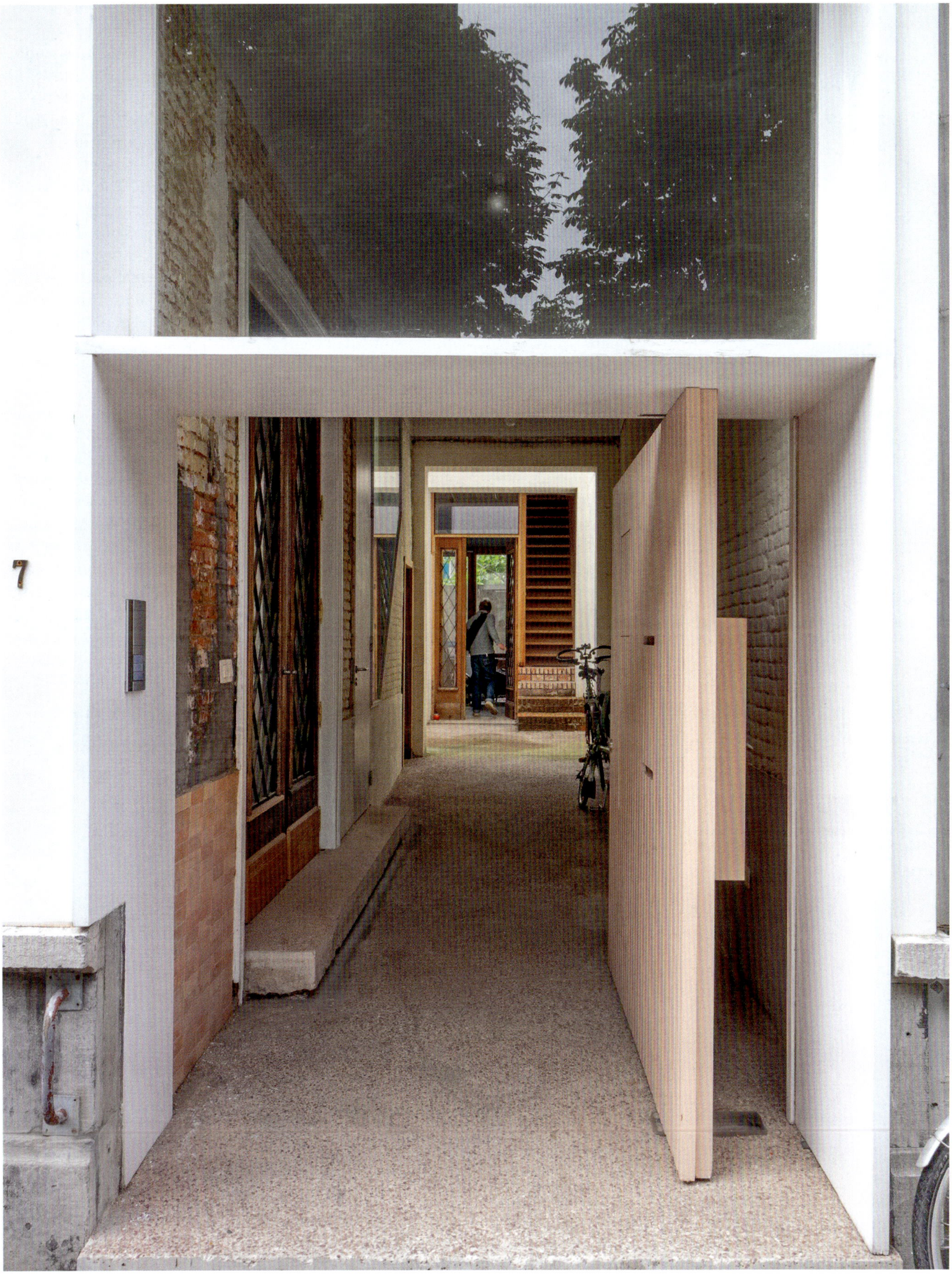

04

4   'Ontdek de geschiedenis – De Sint-Anna Kapel',
    www.sintannakapel.be/geschiedenis-nl.

terraced house and its two-storey extension at the back, inserting a patio in-between. An atelier now occupies the house's ground floor, while its upper floors have been turned into a duplex apartment and the extension into a studio. For the moment, the couple rents out the atelier to young artists; An and Oscar's grown-up children live in the two residential units. This project too could be considered an example of how the creative middle class, looking for affordable places to live and work, has become complicit in gentrification.

Less cynical readers will see a public gesture in the project, if not in terms of functionality, then at least in terms of architecture. The façade was stripped of its stick-on brick tiles to reveal its hidden nineteenth-century articulation, which demarcates the public-commercial ground floor from the private-residential upper floors. This discreet yet noticeable change helped to restore contact between public and private on the small neighbourhood square in a way that goes beyond a single façade. The roller shutter that used to be half-closed here most of the time was replaced by a wooden gate, which opens up invitingly onto the sun-filled central patio. The shopfront window was moved back a few feet, to make way for a mini front garden, a modest oasis amid the otherwise bricks-and-mortar building fronts. New surfaces have been filled with tiles in earthy tones, courtesy of architect/ceramicist An.

At the rear, the façade is set perpendicular to the plot, leaving a space between it and the garden wall on the sloping plot boundary. This tiny back garden – the third outdoor space, besides the front garden and the patio – first and foremost allows light to enter the studio, which used to be a windowless cooling warehouse. At the same time, the garden means the building interrupts the line of extensions along the back of the urban block, thus raising a discreet fist in favour of not-building and greenery across the neighbourhood's garden walls. But above all, the light allows the eye to travel freely through the ground-floor studio, from the square at the front to the back, like a strategically positioned peephole in a boxed-in diorama. All of this illustrates how the order of light, materials and space was designed with a public perspective in mind. While its use may have become more private, the building itself is now a lot more 'public'.

project Renovation of a retail space on Koxplein   **office** import.export Architecture
website www.iea.be   **design team** Oscar Rommens, An Vanderveken, Tim Van Verdegem, Oana Dulvara
address Koxplein 7, 2140 Borgerhout   **client** Rommens-Vanderveken family
design April 2018   **completion** October 2022   **surface area** 260 m²   **volume** 780 m³
total building cost €275,000 excl. VAT   **total building cost per m²** €1,058 excl. VAT
main contractor GBS Bouw, Ranst & Martha, Antwerp   **art integration ceramics** An Vanderveken
stability studies Eddy Henskens, Hemiksem   **EPB studies and safety coordination** Tecclem, Ghent
landscape design import.export Architecture, Antwerp

Added value(able)

The small neo-Gothic St Anne's Chapel stands in the middle of the fields between Tielt and Dentergem. For a century and a half, it has been straddling the public and the private. Throughout history, the building has been prey to the whims of local rulers and has been a silent witness to the intrigues of the nobility, including a few legendary royal escapades![4] The parish that was meant to emerge around it never quite materialized, and the chapel itself was never consecrated. Instead, cattle from the surrounding fields sought shelter in the structure as it slowly fell apart. Yet the chapel remains a familiar element in the landscape. Standing on the intersection of a paved and unpaved road, it is a useful landmark for hikers and cyclists. Born and bred in the region, one of the partners of the Leuven-based architect firm DMOA architecten recognized its potential. (The local authorities, meanwhile, showed no interest in repurposing the chapel.)

DMOA wanted to turn the chapel into the meeting place it had never quite become. The firm added floor slabs to create two spacious rooms inside the ruin. Now, DMOA rents these out for events, as a kind of spin-off of its usual business. The chapel's found architecture and rural surroundings remain its unique selling points. Along one of the side walls, DMOA built a daring extension with support facilities. The extension looks more massive than it really is; to passers-by, it resembles a sculptural multilevel series of staircases.[5] The triangular volume remains confined to the boundaries of a carefully considered envelope, though, to toy with visitors' impressions when they approach from Tieltseweg. From the north, the extension looks like a continuation of the chapel's sloping roof. For those coming from the south, behind the chapel, a sharp curve in the road hides the extension from view. As a result, the building, whose gable roof was never rebuilt, maintains its ruin-like character.

Thanks to the non-existent roof and sculptural staircases, the public can now enjoy the chapel as a lookout tower. This in turn helped the project get financial support from the Province of West Flanders. The latter wants to build twenty-five similar lookout towers along cycle and hiking trails in the province as part of its Horizon 2025 project. In that sense, the architects' plans for the semi-ruined chapel were right up the Province's alley, even before it was turned into an events venue. The firm's private initiative offers unmistakeable added value for the general public. At this scale, public-private partnerships actually make plenty of sense and start looking quite attractive.

[5] While the extension resembles a solid concrete building, it is actually made of bricks. The pattern of its concrete cladding is based on research into 'robotic serendipity' by Lie Bormans, a KU Leuven student who has since joined DMOA. Bormans' research won a Henry van de Velde Award in 2024, in the 'Crafts' category. See 'Robotische serendipiteit | Henry Van de Velde Awards', henryvandevelde.be/nl/awards/24/robot-serendipiteit.

project St Anne's Chapel redevelopment   **office** DMOA architecten
design team Matthias Mattelaer, Benjamin Denef, Lie Bormans   **website** www.dmoa.be
address Tieltseweg 70, 8720 Dentergem   **client** St Anne's Chapel   **design** January 2022   **completion** June 2023   **surface area** 250 m²   **volume** 1,150 m³   **total building cost** €850,000 excl. VAT
total building cost per m² €3,400 excl. VAT   **main contractor** Filip Wiebouw, Danny Kerkhove, Meulebeke
stability studies Ben Verbeeck, Mortsel   **heating and plumbing studies** Bart Cupers, Spalbeek
electricity studies Electro Verhalle, Tielt   **ventilation studies** Comfort Home, Tielt
EPB studies and safety coordination 2B-Safe, Glabbeek

St Anne's Chapel is part of a broader series of DMOA spin-offs. The architects rent out a meeting / events space in their own office Kruul, as well as three short-stay studios in their personal living and working quarters. They sell tamped concrete (specially formulated for Kruul) and have designed two tables. They also developed a portable classroom named Maggie, which was first used while a local school was being renovated and subsequently deployed to crisis areas. All these initiatives are clearly rooted in the architects' regular design work, but also entrepreneurially explore areas like event management, product development and philanthropy.

Like many other architecture firms, DMOA appears to be looking for the right balance – the right 'synergy', in corporate speak – between its entrepreneurship and its societal role. It turns out that a quest for profitability does not need to be incompatible with sustainability, thanks to the architects' fascination for developing new materials and their desire to not just design but also exploit multi-use spaces. The small-scale nature of the firm and its satellite ventures is a key factor in all of this, because it creates the agility to respond to all kinds of opportunities and challenges, just off the beaten track of 'ordinary' architecture.

At the same time, the context in which DMOA engages in entrepreneurship is not entirely unproblematic. Philanthropy was clearly the main goal of the portable classroom. But while the Maggie project led to a non-profit, its work is just a drop in the ocean of global inequality. As early as 2016 (!), a first version of the classroom was erected at the asylum centre in Steenokkerzeel. It has been pointing a finger at the structural migration crisis ever since … It is of course wonderful that architects want to tackle these issues. But what looks like a need for architectural input is actually a symbol of the systemic problems in migration and development-aid policies. And those problems vastly exceed what any one small business owner will ever be able to address.

Even within the field of architecture, a firm like DMOA highlights structural challenges. In spite of all its satellite ventures, the firm still mainly

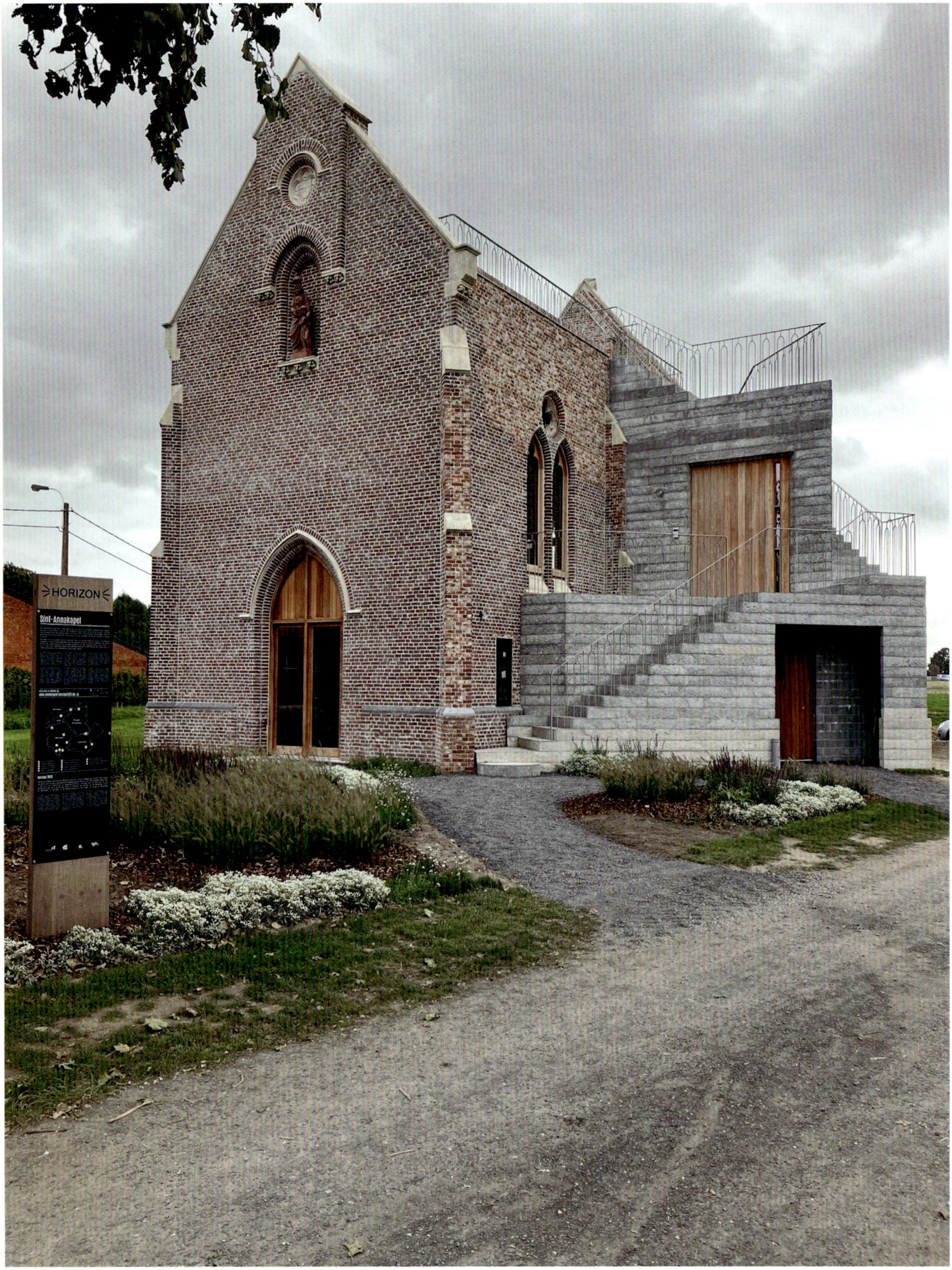

05

06

designs single-family homes, the bread and butter of the local building culture. Ironically, this means that DMOA's rather technology-oriented striving for sustainability still contributes to Flanders' traditionally individualistic way of living, which is anything but sustainable. The architects themselves link their disinterest in competitions and public procurements to responsible entrepreneurship (paying their staff fairly) and architectural freedom (getting to experiment with alternative materials, use scenarios and roles in their spin-offs). Entrepreneurs need to balance the books, and societal engagement comes at a price, even though that price is rarely validated.

project Maggie goes to Leuven **office** Maggie Program vzw and DMOA architecten
design team Benjamin Denef, Matthias Mattelaer, Florence Vermeersch
website www.maggie-program.org, www.dmoa.be **address** Geldenaaksebaan 200, 3001 Heverlee
client VZW Comité voor Onderwijs Annuntiaten Heverlee voor de Vrije Basisschool Sint-Norbertus Heverlee
design March 2020 **completion** July 2020 **surface area** 350 m² **volume** 1,500 m³
total building cost €215,000 excl. VAT **total building cost per m²** €615 excl. VAT
main contractor Maggie Program vzw **stability studies** Engineering firm Ben Verbeeck and Partners, Mortsel **engineering studies** VDM Technics, Tielt-Winge & VDL Electrics, Aarschot & Tim Arnoys Technieken, Herk-de-Stad **EPB studies** 2B-Safe, Glabbeek
landscape (design) Atelier Parkoer, Antwerp (execution) Campo & Jacoby, Mechelen

Fit and form

Irrespective of good intentions, architectural practices still develop within the framework of a building culture that is both socio-economically and culturally intertwined with a tradition of small businesses. As they do, they have to navigate a space that is shaped by local (mis)management and broader socioeconomic force fields, looking for cracks in the system that they might be able to benefit from. For some, 'benefit' equals economic profit; for others, it is social added value. Either way, in their development within that mould, they tend to confirm the familiar manifestation of the architect as one small entrepreneur among countless others. And thus also the sociocultural privilege attached to the architectural sector, regardless of pay discussions.

Within this framework, small-business entrepreneurship sprouts from the seed of ambition, not necessarily from any kind of public commitment. The interwovenness of our architectural culture and small-business entrepreneurship creates immense potential but is not without risk. The collective choices of architects and other small business owners can result in major steps forward or backward in terms of public interests such as sustainability (beyond the purely technological) and socio-economic accessibility. In that sense, we can only hope that government policies will validate small business owners (architectural or otherwise) with a social conscience.

In architecture at least, there is a promising tradition of designers putting pressure on the framework of the architect-as-small-business-owner from the outside, to protect and promote various public interests. Designers have been collectively organizing in a myriad ways, not just setting up traditional firms, but also forming cooperatives and non-profits. Many have also entered related fields, like activism, research and the circular economy. Perhaps the framework could also be challenged from within. A shared ambition of architectural small-business owners to have their social commitment valued could be a means of exerting pressure. So that we may witness a genuine transformation of the above framework, for the sake of architects themselves and of the general public, and so that their ambition may focus on the most pressing challenges we face today. Towards a well-placed opportunism, if you like.

photography
01, Letters & Co bookshop and group housing, Deinze – NERO © Victor De Smet
02, Corner building on Peperstraat, Aalst – Architecten De Bruyn © Johnny Umans
03, Household practice, Ghent – FELT architecture & design © Stijn Bollaert
04, Renovation of a retail space on Koxplein, Antwerp – import.export Architecture © Nathalie Lievens
05, St Anne's Chapel redevelopment, Dentergem – DMOA architecten © DMOA architecten
06, Maggie goes to Leuven, Leuven – Maggie Program vzw, DMOA architecten © DMOA architecten

PROJECT OFFICE Kersten Geers David Van Severen

PROJECT

Brussels Beer Project Brewery, Anderlecht

74

Brussels Beer Project (BBP) is a hip brewery which established itself in the city landscape through strong visual branding based on a palette of flat colours that differ from the usual aesthetics of both commercial and independent beer manufacturers. Following the same logic, it took over strategic locations in Brussels, on Dansaertstraat, on Louizalaan (where it transformed a more traditional Irish pub), and now along the Canal, more precisely on Biestebroekkaai, where it has its operating base and flagship building assorted with a weekend 'beer garden'. Commissioned from OFFICE Kersten Geers David Van Severen, the building both responds to the industrial logic of the area and addresses, through its north façade (the tallest), the large Kureghem crossroads some 200 metres away.

situation plan 0 10 50

03

04

The building is compact with regard to the production volume of about 60,000 litres per week, brewed and bottled on-site. It was designed following the counter-intuitive principle – not uncommon in the industry – of stacking the brewery silos on a raised 'table', liberating the ground floor for bottling and stock. The building also continues the architects' investigation of pure geometry and its deformations, following their principle of the 'Architecture Without Content' series (a pedagogic programme turned into a design principle). Here dubbed *boîte magique*, or magic box, the building is reduced to a consistent and carefully designed empty box, able to accommodate changes in use without giving up its relevance as an everyday monument in the city – a concept made famous by Aldo Rossi, tapping into the long European tradition, in particular Andrea Palladio's Palazzo della Ragione in Padua.[1]

The main façades and the large inclined roof are set perpendicularly to the Canal, while the shortest sides are tilted along the north-south axis, creating corner accidents that slightly deform perspective while retaining the impression of a simple plan. All these geometrical operations are clearly legible through the layout of the exposed prefabricated concrete panels and the glass panels, as well as through the painting of the nine roof spans in steel with the brand colours.

---

1   For an in-depth analysis of their design research, see Roberto Gargiani, *The Incomplete Rationalism of OFFICE Kersten Geers David Van Severen* (Cologne: Verlag der Buchhandlung Walther und Franz König, 2023), 222–23.

PROJECT   **OFFICE Kersten Geers David Van Severen**

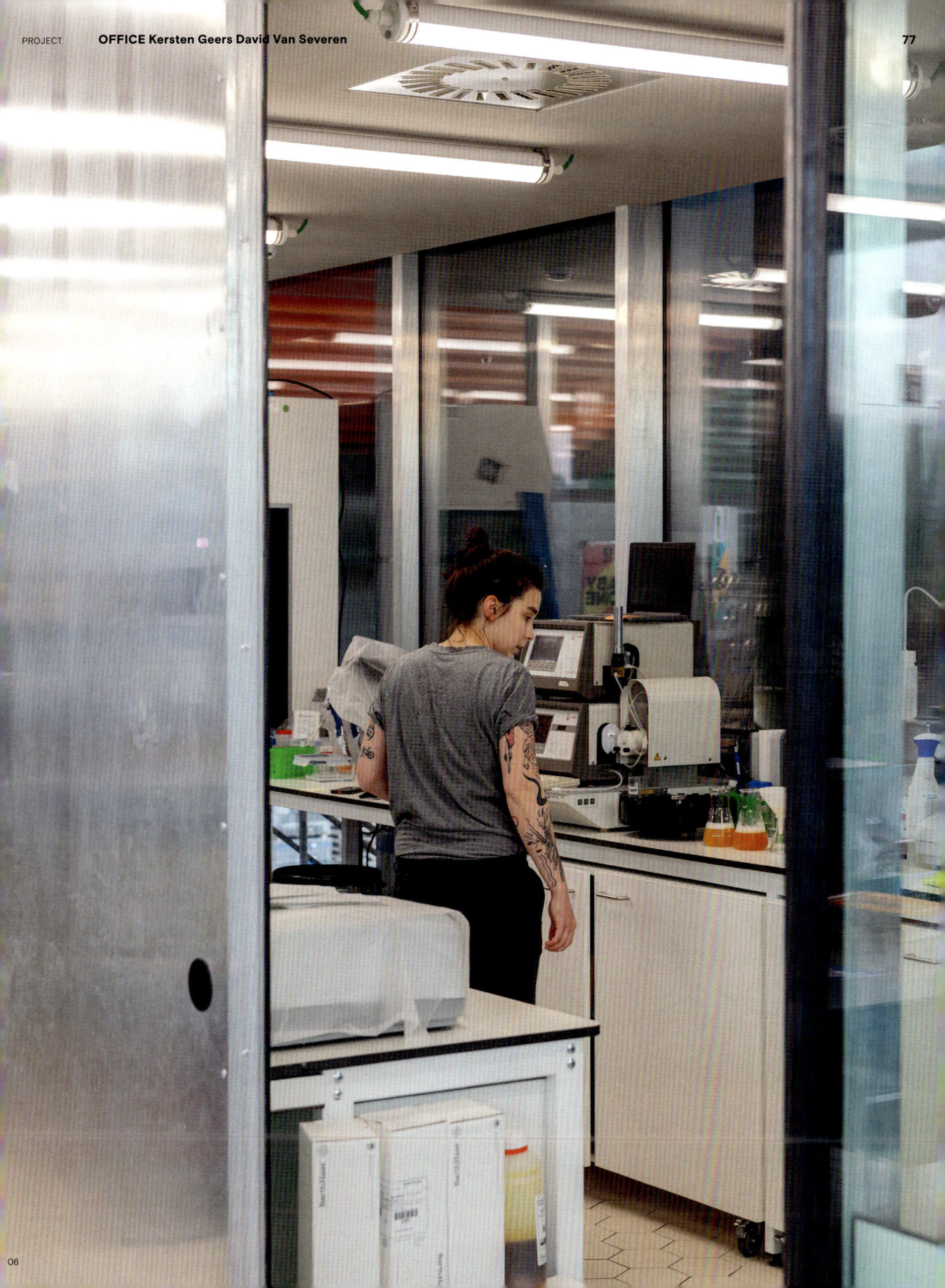

06

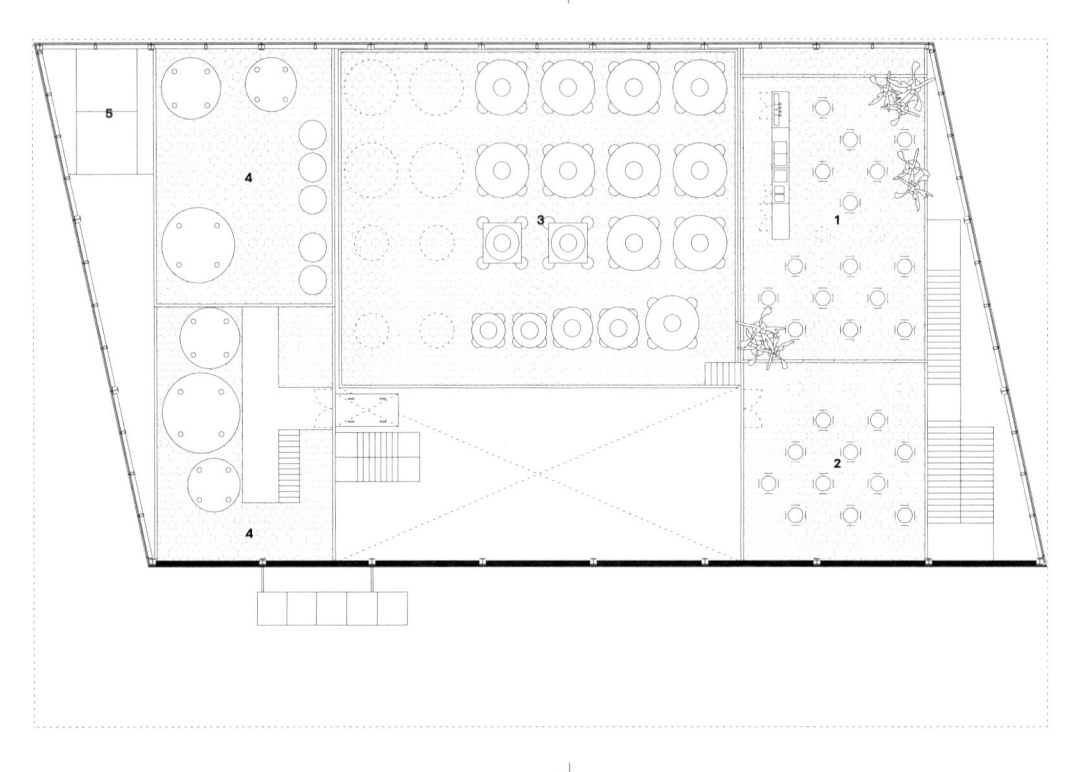

PROJECT **Brussels Beer Project Brewery**

level 3
1 tasting platform, **2** observation platform, **3** fermentation platform, **4** brewing platform, **5** grain silo

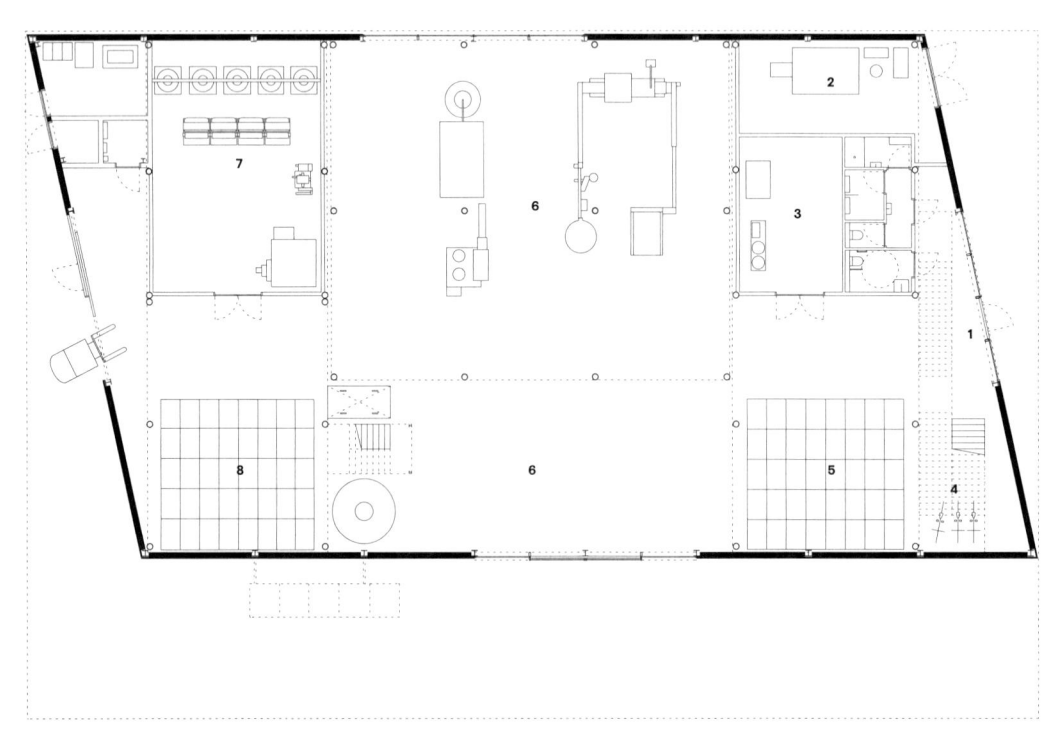

ground floor
1 entrance hall, **2** boiler room, **3** technical room, **4** bicycle storage, **5** storage area incoming, **6** packaging area, **7** malt storage, **8** storage area outgoing, **9** loading and unloading quay

Brussels Beer Project Brewery

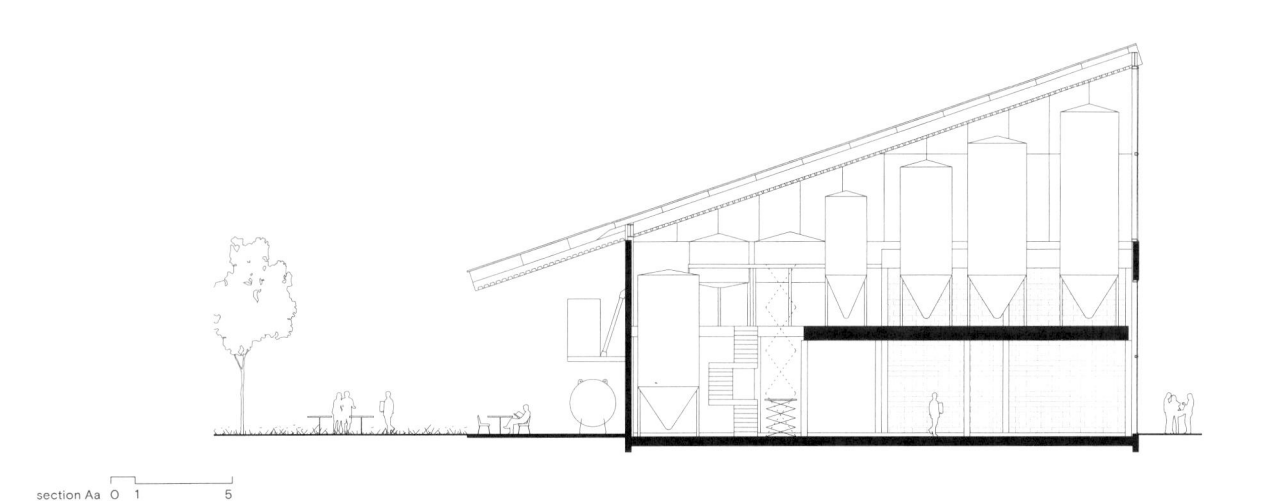

section Aa 0 1 5

project Brussels Beer Project Brewery **office** OFFICE Kersten Geers David Van Severen
design team Kersten Geers, David Van Severen, Alexander Smedts, Henri de Chassey, Steven Bosmans, Linea Dyrbye Jensen, Ziou Gao, Enea Facoetti **website** www.officekgdvs.com
address Biestebroekkaai 23, 1070 Anderlecht **client** Brussels Beer Project
design October 2018 **completion** May 2022 **surface area** 1,600 m² **volume** 9,500 m³
total building cost €1,900,000 excl. VAT **total building cost per m²** €1,187.50 excl. VAT
main contractor Beeuwsaert Construct, Ledegem & Decat, Veurne **stability studies** UTIL Struktuurstudies, Brussels **engineering and EPB studies** Boydens Engineering, Brussels
brewing technology consultant Zymo, Antwerp **landscape design** Jeroen Provoost, Brussels
safety coordination Peritas, Antwerp

text
Carlo Menon
photography
01, 05–06, 08 © Delphine Mathy
02–04, 07 © Bas Princen

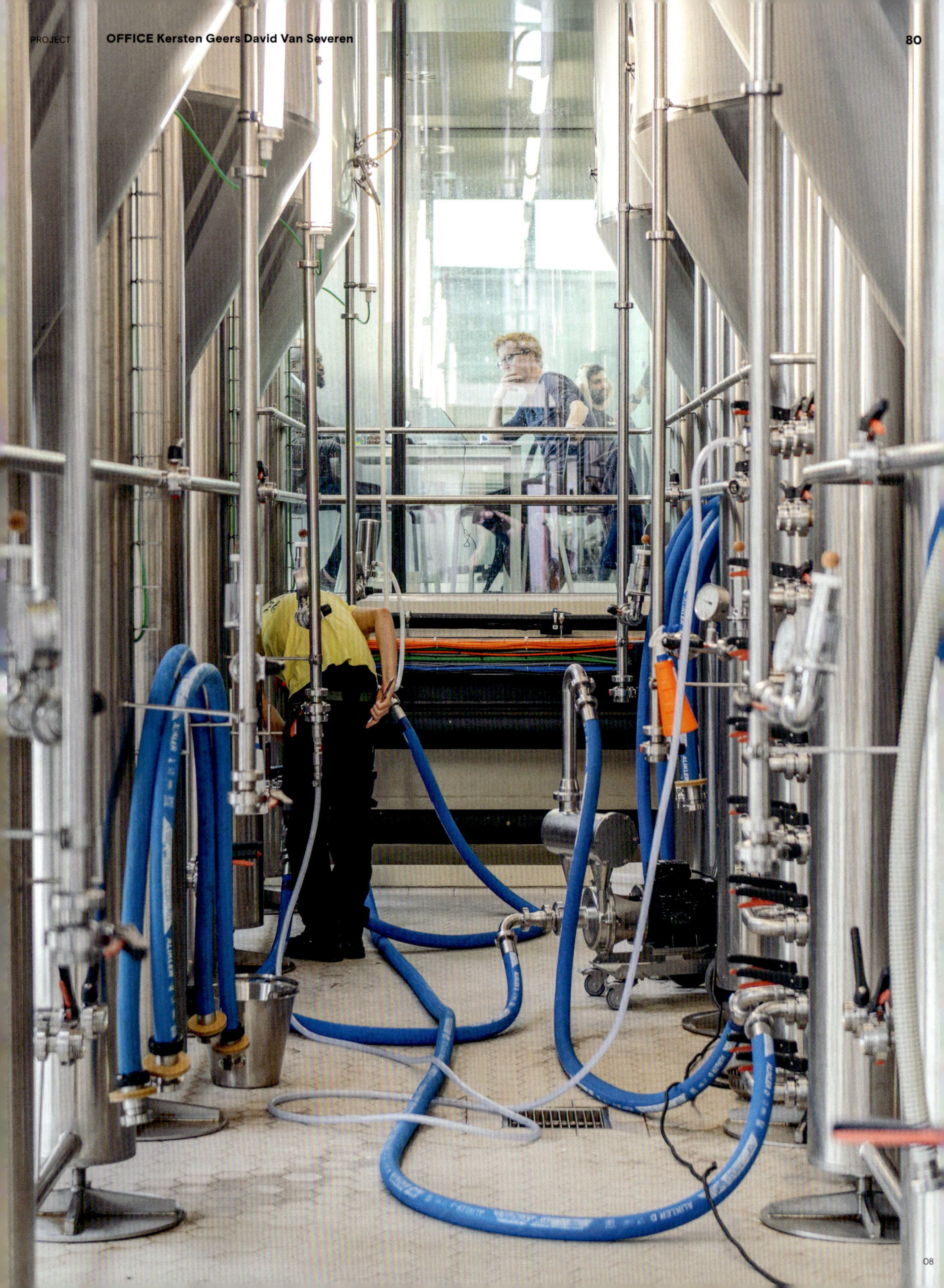

PROJECT **murmuur architecten, Mattias Deboutte**

PROJECT · **Verwerft carpentry workshop, Herentals**

After the sudden death of Jan Verwerft, his son Bart Verwerft and his son-in-law Mattias Deboutte unexpectedly took over the helm of Schrijnwerkerij Verwerft. Bart is a marine engineer, Mattias an architect who gained experience at Marie-José Van Hee architecten and Macken & Macken. Together, they embody a unique symbiosis between architecture and craft. Around the same time, the company moved to a new location on the Albert Canal.

Right along the canal stands a large brick shed with several outbuildings and an outdated office building. Driven by a vision of circular construction, the idea arose to renovate the large shed, together with murmuur architecten (jointly headed by sister Tinne Verwerft). The offices and showrooms were erected as an independent volume within the shed in CLT (Cross-Laminated Timber). A covered outdoor room took shape between the office volume and the exposed façade facing the canal, a room which also serves as a reception area and laboratory for architectural and carpentry experiments. The raised terrace of the staff refectory overlooks it. The view of the canal and the greenery of the military domain opposite contribute to the pleasant work environment, as does the generous inflow of light and air. 'Inland', the heart of the carpentry workshop is mainly formed by the heavy brick walls and delicate rafters of the main shed.

05

A secondary assembly shed was raised against the east flank, again with a panoramic window overlooking the canal. On the west flank, a garden has been fashioned in the remnants of a side building, which simultaneously forms a fire safety buffer with regard to the neighbours. The former office building on the street side should in future accommodate workshops or start-up businesses, facilitating cross-pollination between the various residents/users.

The redevelopment of the business site combines functionality with subtle aesthetics. The design contains allusions to the architecture of Jean Prouvé, as in the round windows and slender columns on a space of the wall. Each element is given its own place within a harmonious workspace, resulting in an inspiring and forward-looking environment.

PROJECT **murmuur architecten, Mattias Deboutte**

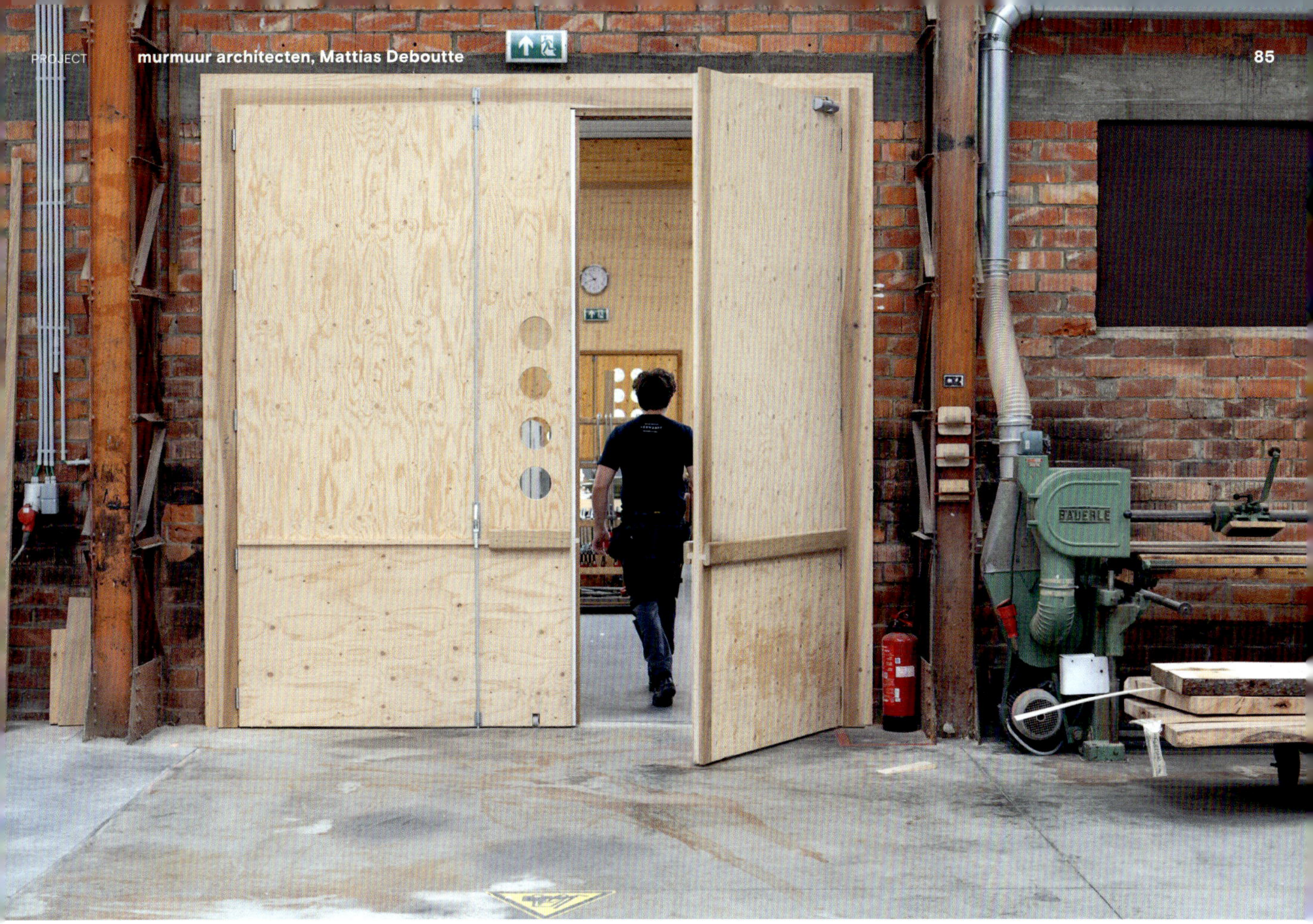
BAUERLE

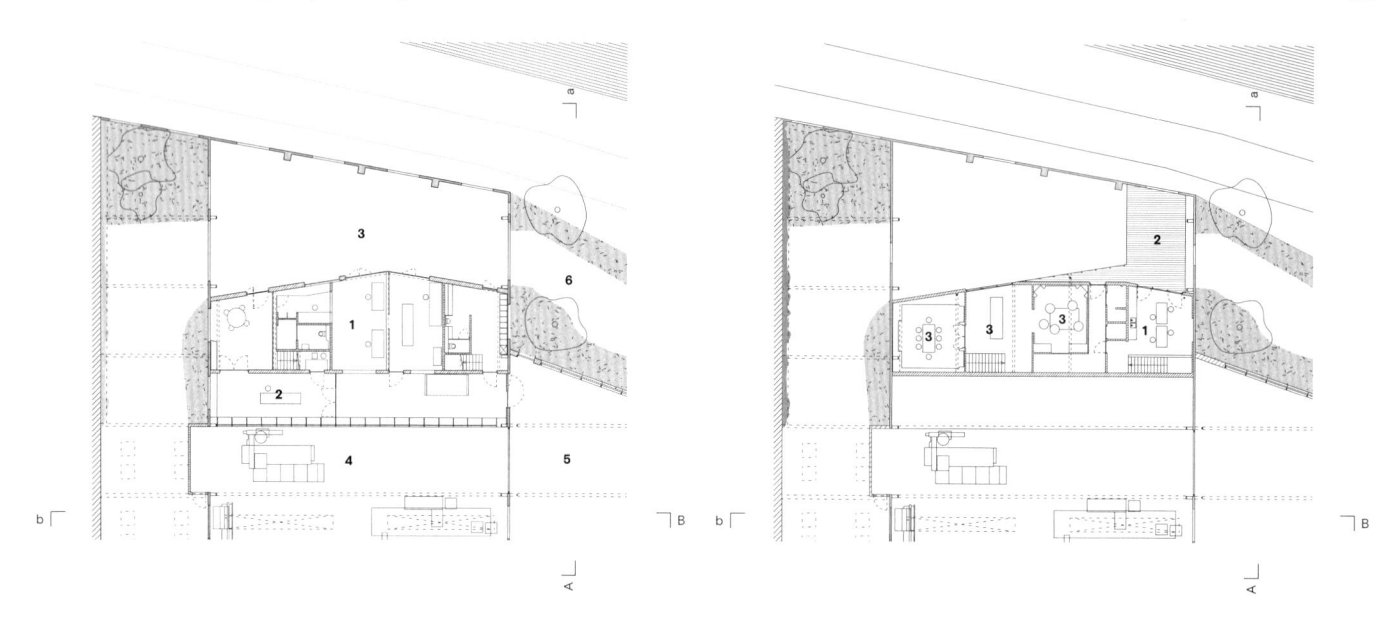

PROJECT **Verwerft carpentry workshop**

ground floor 0 2 10
1 office space, **2** drawing room, **3** reception and multipurpose hall, **4** machines hall, **5** assembly hall, **6** garden

level 1
1 staff room, **2** terrace, **3** showroom

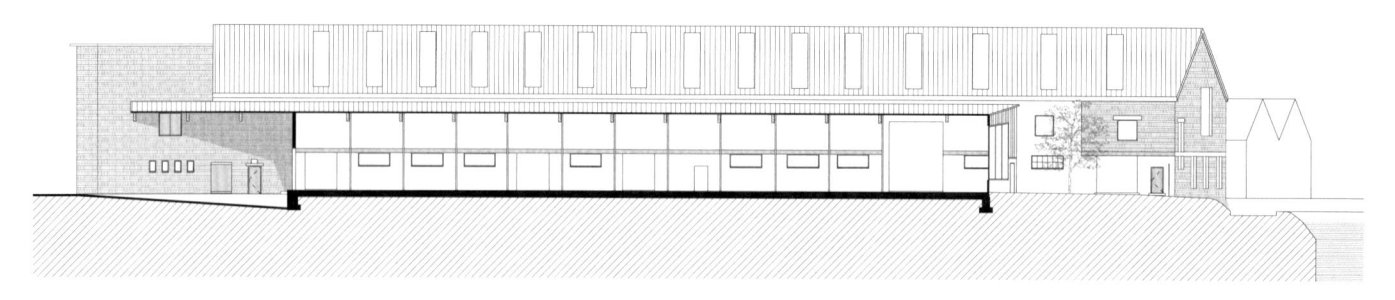

section Aa

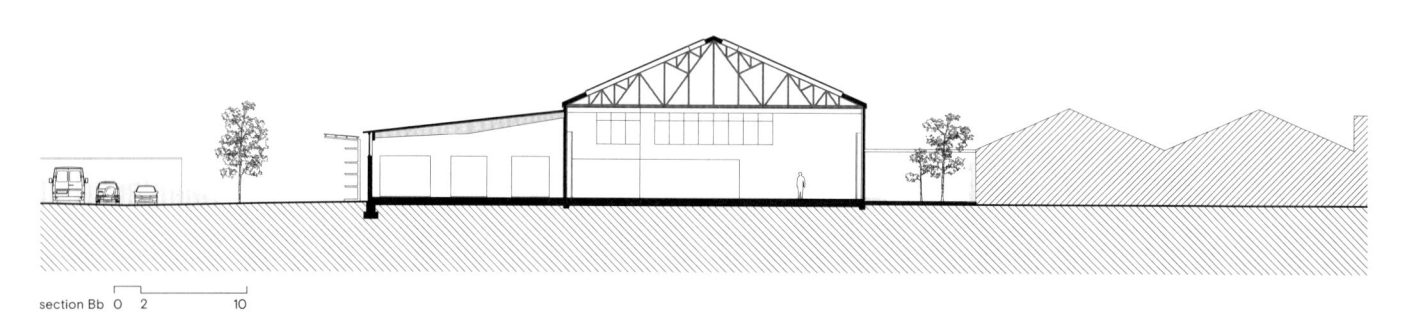

section Bb 0 2 10

PROJECT **Verwerft carpentry workshop**

project Verwerft carpentry workshop   **office** murmuur architecten with Mattias Deboutte
design team (murmuur) Emanuel Verstraete, Silke Van Damme, Joana Martins, Tinne Verwerft (Verwerft Schrijnwerkerij) Mattias Deboutte   **website** www.murmuur.eu
address Lierseweg 298, 2200 Herentals   **client** Verwerft Schrijnwerkerij   **design** August 2019
completion June 2022   **surface area** 3,481.50 m²   **volume** 24,595.60 m³
total building cost €1,002,235.23 excl. VAT   **total building cost per m²** (total) €287.87 excl. VAT
(new shed) €700 excl. VAT (office) €1,600 excl. VAT   **general contractor** Mathieu Gijbels, Oudsbergen
joinery and furnishings Verwerft Schrijnwerkerij, Herentals   **CLT construction** Arwo, Arendonk
electricity Welec, Westerlo   **stability studies** Gijbels Mathieu, Oudsbergen & Stabimi, Zwalm (in part)   **EPB studies** EMS, Deinze   **safety coordination** 2B-Safe, Glabbeek

text
Sophie Bresseleers
photography
01, 06–07, 09 © Delphine Mathy
02–05, 08 © Michiel De Cleene

PROJECT   **murmuur architecten, Mattias Deboutte**

ESSAY — An Editorial Mode of Practice

Architecture as a Story of Existing Elements, Topical Issues and Future Possibilities

Carlo Menon

This essay proposes to make a conceptual shift and consider architectural practice in terms of editorship rather than authorship. Although architectural work has always implied such editorial tasks as orchestrating design consultants and other stakeholders as well as negotiating their requirements, shifting the focus from author to editor makes it possible to grasp ongoing trends within some architectural offices, in Belgium and elsewhere.

  Author and editor are notions borrowed from the fields of literature and media studies. Although they undergo some changes in the transfer to architecture, the difference between them mostly remains. In literature, authors are considered as creative agents who fill the empty page, invent narratives from scratch and shape language into something original and unique. Editors are generally subs. They only work in relation to other people – authors, practitioners, technicians – and they mostly handle pre-existing material, including drafts, manuscript fragments, found correspondence and other broken prose. They mediate between author and reader, as their work responds to both.

  In architecture, editorship can concern the architects' attitude with regard to the existing site and other found materials; a wilfulness to understand the project as a collective process that involves people other than themselves; sometimes the way of using the budget; often, a taste for assembling existing components and found forms. Generally, it means accepting that the end result will not boast the architects' name in capital letters as a distinct piece of their oeuvre, since the outcome depends on many circumstances which the architects don't attempt to bend to their own idiom.

  This is not to say that architects who operate in an editorial mode of practice have renounced authorship. Authorship has been hardwired into architecture ever since this discipline formed in the Renaissance, with printing, perspective and Vasari's *Lives*: the architectural intervention is expected to be legible, coherent and often dominant in relation to its context, so as to 'sign' it, a reflection of the architect's persona. In an editorial mode of practice, by contrast, authorship is somehow fragmented, lessened, compromised: Fragmented, as the design is often the result of parallel questions tackled with their own tools and narratives, without hierarchy. Lessened, as a consequence of a renewed, inclusive if not pervasive acceptance of what is already there. Compromised, because the project is driven by different concerns and demands which the architects must accommodate, not the other way round. Rather than a clear 'statement', however subtle or bold, the resulting architectural language can be contradictory and can even welcome forms of bad taste (relatively speaking, as taste is also collectivized and not uniquely seen from a disciplinary perspective).

  Whereas such an editorial mode would have clashed with the celebrity architecture prevalent at the turn of the century, over the past fifteen years it has become more common, at least in Europe and certainly in Belgium, in line with the planetary and disciplinary crises that have progressively taken a central place in architectural discourse. It is not a pledge for architectural quality per se, but it is perhaps a sign of a different sensibility that rather suits the contemporary condition of architecture. If Europe is already and entirely built, if demolitions and new constructions are like a guilty, 'enormous breath of CO_2',[1] if increased norms and rules require spending a larger part of the budget on technicalities, and if budgets themselves require a lot of creativity

[1] Charlotte Malterre-Barthes speaking to students at ÉNSA Versailles on 2 February 2023.

ESSAY Carlo Menon

01

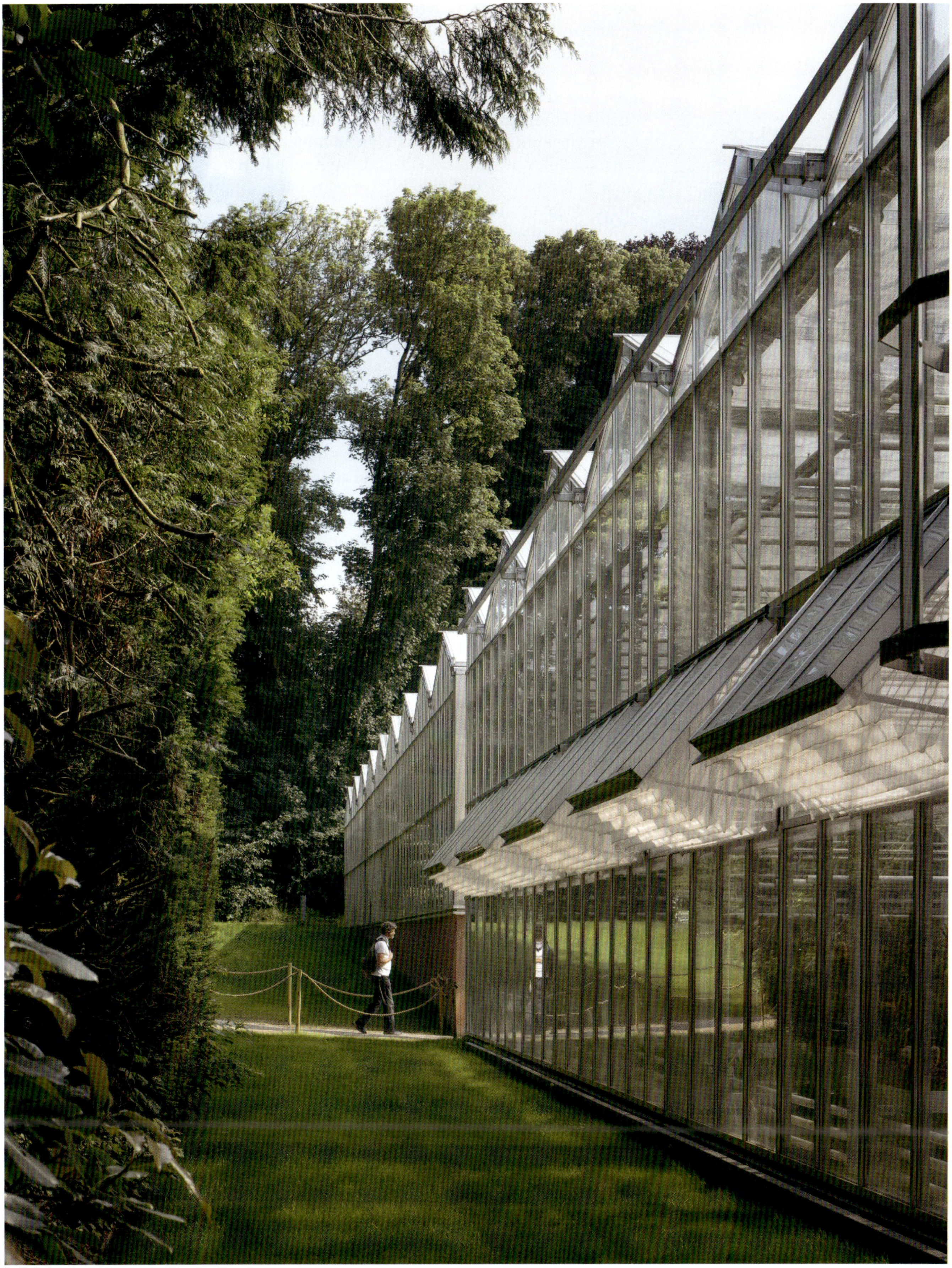

02

to meet the project's ambition, then this attitude can almost be seen as a 'natural' adaptation to the changing professional environment which architects are operating in, as the two projects reviewed below show.

Such a distinction is not equivalent to the difference between the architecture of Zaha Hadid Architects and that of Lacaton & Vassal, but the latter can be taken as a good example. Among their 'editorial' strategies, they refused to alter a public square, preferring instead an ordinary maintenance programme (Place Léon Aucoc in Bordeaux). They borrowed cheap, readymade technology to provide users with more free space in both new designs and renovations (from Latapie House to the Cité manifeste in Mulhouse, the Grand Parc in Bordeaux and the Tour Bois le Prêtre in Paris, both in collaboration with Frédéric Druot). And they spread out the budget to the point of renouncing any architectural imageability so as to provide the maximum space for exhibiting art at the Palais de Tokyo, challenging the standards for an art institution.

In literature, editing can take many forms and tones. In terms of intensity, it can range from delicate to authoritarian, overpowering the expression of the author. In tone, it can accentuate, or conversely neutralize, the accidents and non-canonical strengths of the existing text. In this book, the Zinneke project in Brussels by Ouest Architecture and Rotor combines an aesthetics of the as-found, at times ostentatious for the dissonances it creates between existing spaces and added reused material, with an expanded design process involving a close, day-by-day collaboration between architects, users and builders – with overlapping roles (see p. 161). More sober in outlook but equally outspoken in the redefinition of the architect's tasks, B-ILD engaged in a sort of self-editing practice whereby technical specifications and detailing are overtly reused from project to project, with the exception only of one or two 'new entries'. This enables the architects to save time for greater involvement upstream – in the project's stakes, its brief, its potential links to surrounding buildings and neighbouring institutions (see p. 197).

Among the built projects submitted for this book, a focus on two projects makes it possible to discuss architecture in an editorial mode of practice in more detail, not as a solution, but as a method with its own assets and grey areas.

Projects within a project

The Meise Botanic Garden extends over a large site with a castle, ponds, greenhouses, an orangery and arboretums. Like a museum, besides welcoming the general public it hosts renowned scientific activities based on its collections, nurseries and seed bank. Since 2016, NU architectuuratelier and Archipelago have been in charge of three projects: in 2021 they completed the entrance building, an open roof structure in precast concrete covered in timber; this year they delivered the Green Ark project, an event pavilion inserted within large new conservatories; and soon they will be renovating the farm and castle to encourage public use and venue rental – fundamental activities to help finance the scientific programmes.

A simple comparison between these projects shows a variety of approaches that cannot be traced back with certainty to one and the same hand. Rather, it seems that each project demanded a new toolkit. Zooming in, the Green Ark project itself can be seen as a combination of several interventions, each with its own language. The regular steel structure of the greenhouses sits on a basement construction in concrete which forms the floors and retaining wall. The whole looks at once practical and economical, only enhanced by its monumental size. A change in the cast concrete, highlighted by red pigment and vertical wood formwork, signals the narrow path that slopes down, through the conservatories, leading visitors towards the public

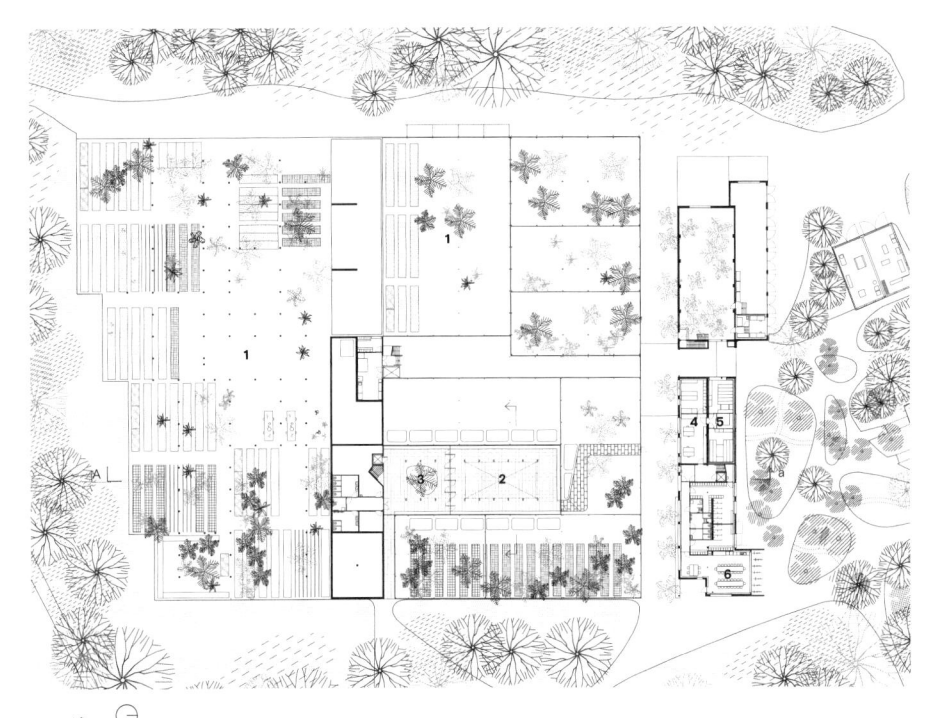

ground floor
1 collection greenhouse, **2** Green Ark visitor pavilion, **3** courtyard, **4** laboratory, **5** cold-store seed collection, **6** staff room

section Aa   0   5   25

area and pavilion. Here, on the ground level, space is organized by a colonnade in concrete that supports a robust deck in timber (the only formal resemblance with the entrance building). Surprisingly, then, the interior space above the colonnade is topped by a sophisticated timber hyperbolic paraboloid that reaches double or triple height and provides the project with its title, Green Ark. A second opening in the deck corresponds to a reservation made in the concrete floor to plant a tree, creating a courtyard in front of the ark. This time, both cuttings are kidney-shaped. To access the deck from the courtyard and so get closer to the outer shell of the ark, the red concrete wall forms a brutal, monochrome niche fitted with a diagonal stair that leads to a big window offering an immersive diagonal view into the conservatories, transforming them into a museum diorama. This series of architectural features is mostly hidden from the park, as it was set among the greenhouses in order to maximize visual contact with the plants. As said, the modernization and maintenance of the Botanic Garden comes with strategic marketing in mind: as 'editors' of the brief, the architects seem to have concentrated architectural spectacle at this particular spot of the project only, considering it one requirement among others, not an end in itself for the whole project.

The renovation of the service building nearby takes two other approaches, with both legible and mimetic interventions to improve the daily use of an unremarkable two-floor building with gabled roof. As the building blocked the walk towards the farm and castle, a large passage has been carved through it on the ground floor, offering views of the seed bank inside through large new openings. It could be argued that this operation is mimetic, as if the passage had always existed. Conversely, on the east side of the building, a shell in red concrete has been used to insert a trapezoidal volume to host a refectory for thirty-six members of staff – the same material, but a very different language than the staircase in the public pavilion.

ESSAY Carlo Menon 94

ESSAY **Carlo Menon** 95

These observations suggest that the architects may have been less concerned with containing the entire project within one coherent gesture than with accommodating an ad hoc approach befitting the management of the site and its existing structures, using architecture in various intensities and forms of expression. Given the number of projects and the progressive competence they must have acquired in regard to the Botanic Garden, the editorial role of the architects might even include a broader consulting activity across the entire site: to maintain its prestige and calm hospitality across time, it needs expertise from within and without.

project Botanic Garden greenhouses   **office** NU architectuuratelier with Archipelago
design team Sarah Callewaert, Armand Eeckels, Iwein Meyskens, Yannick Veny, Laura Béltran Gonzalez, Louise Vanderlinden, Zora Starcevic, Halewijn Lievens   **website** www.nuarchitectuuratelier.com, www.archipelago.be   **address** Nieuwelaan 38, 1860 Meise   **client** Meise Botanic Garden Agency
design November 2016   **completion** May 2024   **surface area** 10,280 m²   **volume** 5,580 m³
total building cost €14,658,495 excl. VAT   **total building cost per m²** €1,425 excl. VAT
main contractor Van Poppel, Mechelen   **stability studies** Mouton, Ghent
engineering studies Frans Zwinkels, Monster & Boydens Engineering, Brussels
greenhouse techniques Bosman Van Zaal, Aalsmeer

Tolerance

The repurposing of the Cordonnier factory in Wetteren by De Smet Vermeulen architecten underwent a long process after they won the competition in 2013, including several reversals regarding the budget and its purpose, from business centre to a well-equipped fine art academy coupled with a basement youth club. Most of the project is invisible today: the architects planned to demolish the large warehouse next to the taller factory so as to open up the block and create a large public passage around which several other buildings could be refurbished or added in the future. The make-do attitude often associated with De Smet Vermeulen is not equivalent to saving what exists at all costs (see also their repurposing of the Sacred Heart Church, p. 101). On the contrary, 'redacting' the warehouse constitutes the fundamental act that enables a totally original urban reconfiguration of the site, and the editorial skills of the architects must be credited at least as much as the respectful, queer attitude they deployed towards the building that was kept, taller and quirkier than the one that was demolished.

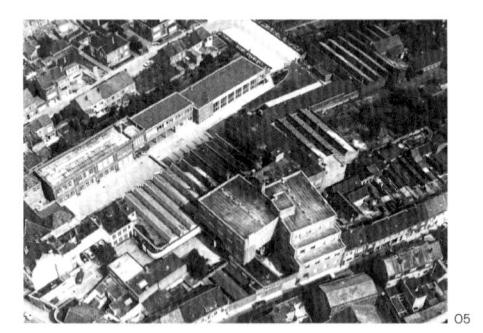

05

The building is recognizable in terms of volume, but it is difficult to say in one sentence whether the editing it underwent was light or heavy. Both inside and outside, the project rests on an (editorial) weaving between the existing, the repaired, the demolished, the added and the refurbished. The thin original strip windows placed on the top part of the manufacturing spaces have been lowered to let in more light. On the outside, a new terracotta-coloured cladding in fibre cement covers the original brickwork. A necessary external fire staircase proudly supports the new building sign. The entrance to the art academy, at the rear of the building, only seems to have been refreshed, while a separate one has been provided for the youth centre in the basement: large stairs descend from the street level and continue in an atrium defined by a retaining wall, with a protruding steel staircase leading back to the ground floor. In the basement, steel beams and braces reinforce the existing concrete slab – probably to comply with new statics standards – as well as the intricacy of the original plan, based on the encounter between two squarish volumes rotated at an angle to one another.

2   From the architects' submission for this book.

3   'Untimely' is used here in reference to Friedrich Nietzsche's *Untimely Meditations* (1873–76; Cambridge: Cambridge University Press, 1983), while 'untamed' is taken from Paul Vermeulen's essay on Architecten De Vylder Vinck Taillieu, 'Wild denken / The Untamed Mind', in *1 boek 2* (Antwerp: De Singel, 2011).

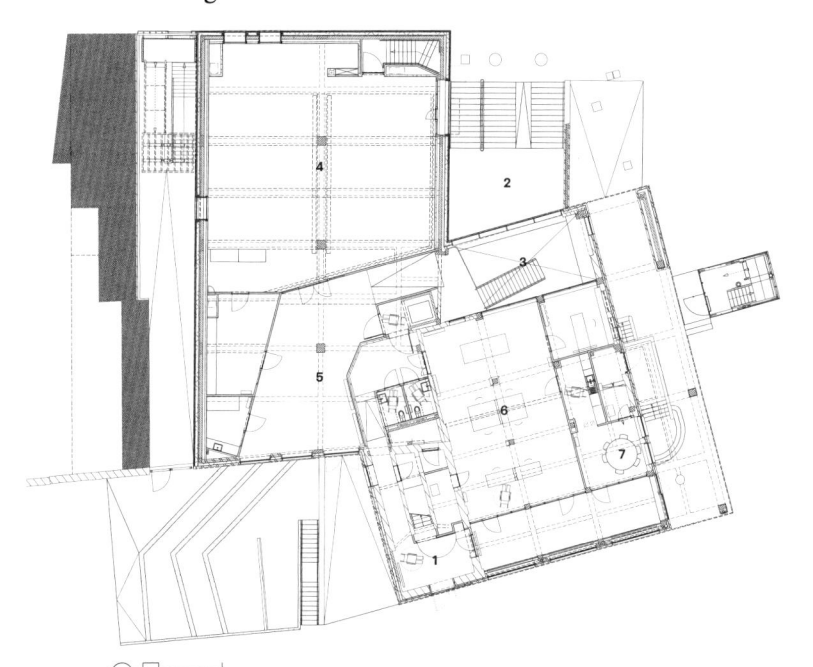

ground floor   0 1   5
1 workshop, **2** entrance hall art academy, **3** entrance hall youth centre, **4** atrium, **5** multipurpose hall, **6** foyer, **7** landscape office, **8** staff room

In short, a foreigner visiting Wetteren for the first time would have a hard time separating the old from the new and dating the interventions, as they do not use the same language everywhere. Some might even have been made decades ago, had the building already been in use. This seems to be the point the architects intended to make: 'Instead of a unifying approach, motifs and surprises surfaced, old and new, with just enough clarity to work as a public building … The unpredictable geometry and the polyphonic palette of old and new produce *tolerant interiors* where the creative work of the students can find a place' (my emphasis).[2] Here lies the difficulty that one might have with receiving the project. Other architects would probably have insisted on the play between old and new so as to make it the image of the building, 'the project'. In this regard, the Cordonnier factory is neither the clean cut of the Deelfabriek in Kortrijk (see p. 9) nor the assumed double face of the Winter Circus in Ghent (see p. 121), projects which capitalize on a pretty much established aesthetics of the as-found – all about boundaries. The Cordonnier factory defies categorization and remains somehow untimely, untamed.[3] De Smet Vermeulen are resistant to fashion and refrain from easy satisfaction. They have integrated Adolf Loos's anathema against architecture that cries for attention. Can this project be read as an immanent critique, in built form, of some contemporary tendencies in European architecture? It might also simply be the result of their diligence towards the project's specificities coupled with a certain nonchalance towards, if not disregard for, the effect it might have in other contexts than the very building itself and its users, an extreme form of ad hoc-ism. Indeed, this project calls for a non-judgemental architecture, one that supports daily use, aesthetically withdrawn but serene and joyful, ready to be experienced in a state of distraction. ▸

project Repurposing of the Cordonnier factory   **office** De Smet Vermeulen architecten
design team Peter Geens, Anabel Houtekier, Philine Vanrafelghem, Jantje Engels
website www.hdspv.be   **address** Lange Kouterstraat 1, 9230 Wetteren   **client** Municipality of Wetteren
design July 2019   **completion** December 2022   **surface area** 3,950 m²   **volume** 15,500 m³
total building cost €5,511,758 excl. VAT   **total building cost per m²** €1,600 excl. VAT
main contractor Himpe, Loppem   **stability studies** Norbert Provoost Engineering, Ghent
EPB and engineering studies HP Engineering, Oudenaarde
acoustics studies Daidalos Peutz, Leuven   **safety coordination** VETO & Partners, Oosterzele

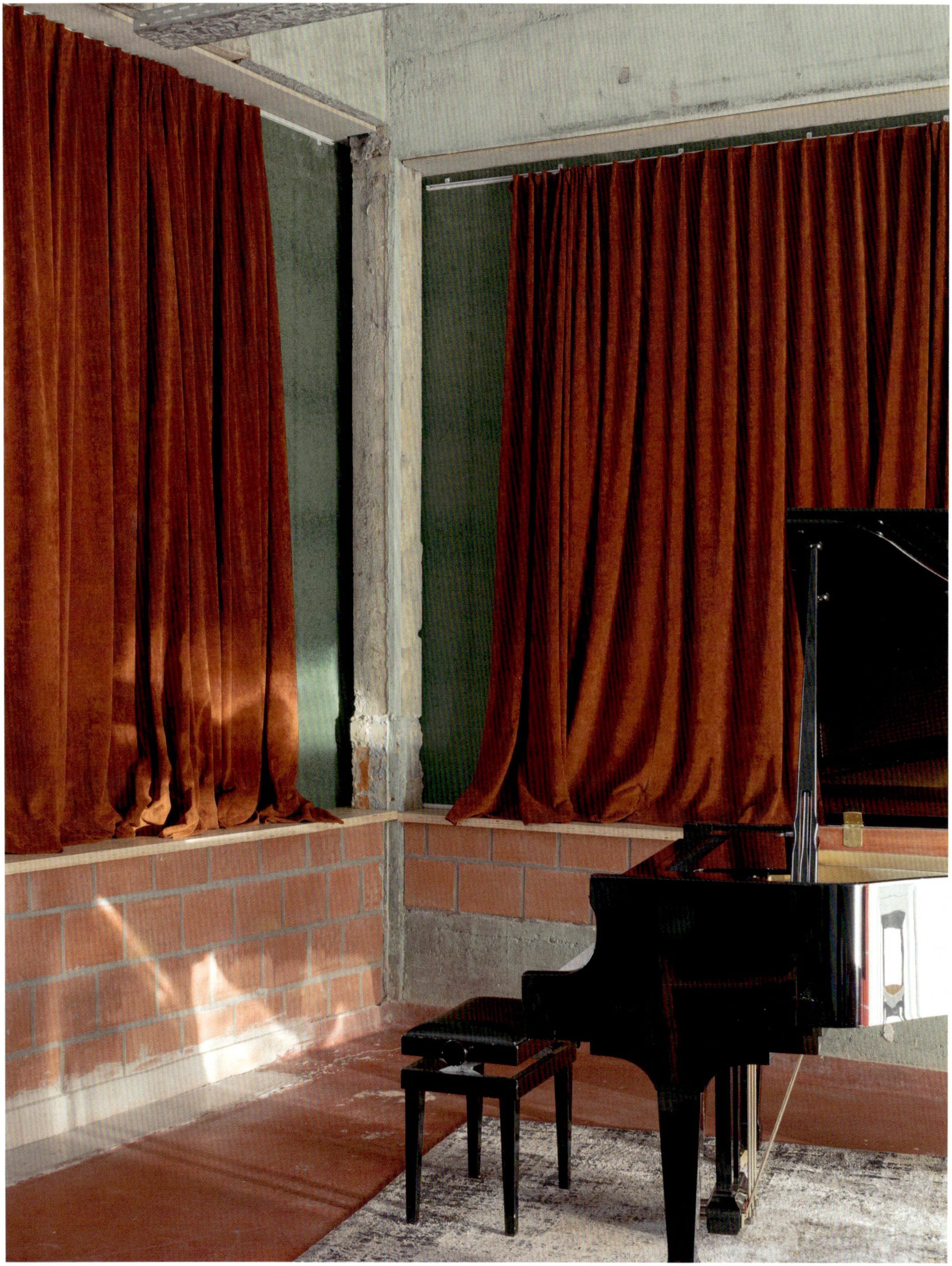

06

ESSAY **Carlo Menon** 99

To conclude, both the Botanic Garden greenhouses and the Cordonnier factory in Wetteren represent cases that question the design approach and the values that define architectural quality. Their design choices swing between ethics and aesthetics; populism, popularity and the rejection of a canon; use and exchange value. Looking at these projects from an editorial perspective makes it possible to accommodate some of the questions they raise within a larger trend in architectural practice, engaging the architectural audience to tune in at different frequencies than what is usually considered to be 'the job'.

photography
01–03, Botanic Garden greenhouses, Meise – NU architectuuratelier with Archipelago © Stijn Bollaert
04, 06–07, Repurposing of the Cordonnier factory, Wetteren – De Smet Vermeulen architecten © Dennis De Smet
05, aerial photo of Cordonnier factory, Wetteren © Wetteren municipal archive – private archive Paul Cordonnier, 1970

PROJECT   De Smet Vermeulen architecten

PROJECT

Repurposing of the Sacred Heart Church, Ghent

The repurposing of the Sacred Heart Church in the Ghent municipality of Sint-Amandsberg is part of the city's *En Route* strategy to revitalize less affluent neighbourhoods and improve public space. Centrally located in the district, the Sacred Heart Church offered opportunities to establish connections with the area and accommodate various social programmes.

After a competition, the assignment was awarded to De Smet Vermeulen architecten, who set themselves the goal of renovating the church in such a way that it would literally and figuratively generate connections: by activating the sides of the church and by creating spaces for different initiatives. Both sides of the church now form a new entrance: one leading to a car-free urban square with room for a market and other activities; and one to the garden, which is connected to the presbytery and the school located at the back. The covered gallery means that the church is a place where people can spend time even outside opening hours.

In the church itself, an extra floor has been inserted in the nave. The ground floor houses a community room and restaurant, while a multipurpose room is to be found on the floor above. The chapel has been left intact so that church services can still be held. In terms of materials, wooden built-in components were chosen for the floors and ceilings, and glass for the partitions, allowing for visibility between the different spaces. The presbytery was also included in the project: among other things, it received a new entrance on the garden side.

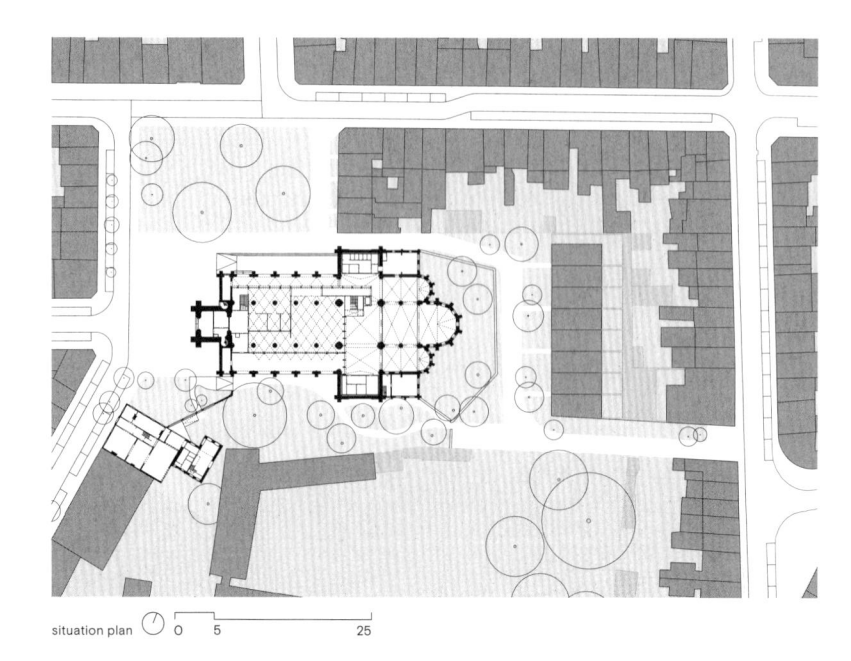

situation plan 0 5 25

PROJECT **Repurposing of the Sacred Heart Church** 103

With its new name, the Hartetroef project promises to become the heart of the neighbourhood, a place in and around which many different initiatives can unfold. The intervention therefore goes beyond just the building and offers Sint-Amandsberg social and spatial potential.

PROJECT   De Smet Vermeulen architecten   104

PROJECT   De Smet Vermeulen architecten

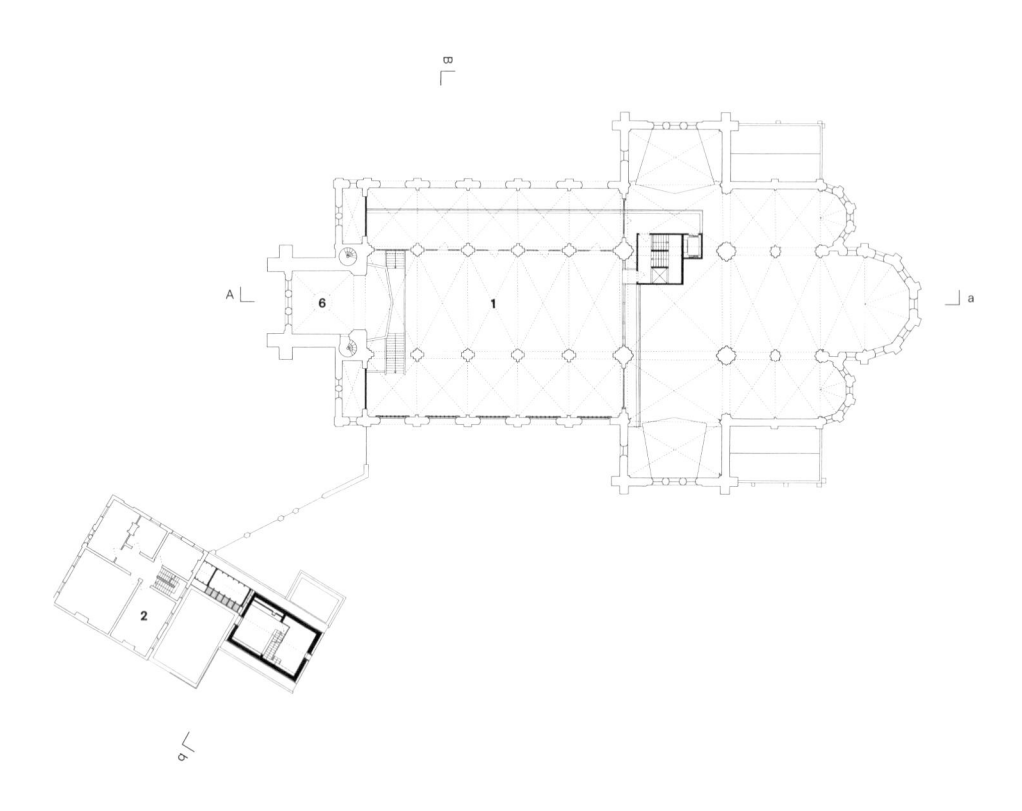

PROJECT **Repurposing of the Sacred Heart Church** 106

level 1
1 multipurpose hall, **2** community centre De Pastorie, **3** organ

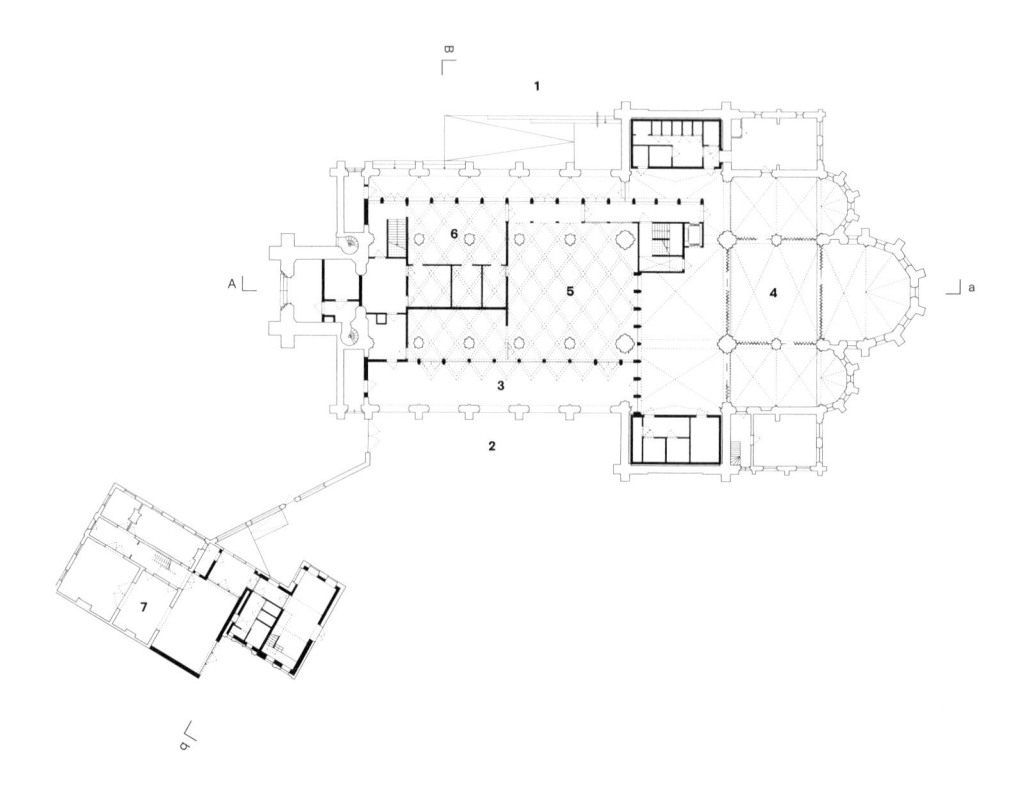

ground floor
1 Heilig Hartplein, **2** garden, **3** covered gallery, **4** multipurpose hall, **5** social restaurant, **6** kitchen, **7** community centre De Pastorie

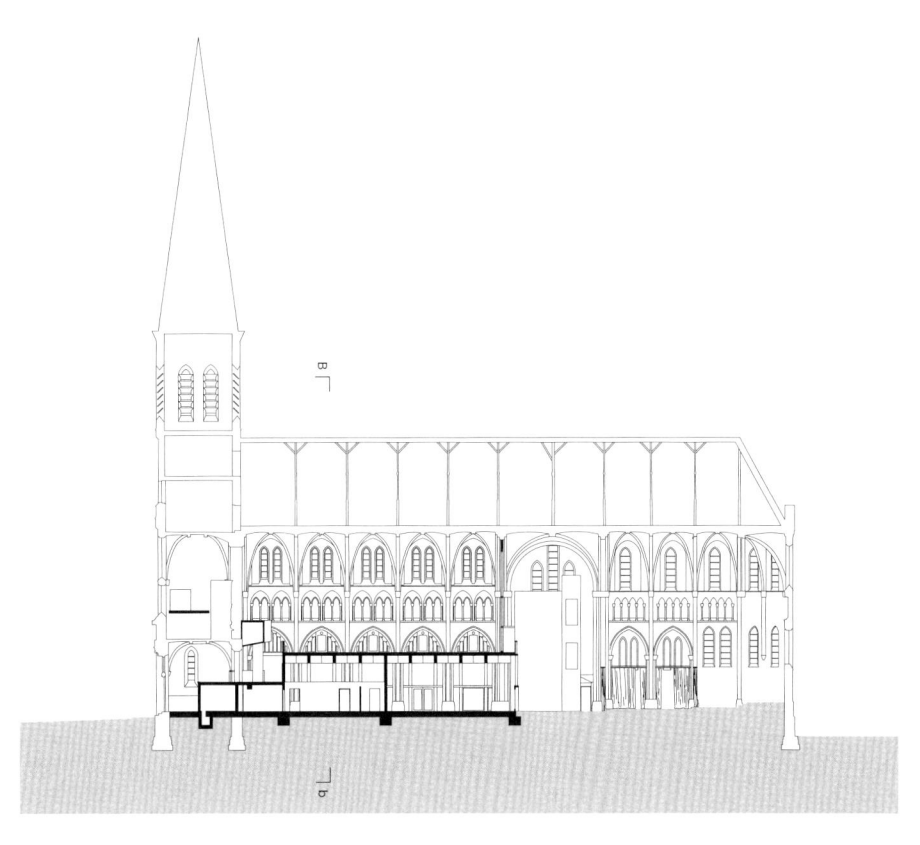

PROJECT **Repurposing of the Sacred Heart Church** 107

section Aa

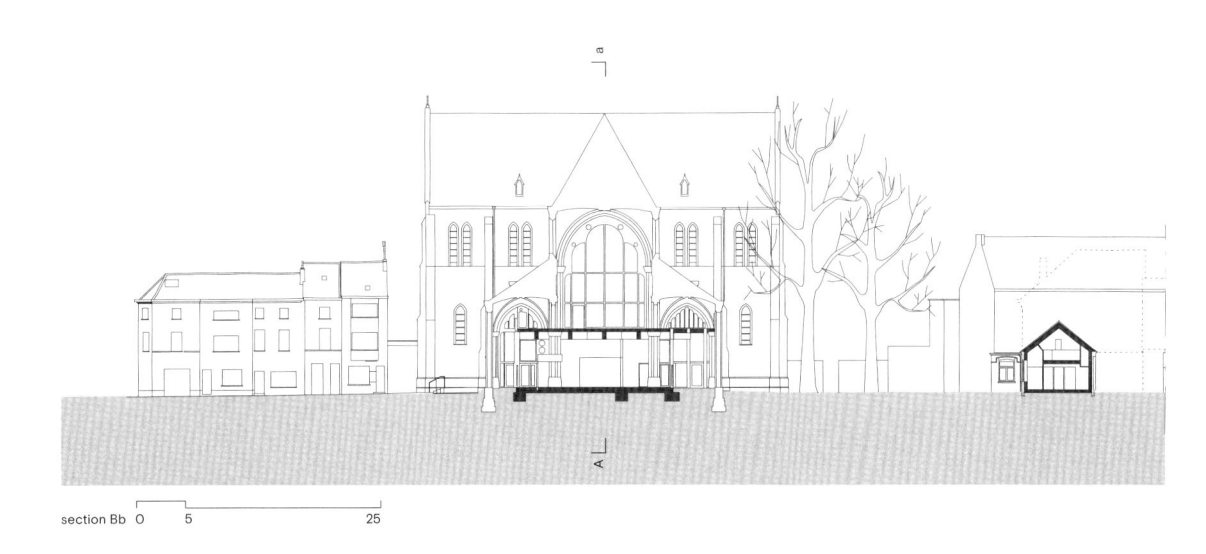

section Bb 0 5 25

project Repurposing of the Sacred Heart Church **office** De Smet Vermeulen architecten
design team Toon Vermeir, Aaron Derie, Jorge Reis, Joana Martins, Ruth Kennivé **website** www.hdspv.be
address Heilig Hartplein, 9040 Ghent **client** sogent **design** July 2019
completion December 2022 **surface area** (church) 1,550 m² (presbytery) 275 m²
total building cost (church) €3,530,000 excl. VAT (presbytery) €835,000 excl. VAT
main contractor (church) TM Vandendorpe, Zedelgem – Van Laere, Zwijndrecht (presbytery) Monument
Vandekerckhove, Ingelmunster **restoration studies** Juxta, Ghent
stability, engineering and EPB studies Tractebel, Antwerp **landscape design** Tractebel, Antwerp (next phase)
safety coordination VETO & Partners, Oosterzele

text
Klaske Havik
photography
01, 07-09 © Illias Teirlinck
02-06 © Dennis De Smet

PROJECT   De Smet Vermeulen architecten

ESSAY **Subtilitas**

In Search of Strategies for a New Building Culture

Sofie De Caigny

As sweeping transitions unfold in terms of climate, migration, a shifting world order and resource scarcity, a different building culture is emerging, one whose focus is shifting away from new build to alternative forms of engagement with existing structures. Despite such widely praised international commitments as the Davos Declaration (2018) and the New European Bauhaus (2020), which both advocate respectful treatment of our existing heritage, curbing the hunger for new buildings – all too often still constructed with toxic, non-circular and energy-guzzling materials – remains a tricky process. Demolition, still witnessed daily, makes this all too apparent. Tearing down and rebuilding from the ground up usually consumes far more energy than a gentler approach based on acceptance and targeted adjustment. A truly different building culture needs new design strategies. During the many site visits to projects submitted for this publication, I was struck by the apparent self-evidence of certain transformations. They seem to have arisen naturally and with minimal design intervention. In this essay, I suggest that this reluctance is an important ingredient within the much-needed changes occurring in building culture. I will argue this by analysing four projects.

Tailor-made exercises

An elegant pavilion stands on a plateau of sand-yellow tiles beside Rotselaar Lake. The rescue post with changing cubicles is busy in the summer. The pavilion stands on the same spot as its predecessor, whose structural elements it reuses. It is at once familiar and unmistakably new. Yet the location of the programme elements differs, as do some of the materials. Showering takes place behind a simple curved steel screen, an elegant, free-standing figure beside the pavilion which offers sufficient privacy. The position of the showers in Rotselaar not only increases user comfort and privacy, but also elevates the slim steel screen to an autonomous landscape element.

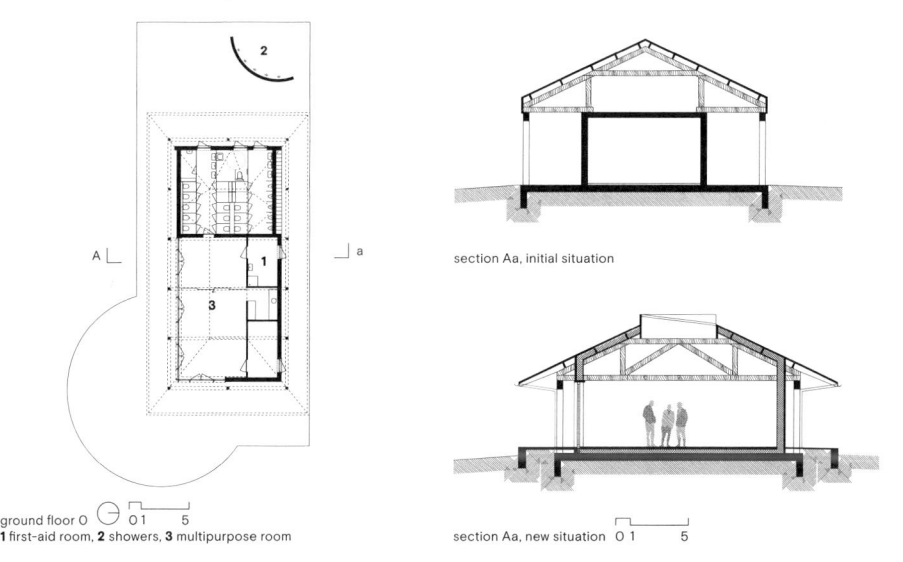

ground floor 0 0 1 5
1 first-aid room, **2** showers, **3** multipurpose room

section Aa, initial situation

section Aa, new situation 0 1 5

Beneath the pavilion's overarching hip roof are fixed benches that offer a view of the lake, sheltered from sun and rain. The zinc roof sits atop the concrete construction of the previous pavilion, which the designer, fijn architectuur atelier, ▶

ESSAY **Sofie De Caigny**

ESSAY **Sofie De Caigny** 111

ESSAY Subtilitas 112

decided to preserve. The wooden roof truss of the old pavilion has been reused, after being truncated in the ridge to provide the entire building with daylight. Future adaptations have been factored in by ensuring that neither internal walls nor façades are load-bearing. A restrained colour palette of blue, grey and yellow invokes associations with beach tourism, strengthening the overall cohesion. Behind the modest and clearly legible appearance lie ingenious design decisions and complex negotiation processes with the contractor. Yet the pavilion appears self-evident to users. The experience is one of familiarity.

project De Plas swimming pavilion **office** fijn architectuur atelier **design team** Liesbeth Put, Peter-Jan Depreeuw, Jonas Van Molle **website** www.fijnatelier.be **address** Vakenstraat 18, 3110 Rotselaar **client** AGB Rotselaar **design** January 2021 **completion** June 2023 **surface area** 162 m² **volume** 576 m³ **total building cost** (building) €595,000 excl. VAT (surroundings) €110,000 excl. VAT **total building cost per m²** €3,675 excl. VAT **main contractor** Coordinat-ed, Mechelen **stability studies** BAS, Leuven **engineering studies** VDB Engineering, Mechelen

Studio Paola Viganò and vvv architecture urbanisme applied a similar strategy to Marie Jansonplein in the Brussels municipality of Saint-Gilles. Here too, the design was based on a thorough reading of the existing site. This 'reading' ranged from the smallest detail to an embedding within the broader context of the urban ecological structure. Most of the trees were preserved and plotted onto a grid. Their positions determined the future development of the square and the soft division of the terrain into discrete zones, each of which facilitates a different type of usage: from play area to sunbathing spot or market. To determine these functions, the designers conducted an analysis of the various local users at different moments of the day and night.

More than half of the pre-existing paving stones have been used in a new configuration. Covered kiosks have been placed on three of the square's corners. These are clearly interrelated in terms of colour and materiality, but each has its own shape that chimes with its respective function. The project recognizes that some of the site's key characteristics have a much longer history: the existing materials, the trees and the park's urban figure and location as a connection between the mineral grey, paved Parvis de Saint-Gilles and the small parks and green squares in the upper part of the municipality. The design has been conceived in such a way that it will gain in quality over time: the trees and plants will grow and enhance the ecosystem of small urban green spaces in Saint-Gilles. As in Rotselaar, there is a tension between the self-evidence with which the project presents itself and the time and cost invested. It is a form of inconspicuous attentiveness that to this day garners scant recognition in the architectural discourse.

project Marie Jansonplein **office** Studio Paola Viganò and vvv architecture urbanisme **design team** Paola Viganò, Guillaume Vanneste, Nicolas Willemet, Bertrand Plewinski, Manu Vanderveken **website** www.studiopaolavigano.eu, www.vvvarchitectes.be **address** Marie Jansonplein, 1060 Sint-Gillis **client** Municipality of Sint-Gillis **design** January 2019 **completion** June 2023 **surface area** 15,250 m² **total building cost** €3,600,000 excl. VAT **total building cost per m²** €236 excl. VAT **main contractor** Colas, Brussels **stability studies** BAS, Leuven **landscape design** ARA, Antwerp

As soon as you enter the Balschool in Berchem, with its newly restored early-twentieth-century façade, you can see that a new layer has been woven through the building. A grey-green tile pattern, a door to the playground drilled through an existing window, and striking yellow-painted gas pipes all convey coherence and playfulness. Starting at the entrance, a green skirting board runs throughout the complex: in the corridors, in new joinery details, in the gym, the refectory and the fixed playground furniture. Residual spaces have been upgraded to pleasant hang-out spots thanks to the inclusion of green tiled benches. The matching skirting board creates unity across the complex, which had undergone ad hoc expansion over time.

The project aligns with Stedelijk Onderwijs Antwerpen's broader mission of tackling its outdated heritage. import.export Architecture updated the school by excising volumes in the silted-up complex with surgical precision and by making existing characteristics visible again. Much of the original building has retained its intrinsic value for the past century: façade, tall windows, large classrooms, wide corridors, durable cement tiles, fixed furniture in the corridors and stairs, and so on. The building can last another century at least. The approach taken was more of a restoration. To improve circulation and increase the legibility of the school complex, import.export removed the building extensions. The designers created architecture by shaping the demolition and removal process. Not unlike the post-war Italian *restauro critico*, the equivalent treatment of cutting away, repairing, adding and restoring creates moments of poetry. In the Balschool, this is expressed in a window that becomes a showcase, in an exceptionally detailed corner window that visually links two play areas, and in the emphatic accentuation when existing façade openings have been breached.[1]

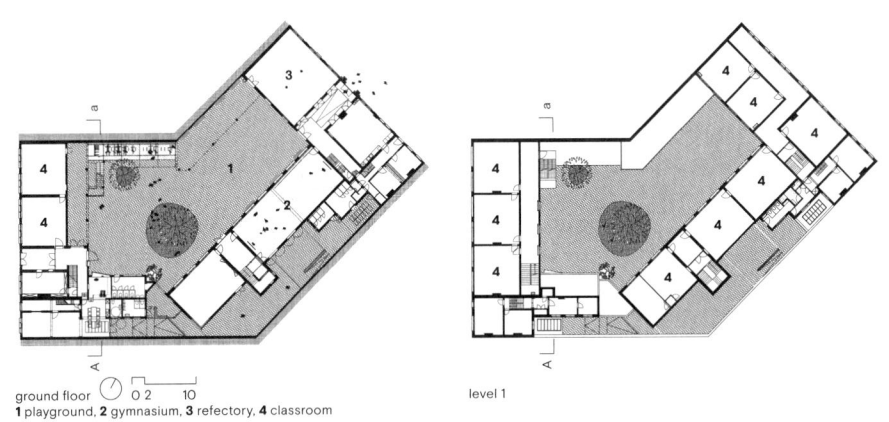

1 Jean-François Bédard et al., eds., *Carlo Scarpa Architect: Intervening with History* (Quebec: Canadian Centre for Architecture, Montreal in collaboration with Monacelli Press, 1999).

ground floor 0 2 10
1 playground, **2** gymnasium, **3** refectory, **4** classroom

level 1

The result is both expressive and honest, and also more ecological thanks to improved insulation and a partly depaved playground. The interventions fit within a continuum of changes to the building. import.export is aware that they will not be the last designers to make alterations to the school. This sense of reality does not rule out ambition. While the assignment was initially smaller, the architects convinced the clients of the added value that could be achieved with a broader renovation. In so doing, they were driven as much by their love of heritage as by their intention to establish a pathway with the users that would translate their needs into the project.

project Klavertjevier primary school (Balschool) **office** import.export Architecture
design team Oscar Rommens, An Vanderveken, Diede Ramakers, Bart Biesemans, Renee Favere
website www.iea.be **address** Jozef Balstraat 6, 2600 Berchem **client** AG Stedelijk Onderwijs Antwerpen
design September 2017 **completion** January 2022 **surface area** (built) 2,225 m² (playground) 659 m²
volume 12,228 m³ **total building cost** €2,167,081 excl. VAT **total building cost per m²** €970 excl. VAT
main contractor Monument Goedleven, Brasschaat **stability studies** Eddy Henskens, Hemiksem
EPB studies and safety coordination Eveka, Sint-Niklaas **acoustics studies** Dox Acoustics, Wommelgem **landscape design** import.export Architecture, Antwerp

In Antwerp's Zuid quarter, Poot Architectuur has also renovated a twentieth-century school building. Here too, you experience the silent power of the transformation when the entrance gate swings shut. Fixed burgundy benches turn the passage into a place where students can congregate. Along a depaved patio, a covered internal street leads to the central playground via the secretariat. A new canopy in the same colour borders the playground. This has significantly improved circulation. Indeed, the school has no corridors; all classes are *en enfilade* and give onto three stairwells that lead to the playground, through which all the circulation in the building is routed.

The same burgundy colour sets the tone throughout the school and weaves all the new interventions together. This makes Poot's intervention highly legible and present. At the same time, it is so self-evident as to be almost imperceptible. The core of the design lies in reading and making legible, enhancing coherence by both removing and adding a new layer in a highly controlled manner. Fixed furniture plays a leading role in the process.

ESSAY **Sofie De Caigny** 114

ESSAY **Sofie De Caigny**

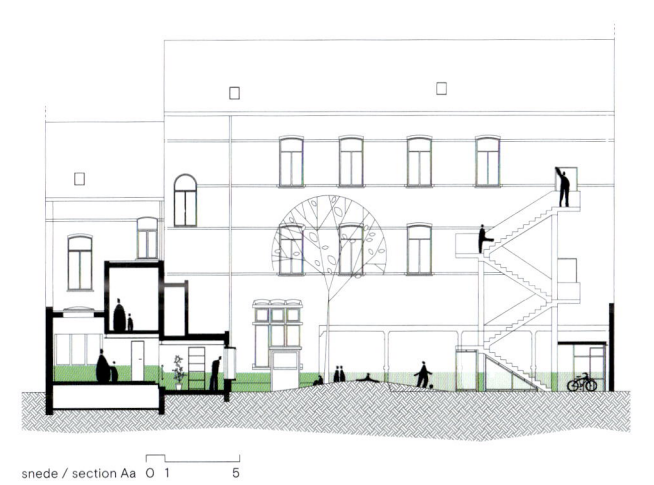

snede / section Aa 0 1 5

ground floor 0 2 10
1 bicycle shed, 2 changing room, 3 entrance, 4 teachers' room, 5 secretariat, 6 sports hall, 7 classroom, 8 covered playground, 9 teachers' house, 10 science room, 11 dance hall, 12 recording studio

The school was given a tactile and user-friendly layer in the form of wall coverings with storage areas, sinks and seating. It incorporates new connections between classrooms, which enable inter-class lessons and project work. The upgrading of residual spaces beside the sports and dance hall into changing and seating areas has also been achieved using fixed furniture. The knowledge that interiors have an average lifespan of fifty years, while the shell and structure of the building will last for hundreds, makes the choice to upgrade the school through the furniture not only generous but also unpretentious.

project Groenhout secondary school Vjera Sleutel, Gaëlle Degezelle, Matilde Everaert **address** Kasteelstraat 17, 2000 Antwerp **completion** October 2023 **surface area** 3,496 m² **volume** 14,261 m³ **total building cost** €3,843,951 excl. VAT **total building cost per m²** €1,100 excl. VAT **stability studies** Raymond Van Soens, Schilde **EPB studies** Vicave, Wuustwezel **landscape design** Poot Architectuur, Antwerp **office** Poot Architectuur **design team** Sarah Poot, **website** www.poot-architectuur.be **client** AG Vespa & AGSO **design** March 2018 **main contractor** Brebuild, Antwerp **engineering studies** Botec, Wommelgem **acoustics studies** Venac, Anderlecht **safety coordination** Eveka, Sint-Niklaas

Minimal intervention

2 André Loeckx, 'LABO RUIMTE, drie verkenningen in radicaal realisme', in *Bouwmeesterrapport* (Brussels: Team Flemish Government Architect, 2020), 176.

The four projects all share the ambition to bring about the greatest possible spatial improvement with as few material resources as possible (demolition and new materials and their transport, CO_2 emissions, etc.), an aim fulfilled by combining several design strategies. An initial strategy comprises an intense search for the existing characteristics, a '"neorealistic" attitude to work with "the things that are there"'.[2] A second strategy presupposes that much of the design effort will remain invisible. Behind the apparent self-evidence of the four projects lies much invisible design work: complex processes of separating, repairing, breaking through, connecting, cutting loose and reconfiguring. In Saint-Gilles, the intention to limit the ecological impact involved convincing contractors to break out, clean and rearrange paving stones on-site; in Rotselaar, sawing and reassembling a twenty-five-year-old wooden roof truss on the premises; and in the Balschool persuading the public client to green-light a process that would take twice as long as originally envisaged. The invisible work also involves the 'dirty' job of evaluating used materials on their current performance. Tasks entrusted to architects for centuries, but taken away from them after World War II. In the current circumstances, which call for reuse, this challenges the role of the architect.

The third strategy is to realize that nothing lasts forever and that, as an architect, you are merely a passer-by in a building or place. The simple fact of recognizing that reality and acting on it facilitates future developments: no load-bearing walls in the swimming pavilion, responding to the as-yet-unknown needs of future users; leaving pipes exposed in the Balschool and painting them a contrasting yellow, aware that they will be replaced in a few decades anyway; and anticipating where future trees can grow in Saint-Gilles. Poot gives a school building a second life when it is still unclear what kind of school it will house. This requires a design that can support a variety of teaching methods without sacrificing eloquence. In so doing, all these designers accept imperfection, are willing to deal with surprises and to make adjustments, but also to let go when the time is right. The answer is not always architecture.

The reluctance to make overpowering architectural gestures recalls the work of Swiss sociologist Lucius Burckhardt (1925–2003). He advocated a minimalist design approach. In contrast to the iconic structures created by 'starchitects', which emphatically carry the contemporary architect's signature, he posits the alternative of soft, almost invisible design approaches. Like the four projects, his ideas about minimal intervention begin with a very precise mapping and reading of the pre-existing situation.[3] For Burckhardt, these comprise the needs of users, the financial, social and spatial conditions, and the materials. His theory departs from the spatial experience, which he views as having a clear aesthetic dimension. Burckhardt describes how minimal interventions enhance this experience and, in turn, the spatial quality.

Material literacy plays a hugely important role.[4] I call it the last strategy. It refers to an excellent understanding of construction elements, both in terms of their durability, quality and aesthetic expression, and in terms of how users might react to them and interact with them. This literacy does not express itself in words, but is internalized. It is the skill of architects who can gauge the effects of materials on users. To achieve these effects, designers focus on colour, rhythm, tactility, patina, texture, association, tone. They promote coherence and legibility, and enable the user to experience an ensemble. According to Pallasmaa,[5] they use the sensory power of materiality and spaces to indicate which places are more intimate or public. This material literacy seems to be a necessary precursor to the success of minimal interventions.

Finally, and underlying all other strategies, I read in the projects a mild and modest attitude reminiscent of the value system of bell hooks. She championed a culture of love, cooperation and understanding of the other.[6] When translating this perspective into architectural practice, 'the other' takes shape in the user, the client, the maker, the employee, the non-human occupants such as plants and animals, and the layered memory of the place. Her theory encourages the expansion of the Vitruvian triangle with a fourth element, *subtilitas* to be added to *firmitas*, *utilitas* and *venustas*,[7] thus arriving at a truly new building culture. This value expresses how to create architecture: not by making hard and indelible gestures, but by perceptively reading and appreciating the existing characteristics. It involves a targeted approach to the investment of materials, time and energy; and knowing where and how to subtract instead of adding, and when to be cautious. *Subtilitas* thus means to make architecture that subtly and decisively enhances spatial quality in terms of usage, ecology and experience.

3 Markus Ritter and Martin Schmitz, ed., *Lucius Burckhardt: The Minimal Interventions* (Basel: Birkhauser, 2022).

4 Mara Trübenbach, *Material Dramaturgy: Tracing Trails of Dust in the Architectural Design Process* (PhD diss., Oslo School of Architecture and Design, 2024), 45.

5 Juhani Pallasmaa, *The Eyes of the Skin: Architecture and the Senses* (Chichester: Wiley, 1996).

6 Lara Schrijver, 'Van rivaliteit naar ruimhartigheid: feministische notities voor de architectuur', in *Vrouwen in architectuur* (Rotterdam: nai010 uitgevers, 2023), 158–73.

7 An exercise was conducted in 2001 into the importance of architectural quality in Flanders today. The authors argue that the Vitruvian triangle is still useful for ascribing architectural quality when the values are considered to be the future value, utility value and experiential value of buildings and places. See Hilde Heynen et al., *Architectuurkwaliteit vandaag: Reflecties over architectuur in Vlaanderen* (Brussels: Royal Flemish Academy of Belgium for Science and the Arts, 2021).

ESSAY **Sofie De Caigny** 118

snede / section Aa   0 1   5

ESSAY **Sofie De Caigny**

photography
01, De Plas swimming pavilion, Rotselaar – fijn architectuur atelier © Jeroen Verrecht
02, Marie Jansonplein, Sint-Gillis – Studio Paola Viganò with vvv architecture urbanisme © Michiel De Cleene
03-04, Klavertjevier primary school (Balschool), Antwerp – import.export Architecture © Tim Van de Velde
05-06, Groenhout secondary school, Antwerp – Poot Architectuur © Stijn Bollaert

PROJECT

Atelier Kempe Thill, aNNo (concept)
Baro Architectuur, SumProject (architect)

PROJECT # Winter Circus, Ghent   122

In 2005 sogent bought the Winter Circus in Ghent on behalf of the city authorities. Erected in the late nineteenth century as a covered circus for urban entertainment and large-scale events, the monument had been empty for several years by then already. The building's appearance today is the result of restoration work carried out in 1923 after a fire in 1920. After World War II, the former circus became a garage. The owner, Mahy, redesigned the internal circulation so that vehicles could reach the top of the building. In the late 1990s, the building was vacated and the search began for a new meaning for the city.

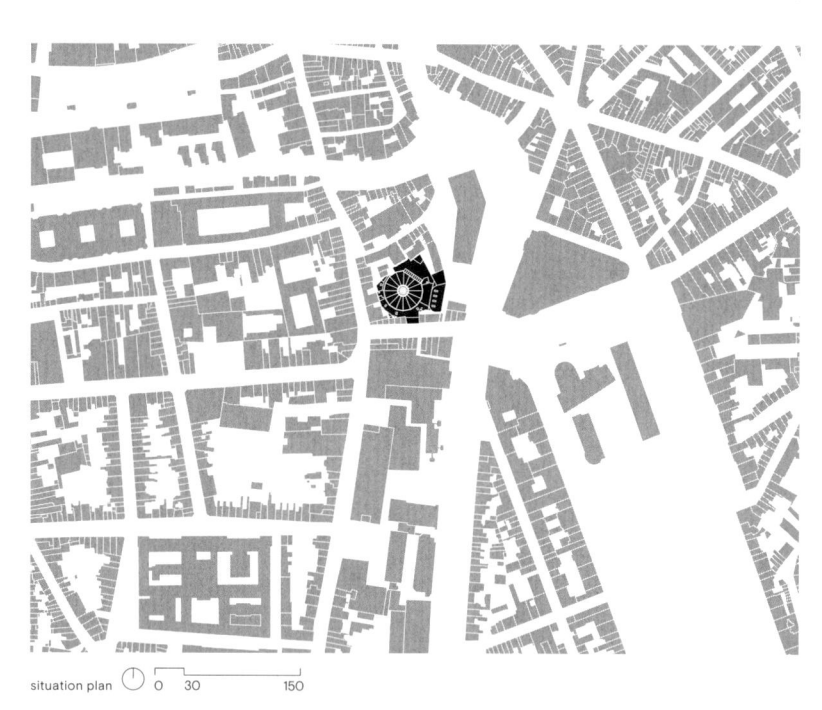

sogent launched an architectural competition to redevelop the Winter Circus and adapt it to the needs of the future concession holder. The latter aspired to turn it into an urban hub with a café and a restaurant, spaces for innovative or emerging companies, and a large events hall. The team made up of Atelier Kempe Thill and aNNo won the competition with a proposal that focused on preserving the large open central hall and the building's rough and weathered character.

situation plan   0   30   150

PROJECT **Winter Circus**

All the building phases of the Winter Circus have left traces. Nevertheless, this huge urban palimpsest is remarkably coherent. The earthen-red factory floors of the former Mahy garage and the weathered plaster on the walls contribute to this overall impression. The designers gave the new concrete floor of the central hall the same colour. When Baro, SumProject and VK Engineering took over in the final phase of the conversion, they added skirting boards, stairs and benches around the central arena in the same colour again, refining the approach of Atelier Kempe Thill and aNNo.

The heart of the project is the hall or central arena. All spaces on the fourteen floors feed into it or look out onto it. Beneath the arena is an events hall with seating for 500 people, like a box in a box. The building is accessible on three floors from the surrounding streets. A rising cylindrical spiral starts on the level of the central arena, leading up to the roof terrace – the route the cars followed at the time of Garage Mahy still steers the way the building is experienced and read.

Getting the Winter Circus ready for its new functions involved a lot of invisible work. More than 125 years old, the building now conforms to ▶

PROJECT   **Atelier Kempe Thill, aNNo (concept), Baro Architectuur, SumProject (architect)**

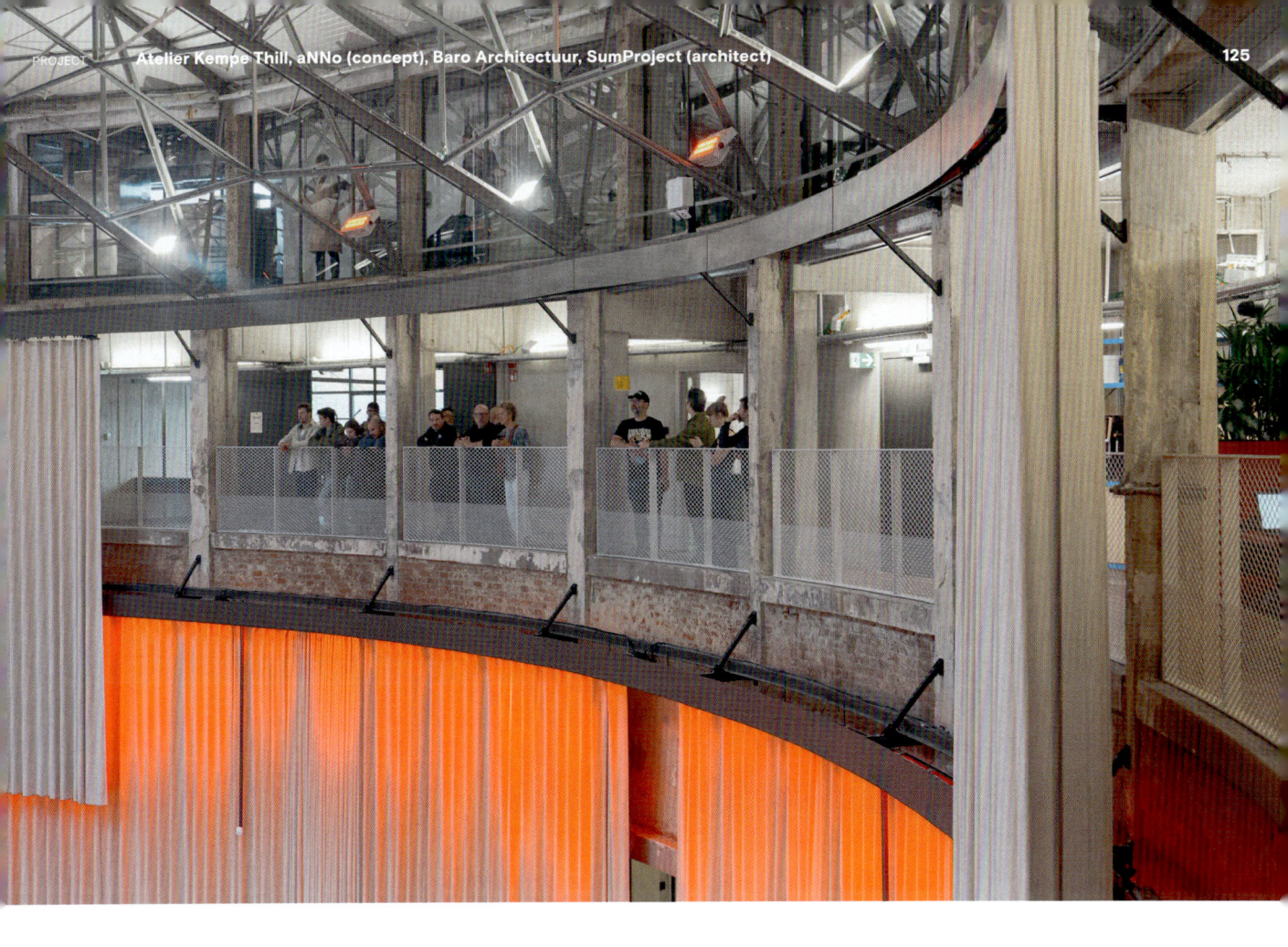

Atelier Kempe Thill, aNNo (concept), Baro Architectuur, SumProject (architect)

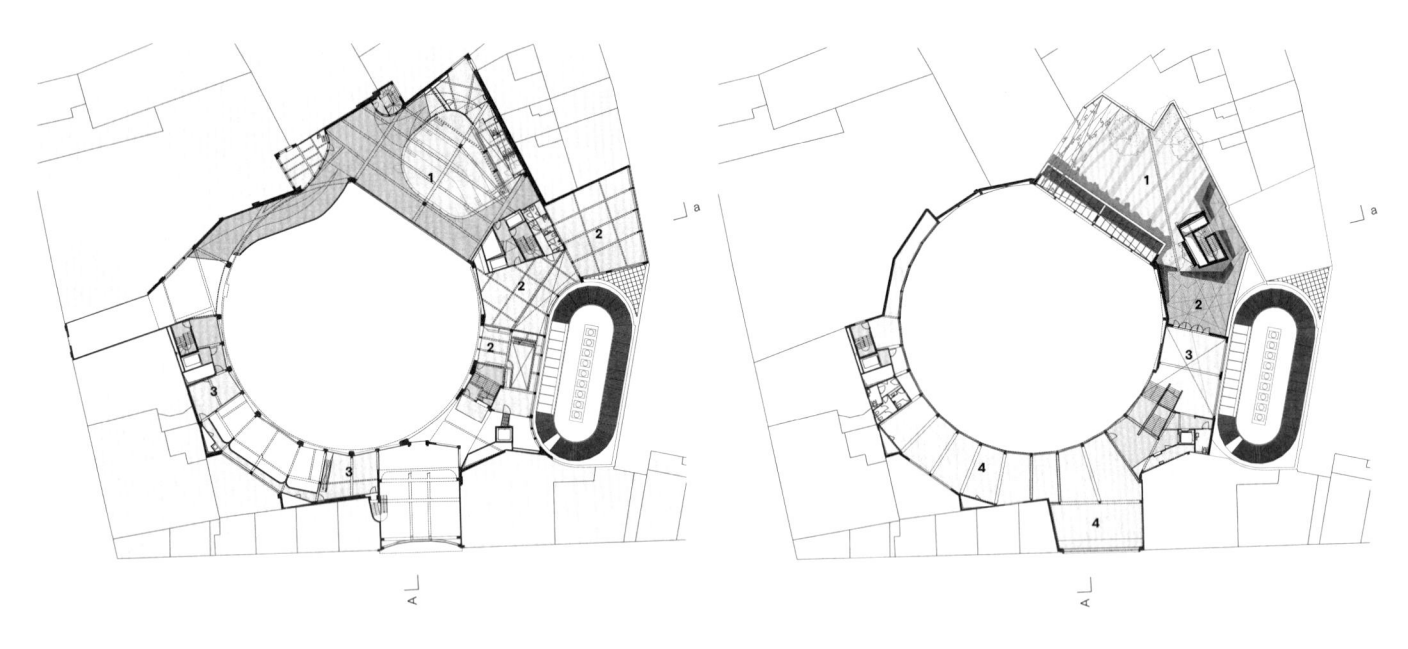

PROJECT **Winter Circus** 126

level 1
1 auditorium, **2** office space, **3** bar

level 3
1 roof garden, **2** roof terrace, **3** bar, **4** office space

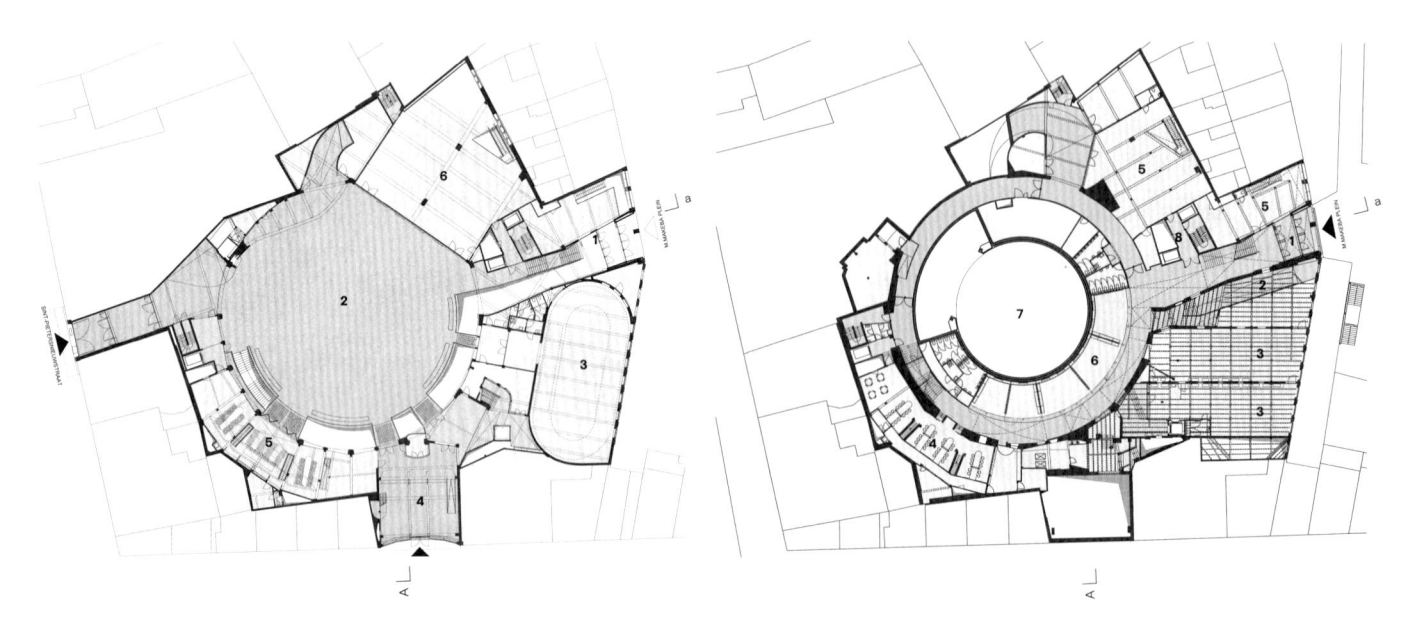

ground floor
1 vestibule, **2** central courtyard, **3** former hippodrome / multipurpose hall, **4** entrance hall, **5** bar, **6** commercial area

level -1
1 vestibule, **2** elephant ramp, **3** artist studios / fablabs, **4** bar, **5** commercial space, **6** meeting room, **7** concert hall (level -2)

PROJECT **Winter Circus**

requirements for contemporary public buildings in terms of fire stability, acoustics and load-bearing capacity. The roof has been sound-proofed and insulated. Below the building is a Borehole Thermal Energy Storage (BETS) system shared with the nearby De Krook city library.

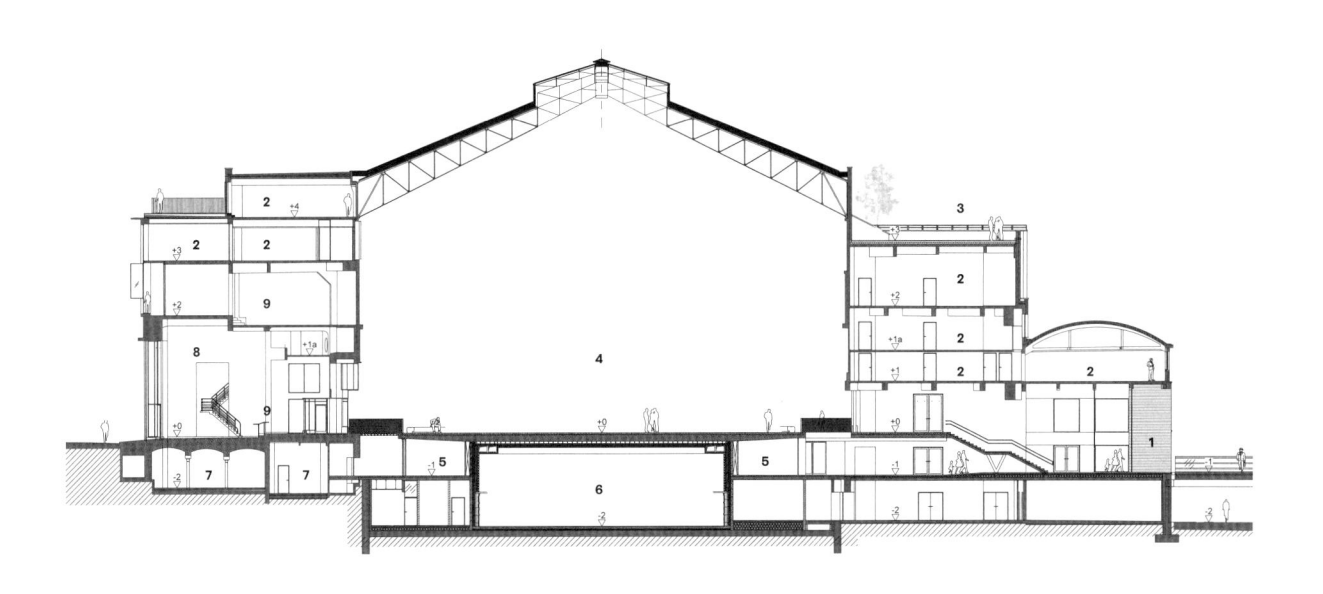

section Aa 0 2 10
1 vestibule, **2** office space, **3** roof garden and terrace, **4** central courtyard, **5** meeting room, **6** concert hall, **7** commercial space, **8** entrance hall, **9** office space

project Winter Circus **office** Atelier Kempe Thill with aNNo (architect-concept designer) Baro Architectuur with SumProject (architect) **design team** (Atelier Kempe Thill) André Kempe, Oliver Thill, Marc van Bemmel, Karin Wolf, Charline Busson, Renzo Sgolacchia, Pauline Durand, Valérie Van de Velde, Andrius Raguotis, Nynke Bergstra, Jeroen de Waal, Cormac Murray, Martins Duselis, Guillem Lopez (aNNo) Stijns Cools, Sofie de Ridder, Elisabeth Lehouck, Barbara Joseph, Kelly de Scheemaker, Nele Vancaeysele (Baro) Geert Willemyns, Klaas Van de Sompel, Liesbet Vandenbussche, Feije Gijsen, Aglaia Vannieuwenhuyse (SumProject) Paul Lievevrouw, Jean-Pierre Mariën, Niels De Luyck, Nikolas Debrauwer, Thijs De Pauw **website** www.atelierkempethill.com, www.annoarchitecten.be, www.baro-architectuur.be, www.sum.be **address** Lammerstraat 13, 9000 Ghent **client** sogent **design** October 2012 **completion** 8 June 2022 **surface area** 14,297 m² **volume** 67,207 m³ **total building cost** €21,000,000 excl. VAT **total building cost per m²** €1,468 excl. VAT **main contractor** Furnibo, Veurne **lighting design** NO4MAD, Jan Dekeyser, Ghent **stability studies** (design and execution) VK Architects & Engineers, Ghent (preliminary studies) BAS, Leuven **engineering studies** (design and execution) VK Architects & Engineers, Ghent (preliminary studies) Arch & Teco, Ghent **EPB studies** VK Architects & Engineers, Ghent **acoustics studies** (design and execution) VK Architects & Engineers (preliminary studies) Scala Consultants, Leuven **landscape design** Omgeving, Ghent **safety coordination** VETO & Partners, Oosterzele

text Sofie De Caigny
photography
01, 07-09 © Illias Teirlinck
02-06 © Ulrich Schwarz, Berlin

PROJECT   Atelier Kempe Thill, aNNo (concept), Baro Architectuur, SumProject (architect)

Responsibility and Equity

Feminist Notes on Gender and Diversity in the Flemish Architectural Sector

Evelien Pieters

In this edition of the *Flanders Architectural Review*, we seek out an architecture that takes responsibility for today's social and environmental crises, analyses them critically, and strives to provide answers. How are these values reflected in the way architectural practices are organized? Is there a distinct work environment or architecture culture linked to the values we have formulated as editors? Who belongs to this architecture culture? A diversity of voices is not yet a reality in our sector. More women than men are leaving the architectural profession. People with a migratory background are under-represented. And the lack of diversity stretches further: consider, for example, the paucity of architects with a disability. This article, together with that of Vjera Sleutel, focuses on the conditions in which architecture is created in Flanders and Brussels. In particular, I advance a feminist framework that can offer alternative values to the masculine and competitive culture that characterizes the architecture sector.[1]

Gender and diversity in the architecture sector: A summary

The Order of Architects' most recent annual report shows that in Flanders, 40 per cent of registered architects are now women.[2] This represents a significant increase compared to ten years ago, when that percentage was only 31. The gender balance per age category reveals a different picture: up to the age of 35, women are in the majority at 55 per cent, but in the 35 to 39 age category, the figure suddenly drops to 46 per cent. If we examine this in more detail, we see that in 2023, female architects up to the age of 33 were in the majority, and after that we see a turnaround.[3] In the 40 to 49 age category, the percentage of women drops still further to 37, and from age 50 to 59 to 29. The same report shows that gender distribution among trainee architects in 2010 – that is, those in their thirties – was already 50/50, and in the Flemish architectural courses the number of female and male students has been more or less balanced for several decades.[4] So far, more women than men leave the architectural profession.[5] This phenomenon is known as the 'leaky pipeline', an allusion to the structural mechanisms that, often unnoticed, push women out of architecture.[6] Alongside the leaky pipeline, there is also a glass ceiling that continues to be difficult to break.[7] On this, there are no clear figures. A sample of the fifty largest offices affiliated with Netwerk Architecten Vlaanderen (NAV) shows that half of the firms have both men and women in leadership positions (although at many of them, women are in the minority), while almost the entire other half has exclusively men as directors or board members. Just a few firms have a solely female management team.[8]

These figures relate solely to gender.[9] Data on other kinds of diversity, such as social class, ethnicity, disability or sexual orientation, barely exist. Recently, the Order of Architects has begun keeping records of the number of architects born outside Belgium. In 2023, 12 per cent of trainee architects were born outside the EU, compared to 2 per cent of architects. These figures paint only a limited picture because people born in Belgium with a migratory or bicultural background are not included, while these groups have to contend with comparable barriers. A 2021 article in *Knack Weekend* reports that 16 per cent of architecture students at Antwerp University and KU Leuven have a migratory background.[10] It is from precisely this group that relatively more students drop out of the course.[11]

---

[1] In the footnotes to this text, I reference multiple sources that can serve as a starting point for anyone in architecture looking to engage with these themes themselves. I refer to academic and popular feminist literature, to studies and toolkits that aim to change the work culture, and to various studies and initiatives. I mainly try to quote women and minority group sources, so as to extend the frame of reference in this type of publication. I draw on feminist thinker Sara Ahmed who, in *Living a Feminist Life* (Durham, NC: Duke University Press, 2017), challenges the academic standard with a feminist quotation policy by not quoting 'white men', where 'white men' stands for an institution. She writes: 'Feminism is at stake in how we generate knowledge; in how we write, in who we cite. I think of feminism as a building project: if our texts are worlds, they need to be made out of feminist materials. Feminist theory is world making.'

[2] Annual Report 2023, Order of Architects – Flemish Council. When registering, the Order only uses the categories of male and female.

[3] This is evident from the number of registered male and female architects per age group in 2023. These figures were emailed to me by the Order of Architects, in anticipation of the publication of the 2023 Annual Report.

[4] In '(Onder)vertegenwoordiging van vrouwen in de architectuur in Vlaanderen' ([Under] representation of women in architecture in Flanders) (master's thesis, KU Leuven et al., 2017), Caroline Vermeiren shows that the number of women graduating from architectural courses in Flanders has been about 50 per cent since 2005. In 'Vrouwen in de architectuur. De vertegenwoordiging van vrouwen in de architecturale opleidingen en het belang van rolmodellen' (Women in architecture: The representation of women in architectural courses and the importance of role models) (master's thesis, University of Antwerp, 2023), Eva Lapage shows figures from 2013 in which the number of female and male students is the same, with the percentage of women even increasing in recent years.

[5] Where are these women, as well as minority groups? It would be overly simplistic to claim that they leave the profession entirely, because many remain active in the architectural sector or in urban planning, but then in other roles, for example with government agencies, as clients or in cultural organizations, among others – positions that frequently offer better work conditions and have a different work culture. They can also have a major impact from these positions. One of the tasks is therefore to broaden our picture of 'the architect' and also to consider these other impactful roles.

[6] There are multiple sources available regarding the leaky pipeline, in Flanders the above thesis of Caroline Vermeiren, among others. She already noted in 2017 that the percentage of young women in architecture is even greater than the number of men, but that many individuals from this group leave the practice.

[7] Vermeiren, '(Onder)vertegenwoordiging'.

SURVEY **Statuut / Status**

In het voorjaar van 2024 vroeg het Vlaams Architectuurinstituut gepubliceerde architecten uit het *Architectuurboek Vlaanderen N°16* om een anonieme bevraging in te vullen. Van de 49 aangeschreven bureaus reageerden er 25, die een totaal van ongeveer 250 architectuurwerkers representeren. Hoewel dit geen uitgebreid onderzoek is, geeft het inzicht in de samenstelling van de bureaus, toewijzingsprocessen en verloning achter de architectuur in deze publicatie. Geen enkele ondervraagde identificeerde zich als non-binair, daarom zijn enkel de categorieën 'man' en 'vrouw' gebruikt.

In spring 2024 the Flanders Architecture Institute asked architects published in the *Flanders Architectural Review N°16* to complete an anonymous survey. Of the 49 firms contacted, 25 responded, representing a total of approximately 250 architectural workers. While this is not a comprehensive survey, it provides insight into the composition of the firms, assignment processes and remuneration behind the architecture in this publication. No interviewees identified themselves as non-binary, therefore only the categories 'male' and 'female' were used.

Bureaus met mannelijke en vrouwelijke vennoten
Firms with male and female associates 50%

Bureaus met enkel vrouwelijke vennoten
Firms with only female associates 17%

Bureaus met enkel mannelijke vennoten
Firms with only male associates 33%

Bureaus die geen architecten als bediende onder contract hebben
Firms that don't contract architects as employees 88%

Bureaus die architecten als bediende onder contract hebben
Firms that contract architects as employees 12%

Bureaus die nooit overwogen om architecten bediendecontracten aan te bieden
Firms that have never considered offering architects employment contracts 20%

Bureaus die overwogen om architecten bediendecontracten aan te bieden
Firms that considered offering architects employment contracts 80%

SURVEY **Samenstelling / Composition**

Zelfstandig
Self-employed

Vrouw Female 108

Man Male 121

Bedienden
Employees

Vrouw Female 14
Man / Male 4

Vennoten
Associates

Vrouw Female 17

Stagiairs
Interns

Vrouw Female 22

Man Male 38
Man Male 21

Gediplomeerde architecten
Licensed architects

Vrouw Female 107

Man Male 130

Andere functies
Other functions

Vrouw Female 13
Man / Male 4

8   There are no clear figures on leadership positions in architecture firms. The Order of Architects does not record this kind of data, nor does the NAV have a full overview. The figures mentioned here are based on a sample I made from a list of the fifty largest affiliated firms, as provided to me by NAV. For figures on men and women in management roles or on the boards of these firms, I consulted the information available on their websites. In researching this, I encountered a great many difficulties, because the information on the websites is not always clear, and each office has its own terminology. NAV's list of members also includes some public agencies and property developers that I have not considered. I have included some large companies that we would usually consider to be engineering firms. The largest offices are something of an exception in the Flemish architecture landscape with its many small firms, so this sample is certainly not representative of the whole sector. Even without a full overview, however, the insight this sample provides is still important enough to mention here.

9   In this essay I mostly use the binary terms 'man' and 'woman' because most available data only contains these categories. The call in this text to question exclusion mechanisms is intended to include non-binary persons, as well as other marginalized groups, in addition to women, with the aim of embracing society's full diversity.

10 Wided Bouchrika, 'Architect is nog steeds een erg "wit" beroep. Hoe zorgen we voor meer diversiteit?' (Architect is still a very 'white' profession: How do we ensure more diversity?), *Knack Weekend*, 21 April 2024. These figures are compared to one in four residents of Flanders with a migratory background.

11 This emerged during a discussion evening organized by PAF (Platform for Architecture & Feminism) on gender and diversity in architecture courses on 26 February 2024.

12 Jolien Verlinden, '(Vrouwelijke) architecten. Gender in hedendaagse architectuurpublicaties en architectuurcultuur' ([Female] architects: Gender in contemporary architectural publications and architectural culture) (master's thesis, Ghent University, 2023). She counted the number of women featured in issues of *A+* between 2018 and 2020 (18 editions) and in the past three editions of the *Flanders Architectural Review* (2018, 2020, 2022).

13 For this count, I based myself on the information given on the firms' websites about their managers/partners. It therefore does not relate to the people in the team; this data was not available for all submitted projects.

14 Karin Hartmann, *Black Turtleneck Round Glasses* (Berlin: Jovis, 2023). Sara Ahmed also writes about this in *Living a Feminist Life*: 'The personal is structural.' Caroline Vermeiren's thesis focuses on barriers at an individual, organizational and sociocultural level.

15 In heterosexual couples, men spend an average of 13 hours and 35 minutes per week on care tasks and women an average of almost 22 hours, according to time usage research in Flanders, conducted by research group TOR at Vrije Universiteit Brussel (VUB). See torvub.be/het-huishouddeul-anno-2020.

16 The Flemish initiative Dear Architects by Paulien Gekiere conducted an internet survey in 2023, in which 36 per cent of the sixty-four mothers reported having quit as a freelance architect because of motherhood, while only 9 per cent of the forty-seven fathers reported having quit as a freelance architect after becoming fathers.

We see the situation in the sector reflected in the representation figures. Who do we see at architecture exhibitions and lectures, in magazines and books? From a student thesis that counted the number of women appearing in the architecture magazine *A+* (2018–20 editions) and in the past three editions of *the Flanders Architectural Review*, it emerges that just 9 per cent of the firms discussed have exclusively female managers and about a third mixed management. The majority of the firms discussed therefore have exclusively male managers (59 per cent for *A+* and 54 per cent for the *Flanders Architectural Review*). Of the architects interviewed in *A+* in 2018–20, 26 per cent were women.[12] There are no figures on people with a migratory background, but those who work in the architecture sector know that their representation is minimal. The image of the architect in Flanders is therefore still mainly white and male.

And what about the book you now have open in front of you? Of the just under 300 projects submitted, around 5 per cent were designed by firms or teams headed exclusively by women, and 39 per cent by a mix of men and women. In about 56 per cent of the projects submitted, the managers of the firms were exclusively men.[13] A total of about sixty architectural firms worked on the projects ultimately covered in this book. Of these, about 12 per cent have only female partners, 45 per cent both men and women among their managers, and 43 per cent only men. We questioned the firms behind the selected projects about the composition of their teams in greater depth. A total of about sixty architecture firms worked on the projects ultimately reviewed in the book. Of these, about 12 per cent have only female partners, 45 per cent have both men and women on their boards, and 43 per cent have only men. We further surveyed the architects of the published projects about the staff composition of their firm, to which almost half responded. You will find the results in the pages between this article. The total number of men and women working in the firms is distributed roughly evenly, but the leaky pipeline is visible in the male-female distribution by age category. It is notable that, among staff with children, more than 60 per cent are male. The representation of minorities also stands out: 16 per cent of of architects working in these firms identify as bicultural or from a migrant background, 11 per cent as belonging to the LGBTQI+ community, and only 2 per cent report having a disability or handicap.

You could see the representation in architectural publications as a reflection of the state of gender balance in the sector. But as an architectural sector, should we be choosing to reflect this situation unquestioningly, because we believe these projects and firms to be of the highest quality? Or should we in fact be using our positions as gatekeepers to challenge the norms and put forward a more diverse overview of voices? What's more, gatekeepers who help to determine the architectural discourse themselves occupy different positions in the field: from an editorial team looking at the projects completed over the past two years to the city and government architects who shape architectural policy and select architects. What (often subconscious) position do we take in these roles?

Exclusion mechanisms

The figures show that we cannot simply interpret the departure of people from training or work practice as individual decisions. While people may face individual choices, when we individualize the causes, the systemic influences are kept out of the picture.[14] In Flanders, the precariousness of the profession with low pay and tolerated bogus self-employment, is a heavy weight to bear. This certainly holds true for those in a less favourable socio-economic position, and most definitely holds true in a society where women still take on a far greater share of (often unpaid) care.[15] When it comes to family expansion, it is mainly women who make the choice to leave the architectural profession.[16]

As a sector, we must problematize and tackle the poor socio-economic position of architects; see also the article by Vjera Sleutel on this issue in this volume.

At the same time, it is too restrictive to look solely at the self-employed status as an exclusion mechanism. We also see comparable figures in neighbouring countries where architects are employed on permanent contracts. The reasons for a lack of gender balance and diversity are broader and ingrained in the architecture and work culture, where anything 'different' is still often excluded.[17] It is by stipulating what the norm is, and who falls outside it, that this culture perpetuates power imbalances.[18]

A 2018 survey of gender in the creative sector shows that a large proportion of female architects are faced with gender stereotyping and sexism.[19] The survey looked at experiences in the previous year, with more than half of the architects being confronted 'sometimes or often' with sexist jokes or comments, and 29 per cent of female architects surveyed finding that they themselves were the subject of those comments. Around a third of female architects reported being infantilized, or treated as stupid and incompetent. Moreover, a quarter of women endured discrimination related to motherhood.[20] A survey of architects in the United States that specifically addressed racism shows that people of colour in the architecture sector experience exclusion on more grounds than just gender differences.[21] Sexism and discrimination are often expressed by us as implicit preconceptions, entrenched in a culture we regard as normal.[22]

The romantic image of the architect as an artist genius still prevails and contributes to the masculine work culture. Hilde Heynen describes how the 'mystique' of individual authorship plays a role, as if the qualities of the work can be traced back to the creativity of a single person.[23] There is often still the image of the ever-present architect with total dedication to their 'calling' and, self-evidently, long working days. During training, we are already taught that this is the norm. 'Talk over the drawing boards includes a hidden curriculum on how to behave as an architect', the feminist architecture collective Matrix wrote as early as 1984.[24]

One aspect of the masculine norm in architecture is competition culture. What effect does that have on the work culture and on the resulting designs and built environment? On this subject, Lara Schrijver says: 'The profession is full of exclusionary practices such as rivalry, based on an underlying narrative about power and domination. If practices compete and the historiography is based on exclusion, then it becomes self-evident to approach the built environment via a comparably reductive narrative.'[25]

In search of change

What do those numbers and causes tell us? Is striving for more gender balance and diversity an end in itself? Does this not divert attention from what truly matters? The answers to these frequently asked questions are not self-evident.

First and foremost, it is about involving a wider variety of perspectives in architectural assignments. This reduces the number of blind spots, enabling us to create better environments for users.[26] It seems obvious that the group of people who shape the built environment should be as diverse as the people who use it.[27] At the same time, a broadening of perspectives can contribute to much-needed innovation and solutions in the light of the climate crisis. Because research has shown that diverse teams perform better.[28]

Yet there is also the importance of representation. Who determines our image of 'the architect'? Who do we see working for and managing architectural firms, and on platforms and in publications in architectural culture? In image-defining positions such as the 'government architect' roles? In the course material ▶

---

17 Lara Schrijver, 'Van rivaliteit naar ruimhartigheid. Feministische notities voor de architectuur' (From rivalry to generosity: Feminist notes for architecture), in *Vrouwen in Architectuur* (Rotterdam: nai010 uitgevers, 2023), 158–73.

18 This is evident from the literature and can also be heard in many testimonials. I base myself on conversations we had in 2023 and 2024 within the PAF project as well as on conversations held during various lecture and debate evenings, including those organized by the Flanders Architecture Institute, and on experiences shared during interviews recorded in student theses, such as those in Lotte Kerkhofs' 'Vrouwen in de architectuur. Een verkenning van Vlaamse casussen in een door mannen gedomineerde sector' (Women in architecture: An exploration of Flemish case studies in a male-dominated sector) (master's thesis, University of Antwerp, 2021).

19 CuDOS UGent, *Zo man, zo vrouw? Gender en de creatieve sector in Vlaanderen* (2017), including findings about experiences of sexism among Flemish architects.

20 Twenty-four per cent of women sometimes or often heard people say that mothers are less productive at work. See CuDOS UGent (2017).

21 *The Elephant in the (Well-Designed) Room: An Investigation into Bias in the Architecture Profession* (2021) by the American Institute of Architects: content.aia.org/sites/default/files/2021-12/AIA_Bias_Interrupters_FINAL.pdf.

22 The survey by Ghent University did not address exclusion due to ethnicity or other marginalized identities. The American Institute of Architects' research into 'implicit bias' shows that the accumulation of marginalized identities has a big impact. People of colour experience many barriers and prejudices in the architectural sector.

23 Hilde Heynen, 'The Gender of Genius', *Architectural Review* (March 2020): 331–45.

24 Matrix, *Making Space: Women and the Man-Made Environment* (London: Pluto Press, 1984).

25 Schrijver, 'Van rivaliteit naar ruimhartigheid'.

26 Arna Mačkić writes: 'By looking at the same problem with a greater number of different eyes, more blind spots are eliminated, and we can more effectively learn what users need.' See Arna Mačkić, 'De ogen van de architect' (The architect's eyes), in *Architectuur in Nederland Jaarboek 2019/2020* (Rotterdam: nai010 uitgevers, 2020). The essay was also published as a series of columns on Archined: www.archined.nl/2020/09/door-de-ogen-van-de-architect-i-representatie-in-werkwijze-en-architectuur.

27 Statement by Naomi Stead and Justine Clark of Parlour, Australia, during the 'Gender Equity in Irish Architecture' conference on 16 February 2024: 'We believe the people who design the built environment should be as diverse a group as those who use it.'

28 David Rock and Heidi Grant, 'Why Diverse Teams Are Smarter', *Harvard Business Review* (2016). See hbr.org/2016/11/why-diverse-teams-are-smarter.

SURVEY **Verdeling in leeftijd en gender / Age and gender distribution**

30–39 **37%**

25–29 **33%**

Vrouw Female 48
Man Male 43

Vrouw Female 44
Man Male 39

<25 **10%**

Vrouw Female 13
Man Male 12

SURVEY **Verdeling in leeftijd en gender / Age and gender distribution** 135

40–49 **16%**

Vrouw
Female **14**

Man
Male **27**

50–59 **3%**

Female / Vrouw **2**

Man
Male **6**

60+ **0%**

Man / Male **1**

29 In 'How Wide Is the Gap? Evaluating Current Documentation of Women Architects in Modern Architecture History Books (2004–2014)' (2017), Florencia Fernandez Cardoso counts the number of women that are named in ten frequently read books on architectural history. Of the 1,063 architects and designers listed on more than one page, 61 (5.7 per cent) are women.

30 Hélène Frichot, *How to Make Yourself a Feminist Design Power Tool* (AADR, 2016).

31 Denise Scott Brown, 'Room at the Top? Sexism and the Star System in Architecture', in *Architecture: A Place for Women*, ed. Ellen Perry Berkeley and Matilda McQuaid (Washington, DC: Smithsonian Institution Press, 1989), 237–46.

32 See, among others, the text by Sofie De Caigny on minimal interventions in which she also refers to the love ethic of bell hooks, and the article by Els Nulens in which she discusses the importance of commitment and the relational in the creation of high quality architecture.

33 Schrijver, 'Van rivaliteit naar ruimhartigheid'.

34 'To begin by always thinking of love as an action rather than a feeling is one way in which anyone using the word in this manner automatically assumes accountability and responsibility.' bell hooks, *all about love: new visions* (New York: Harper, 2000).

35 Hélène Frichot, 'Mottos for Maintenance as Care Work', in *ARCH+ #252 Open for Maintenance – Wegen umbau geöffnet* (2023). In this, Frichot bases herself on the essay 'Maintenance and Care' (2018) by Shannon Mattern and on feminist artistic practice and the 'Maintenance Art Manifesto, 1969!' (1969) by Mieke Laderman Ukeles.

36 See, e.g., 'Feminisme voor de 99%. Een manifest' (Feminism for the 99%: A manifesto) (2019) by Cinzia Arruzza, Tithi Bhattacharya and Nancy Fraser. See also rosavzw.be/nl/themas/feminisme/feministische-stromingen/marxistisch-en-socialistisch-feminisme.

when students are learning and in the canon?[29] Representation is important to smooth the path for the young generation. To ensure that they feel at home and to show that these roles are open to them too. For this reason, figures remain important. How many men are there, and how many women? How many people of colour? Hélène Frichot calls this 'the count' and emphasizes the necessity and political importance of this counting.[30] It does not distract us, but rather forces us to confront the facts.

Reinforcing a feminist awareness, however, is far more crucial than striving for balanced figures. 'On seeing their male colleagues draw out in front of them, women who lack a feminist awareness are likely to feel that their failure to achieve is their own fault', Denise Scott Brown wrote back in 1989 in 'Room at the Top?'.[31] I still hear people explaining women's decisions to leave architecture purely in terms of individual circumstances, instead of seeing it as a collective issue. In *Feminism Is for Everybody*, bell hooks emphasizes that the feminist movement is focused on ending sexism, or the patriarchal system, or oppression, also of other marginalized groups. It is not about a movement 'against men', but against the very system in which we are all socialized and raised. A feminist frame of mind refuses to simply accept and reproduce social norms and conventions. It provides us with a language to question prevailing structures and to put forward an alternative value framework. What values do we wish to prioritize? What answers will we formulate? Where do our responsibilities lie?

The other authors in this book cite a great deal in relation to these values: justice, concern and care for people and the planet.[32] In the recently published book *Vrouwen in Architectuur* (Women in architecture), Lara Schrijver writes about open-heartedness as a counterbalance to rivalry.[33] She thereby bases herself on what bell hooks describes as a 'love ethic'. She is not referring to romantic love here, but a love that is all about connection and responsibility as a basis for social justice.[34] What if we were to shape architecture and architectural practice based on this love ethic?

'Maintenance' as a feminist design principle

A recent project centred around staunch feminist values as an alternative approach to architectural practice was the German Pavilion at the Venice International Architecture Biennale in 2023. It was designed by Ghent-based Büro Juliane Greb and the German partners Summacumfemmer and *ARCH+*. The concept of 'maintenance' was a core design tenet. 'Rather than heroic acts of construction and infrastructural connection, ribbon-cutting and expressions of rude wealth inscribed into façades rising dizzyingly high, it's the minor, everyday acts of maintenance, repair and making do that matter', wrote Hélène Frichot in the catalogue.[35] The curatorial team thus endorsed the feminist concept of 'reproductive' labour, everyday care and maintenance tasks as an essential support for society and the economy.[36] The team translated this into architectural practice by radically embracing architecture as a caring practice.

They transformed the pavilion into a designated space for reproductive work. The starting point was the condition of the building following the previous year's art biennale, with a central storeroom for the materials used for more than forty pavilions. They sought to connect with the local issues, such as the shortage of affordable homes and mass tourism, and collaborated with local activist groups on a programme of workshops that uses the material for buildings in the city. They made room for those groups by setting up a workplace, kitchen and meeting space inside the pavilion. They addressed contextual needs, such as the lack of sanitary facilities on the site of the Biennale, and installed a public dry toilet, unisex urinal and baby changing tables, which at once rendered visible the connection between ecology, social justice and care

37 Especially sensitive is the fact that at the time, the German pavilion had been converted to its current state in line with the Nazi ideology.
38 See vai.be.
39 See civa.brussels and architecturequidegenre.be.
40 In 1978 the National Union of Women Architects of Belgium was founded as the Belgian arm of the International Union of Women Architects (UIFA), established in Paris in 1965. Out of this grew ufvAb, which recently changed its name to Women* in Architecture Belgium. See wiab.be.
41 See paf.community.

work. With the architectural intervention of a semicircular ramp with stage (also using recycled material), they solved the lack of accessibility, while at the same time problematizing the social perspective behind it.[37] For bodies that fall outside the norm – people who are less mobile, people with a pushchair, or cleaning staff with heavy equipment –, only temporary access was available, hidden away at the back. The project shows how you can take responsibility in design and process. Instead of a strong visual concept, the result is rather an architectural interlacing of carefully balanced choices and interventions that seek to have an impact at a spatial and societal level.

Advocates of change

Shaping alternative practices and doing things in a radically different manner, as the work of Büro Juliane Greb and partners shows, is a way of experimenting and showing how we can drive change in the sector. But structural change can only succeed if we work at many different levels simultaneously, both in research and in practice, in the cultural field, and with policy preparation and activist work. It is a hopeful sign that the seeds of change can be discerned at different levels in Flanders, Brussels and beyond.

In the cultural field, for example, we have seen a shift in discourse in recent years, whereby institutions are starting to critically question their role as gatekeepers. The Flanders Architecture Institute organized the agenda-setting and network-strengthening project Wiki Women Design and took the curatorial decision to work for several years on the theme of care.[38] The Brussels CIVA also questioned the colonial roots of architectural heritage in the exhibition *Style Congo*, among other things, while the Brussels feminist initiative *L'Architecture qui dégenre* interrogates the accessibility and intersectionality of the city through initiatives such as their Matrimony Days.[39] The union of women Architects of belgium (ufvAb), founded in the 1970s, was also revitalized as Women* in Architecture Belgium.[40] Last year in Flanders, I myself launched the Platform for Architecture & Feminism (PAF) initiative, which organizes intergenerational conversations and aims to boost feminist awareness.[41]

In the field of academia, Hilde Heynen has been conducting groundbreaking work for decades around the theme of gender and women in architecture. Other academics, such as Lara Schrijver and Luce Beeckmans, have also embraced themes such as feminism and decolonization in architecture, ▸

Hoeveel architectuurwerkers op het bureau zijn ouder van minstens 1 kind?
How many architectural workers are parents of at least 1 child?

Vrouw
Female 39

Man
Male 62

Geen ouder
Not a parent 149

SURVEY **Representatie / Representation** 139

Niet van toepassing
Not applicable

Hoeveel architectuurwerkers zijn geboren buiten België? 55
How many architectural workers are born outside of Belgium?

Hoeveel architectuurwerkers hebben geen financiële of logistieke steun ontvangen van hun ouders of voogd tijdens de studies? 10
How many architectural workers did not receive financial or logistical support from their parents or guardians during their studies?

Hoeveel architectuurwerkers hebben een biculturele of migratieachtergrond? 40
How many architectural workers have a bicultural or migration background?

Hoeveel architectuurwerkers identificeren zich met de LGBTQI+-gemeenschap? 26
How many architectural workers identify themselves as part of the LGBTQI+-community?

Hoeveel architectuurwerkers hebben een beperking of een handicap? 6
How many architectural workers have an impairment or disability?

and in recent years more and more master's theses have been appearing on related subjects.[42] However, the insights from the academic field are not really trickling down into practice in any specific way. In architecture firms we see the search for positive change, navigating within structural constraints. We see architects seeking collaboration and collectivity as a countermovement of rivalry, a concept with which we are also conversant thanks to feminist initiatives in the 1980s, including the London-based Matrix. And yet these are still exceptions. There is a lack of policy that focuses on gender and diversity on the work floor. NAV set up a work group in 2023 entitled 'Women in architecture'; the Order of Architects reports on the percentage of women, but the insights rarely translate into concrete policy actions; most importantly, greater diversity barely surfaces as a theme.

And yet there are plenty of shining examples if one looks abroad. The Australian initiative Parlour, created on the interface between academic research and practice, has been working on gender, equity and architecture for twelve years.[43] With the Australian Institute of Architects, Parlour has formulated a 'Gender Equity Policy'[44] and published 'Guides to Equitable Practice' around themes such as equal pay, the long-hours culture, part-time work, and application processes.[45] With such guidelines to hand, architectural firms can get to work themselves, or disgruntled employees can more easily make their point. The American Institute of Architects published comparable guidelines in late 2023, based on Parlour's preparatory work.[46] This highlights a useful lesson: do not reinvent the wheel yourself, but continue building on the work of others.

'There is still only a minimal focus on gender balance in the architecture sector. We could certainly use a dose of activism', Hilde Heynen commented in 2021.[47] Since then, the focus on gender balance seems to have sharpened; but when it comes to exclusionary mechanisms which keep or push people from (previously) marginalized groups out of the sector, there is still only minimal attention. This burst of activism to drive actual change is something that we still sorely need. Although there are sufficient starting points and opportunities for change, there is no easy solution, no straightforward checklist. There will need to be many initiatives that simultaneously focus on raising awareness, representation, making room for diverse voices, policy, improvement in pay, and changes to the training and work culture. So let's keep on 'counting', and let's continue to focus on enhancing our feminist awareness with alternative values that influence how we shape our profession and practice.

---

42 See, e.g., the theses cited in this essay.

43 See parlour.org.au/.

44 See parlour.org.au/noticeboard/notices/australian-institute-of-architects-gender-equity-policy.

45 See parlour.org.au/parlour-guides/. Also, the Architect's Council of Europe (ACE) published a brief inspiration collection 'Gender Balance, Diversity & Inclusion in Architecture' in 2023; see www.ace-cae.eu/activities/publications/abc-gender-balance-diversity-and-inclusion-in-architecture.

46 These can be downloaded on www.aia.org/resource-center/guides-equitable-practice. The American Institute also has other tools available, such as the 'bias interrupters' as part of the research 'The Elephant in the (Well-Designed) Room' into sexism and discrimination in architecture.

47 She made this statement in the podcast episode 'Zijn vrouwen ondervertegenwoordigd in de architectuur?' (Are women under-represented in architecture?) from architectura.be (September 2021).

Architecture Works

A Critical Note on the Socio-Economic Position of Architects in Flanders and Brussels

Vjera Sleutel

The *Flanders Architectural Review* is the place to proudly survey the exceptional projects completed in Flanders and Brussels in the two preceding years. Architecture from this corner of the world is such a success! Acclaimed, daring and sustainable projects offer responses to a range of social and societal issues. But is everything as good as it seems? Amidst the acclaim, cries of distress can be heard from within the sector. The rapid succession of critical news articles has shown that it is time to reflect on working conditions in the architectural field. Indeed, numerous articles specifically expose the terms under which emerging architects are expected to work. What are these conditions? How did they infiltrate our architectural culture? How are we to deal with these pleas for help? This essay considers some of the problems that the sector has been grappling with. It does so from my point of view, that of a young, post-internship architect at the start of her career.

Working conditions for beginners

After five years of university, a young graduate, with no practical experience, approaches a firm.[1] A Belgian architect's career begins with a two-year internship, according to the model career path.[2] They will either be an employee or self-employed during this time. The majority of recent graduates opt for self-employment, but without having much say in the matter.[3] This comes with a number of disadvantages. The first complaint, therefore, is young architects working for firms on a self-employed basis. This increases the number of responsibilities during the internship: the intern needs to open a professional bank account, register with the Crossroads Bank for Enterprises, join a health and social security fund, make the corresponding social contributions, write invoices, maintain accounts (including VAT declarations) and pay their annual membership fee to the Order of Architects … What's more, the intern will have limited social security protection: self-employed people only receive sick pay after the second month of being declared unfit for work – and then, only at a flat rate.[4] Young interns who lose their jobs cannot claim unemployment benefits. And lastly, on average, self-employed workers tend to fare less well in terms of pension provision than employees. Retirement and sickness might be the last things on the minds of healthy twenty-somethings, but insurance premiums that offer a guaranteed income and optional supplementary pensions come at a high price. As a result, many budding architects dive into self-employment involuntarily and without being properly insured.

Working for a permanent employer who dictates your working hours and tasks while registered as self-employed is officially classified as false self-employment – social fraud, in other words. Yet the architecture sector in Flanders and Brussels has systematically turned a blind eye to the practice.[5] And that is not all: false self-employment seems to be ingrained in the system. An intern must work 120 hours per month with a master architect; at the same time, the Order of Architects publishes a list detailing the minimum hourly wage that young architects ought to receive while self-employed.[6]

This list states that the minimum hourly rate for an entry-level intern is 14.16 euros (gross) during the first six months.[7] A sum that increases every six months by an average of 2.85 euros per hour. The rates form the second complaint. In theory, the minimum scale set by the Order of Architects ▸

---

1 Practical experience is not part of the graduate degree in Flanders and Brussels.

2 According to the model career path, you will start your internship at an architectural firm immediately after your studies, where an architect who has been registered with the Order of Architects for at least ten years can supervise a maximum of two interns. You can, however, start your architectural internship at any time. An internship is not a compulsory requirement for architecture graduates entering the construction industry. It is compulsory if you wish to work as an architect, as stipulated in the law of 20 February 1939 regarding the 'title and profession of architect'.

3 In 2022, 92 per cent of trainee architects were self-employed, 7 per cent were salaried, and 1 per cent were civil servants, according to the annual report of the Order of Architects.

4 A white-collar worker receives their usual salary from their employer during the first month of sick leave, and thereafter receives a benefit from the health insurance fund that is based on the gross salary.

5 This is also a known problem in other sectors, with an emphasis on the liberal professions. A natural person practising a liberal profession is deemed to exercise it as a self-employed person, regardless of whether they are working as a manager, subordinate or trainee. Even trainee lawyers or doctors usually do their traineeships under self-employed status.

6 Dear Architects launched 'De Loonbarometer' (The wage barometer) in early 2024, an online survey focusing on the socio-economic position of 'architectural workers', specifically targeting self-employed people working for a Belgian architectural firm. Among other things, participants were asked whether they thought their self-employed status was false: 80.5% of participants answered 'yes' to this question. See deararchitects.be/loonbarometer.

7 This list can be found at: www.architect.be/stagiairs/vergoeding.

Uurtarieven / Hourly Rates

€10-15 2% | €15-20 9% | €20-25 13% | €25-30

SURVEY **Uurtarieven / Hourly Rates**

| 29% | €30–35 | 24% | €35–40 | 11% | €40–45 | 7% | €45–50 | 1% | €50+ | 3% |

8   Guaranteed minimum average monthly income on 15 May 2024. Dear Architects took the test: Case study 'Amber' would need to earn 21.03 euros/hour as an unmarried and childless self-employed person to be above the Guaranteed Average Minimum Monthly Income. The calculations can be found at: deararchitects.be/wasl.

9   Although for many young architects working in an architectural firm, the term 'employee' is incorrect (see also the section on false self-employment), I use the term to emphasize the de facto subordinate position vis-à-vis an employer.

10 The European Working Time Directive can be read at: ec.europa.eu/social/main.jsp?catId=706&langId=en&intPageId=205.

11 In 2023 Dear Architects conducted an Instagram survey with the following result, among others: the median hourly wage of ninety respondents aged between 27 and 29 was a paltry 25.55 euros/hour.

12 The biennial survey by the Architects' Council of Europe (ACE) provides a comprehensive report on the state of the architectural profession in Europe. Belgium performs worst at 16 per cent. Poland is just above them in the list, with 27 per cent. See also www.ace-cae.eu/fileadmin/user_upload/2020ACESECTORSTUDY.pdf.

13 The research group CuDOS collected online survey data from 1,840 architects (25 per cent of the total number of architects in Flanders) and 578 designers in a paper entitled 'Wie heeft het gemaakt? Een onderzoek naar de sociaaleconomische positie van architecten en designers in Vlaanderen' (Who made it? A study on the socio-economic position of architects and designers in Flanders). They found a sharp decline in the number of women across all age ranges. See publicaties.vlaanderen.be/view-file/32565.

14 'Enquête NAV', www.vai.be/nieuws/enqu%C3%AAte-nav-meer-afstemming-tussen-architectuuronderwijs-en-sector-broodnodig.

is typically considered the norm. In practice, young architects are routinely paid less. I have yet to meet an intern who earned more than the minimum rate at the start. Subtract all the above costs, taxes, unpaid holidays and sick days from the hourly rate, and you are left with an embarrassingly low income. Although self-employed workers are not bound by the minimum wage, it is clear that the stated figures are less than the statutory guaranteed income of €1,954.99 gross per month.[8] Young architects have to work long hours to be able to submit a high enough invoice at the end of each month.

This leads seamlessly to complaint number three: working at an architecture firm generally involves a high workload. You stay as long as it takes to get the job done, even if it means working evenings, nights and weekends. Official holidays are not respected. As an 'employee', it goes without saying that you make sure the project gets done, even if you have to work beyond your contracted hours.[9] The European Working Time Directive is shamelessly flouted and nobody bats an eyelid.[10] While few concrete figures are available, high workloads and minimum rates of pay are the norm in the architecture sector.

Once you have completed your internship, you can register with the Order of Architects and officially start working as an architect. But even then, your salary will probably be low and your workload high.[11] The survey conducted for this *Review* shows that 53 per cent of the (self-employed) staff of the offices that replied are paid less than 30 euros gross per hour. With foreseeable consequences, as people leave in droves. While there are no concrete figures with which to contextualize the dropout rate among architects in Flanders and Brussels, a European study from 2020 shows that barely 16 per cent of Belgian architects expect to remain in the profession until retirement.[12] My own ad hoc research shows that despite the huge investment in an expensive five-year degree, barely two-thirds of the friends I graduated with in 2017 are still working in architecture. The dropout rate is even higher among young female architects (more on this in Evelien Pieters' essay in this publication, see p. 129).[13]

Where did it all go wrong? A sector in crisis

Low wages are often justified by the fact that interns are unable to work independently. A survey by Netwerk Architecten Vlaanderen (NAV),[14] the largest professional association in Flanders, showed that the technical skills of recent graduates often fall short of their mentors' expectations. Are architecture students insufficiently prepared for the professional field? Few people hit the ground running straight after university: graduates need time to learn how to work independently or to complete on-the-job training. Do we expect a bioengineering graduate to join a pharmaceutical company, or a language and literature graduate to join a publisher, and for them to know all the tricks of the trade from day one? Moreover, what is the function of an internship if the intern is expected to work independently from the get-go? But if the internship is viewed as an extension of a student's academic training, and thus as a period of hands-on practice, then it is inherently a learning process. Expecting the mentor to invest time in the intern is not unreasonable. Finally, it is important to emphasize that students follow an architecture course rather than one specifically geared to building. Graduates have multiple career options: consultant at a construction company, spatial policy architect, academic researcher, curator or author, spatial installation designer, project manager for a developer – the list goes on. I myself work simultaneously as an architect for a firm and as an author-researcher and lecturer, for example. The university course is akin to a haven: in addition to technical skills, students learn, above all, the basic principles of architecture, such as critical and creative thinking, positioning within society, cultural baggage and the potential for synthesis. We might well criticize architecture training, what it represents and what it should be, but technical skills are only one aspect of the training, not the sum total.

Why do employers lack the resources to pay their staff a decent wage, train them and provide good working conditions? A potted history: until June 2004, the fee calculation scale was set by the Professional Code of Ethics, specifically Ethical Standard 2. Fees were based on a building's cost and the architect's corresponding services. The Order of Architects was forced to scrap the list under pressure from the European Commission,[15] the verdict being that architectural firms are commercial enterprises and must therefore comply with competition rules. Rates should certainly not be determined by a professional code. Fees plummeted as a consequence and the race to the bottom began.[16]

In many cases, private individuals are obliged to hire architects; only their building and renovation budgets often do not allow for sufficient support.[17] Skimping on the architect's fee is now a common phenomenon, whereas negotiating the salary of your doctor or lawyer is anathema. Less pay means fewer hours. Detailing, dossier compilation and site supervision are labour-intensive tasks. Yet the architect shoulders all these responsibilities and associated risks: legal fees and damages are a constant concern. In 2019, for every forty building permits issued, one construction project ended up in court.[18]

Most large-scale and public contracts are still awarded via the standard mechanism of an architectural competition.[19] While government architects in Flanders and Brussels have fought a unique battle in recent years to make quality the decisive award criterion,[20] fees still tend to receive a relatively high percentage weighting, often as much as 40 per cent.[21] Architectural offices consequently tender at too low a fee. Huge strides have also been made in the local context in terms of competition fees – guidelines for minimum tariffs in tandem with workload reduction – but have not gone far enough. The competitive culture of overperforming shows no sign of abating. Research demonstrates that architectural firms participating in competitions spend between 5 and 15 per cent of their annual turnover on the task, without any guarantee of winning a single project.[22] Even worse, 73 per cent of entries will not result in any award at all.[23]

The method of setting and paying fees – at the client's instigation in large projects – also has a major impact on the financing of the work. A fee can be predicated on a budget estimate that ultimately bears no resemblance to the final cost of the building. For example, 54 per cent of the salaries paid to the respondents of the survey carried out for this *Review* consisted of a fixed sum, at some point in the process. In some cases, participation in the award procedure is not remunerated. In this book, 44 per cent of projects were not remunerated before the award (not to mention all the firms that missed out on the project). Or a percentage of the construction cost can be agreed, but fixed at the final design stage rather than at completion. Fees might not be index-linked on a project that takes years to complete. Payment in instalments after approval of a phase requires a considerable degree of pre-financing in complex cases.

Low fees must also be set against a backdrop of increasingly complicated assignments and an exponential expansion of the architect's remit. Those who still believe that an architect spends most of their working hours behind a drawing board are sorely mistaken. Today's architects are project coordinators with entire teams of external partners under them. They organize participation processes, collaborate on subsidy requests, and are expected to have all the latest information on the norms and legislation pertaining to acoustics, accessibility, heritage, environment, safety, etc. In the survey

15 The decision of the European Commission can be read at: ec.europa.eu/competition/antitrust/cases/dec_docs/38549/38549_74_1.pdf.

16 This term refers to a competitive situation where companies try to undercut competitors' prices by compromising on quality or reducing labour costs.

17 For works requiring planning permission, an architect's services are mandatory under the law of 20 February 1939 (art. 4) on the protection of the title and profession of architect. A number of these interventions have been exempted from supervision by an architect by decision of the Flemish Government (BVR 29 May 2009, art. 1).

18 From the article 'Naar een echte bescherming van het architectenberoep' (Towards real protection of the architectural profession), by Kurt Van Merode, published on 20 October 2022 in *architectura*. The government publishes the number of building permits per year and month on the website: statbel.fgov.be/nl/themas/bouwen-wonen/bouwvergunningen#figures.

19 The European Directive of 18 June 1992 (on the coordination of procedures for the award of public service contracts) requires public authorities to establish procedures for competition.

20 The team of the Flemish Government Architect has been fighting for a better competition culture via the Open Call procedure for more than twenty years, for example, while the Brussels Government Architect (BMA) launched '10 punten van BMA voor een goede wedstrijd' (10 points from the BMA for a good competition) as recently as 2023.

21 'Bevoegd minister Clarinval reageert op klachten en bedenkingen van jonge architecten' (Competent minister Clarinval responds to complaints and concerns from young architects), see www.architect.be/nieuws/bevoegd-minister-clarinval-reageert-op-klachten-en-bedenkingen-van-jonge-architecten.

22 Research shows that architecture firms that participate in competitions spend between 5 and 15 per cent of their annual turnover on the task and might not win a single one. See the article 'Lage vergoeding stagiaires-architecten besmet de hele sector' (Low-paid trainee architects infect the entire sector') on the NAV website, 29 September 2023.

23 This is one of the results of a 2015 study on the economic footprint of public procurement conducted by research and consultancy firm Ecorys on behalf of G30, a non-profit organization founded in 2007 by a number of Belgian architectural firms to improve conditions in the profession.

SURVEY **Gunning / Procurement**

Via welke procedure is het project aan jullie gegund?
How was the project awarded to you?

Wedstrijden / Competitions	48%
Open Oproepen / Open Calls	4%
Ontwerperspoule / Designer pool	8%
Design-and-Build procedure	4%
Offertevragen / Quotations	12%
Privé opdrachten / Private assignments	20%
Eigen projecten / Own projects	4%

Werden de prestaties binnen de gunningsprocedure vergoed?
Zo ja, op welke manier?
Were the services in the award procedure remunerated?
If so, in what way?

Nee / No	44%
Ja, als deel van het ereloon / Yes, as part of the fee	4%
Ja, vergoeding voor een conforme, volwaardige en kwalitatieve offerte / Yes, a fee for a compliant and quality quotation	4%
Ja, via een wedstrijdvergoeding / Yes, via a competition fee	24%
Niet van toepassing / Not applicable	24%

SURVEY Gunning / Procurement

Op welke manier werd het ereloon vastgelegd?
How was the fee determined?

Als percentage van de bouwsom
As a percentage of the building sum — 44%

In functie van oppervlakte per programma, vervolgens geforfaitiseerd
Depending on the surface area of each programme, then fixed — 4%

Als percentage van de bouwsom, vervolgens geforfaitiseerd
As a percentage of the building sum, then fixed — 24%

Forfaitair met surplus werfopvolging in regie
Fixed with surplus on site follow-up in direction — 4%

Forfaitair
Fixed — 16%

Forfaitair met surplus op meerwerken
Fixed with surplus on additional work — 4%

Niet van toepassing
Not applicable — 4%

Stond het ereloon, wat jullie betreft, in verhouding tot de gevraagde prestaties?
In your opinion, was the fee commensurate with the services you provided?

Nee
No — 71%

Ongeveer
Approximately — 4%

Ja
yes — 25%

[24] The KU Leuven Faculty of Architecture presented a major study on architectural performance in 2016. Hourly records of 687 architects were processed and interpreted in the paper 'Onderzoek nacalculatie van de architectenopdracht, faculteit architectuur, vakgroep mens & wetenschap, vakgroep management, onderzoek Johan Rutgeerts – Hoofddocent' (Post-calculation research of the architectural assignment, Faculty of Architecture, Department of People & Science, Department of Management, research by Johan Rutgeerts, Senior Lecturer), archimath.systeme-d.com/BRADA_HET_RAPPORT_20160126_JR.pdf.

[25] See failedarchitecture.com/death-to-the-calling-a-job-in-architecture-is-still-a-job.

[26] Quote from 'Death to the Calling: A Job in Architecture Is Still a Job' by Marisa Cortwright.

[27] In many European schools, a period of practical experience between undergraduate and graduate courses is encouraged. Students regularly gain this experience abroad.

conducted for this *Review*, seventeen out of twenty-five respondents stated that the fee was not commensurate with the service they provided. That corresponds to 68 per cent. When asked what the most pressing work issues were within the architecture sector, 67 per cent mention remuneration. A large-scale 2015 study by KU Leuven revealed a huge discrepancy, on average, between the hours that architects work and their remuneration – with those at the bottom of the ladder paying the price.[24]

Low pay is not the only problem facing young architects: they are self-employed workers but the pressure of the job can be intense. Competition culture only exacerbates the stress. A huge amount of work has to be completed to very tight deadlines, all in addition to running the projects currently in progress. Nor is winning a commission a guarantee that it will not falter. Once a public or private contract has been awarded or a competition won, the parties involved often expect quick results. Grant deadlines and budget allocation both ramp up the sense of urgency. If the client fails to award the contract on time, it is often the architect who will suffer. The predetermined deadlines do not slide; the schedule is merely tightened. Architectural firms do not have a reserve bench of employees ready to deploy at a moment's notice. On the contrary, low company reserves dictate that every workforce operates at maximum capacity. The idea that architects can somehow hire an extra pair of hands from one day to the next and that the recruit will be familiar with the workplace culture and the ins and outs of the new commission is a utopian dream. Winning a commission equates to a massive amount of extra work. Conversely, if none of the submissions, tenders or competitions yield a result, the only way to 'lay off' workers in the short term is to have hired freelancers in the first place. Firing two permanent employees would mean paying their notice or severance pay; this places a stranglehold on many small offices. In a profession characterized by great uncertainty, therefore, offices often opt to engage self-employed workers and to absorb spikes in the workload with limited staffing.

Why participate?

This all begs the question: why do young architects tolerate such poor working conditions? Author Marisa Cortright hit the nail on the head in her article 'Death to the Calling: A Job in Architecture Is Still a Job'.[25] A deep-rooted culture exists among architects that their job is a calling: architecture is the most beautiful profession, and long hours and low pay are par for the course, best accepted graciously. If architecture is your vocation, then why not work on Sundays as well? In Cortright's words, 'The calling is not to complete some task or travel somewhere: it is to become something.'[26] Being an architect is part of your personality. The office in which you work is about more than just finding good employment terms, it also says something about your identity. New 'employees' become part of a collective or family, where only the best – read, the hardest – workers are allowed to stay. As attractive as this sense of a calling and belonging might seem, it also opens the door to abuse.

Numerous firms motivate the cheap labour with the idea of 'paying your dues'. Many illustrious architecture firms profit from unpaid labour under the guise of it being 'valuable experience'. If you don't want to participate, there are plenty more people in the queue behind you, including foreign architects and students.[27] When designer Adam Nathaniel Furman shared a post by architecture firm Junya Ishigami + Associates on Instagram in March 2019, it quickly became world news. The prestigious firm, then responsible for designing that year's Serpentine Pavilion in London, was offering unpaid internships, six days a week, from 11 a.m. to midnight. To cap it all, interns were expected to use their own laptops and software. Furman made the post, one of a series, under the hashtag #*archislavery*. It could be argued that the practice is peculiar to the country in question (unpaid internships are common practice in Japan), but several posts under the same hashtag reveal that these kinds of deals are made the world over. Given this exchange of workforces and architectural commissions, therefore, we cannot ignore the European and international dimension. The issue is not purely local and requires cross-border scrutiny.

Creating a sustainable work environment together

While the socio-economic position of architectural workers is an overarching, international and complex issue, the consequences are concrete and can result in tragedy. I write this as a young, novice architect, not yet fully versed in the subject, but I speak from experience – my own and that of my fellow architects. Our working conditions are a constant topic of conversation around the dinner table, a difficult subject. How has it come to this? Is architecture really so underappreciated? Do we, as architects, need to unite more?

Much work has already been done both at home and abroad. In the UK, young architects are organizing themselves via associations such as United Voices of the World – Section of Architectural Workers (UVW-SAW) and Future Architects Front (FAF), who are jointly advocating a 'Just Transition'.[28] This resulted in the election in 2022 of Muyiwa Oki as president of the Royal Institute of British Architects (RIBA).[29] He is the youngest ever president, the first black person in the role, and he is also employed by an architectural firm. In the Netherlands too, closer collaborations are emerging between Netherlands Angry Architects (NAA!), representing young workers in architecture, and the Federatie Nederlandse Vakbeweging (FNV), the country's largest trade union.

While Belgium has a high rate of unionization, architects have fallen by the wayside. The country has the largest share of freelancers in the European architectural sector, yet self-employed people seem difficult to unionize. Recently, however, two local initiatives have managed to rally a large number of stakeholders: Dear Architects and Belgian Architects United (BAU) issued an appeal to the Order of Architects on 5 December 2023. In a document entitled 'Voor een betere architectuursector' (For a better architecture sector),[30] they identified four challenges: stopping the race to the bottom; creating stability for architecture workers and associates; redefining the profession; and renewing the Order of Architects. The appeal has since been signed by more than 600 architecture professionals.[31] Also in this book, Evelien Pieters advances an alternative to the competition culture as a way of achieving greater social justice. These voices help us move away from the idea that the situation 'is what it is' and makes it the subject of change.

The term 'architectural worker' was introduced by the American movement, Architectural Workers United (AWU). It has been adopted in Belgium by Dear Architects and BAU as *architectuurwerker*. The word has three important connotations. First, it references a wider audience than the architect who builds, as per traditional considerations. Secondly, it emphasizes the fact that architects are *workers*, people practising a profession. Finally, it distinguishes between people in positions of power (those who can 'hire and fire') and those who are not.[32] Creating this new language helps us to place the emphasis on responsibilities. The higher your position on the ladder, the greater your accountability. Convinced that the 'architectural employer' *(architectuurwerkgever)*[33] has the best interests of the young people in their offices at heart, this essay is an open invitation to collaborate on improving both working conditions and wages. As we reflect on projects

---

28 The Just Transition is an association of various UK-based actors who lobby for urgent changes in the construction industry, united in the belief that a sustainable society presupposes sustainable working conditions. The name of the group refers to the term introduced by labour and environmental activist Tony Mazzocchi.

29 Simeon Shtebunaev et al., 'Reclaiming an Architectural Royal Institution: Mapping the Just Transition Lobby's RIBA Presidential Takeover', *City* 1, no. 11 (25 April 2024).

30 Dear Architects is an association working to improve the socio-economic status of architectural workers. Belgian Architects United (BAU) is a group of young architecture workers lobbying for better employment conditions in the sector.

31 The number of signatures on 15 May 2024. This petition was not only widely signed but was also given a hearing in the federal parliament (www.dekamer.be/doc/CCRI/html/55/ic1280x.html) and at the Order of Architects (www.architect.be/nieuws/perspectief-voor-jonge-architecten-orde-van-architecten-lanceert-actieplan).

32 'Hiring and firing' are not the legally correct terms in this instance, since within an architectural firm, the workers are technically self-employed. These terms do, however, reflect the practical reality.

33 I use the term 'architectural employer' by analogy with the term 'architectural worker', as introduced by AWU.

SURVEY   Verloning / Wages

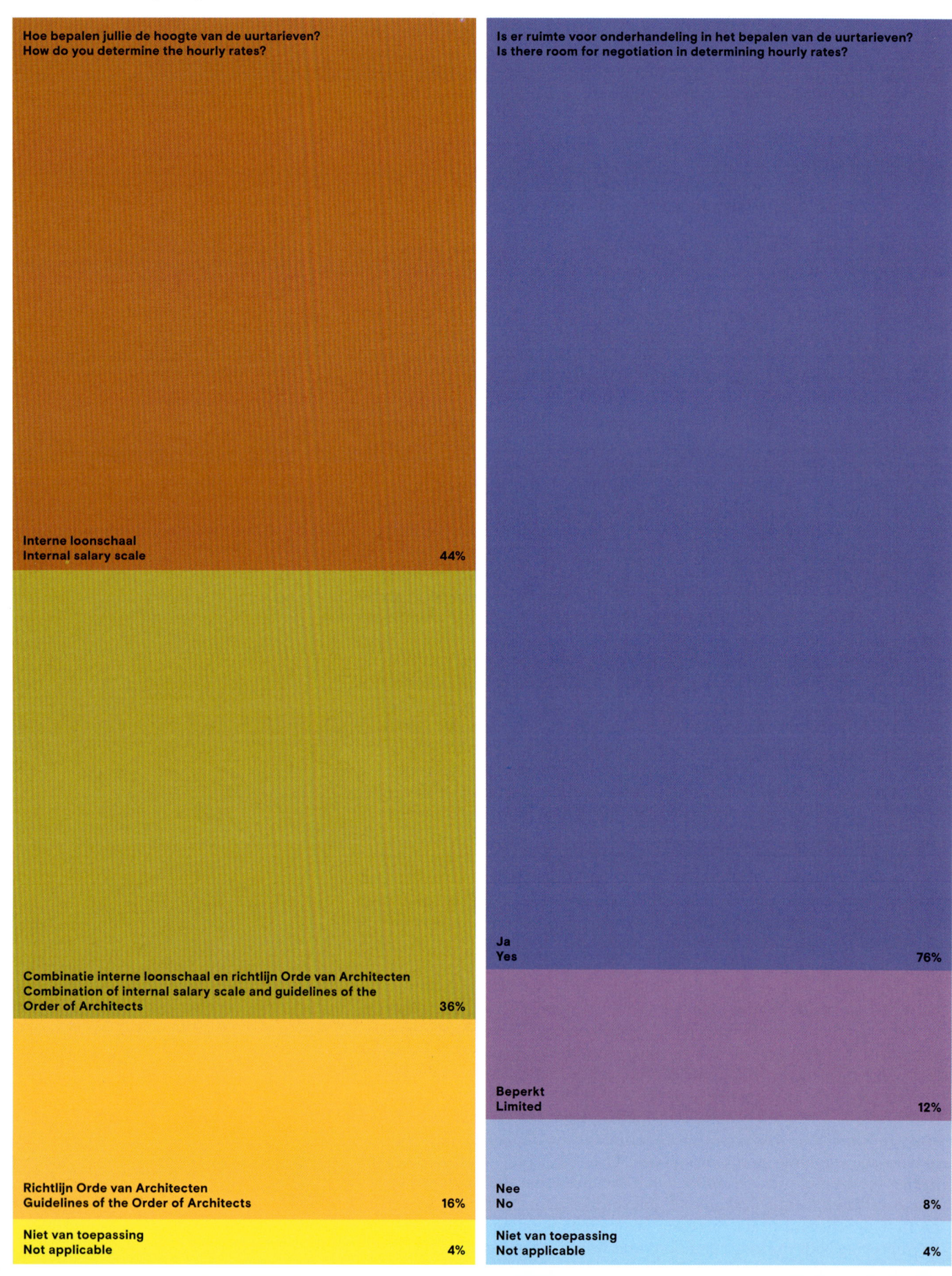

Hoe bepalen jullie de hoogte van de uurtarieven?
How do you determine the hourly rates?

Interne loonschaal
Internal salary scale — **44%**

Combinatie interne loonschaal en richtlijn Orde van Architecten
Combination of internal salary scale and guidelines of the Order of Architects — **36%**

Richtlijn Orde van Architecten
Guidelines of the Order of Architects — **16%**

Niet van toepassing
Not applicable — **4%**

Is er ruimte voor onderhandeling in het bepalen van de uurtarieven?
Is there room for negotiation in determining hourly rates?

Ja
Yes — **76%**

Beperkt
Limited — **12%**

Nee
No — **8%**

Niet van toepassing
Not applicable — **4%**

Verloning / Wages

Hoe vaak worden uurtarieven verhoogd, en wanneer?
How often are hourly rates increased, and when?

Halfjaarlijks / Semi-annual	28%
Halfjaarlijks tot jaarlijks / Semi-annual to annual	24%
Jaarlijks / Annual	24%
Tweejaarlijks / Biennial	16%
Na evaluatiegesprekken / Based on evaluations	4%
Niet van toepassing / Not applicable	4%

Volgen jullie een indexering van de uurtarieven?
Do you follow an indexation of hourly rates?

Ja / Yes	88%
Nee / No	8%
Niet van toepassing / Not applicable	4%

that deliver a social and sustainable result for our communities, let us also work on projects that have been conceived in a social and sustainable way, so that, in the next edition of *Flanders Architectural Review,* we can write, 'Things are going well for architects in our corner of the world!'

PROJECT **MADE architects, Karuur Architecten**

PROJECT **Erasmus primary school, Zelzate**

The spacious campus terrain in Zelzate houses a secondary school, a primary school and a kindergarten. A new primary school was built on the green site, where over the years several school buildings had been constructed, some dilapidated and no longer meeting contemporary requirements. One of the existing buildings, a former boys' school, was listed and had to be preserved; others were ripe for demolition.

MADE architects and Karuur Architecten formed the design team that had to find a balance between the green site, the value of the existing structures, and contemporary requirements for school buildings. Accessibility and fire safety, for instance, were imperative. The architects designed a wooden canopy connecting the gymnasium and the primary school on the site, while the old school building was refurbished with strategically placed wooden elements. The refectory, the multipurpose room and the outdoor areas became key spaces in the project. A number of former classrooms that were no longer required in the programme were repurposed as walled outdoor spaces by removing the windows and adding safety barriers to the open frames instead.

The clients were closely involved in the design decisions throughout the process, and this made it possible to tailor the work to the school's needs. The carefully considered balance between old and new, and between intervening and adding, turned the initially fragmented campus into a more cohesive whole,

situation plan 0 5 25

PROJECT **Erasmus primary school** 155

with both walled play and rest areas as well as squares and playgrounds outside on the site.

PROJECT   MADE architects, Karuur Architecten

PROJECT MADE architects, Karuur Architecten

PROJECT **Erasmus primary school**

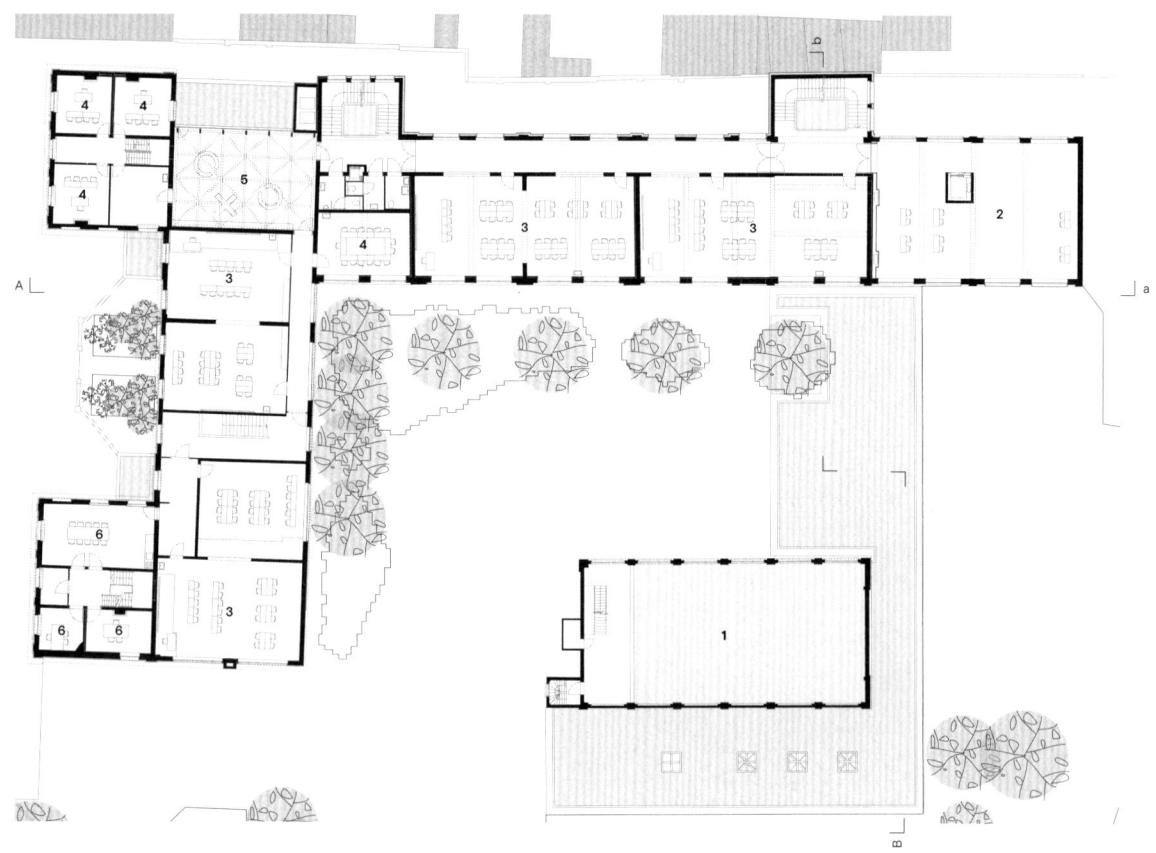

level 1
1 gymnasium, **2** covered play area / outdoor classroom, **3** double class, **4** small class, **5** multipurpose space, **6** teachers' room

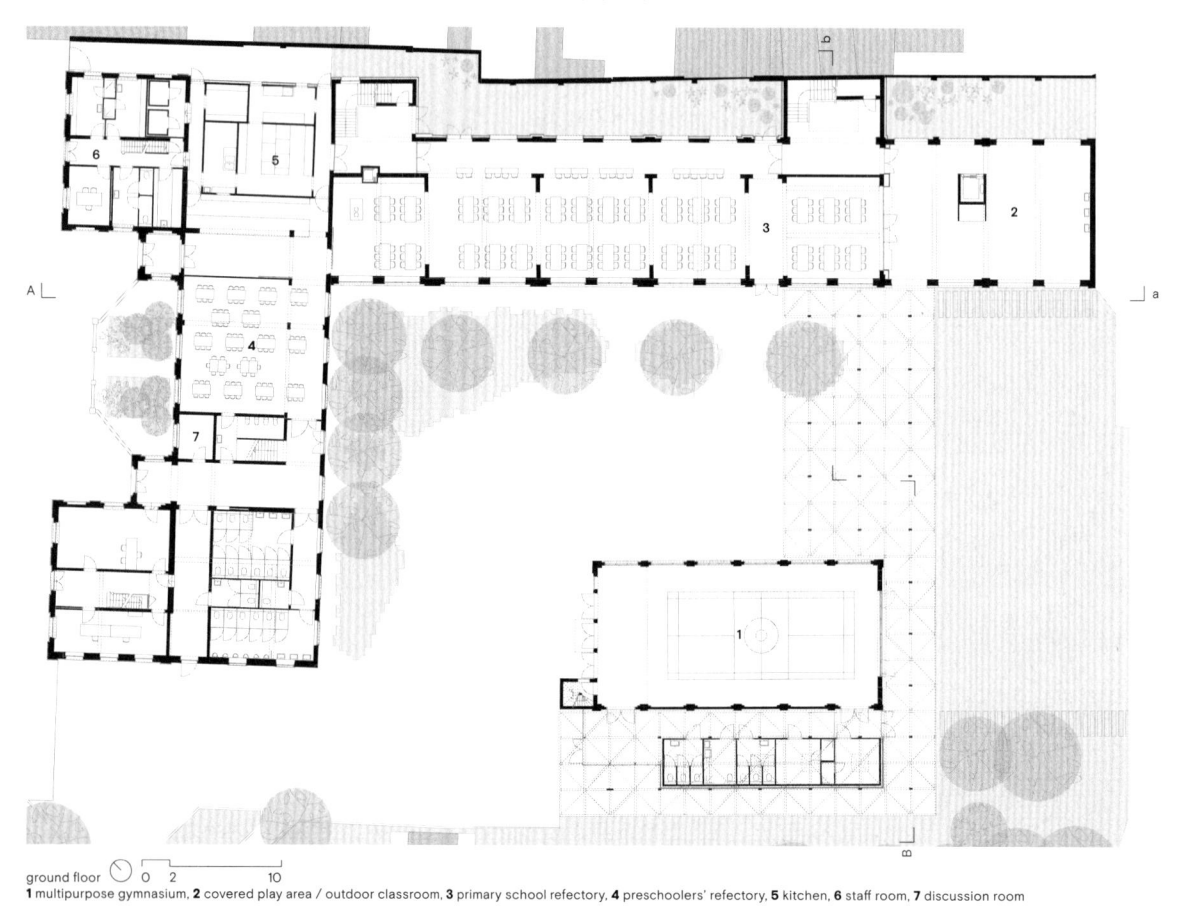

ground floor
1 multipurpose gymnasium, **2** covered play area / outdoor classroom, **3** primary school refectory, **4** preschoolers' refectory, **5** kitchen, **6** staff room, **7** discussion room

PROJECT **Erasmus primary school**

section Aa

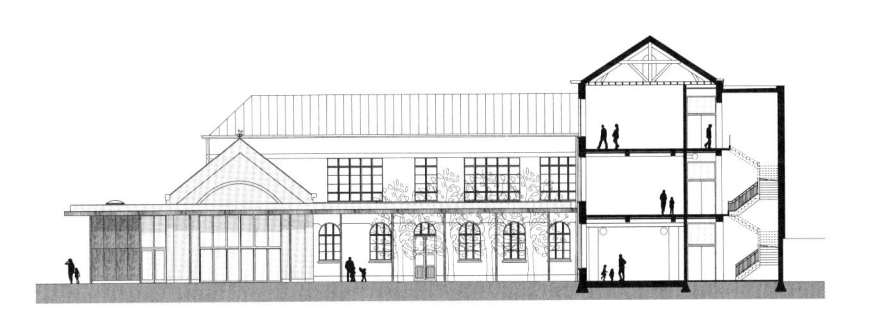

section Bb 0 2 10

project Erasmus primary school **office** MADE architects and Karuur Architecten
design team (MADE) Gill Matthyssen, Liesbeth Storkebaum, Tom Meyvis, Jeroen Van Roie
(Karuur) Thomas Feyen, Babs Geens, Charlotte Vandeplassche, Nina Hooyberghs
website www.madearchitects.be, www.karuurarchitecten.be **address** Leegstraat 2-4, 9060 Zelzate
client GO! Education of the Flemish Community **design** May 2015
completion December 2021 **surface area** 4,110 m² **volume** 20,178 m³
total building cost €5,305,539 excl. VAT **total building cost per m²** €1,291 excl. VAT
main contractor (renovation) VMG-De Cock, Sint Niklaas (restoration) Artes Woudenberg, Bruges
stability studies UTIL Struktuurstudies, Brussels & Denkbar, Mechelen
engineering studies Ingenium, Bruges **acoustics studies** Daidalos Peutz, Leuven

text
Klaske Havik
photography
01, 06–08 © Laura Vleugels
02–04 © Stijn Bollaert
05 © Koen Van Damme

PROJECT   **MADE architects, Karuur Architecten**

PROJECT   Ouest Architecture, Rotor, Zinneke

PROJECT   **Zinneke, Brussels**

Zinneke is best known as a socio-artistic organization for the eponymous procession that meanders through Brussels every two years. The Zinneke Parade is the highlight of a project whose mission is to bring together city residents, associations and artists. Central to its activities are ateliers and workshops which, like the floats, seek to interweave a wide range of technical and creative skills.

In 2013 Zinneke moved into the former printing plant for revenue stamps on Masuiplein in the north of the city. The complex consisted of several sheds, town houses and a central director's residence. Within these given structures, Zinneke set out to redesign the site to suit their purpose, in collaboration with Ouest Architecture and reuse experts Rotor.

Zinneke's ateliers are the result of a groundbreaking design process. There was a clear ambition to go as far as possible in the reuse of materials and installations, both from the site itself and from outside. This allowed the project to benefit from European support. In addition, the values and skills which the association brought with it to the design table of Ouest and Rotor made it a partner in the process rather than a mere client. Zinneke also took matters into its own hands wherever it could in terms of execution.

This design approach led to pushing boundaries beyond the design table. In terms of building permits, for example, the project explored how to deal with the uncertainty that extensive reuse entails as to the final form. For example, a façade drawing in the building permit application shows the maximum and minimum dimensions of window openings in dotted lines. The contractors had to work with the unpredictability of recovered building elements rather than with the predictability of off-the-shelf building materials. In short, Zinneke, Ouest and Rotor saw in the specificity and context of the design question an opportunity to challenge the foundations of the building world.

PROJECT Ouest Architecture, Rotor, Zinneke

PROJECT **Ouest Architecture, Rotor, Zinneke**

PROJECT **Zinneke** 166

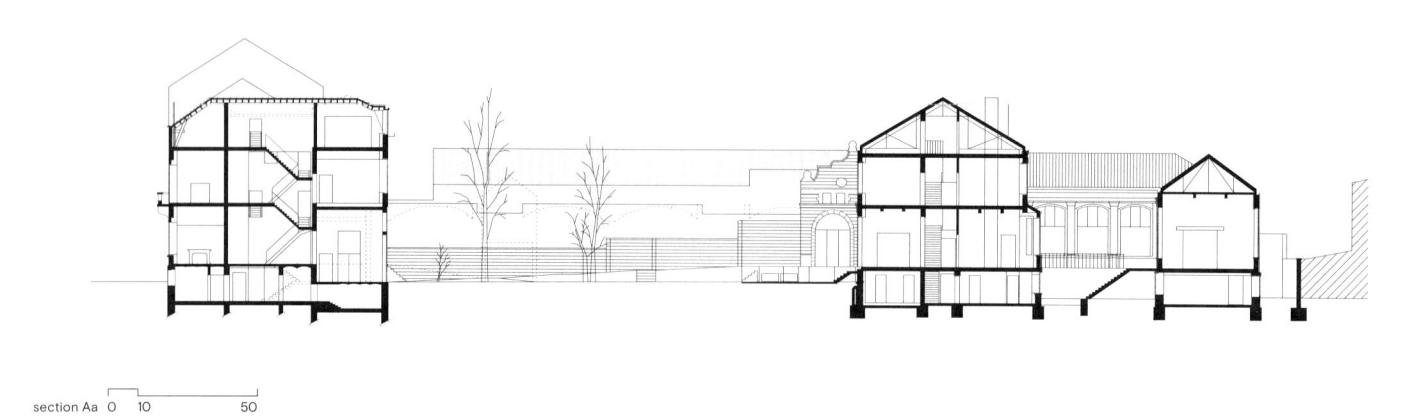

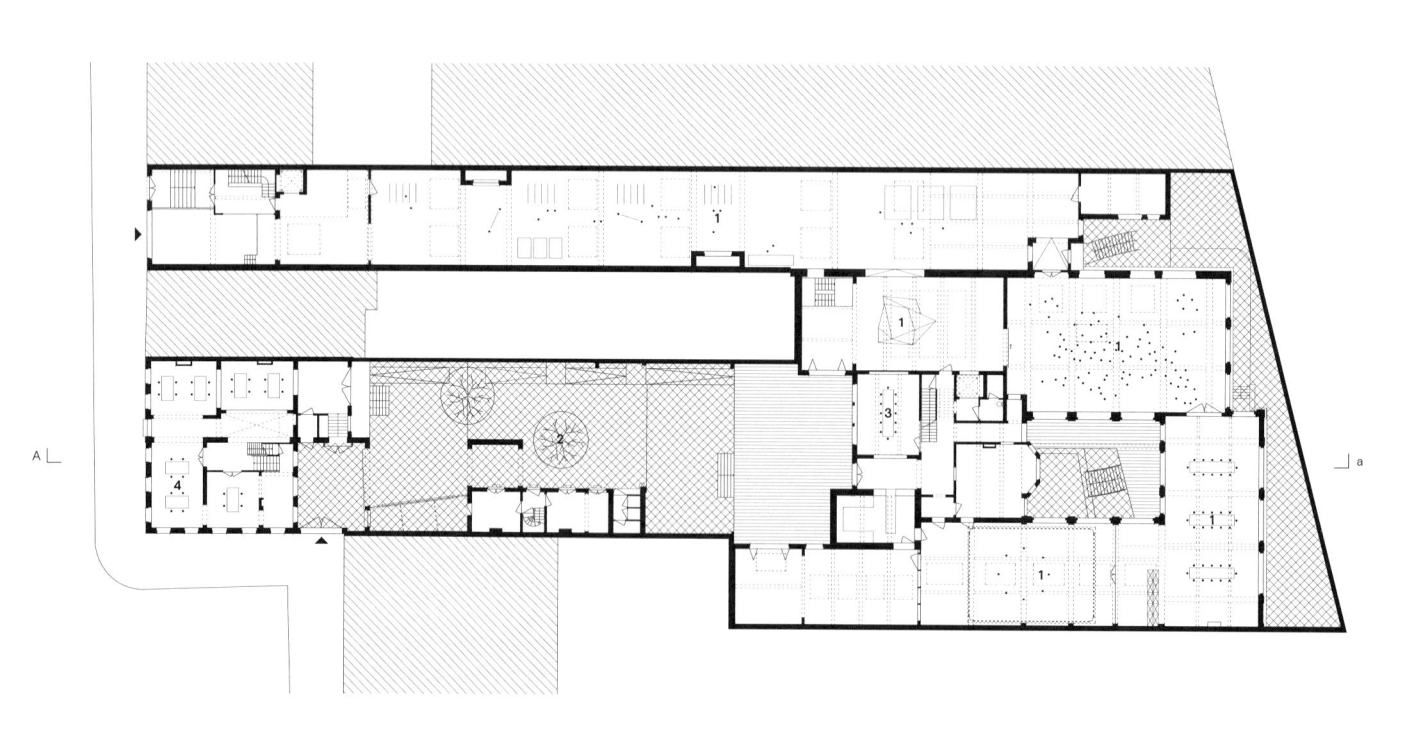

section Aa 0 10 50

ground floor 0 2 10
1 studio, **2** courtyard, **3** meeting room, **4** office space

PROJECT **Zinneke** 167

project Zinneke **office** Ouest Architecture, Rotor and Zinneke
design team (Zinneke) Myriam Stoffen, Sandrine Tonnoir, Marcel Rijdams, Delphine Mathy, Christophe Wullus, Anton Cauvain (Rotor) Benjamin Lasserre, Anne-Lie Bouillon, Arthur Wéry, Renaud Haerlingen, Sophie Boone, Michael Ghyoot, Gaspard Geerts, Alex Basile, Pauline Gonieau (Ouest) Jan Haerens, Stephane Damsin, Matthias Mazelier, Floortje Van Sandick (Matriciel) Fabrice Derny, Arnaud Bricteux, Quentin Remy, Jules Tardy (JZH & Partners) Jeanne Lambeau, Michaël Nguyen (others) Maxime Vanderstraeten, De Coninck, Delta Thermic, Brudex, Collignon **website** www.ouest.be **address** Masuiplein 13, 1000 Brussels **client** Zinneke **design** July 2016 (start) **completion** June 2021 **surface area** 4,000 m² **volume** 14,000 m³ **total building cost** €2,275,000 excl. VAT **total building cost per m²** €570 excl. VAT **main contractor** De Coninck, Herent **stability studies** JZH & Partners, Brussels **engineering and EPB studies** Matriciel, Ottignies-Louvain-la-Neuve

text
Petrus Kemme
photography
01-11 © Delphine Mathy

PROJECT Ouest Architecture, Rotor, Zinneke

Architecture in Conversation

Connecting, Grounding and Improvising as a Response Strategy

Klaske Havik

This is not an architecture of the grand gesture. Nor a diagrammatic concept that can be sketched on a beer mat. At first glance, these are designs that seem reserved and unobtrusive. They are not immediately visible or legible as new buildings. They are multilayered and ambiguous. There is no clear façade, no photogenic frontage to serve as an iconic image of the building. They did not immediately catch our eye during the first selection round for this book, when we encountered the projects through photographs on a digital platform. But when we saw the buildings in reality, we were utterly astounded. It turns out that the buildings have more to say than could ever be conveyed in an image. These are buildings and spatial interventions that speak: to their surroundings, to the communities they bring together, and to the history of the places in which they naturally seem to nestle. This eloquence does not come from nowhere: these buildings are conversations, the answers to the many complex questions of a commission.

During the editorial meetings and site visits for this book, we debated the responsibilities of architects, on various levels, towards complex spatial and social issues: from a lack of housing construction and rising commodity prices to climate change. All these issues brought one burning question to the fore: what is the architect's responsibility? It could be argued that an architect's primary and paramount responsibility is to understand the issues behind a commission and to provide the most precise spatial response. How does the architect answer, through design, the manifold questions, the complexity of the architectural task? An unambiguous concept and a specific visual language are no longer enough when it comes to responsible architectural decision-making. Today, perhaps the measure of success is linked rather to the manner in which the architecture constitutes a response. This essay considers several response strategies that address the changing conditions around the design process. It also considers the social context and various actors that play a role around the project (connecting), the situation, site specificity (grounding), and the unpredictable nature of the commissioning and design process (improvising).

Connecting: Transversal connections between church and community

In a room to the rear of the Sacred Heart Church in Sint-Amandsberg, Ghent, six volunteers are peeling carrots for the local solidarity kitchen. It is nine o'clock on a Monday morning. Boxes of vegetables and pasta cover the table, surplus food that is used to prepare a budget three-course meal for more than fifty local residents on Monday evenings. Sint-Amandsberg is not the wealthiest neighbourhood in Ghent, and these kinds of local initiatives maintain its liveability. Small-scale social enterprises are part of the context to which the HartenTroef project responds.

The repurposing of the Sacred Heart Church, including the presbytery and garden, is one of the key projects in the *En Route* urban renewal strategy aimed at strengthening social cohesion in urban areas through the renovation of squares, streets and parks. In 2020 the design competition for the project, which involved several architectural offices, was won by De Smet Vermeulen architecten. Earlier still, this firm had argued that community functions should be the priority consideration when repurposing churches and that religious architecture allows a degree of flexibility for the insertion of combined programmes.[1]

ESSAY **Klaske Havik** 170

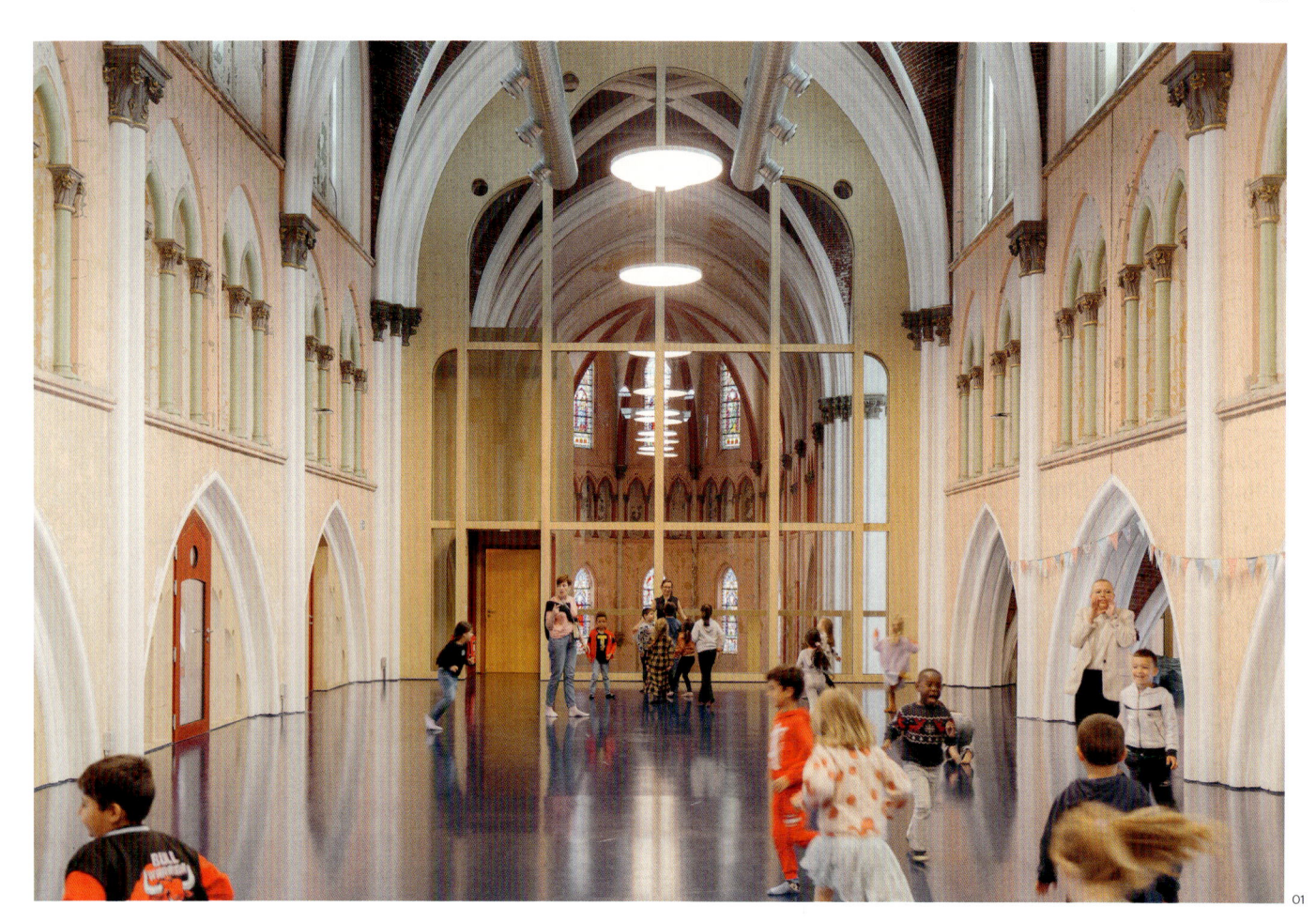

ESSAY **Klaske Havik**

[1] The statement about a social approach to the repurposing of religious heritage is from a comprehensive study on the conversion of churches conducted by the firm with noAarchitecten: *Herbestemming van kerken: twaalf aanbevelingen*, 2014.

The theory was put into practice in the redevelopment design for the Sacred Heart Church.

03

The church space was the starting point for a series of spatial and social connections, each of which offers scope for encounters while simultaneously establishing a relationship between the building's interior and the wider Sint-Amandsberg community. First, the church's side walls were opened and a new timber-frame structure was inserted into the building, leaving a gap between the old and contemporary walls. This created a new space – a connecting zone – while preserving the historic contours of the building. A constant factor in the design is the connection between the church and the outside spaces: the new glass façades open up a view of the garden and presbytery on one side and of the urban square on the other. The redevelopment is not limited, therefore, to the church interior. On the contrary, the relationship to the public space and the presbytery is pivotal. The church turns outward, so to speak: the pulpit, hidden behind the closed walls of a congregation, is no longer the focal point. The side façades now form gateways to the wider community. The new links are transversal connections: the direction has shifted towards the outside, diagonal to the church.

An architectural answer does not always need to be a confirmation, a careful elaboration on the past. In this project, the answer is also a form of respectful contradiction. The design challenges the church's original monumentality and the building's exclusive use by a religious community – everyone facing the pulpit, all looking the same way. In a vertical sense, the wooden insert breaks the monumental height of the nave, while in a horizontal sense, through the transversal axis, the design shifts the focus from a sacred to an urban connection. In this way, De Smet Vermeulen responded to the brief by simultaneously connecting and throwing open, by using transversal alignment and by offering new perspectives. The latter are not just literal, via the new sight lines from the church, but also figurative, since the building can now be used in a myriad of new ways. The community functions that De Smet Vermeulen advocated in their 2014 study are undoubtedly at the heart of this project: the church contains a restaurant and neighbourhood kitchen, and a larger events space was created on the first floor. This intervention, involving a new volume and upper level, punctures the church's monumentality but also delivers a substantial amount of new surface area for the benefit of the local community. The renovated presbytery provides opportunities for various neighbourhood functions to come together, such as office space, community centre and co-working spaces, as well as areas for creative and cultural activities, including a darkroom. The community functions and the vision for the garden and public space were all developed in consultation with the local residents. The church building opens itself up: to its surroundings and to more diverse uses. Together with the garden and presbytery, the Sacred Heart Church has become the beating heart of Sint-Amandsberg.

project Repurposing of the Sacred Heart Church **office** De Smet Vermeulen architecten **location** Ghent
see p. 101

Grounding: Anchored in the heart of the village

Before entering one of the houses, we remove our shoes in the covered walkway on the square. Integrated into the façade next to each front door is a bench: the perfect spot for slipping your shoes on in the dry, putting out a plant, or having a chat with the neighbours. A cat meanders across the square and a child's bicycle lies on the ground. Otherwise, nothing stirs on this weekday afternoon in November. We enter the house on stockinged feet, only to find that the front door conceals a vibrant and spatially exciting home. It is a split-level property and we stand on the steps, looking through the dining room and out into the sheltered garden. From the modest living room at the front, a few steps lead down to the kitchen and garden-facing dining area; on the other side, steps lead to the bedrooms on the upper floor. This house is on the north-east side of the square: here, the terrain slopes gently towards a clearing, where an orchard is due to be planted. The split-level design was prompted by the slight height differential between the square and the lower-lying ground at the rear of the houses.

The restrained intervention by Dierendonckblancke architecten is on the site of an old boys' school in Zomergem. It now contains thirteen houses in three building blocks: one within the contours of the former school and two new wings around the former playground. It is a substantial project in the heart of a small village. The question in this case was how to respect and simultaneously transform the character of this rural locality: after all, several dilapidated buildings needed to be demolished.

Dierendonckblancke departed from a precise reading of the existing composition of the volumes around the communal playground and used this as the basis for the new infill. What was once the schoolyard is now a traffic-free collective space between two rows of low-rise dwellings; people live around a communal square. It is a modest-looking ensemble: a narrow covered walkway runs along the front of each volume, sheltering the front doors. The walkways end at the boundary wall between the square and the park beyond (which, incidentally, begs for a gateway; hopefully the municipality will want to realize this connection). The ground-floor façades below the canopy are all clad in the same glazed tiles, thereby establishing a connection with the new properties within the old school building. The wooden window frames and front doors run from floor to ceiling. Spatially ingenious dwellings are concealed behind these seemingly simple façades. A total of six different housing types have been developed, of which the split-level houses on the north-east side are the most remarkable. The old brick façade of the existing school building has been retained, while on the inside, the old classroom structure has been replaced by new flats. Behind the historic brick façade is a brand-new one, finished with the same white tiles as the contemporary volumes. The gap between these frontages provides each flat with a loggia (on the first floor) or a covered terrace (on the ground floor). The old director's house was preserved and converted into two homes, while a communal area is intended for the community centre. The idea of cloistered communality translates, first and foremost, into the square and community centre. Less visible communal facilities are the rainwater cistern for the toilet grey-water system, the communal installation room and the bicycle storage in the former caretaker's quarters.

ESSAY   **Klaske Havik**   174

04

ESSAY   **Klaske Havik**   175

06

Grounding as a response to a commission can also be understood as a site study, the ground as a layered place on which something is built. This project recognizes the different temporal layers and historical narratives and anchors the design in both, by adding, unearthing, omitting, referencing. By responding to local conditions in a subdued, understated and seemingly simple way, a residential community has been created just a stone's throw from the Zomergem church. The project is a measured answer to the site and its history but it also does justice to the collective principles that underpin a boys' school. Above all, it creates space for a contemporary interpretation of collective and multigenerational living in a vibrant village community.

project Jongensschool group housing **office** Dierendonckblancke architecten **location** Lievegem
see p. 181

Improvising

Perspective is completely tilted in the hall of Zinneke's offices in Brussels. Stairs criss-cross the space, and floor and ceiling heights are out of kilter. Old and new, here and there, high and low, and all kinds of things – from the sleekly modern to the classically decorative – are combined into a remarkable mix. The result is not unlike an Escher drawing. And this is just one of the many episodes in the chain of architectural encounters to be found in the Zinneke building. The office area, situated in two adjacent street-side properties, foreshadows the array of atmospheres that have materialized in the former printworks, which also boasts a courtyard. There is the deep low room with corrugated concrete ceiling and yellow walls which houses the woodworking and metalworking machinery; there is the theatre room with terrazzo floors and original painted walls in beige and turquoise; there are the glass doors around a small courtyard with a staircase leading downwards; and there is the kitchen area that is fully clad in OSB boards.

Zinneke is a 'social-artistic production centre' that houses a collection of creative schools in the north of Brussels with the aim of connecting different socio-economic groups and providing opportunities for young people from less affluent neighbourhoods. The organization is known for its biennial carnivalesque 'Parade' featuring homemade masks and floats with metal sculptures. Zinneke has occupied the building on Masuiplein in

Brussels since 2013. The renovation, which is still partly ongoing, began in 2016. The decision to opt for reuse – in terms of both the building and the materials – was an ethical and political one.

As a subsidized organization with a public function, Zinneke was obliged to follow compulsory competitive tendering procedures. Yet its approach was hard to fit within the existing frameworks. A description of what the process would involve was sent out to tender, therefore, instead of a defined design. Paradoxically, this format ensured that improvisation was almost the only fixed element of the plan. The programme was initially left as open as possible, so that improvisation became the core of the strategy. A strategy of ad hoc responses does not lend itself to the conventional design and construction process, wherein every action, spatial transformation and detail is fixed in advance on drawings and in specifications.

07

No detailed drawings were produced for the building application, for example. Interventions were described in writing instead, with comments such as, 'Second-hand window to be installed here'. The architects were involved from the beginning and were thus participants in this 'as found' approach. It was made clear from the outset that the bulk of materials would come from the on-site workshops and that the metalwork students and participants in the Zinneke projects would contribute to the construction process as part of their training. Such an approach shifted the design and construction process in other ways as well: the financial set-up of the project also had a radically different framework, as the materials were largely harvested on-site and labour was also partly sourced from within Zinneke. With this reorganization of material and labour, the project became a commentary on Western architectural culture, which in many respects has become too far removed from skilled craftsmanship. In this project, the importance of traditional know-how was instead placed at the centre of the process. The building itself steered the design, acting as a substrate to which architect, builders and users formulated responses with the materials and labour that were at hand. The conversion of Zinneke in Brussels is thus a prime example of improvisation as a strategy for dealing with fluctuating conditions and unexpected twists in a design and construction process.

project Zinneke   **office** Ouest Architecture, Rotor and Zinneke   **location** Brussels   see p. 161

All these strategies – connecting, grounding and improvising – are ultimately just some of the many elements that form a well-considered approach towards a commission. Architectural responsibility is here understood to mean a meticulous grasp of the specific characteristics of a place (grounding), an empathetic linking of different social wishes, needs and initiatives (connecting), and a creative and resilient response to uncertainties, using the clues provided by a building or organization during the construction process (improvising). By presenting these strategies individually and illustrating each via a single project, I am in no way suggesting that the approaches are mutually exclusive; on the contrary: aspects of all three perspectives can be found

ESSAY   **Klaske Havik**   178

ESSAY   **Klaske Havik**   179

09

in all three projects. It is the responsive aspect – wanting to enter into a dialogue with the place, the social environment and time – that is precisely what makes these projects so resilient: not an architecture of grand gestures, but an architecture of conversation.

photography
01-02, Repurposing of the Sacred Heart Church, Ghent – De Smet Vermeulen architecten © Illias Teirlinck
03, Repurposing of the Sacred Heart Church, Ghent – De Smet Vermeulen architecten © Dennis De Smet
04-06, Jongensschool group housing, Lievegem – Dierendonckblancke architecten © Filip Dujardin
07-09, Zinneke, Brussels – Ouest Architecture, Rotor and Zinneke © Delphine Mathy

Dierendonckblancke architecten

PROJECT # Jongensschool group housing, Lievegem

The former school site is located in an inner area in the village centre of Zomergem. Dierendonckblancke architecten and local property developer and contractor Arlo repurposed the 'high-rise' at the front and the head teacher's house into five residential units. They converted the former classrooms into eight new dwellings around the old playground.

The playground now functions as a collective square through which the units can be reached. Vehicles are parked centrally behind the entrance gate. Residents also share a bicycle shed and a storage room; a covered outdoor area provides space for a neighbourhood party or barbecue. The canopies and benches along the façades around the square are like a gesture of welcome and serve as a transition to the private dwellings. The covered area can be used by residents to put down a table and chairs or some flower pots, but also to leave out dirty shoes or park a balance bike.

On the south-west side, the dwellings are wide and of little depth; on the north-east side, a number of steps in the living space bridge a height difference, creating a split level. The dwellings each have

PROJECT **Jongensschool group housing** 183

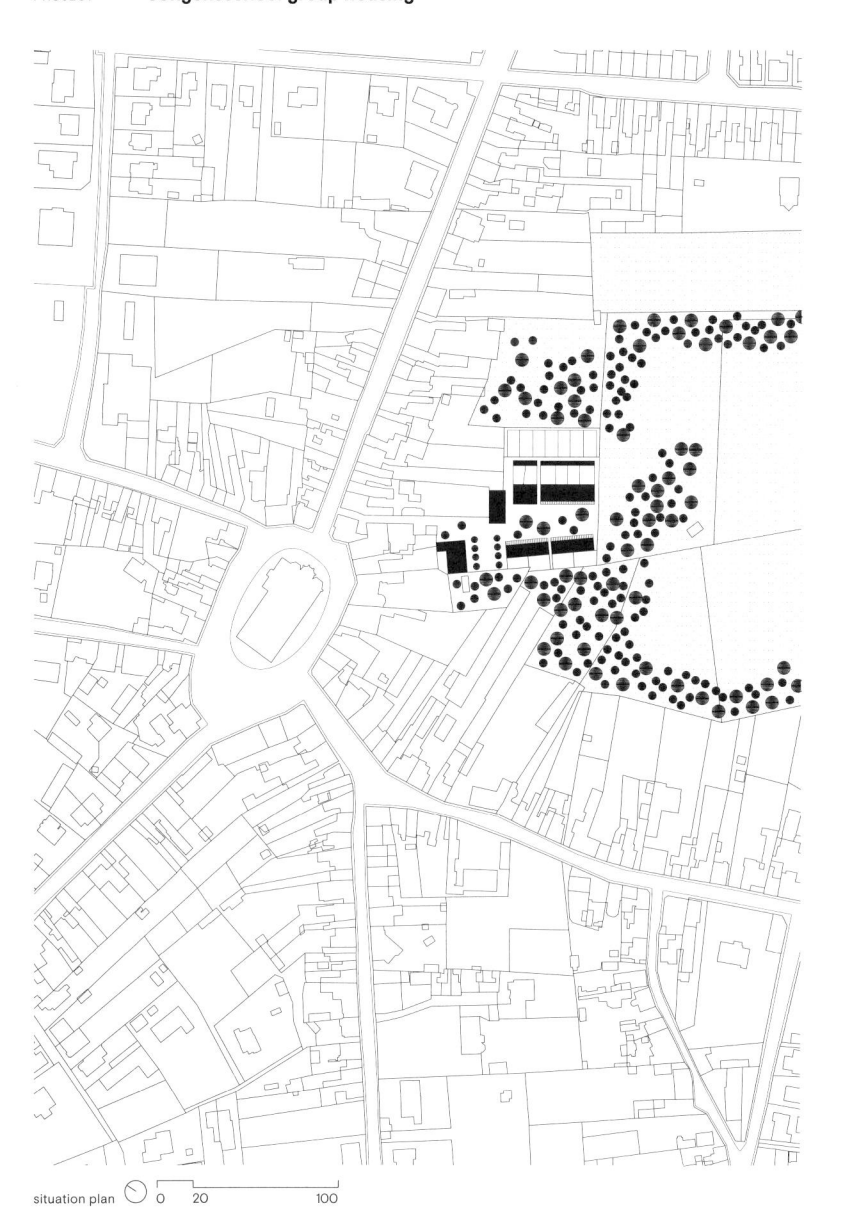

situation plan 0 20 100

05

a private garden at the rear. The simple detailing, with whitewashed façades and garden walls, and the white tiles under the canopies give the project a fresh appearance. The same tiles are also to be found in the high-rise at the front, where the setting back of the façade, behind the opened existing wall, has created spacious private terraces.

Many Flemish villages continue to struggle with the question of how to best shape good housing, somewhere between the detached villa and the umpteenth apartment building. This project, however, is a striking example of a rural way of living with density and collective quality. Although a passage to a green zone at the back and an original idea of a community centre and allotments were not realized (at least, not yet), the project manages to generously fit into the spatial and social fabric of the village.

PROJECT   Dierendonck blancke architecten

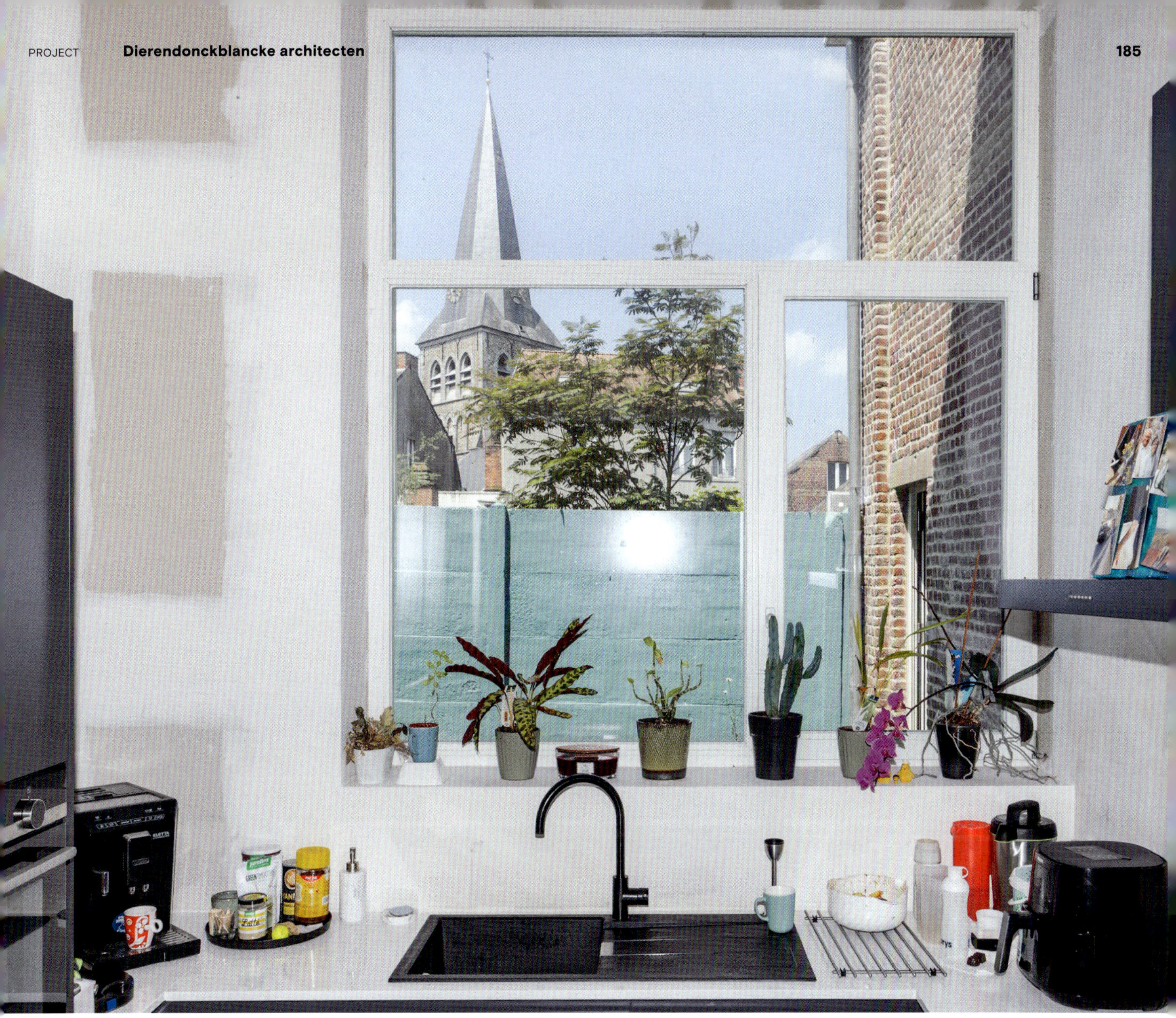

PROJECT   **Jongensschool group housing**   186

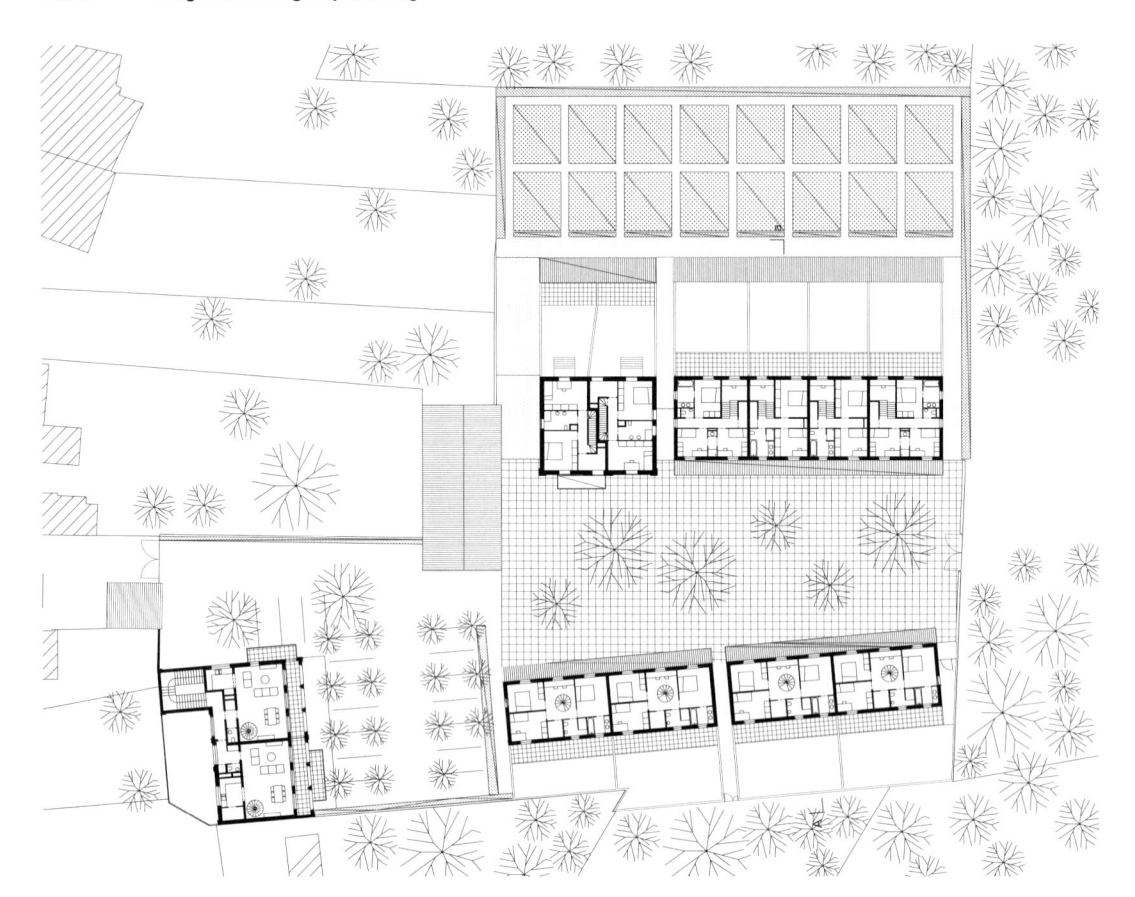

level 1

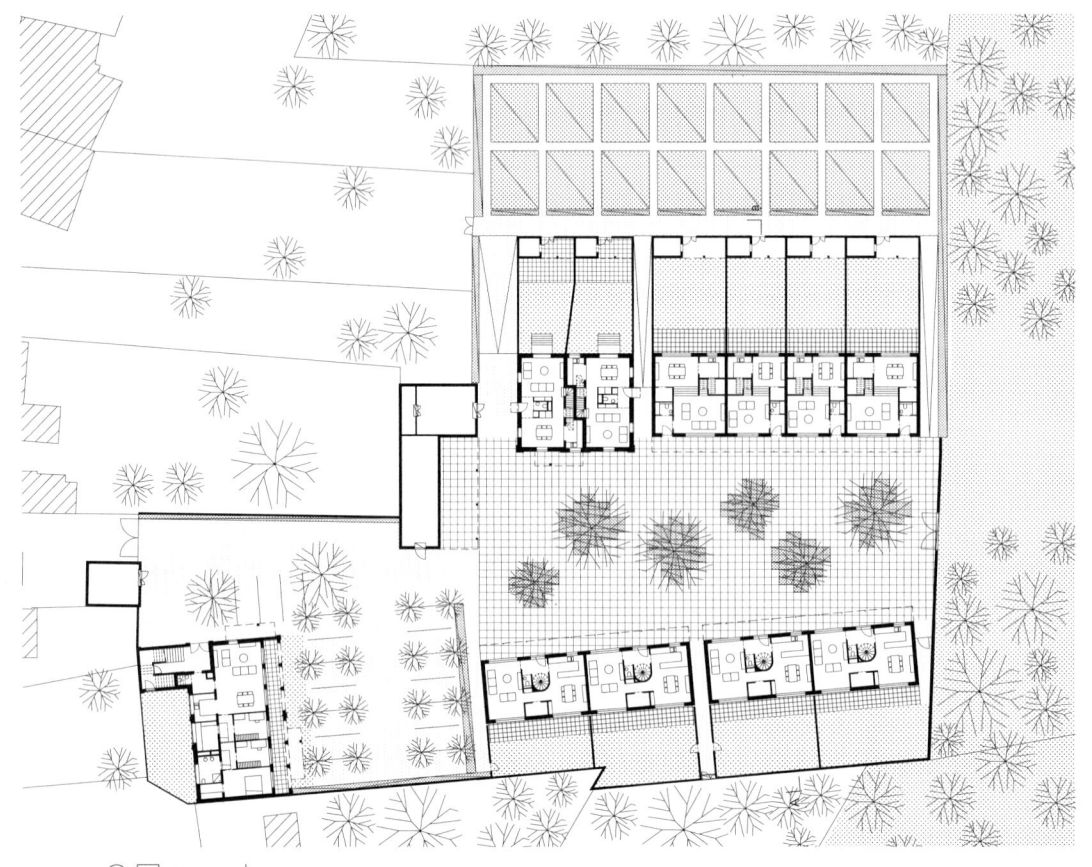

ground floor

PROJECT **Jongensschool group housing** 187

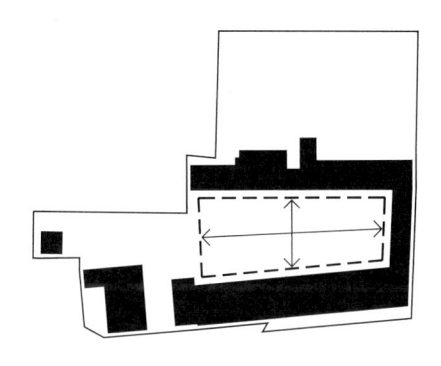

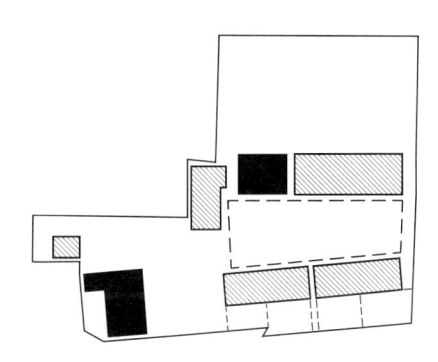

initial situation

new situation

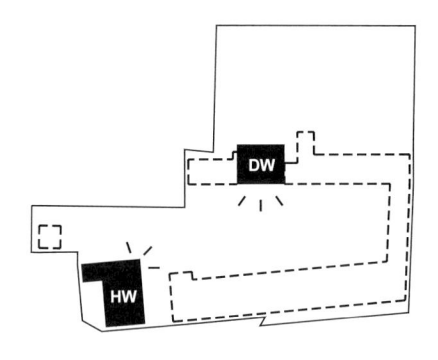

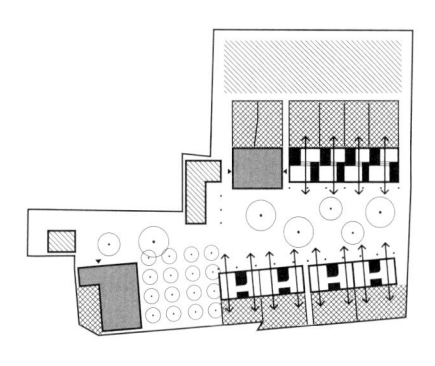

demolition and preservation

transverse living spaces

section Aa 0 1 5

text
Evelien Pieters
photography
01, 06–08 © Nick Moons
02–05 © Filip Dujardin

project Jongensschool group housing
design team Alexander Dierendonck, Isabelle Blancke, Catherine Pyck, Lisa Lu, Lennart Vandewaetere, Arne Standaert, Stijn De Pauw
address Jongensschoolpleintje 1–11, 9930 Lievegem
completion June 2023   **surface area** 2,525 m²
total building cost €4,000,000 excl. VAT
main contractor Arlo, Lievegem
engineering studies Tech3, Ghent
landscape design Lieve Van De Ginste, Ghent

office Dierendonckblancke architecten
website www.dierendonckblancke.eu
client Arlo   **design** May 2016
volume 7,313 m³
total building cost per m² €1,453 excl. VAT
stability studies Cobe ingenieurs, Bruges
EPB studies EA+, Ghent
safety coordination Niveco, Drongen

PROJECT   Dierendonckblancke architecten

PROJECT De Gouden Liniaal Architecten

PROJECT # De Helix school campus, Maasmechelen

Following a merger of three educational institutions, De Helix is by far the largest school in Maasmechelen. The eclectic main building of the former Heilig Hart College dominates the view from the main road. Behind it, a campus unfolds for which De Gouden Liniaal Architecten drew up a master plan to organize the study programmes offered on-site, replace outdated infrastructure and create a new green lung.

The opening move is this building by the same designers where the electricity classes take place. But the building was designed from the idea that, with all the expected developments, another course could also be housed in it with relatively moderate interventions. The plan was conceived as a point-symmetrical framework within which walls, disciplines and users can change. Only two circulation shafts are permanent – at an angle to each other so as to avoid total symmetry.

The core of the building is a generous void. Downstairs, there is a spacious entrance hall with a gallery. Daylight enters through an oculus in the ceiling. On the second floor, the glass area is demarcated by a round study table, the roof above it having been raised to admit a maximum amount of light. In the current arrangement, class modules are gathered in clusters to create spacious and flexible practice rooms that let teachers either face the window or have their backs to it. Elsewhere, this plan form ensures that the workshop layouts have a 'sense of direction', as it were, even when

05

there is no blackboard. In the future, the plan may make up a string of more compact classrooms.

The flexibility of the scheme continues in the simple but effective finishes and equipment. Acoustic ceilings offer admirable resistance to the sound reverberations you would expect in such a concrete structure. That the building does not care about orientation is helped by contemporary insulation standards and automated sun blinds. The industrial impression fits the current occupants like a glove, but also allows for an array of future occupations.

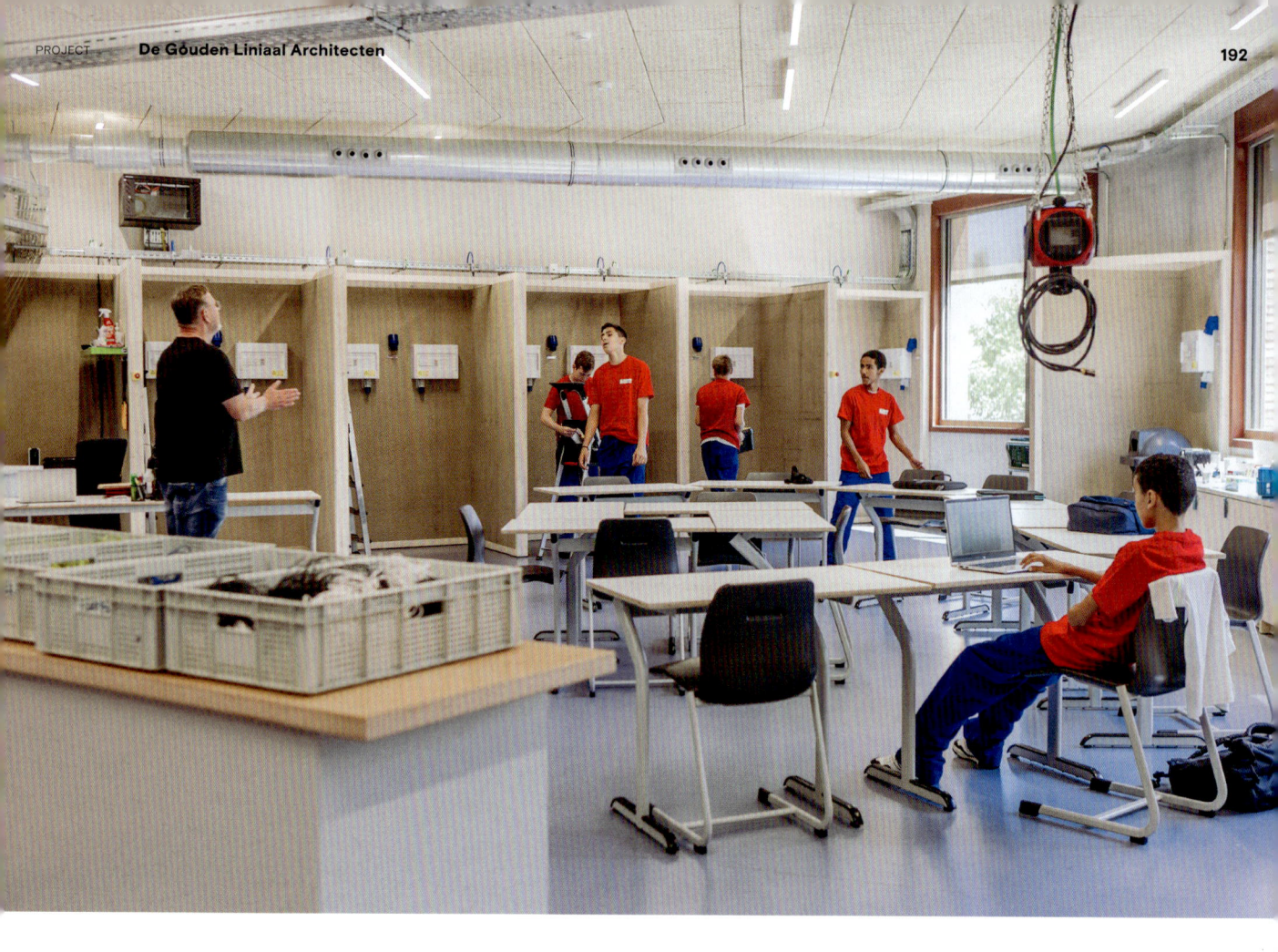

PROJECT   **De Gouden Liniaal Architecten**

PROJECT De Gouden Liniaal Architecten

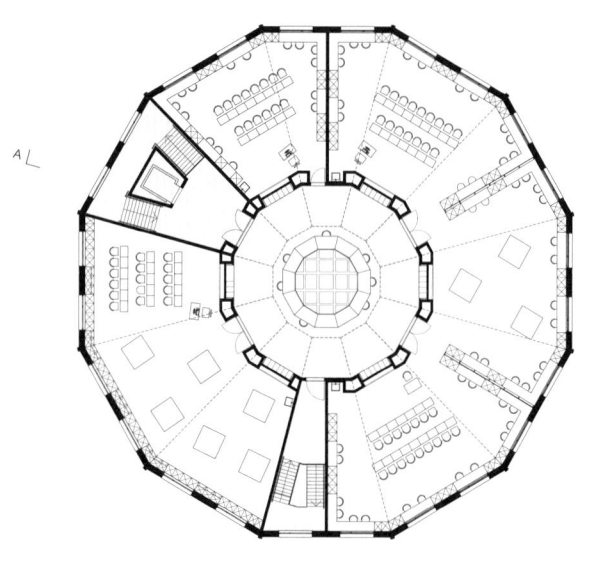

PROJECT **De Helix school campus** 194

level 2

section Aa 0 2 10

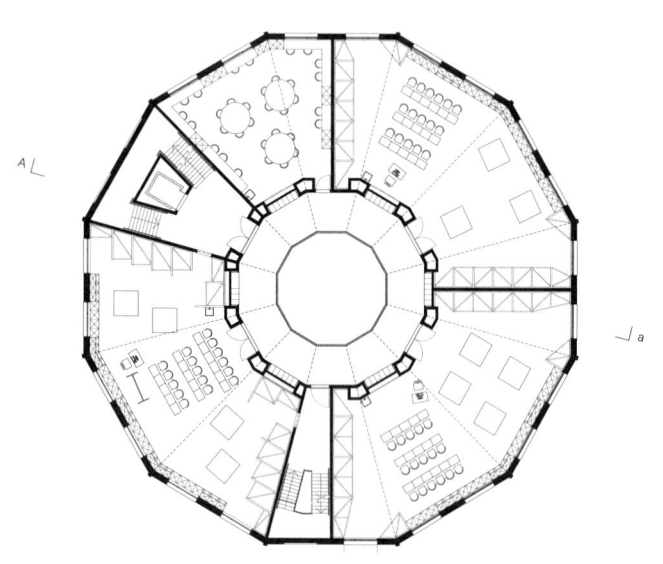

level 1

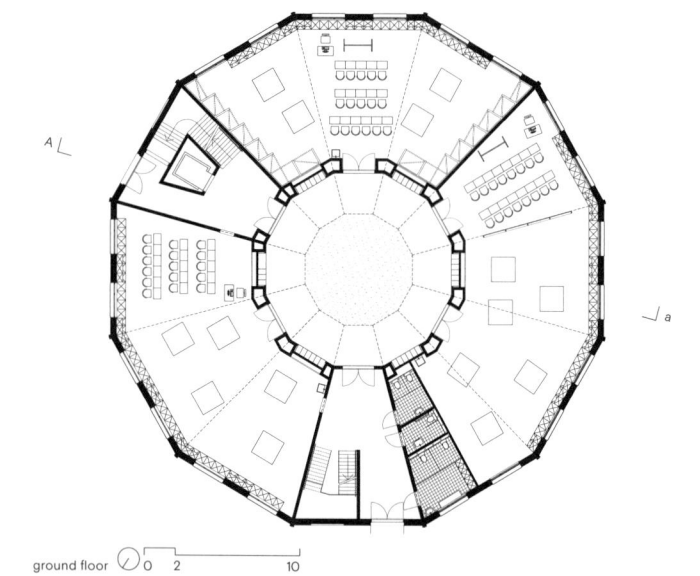

ground floor 0 2 10

PROJECT **De Helix school campus** 195

08

project De Helix school campus **office** De Gouden Liniaal Architecten
design team Sofie Rastelli, Raf Snoekx, Jan Thys, Kristof Benaets, Wim Dirickx, Olivier Eurlings
website www.degoudenliniaal.be **address** Rijksweg 357, 3630 Maasmechelen
client KSOM De Helix vzw **design** October 2019 **completion** August 2023 **surface area** 3,400 m²
volume 12,900 m²
total building cost per m² €1,526 excl. VAT **total building cost** €5,189,000 excl. VAT
main contractor Houben, Hasselt
exterior joinery and aluminium Drijkoningen, Neeroeteren-Maaseik **electricity** E.L. Systems, Zonhoven
heating Cooltech, Alken **plumbing** Luc Vanderhallen, Maasmechelen **interior joinery** Driesen, Pelt
interior metalwork Slegers Metaalwerken, Oudsbergen **stability studies** V2S, Genk
engineering studies AE+ Engineering, Sint-Truiden **acoustics studies** D2S International, Heverlee
EPB studies and safety coordination 2B-Safe, Bilzen

text Petrus Kemme
photography
01, 06-07, 09 © Laura Vleugels
02-05, 08 © Stijn Bollaert

PROJECT **De Gouden Liniaal Architecten**

ESSAY

Generous Sharpness

A Miscellany of Liberality as a Result of Precision

Saar Meganck

When you sharpen a pencil, you remove the excess in order to be able to draw clear lines. A process of elimination to achieve focus. This concentration can go in a number of directions. It is fascinating when the act of 'stripping away' becomes a trigger for 'generosity'. It is then about an attitude in which austerity is a conscious decision, but one that involves transcending sparingness in order to become generous again.

Some thrilling examples of 'generous sharpness' exist in Belgium's contemporary architectural landscape, wherein processes or creations have been 'degreased'. Sometimes these are only linked to a specific project, but they generally manifest themselves as an attitude within the team. They demonstrate a careful management of available resources for a higher purpose. Depending on the project, that management comprises a strict control of time, material or space. It is an attitude that demands a serious commitment and involvement by the architect; after all, waste requires less thought. Moreover, it is only successful if, instead of being 'deboned', the result transcends, in the very breathing space created by its simplicity, the 'lack' both architectonically and socially. There is a fine line to be trod here. When parts are excised thoughtlessly or excessively, the soul can vanish. It is like walking a tightrope.

In Aalbeke, urbain architectencollectief has redesigned and strengthened the village centre in an all but stripped-down language that is strongly aligned with the context. The project exudes a modesty that shows the power of an architectural team that deploys pragmatic logic. Indeed, here the team prioritized taking a critical look at the site and revising the existing 'public heritage' master plan by means of an intensive, participatory, design-based preparatory phase. Two studies were combined: on the one hand, research into the housing of services and associations in several municipalities as well as optimizing heritage by selling empty buildings and plots; on the other, the search for a new purpose for the Church of St Cornelius. Ultimately, the church and the existing meeting centre were linked to some 2,850 m² of shared community space. This volume of meaningful space could not have been achieved without the careful omission of interventions and materials. Simplicity and restraint, in language and approach respectively, to achieve an equilibrium. The 'undressing' of the architectural intervention was particularly successful. Any more 'cutting away' would have made the overall project too meagre and resulted in the loss of its aesthetic enfolding.

project Church of St Cornelius and community centre   **office** urbain architectencollectief   **location** Aalbeke
see p. 37

B-ILD's approach is to 'shift' time, material and space, and thus to free up latitude for a targeted dedication to social engagement. One example being the use of standard details in all the firm's dossiers. The time that is won as a result is used for processes in the preparatory phases of the project. This allows every proposal to be thoroughly reviewed and a decision might be taken, for example, to seek out additional usage partners for the same building, or to rework the commission with all parties, and then to try and find additional financing for vulnerable groups or landscapes. This is a bold position to take in a Flemish architectural scene with a strong focus on 'celebrating and characterizing' the detail. The designs far surpass this standardization, however, and they attest to a refined and clear architectural vision. When designing the new-build Dagpauwoog living school in Koningshooikt, ▸

ESSAY **Saar Meganck**

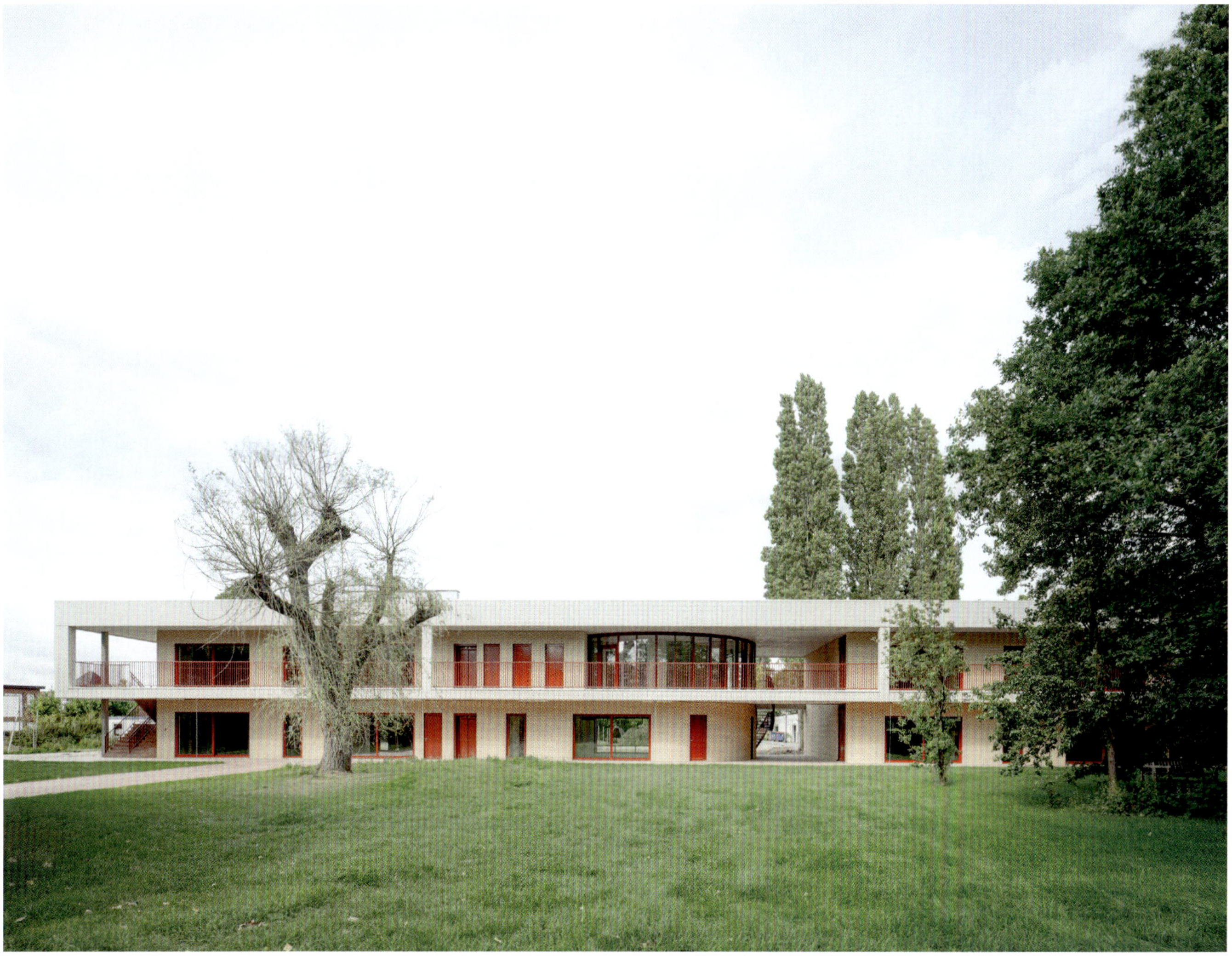

02

ground floor 0 1 5

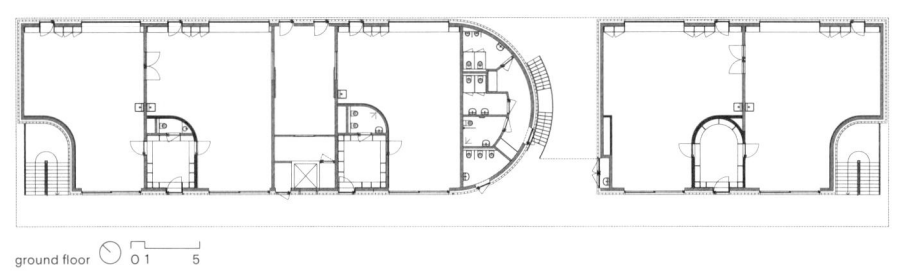

B-ILD explored whether the subsidies left any margin for reinforcing the school's pedagogical project through the architecture. They eliminated as much circulation as possible from the heated volume in order to achieve classrooms with unusual dimensions but which still fall within the regulations governing the surface area that can be subsidized (90 m² as compared to 55 m² for a standard room). Once again, a 'simplification' that restores meaning. This decision simultaneously determines the plan, the cross-section and the appearance of the façade: an organic structure for the community school where an uncomplicated, rigid rectangle is overlaid with circulation.

project Dagpauwoog kindergarten and primary school
design team Kelly Hendriks, Stephanie Vander Goten, Fatme Hassan, Bruno Despierre, Joris Kerremans, Marta Gruca, Linnea Vanden Wyngaerd
address Dorpsstraat 63, 2500 Koningshooikt
design July 2016   **completion** July 2023
total building cost €2,596,000 excl. VAT
main contractor Dhulst', Lier
engineering and EPB studies Studie 10, Lier
office B-ILD
website www.b-ild.com
client GO! Education of the Flemish Community
surface area 1,557 m²   **volume** 5.901 m³
total building cost per m² €1,667 excl. VAT
stability studies UTIL Struktuurstudies, Brussels
safety coordination Be Consult, Geel

At the service centre in Veldegem by Havana architectuur, the simplicity of 'reversing' the building is an act of profound social and urbanistic generosity. It does not stand 'in' the public space; rather, the façade wall forms, as it were, a nurturing boundary around an internal public square. As an open space, the square weaves along the axis of a transverse passage linking the old village centre to a new quarter that is still in development. Together with the car park and retirement flats, the local service centre forms a single connected whole with a legible and open appearance in this introverted figure. This plan drawing is so convincing that the architectural language can once again fall silent in the pared-down, sharp simplicity that is typical of this design team. A mannered complexity in visual language is sought out – detail, materiality, façade drawing, bas-relief, ornamentation, chroma composition, and so on. This puts the emphasis on the overarching purpose: a platform for human actions and encounters. Movements towards the various municipal services, the hairdresser, the boules pitch, the retirement flats and the through-circulation are given an architecturally embraced space as a generous 'lee'.

project Veldegem service centre
see p. 225
office Havana architectuur
location Zedelgem

In complete accordance with their oeuvre, at URA Yves Malysse Kiki Verbeeck's kindergarten and primary school De Telescoop in Brussels we also find this sleek calmness of language, which here goes hand in hand with spatial generosity. This is also a project that folds into an inner area between two streets. However, this 'folding' is achieved in an entirely different way to Havana's service centre in Veldegem. The plan arises from the meeting of the two resolutely rectangular forms of the inner area with the diagonal lines of the site. The spatial richness is celebrated in all the little 'folds' *of*, *in* and *against* one another: a corner that pushes into a space, an entrance that deflects and makes a vestibule to the street, a staircase that organically presses into a thick wall like a poché, a vertical circulation as a theatre façade, and so on. In this way, the overall design succeeds in creating an open experience on a compact plot thanks to a continuous shifting of views and boundaries. The vocabulary supports this via the variation that is still permitted to play out at the margins, within a limited choice of materials and colours. For example, the same window detail offers a completely different view each time through the constant shifting of a yellow front panel; the yellow columns appear to be wandering arbitrarily in the refectory and a single column has 'stepped' outside, where it stands alone in the playground …

project De Telescoop kindergarten and primary school
location Laken

office URA Yves Malysse Kiki Verbeeck
see p. 209

Dierendonckblancke architecten are lord and master of a generous sharpness; they strip down to a core before again deploying a highly deliberate spatial 'generosity', whether in terms of material or detail. The Lange Beeldekensstraat project in Antwerp for AG Vespa is yet another example. The façades are set into an existing corner building as cornerstone. The intention was to acquire the entire corner in order to realize the project, but AG Vespa failed to bring this to fruition. The initial commission was to convert the two buildings into five terraced houses. The architectural team dared to take a critical look at this approach. They convinced the client to switch to a multi-family dwelling that offers the opportunity to live 'together' as a new collective around a courtyard garden. In so doing, they could also place new typologies for other target groups into the gallery around the shared open space. The clear intervention echoes an understated severity in the façades. However, the delicate and precise detailing immediately reveals that not only the plan, but also the language of the elaboration is driven by a balanced choice that embodies both simplicity and peculiarity.

ground floor 0 1 5

project Lange Beeldekensstraat group housing
design team Alexander Dierendonck, Isabelle Blancke, Stijn De Pauw, Carmine Van der Linden, Maarten Thys
website www.dierendonckblancke.eu **address** Lange Beeldekensstraat 76 – Greinstraat 30, 2060 Antwerp
client AG Vespa **design** November 2015
surface area 1,348 m² **volume** 2,848 m³
total building cost per m² €1,439 excl. VAT
stability studies UTIL Struktuurstudies, Brussels
EPB studies EA+, Ghent
landscape design Landinzicht, Brussels

office Dierendonckblancke architecten
completion September 2023
total building cost €2,065,790 excl. VAT
main contractor Huybreckx, Turnhout
engineering studies Boydens Engineering, Dilbeek
acoustics studies Daidalos Peutz, Leuven
safety coordination Eveka, Sint-Niklaas

The Robust housing for the Public Centre for Social Services (OCMW) in Ghent by ae architecten balances simplicity and uniqueness for a very different reason. The project is a 'housing first' project, focused on the reintegration of a vulnerable group of homeless people. The translation of 'living' is fundamentally different here and must encompass alternative orientations. On the one hand, it is very important to enable each resident to have their 'own world' (privacy) and to design this robustly and without overstimulation. On the other hand, there is a significant need for social control and conflict avoidance. Both intentions ▸

ESSAY **Saar Meganck**

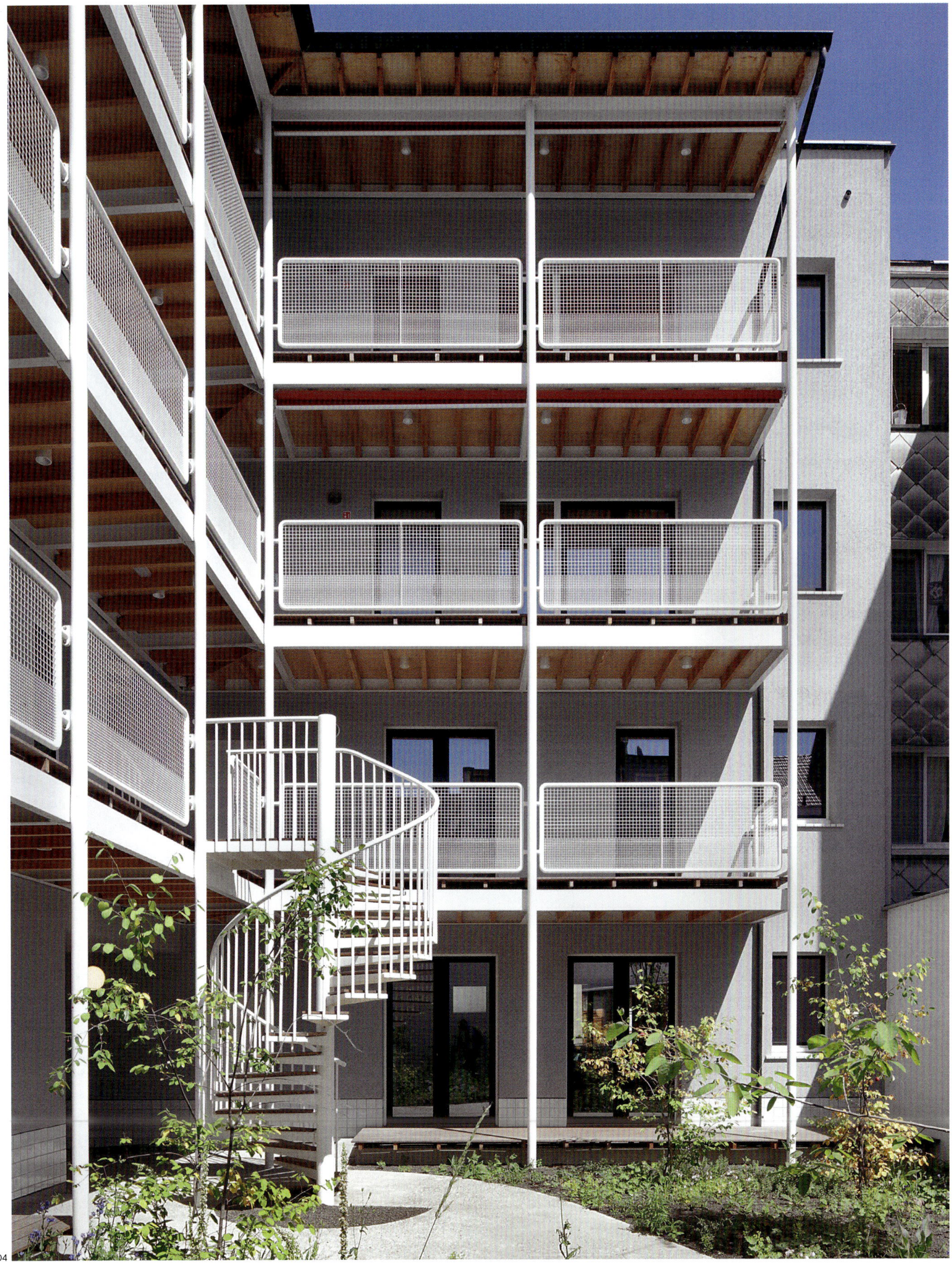

seem contradictory and, moreover, could result in a soulless, robust carcass ready to take punches. In this project, despite these demands, a layering has nevertheless been inserted that both works on a social level and focuses on the details. The architects strove to create social depth by introducing a number of (in)visible boundaries that enable residents to determine their own levels of privacy and social contact. In the collective outdoor area, a decentralized path unfolds with two meeting places beneath the lime trees. This gives the residents a choice between connecting and avoiding. Based on the example of the beguinage typology, the collective transitions into the private through the insertion of personal 'outdoor rooms'. This walled front garden serves as a filter to the outside world and allows the living space on the ground floor to open up through large windows without compromising the sense of security and privacy. The bathroom/bedroom withdraws most from the world and is situated on the first floor.

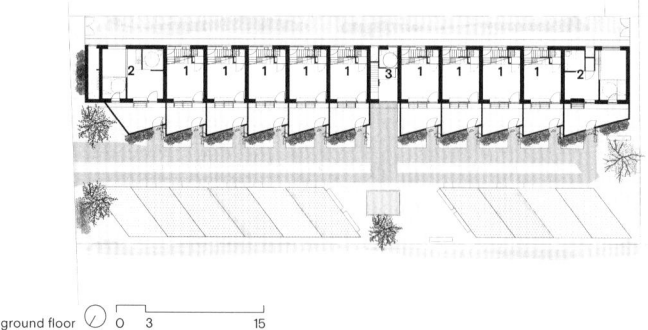

ground floor   0   3   15
1 duplex, **2** accessible unit, **3** municipal services contact point

These very compact units are aligned and meticulously positioned in their context. In the design choices, the volume is elevated above a cheap meagreness with great precision and nuance: the wall of the front garden tilts, creating a fractured zigzag pattern across the masonry; where they transition, the houses are marked with a 'comb' on the façade, so that each home has its own identity; the split outdoor/indoor bench in the transition from garden to living area creates an inviting in-between space; the meeting of staircase and joinery on the rear façade becomes a carefully designed cluster … The gift of small moments of beauty and the attentive architecture attest to a hugely meaningful gesture of empathy. These are signs of care which, through the built environment, can surround and affirm a person.

ESSAY Generous Sharpness 205

project Robust housing **office** ae architecten **design team** Jan Baes, Petra Decouttere **website** ae-architecten.be **address** Hogeweg 96, 9040 Sint-Amandsberg **client** OCMW Ghent **design** February 2020 **completion** December 2023 **surface area** (building) 564 m² (surroundings) 984 m² **volume** 1,571 m³ **total building cost** €1,140,715 excl. VAT **total building cost per m²** (building) €1,968 excl. VAT **main contractor** Siemoens Bouwonderneming, Tielt **art integration** Rudy Luijters: Atelier Veldwerk, Sint-Pieters-Leeuw **stability and EPB studies** H110 Architects And Engineers, Heusden **engineering studies** Declerck en Partners, Waregem **landscape design** Rudy Luijters: Atelier Veldwerk, Sint-Pieters-Leeuw **safety coordination** AB-Solid, Destelbergen

Carton123 architecten, atelier Starzak Strebicki and Natural Born Architects have realized an equally refined enfilade of spaces with the Begijnenborre project in Dilbeek. It houses a kindergarten, a playground and multipurpose rooms. The corridor strings the classrooms and the shared spaces together in a very matter-of-fact way. But by laying the plan upon the site in a folded state, a curved spatial effect is created that introduces the scale and the landscape as protagonists. The architectural team did not want to fell a single tree on the site and at the same time wished to keep the existing school buildings operational during the construction phase. These starting points immediately established the framework for the design. The architectural team asked themselves whether the landscaping generosity of preserving the trees could not be translated differently, namely into a compactly stacked building.

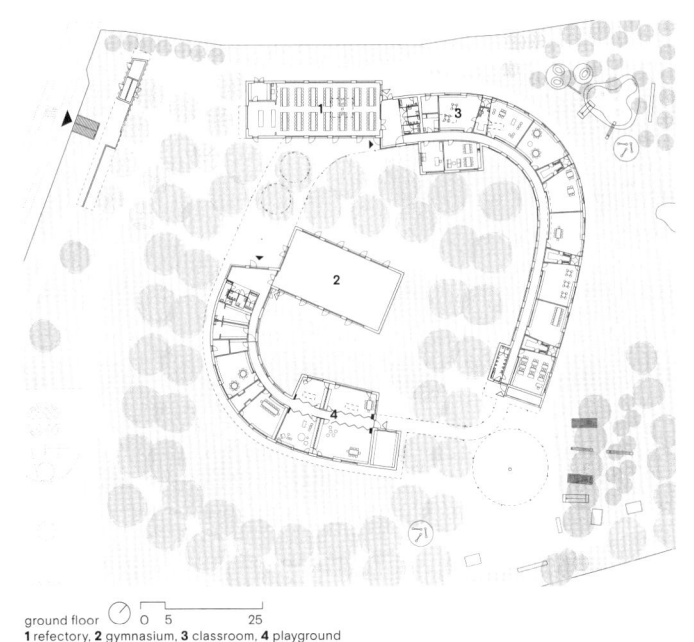

ground floor 0 5 25
1 refectory, **2** gymnasium, **3** classroom, **4** playground

The value of the preschoolers' play and learning environment being in direct contact with 'outside' was the decisive factor for a purely ground-level solution. Highly controlled façades with repeated window details and in a uniform tone gracefully blend into the landscape, enclosing a sheltered inner courtyard. The building does not muscle into the foreground, but adapts to the child and to the landscape in all simplicity.

project Begijnenborre kindergarten and playground **office** Carton123 architecten, atelier Starzak Strebicki and Natural Born Architects **design team** Bartosz Bisaga, Jens De Schutter, Joanna Lewańska, Dominika Lis, Joost Raes, Luis Gómez Soriano, Jola Starzak, Miguel Steel Lebre, Dawid Strębicki, Els Van Meerbeek, Jordy Van Osselaer (project architect) **website** www.carton123.be, www.starzakstrebicki.eu, www.naturalbornarchitects.com **address** Bodegemstraat 113, 1700 Dilbeek **client** Municipality of Dilbeek **design** May 2016 **completion** September 2021 **surface area** 2,300 m² **volume** 8,796 m³ **total building cost** (building) €4,490,000 excl. VAT (landscape) €706,000 excl. VAT **total building cost per m²** €1,952 excl. VAT **main contractor** Brebuild, Antwerp **stability studies** Lambda-max, Aalst **engineering studies** VK Architects & Engineers, Merelbeke **landscape design** Atelier Arne Deruyter, Roeselare **safety coordination** EVOplus, Oudenaarde

A rich spectrum of methodologies is legible within this 'generous sharpness' in the architectural landscape. The attitude is sometimes specific to a project and sometimes particular to the way in which the architectural team works, ▶

ESSAY   Saar Meganck   206

07

ESSAY **Saar Meganck**

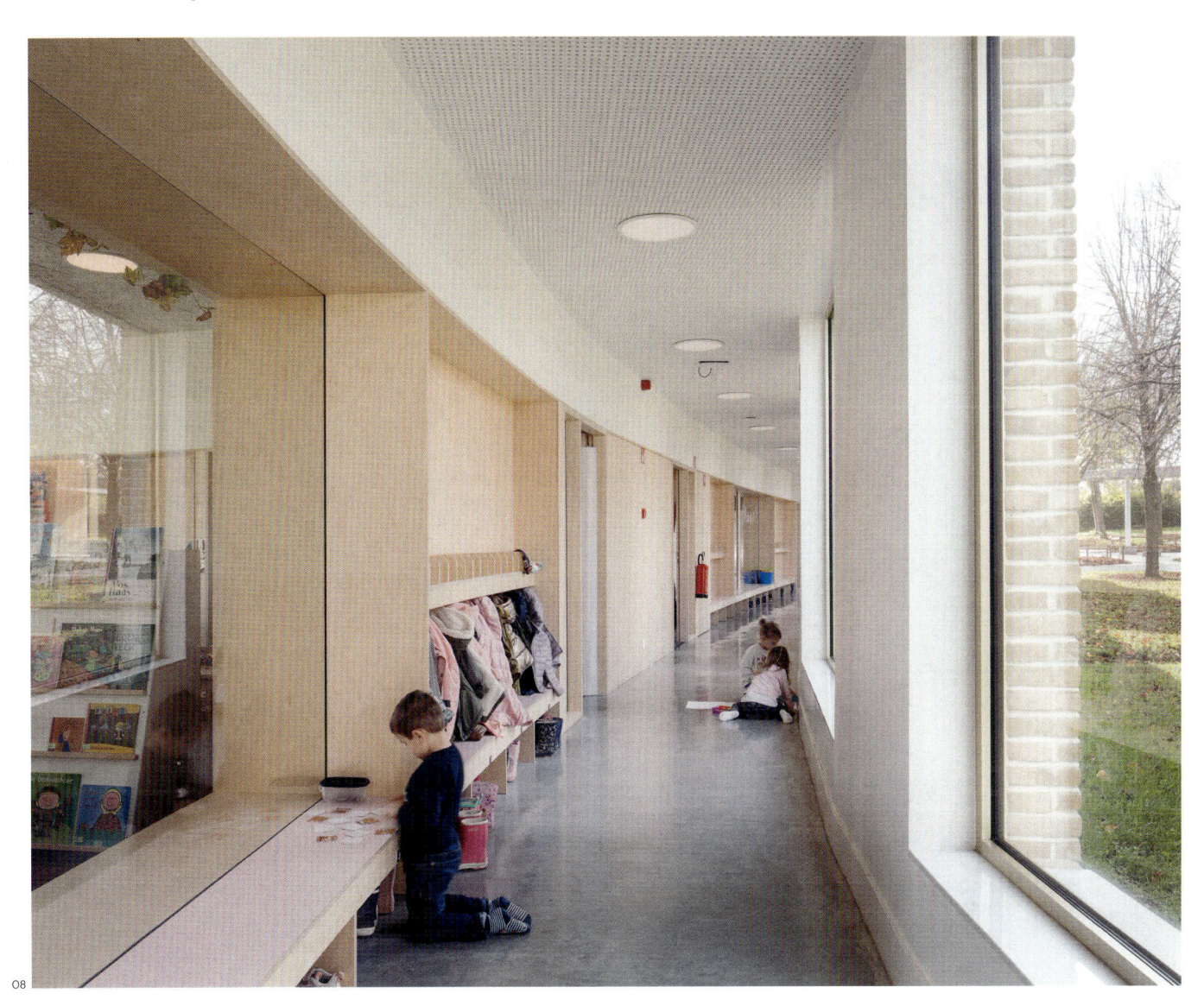

as with B-ILD or Dierendonckblancke. What is clear, however, is that the tone of the process and result resonate with a sincere quest to 'give more' by taking tighter hold of the reins in certain respects. Not being generous by giving out unconsciously and profusely, but by taking a step back – *reculer pour mieux sauter*, as they say in French.

This may be a movement that has acquired its roots and individuality in the zeitgeist. Indeed, we live in a period and amid a succession of generations that must learn to deal with conscious choices about what can and cannot be done. Those willing and able to take responsibility seek an active role. We know that an unbridled 'and, and, and' is no longer justifiable. Fortunately, there is also a general awareness that it is incredibly relevant to preserve social and aesthetic generosity within this act of *cutting*. Architects, as designers of the built context, are exceptionally well placed to make this happen. In the mechanism of 'form and content', they must therefore make very conscious choices, from the start to the completion of a project. The fragility lies in the fact that it is not about the stripping away of spatial and visual beauty in the object. On the contrary, every element is ultimately connected through careful management – of time, material, space – and a balanced aesthetic enthusiasm for a clear social commitment.

Sharpening the pencil to draw a clear, generous line.

PROJECT URA Yves Malysse Kiki Verbeeck

PROJECT
De Telescoop kindergarten and primary school, Laken

GO! Education of the Flemish Community renovated its school in the Brussels municipality of Laken to offer pupils more space and greater spatial quality. It is now a Freinet school, where education is based on the life experiences of the pupils, who shape their curriculum and learning style with the teachers in a practice-based approach. The school grounds are part of the surrounding patchwork morphology, neighbours including the vast Royal Domain, the beautiful retirement home and community centre Mellery, Laeken's Church of Our Lady, the cemetery and the densely built-up residential area.

De Telescoop is located at the corner of a city block, where the school extends from one street to another and forms a triangle with a number of apartment buildings. Two separate volumes border the school. It is in this context that the architectural firm URA Yves Malysse Kiki Verbeeck decided to keep the volume at the back of the site in order to continue the row of houses on Koninklijk Parklaan, while the rear façade giving on to the playground was renewed. This volume now serves as a kindergarten and has a fully transparent rear façade, with the stairwell connected to it, allowing the pupils' movements inside the building to be clearly seen. The classrooms, which are now spacious, lean over to the back and look out onto the street through the windows of the old building. On the other side of the playground, the primary school is housed in the volume overlooking Mathieu Desmaréstraat. The main entrance is also on this street, the kindergarteners being guided to the playground and the

PROJECT **De Telescoop kindergarten and primary school** 211

primary school pupils to the elaborate staircase. Here too, the classrooms face the street and are arranged side by side along the façade. In this block, the volumes looking out onto the playground serve as spacious corridors that can be turned into multipurpose rooms when required.

The project as a whole gives the feeling that the architects found a masterful solution to an intricate spatial puzzle. The density of the programme contrasts with spacious classrooms, a sports hall rich in daylight and the not-so-small playground that is even home to a tree. That playground is cleverly divided into two by a few steps, so that the kindergarteners and primary school children each have their own play area. The refectory overlooking the playground also serves as a multipurpose room for various classes.

PROJECT URA Yves Malysse Kiki Verbeeck

PROJECT URA Yves Malysse Kiki Verbeeck

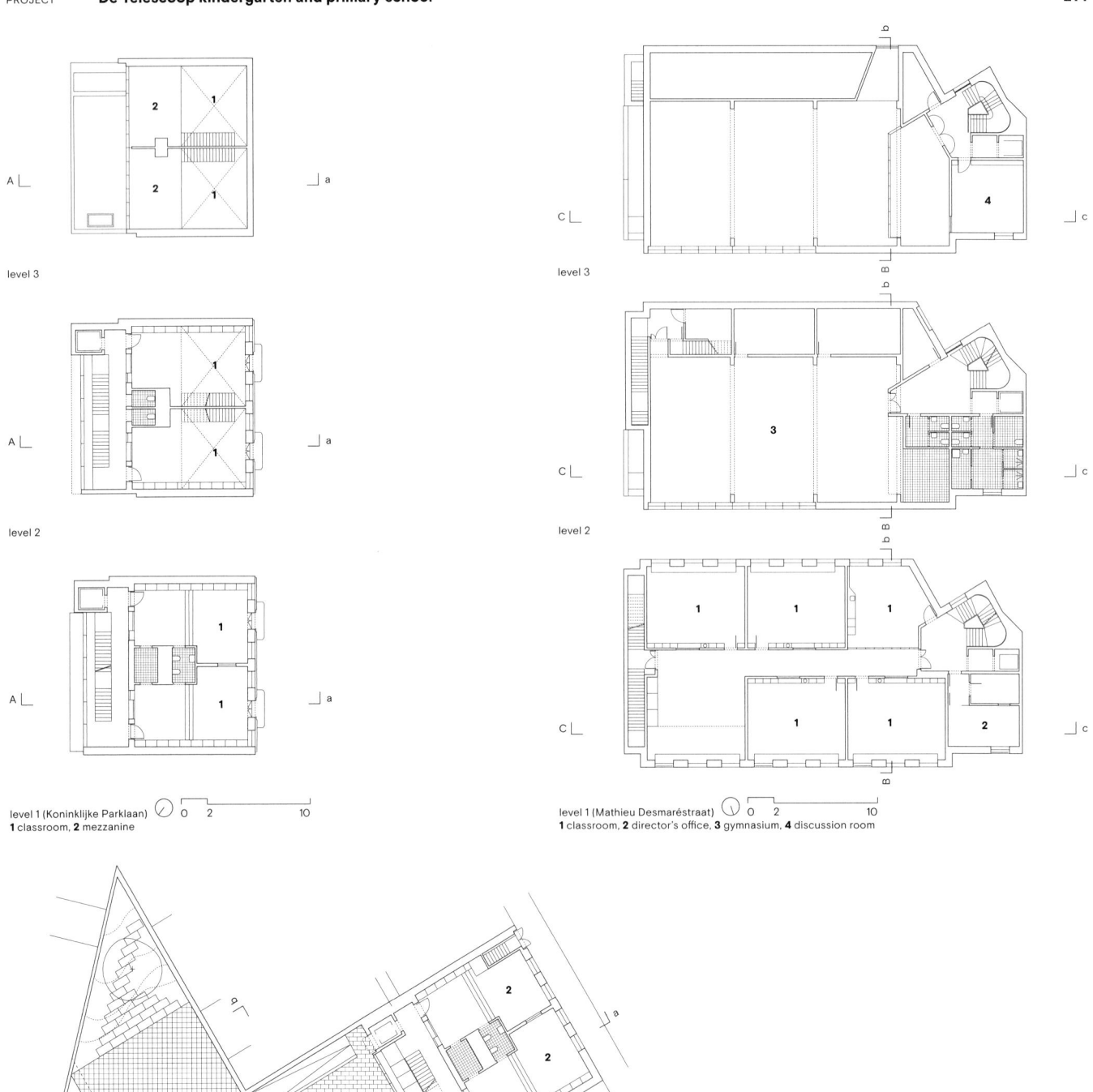

PROJECT **De Telescoop kindergarten and primary school** 214

level 3

level 2

level 1 (Koninklijke Parklaan)   0 2   10
1 classroom, **2** mezzanine

level 3

level 2

level 1 (Mathieu Desmaréstraat)   0 2   10
1 classroom, **2** director's office, **3** gymnasium, **4** discussion room

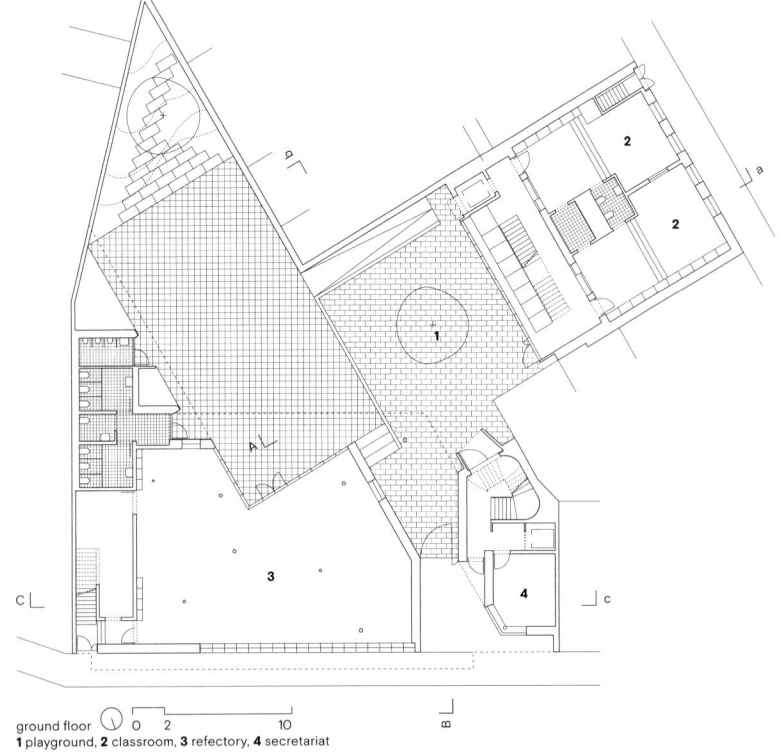

ground floor   0 2   10
1 playground, **2** classroom, **3** refectory, **4** secretariat

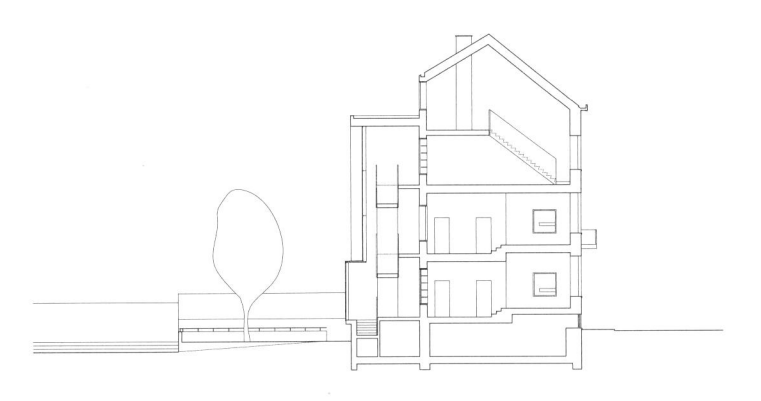

PROJECT **De Telescoop kindergarten and primary school** 215

section Aa (Mathieu Desmaréstraat)

section Bb (Mathieu Desmaréstraat)

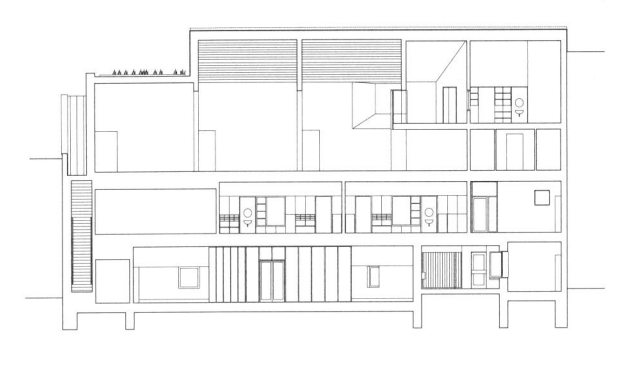

section Cc (Mathieu Desmaréstraat)   0   2   10

09

The soft boundaries create unconventional teaching spaces and make appropriation or reinterpretation possible. This is especially the case in the intermediate spaces between the corridors and classrooms. Following on from the pedagogical approach of this active-learning school, the design plays with the spatial possibilities in its compact context.

project De Telescoop kindergarten and primary school
design team Yves Malysse, Kiki Verbeeck, Benny Geerinckx, Eva Lo, Carmen Vandermolen, Jonathan Robert Maj, Isaura Doumen, Harold Vermeiren
address Mathieu Desmaréstraat 14, 1020 Brussels
design October 2015
surface area 1,800 m² **volume** 11,000 m³
total building cost per m² €1,880 excl. VAT
stability studies UTIL Struktuurstudies, Brussels
EPB studies Bureau Bouwtechniek, Antwerp
landscape design Landinzicht, Brussels
office URA Yves Malysse Kiki Verbeeck
website www.ura.be
client GO! Education of the Flemish Community
completion (provisional) August 2020 (final) January 2023
total building cost €3,400,000 excl. VAT & fees
main contractor Strabag, Antwerp
engineering studies HP Engineers, Ghent
acoustics studies Daidalos Peutz, Leuven
safety coordination VC-CS, Halle

text Hülya Ertas
photography 01, 07–08, 10 © Laura Vleugels
02–06, 09 © Filip Dujardin

PROJECT   URA Yves Malysse Kiki Verbee

PROJECT **Raamwerk**

PROJECT **Duinhelm residential care centre, Ostend** 218

Duinhelm is a care institution for people with mental disabilities on the outskirts of Ostend. Like many contemporary care institutions in Flanders, Duinhelm seeks to create a homely atmosphere and sense of community for its residents. In 2017, together with the Flemish Government Architect, Duinhelm launched an Open Call for residential premises for forty residents, planned in two phases. The design by Raamwerk, with two curved volumes, was selected; today, the first phase has been completed and twenty people live there.

The choice of materials and tectonics does not spell out the building's function to passers-by. The prominent, asymmetrically sloping roof structure, wooden cladding, robust brickwork and refined details all merge into a gently undulating volume. The surrounding area, a fifteen-minute bicycle ride from the railway station, is predominantly residential. The institution is right opposite the striking brutalist social housing estate Mimosa, but also counts among its neighbours detached houses of all styles, as well as several residential projects (under construction or recently completed). This spatial context is not so obvious. In this reality, Raamwerk's ground plan with two curved volumes (only one of them having been realized so far, therefore) offers a hierarchy of open spaces. The spaces enclosed by the curved volumes imply a more intimate use of the gardens, while the surrounding open park remains public. As such, this care facility is not cut off from its context but still offers its residents some privacy.

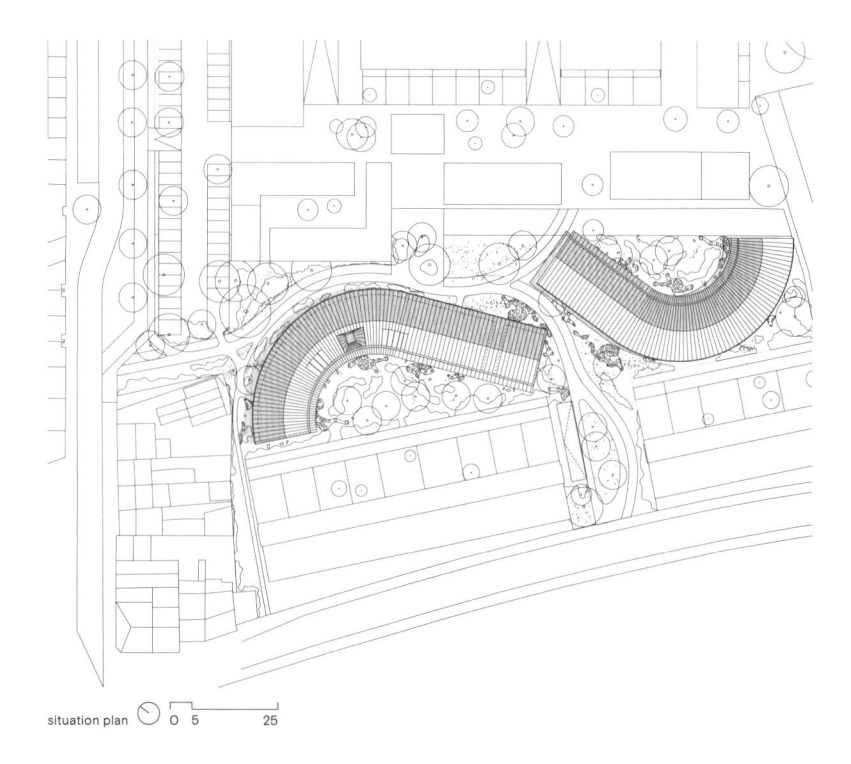

situation plan 0 5 25

PROJECT **Duinhelm residential care centre** 219

Another design advantage of the curve is noticeable in the rooms. There are sixteen rooms on the first floor and four on the ground floor, with different views and configurations. On the ground floor, there are mainly communal rooms, such as living areas and kitchens, which feature double-height ceilings and overlook the enclosed garden at the rear. The central core with lift, laundry room and staff bedroom can be closed off on both floors with the doors in the corridors. This means the long volume can be divided into two smaller blocks to meet the residents' need for privacy and intimacy.

Duinhelm can be seen as a continuation of the pioneering spatial innovation in healthcare facilities that has taken place in Flanders over the past decade. The concept of extending medical care spaces to a domestic living environment is architecturally supported by careful design decisions.

PROJECT **Raamwerk**

PROJECT **Raamwerk**

PROJECT **Duinhelm residential care centre** 222

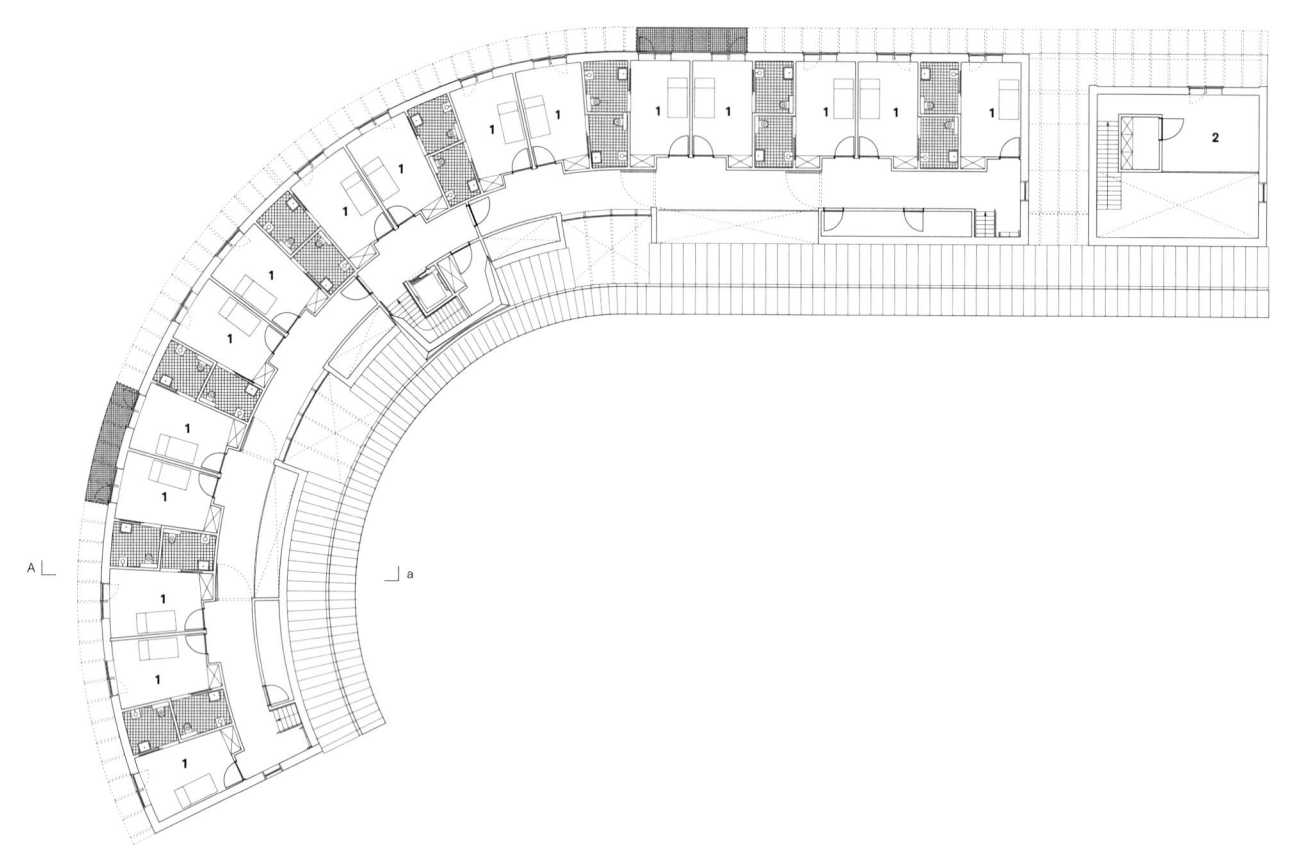

level 1
1 bedroom, **2** multipurpose space

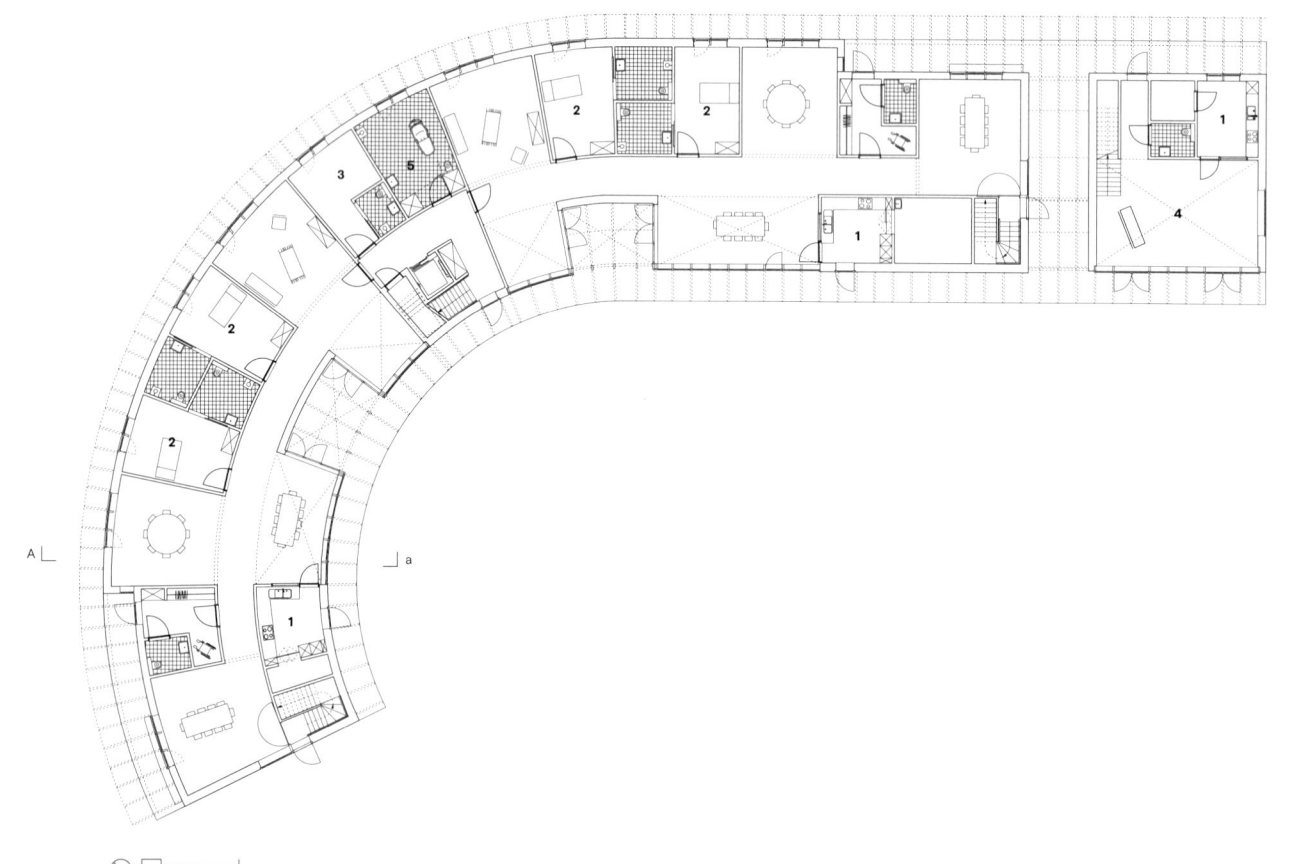

ground floor 0 1 5
1 living area, **2** bedroom, **3** staff bedroom, **4** multipurpose space, **5** care bathroom

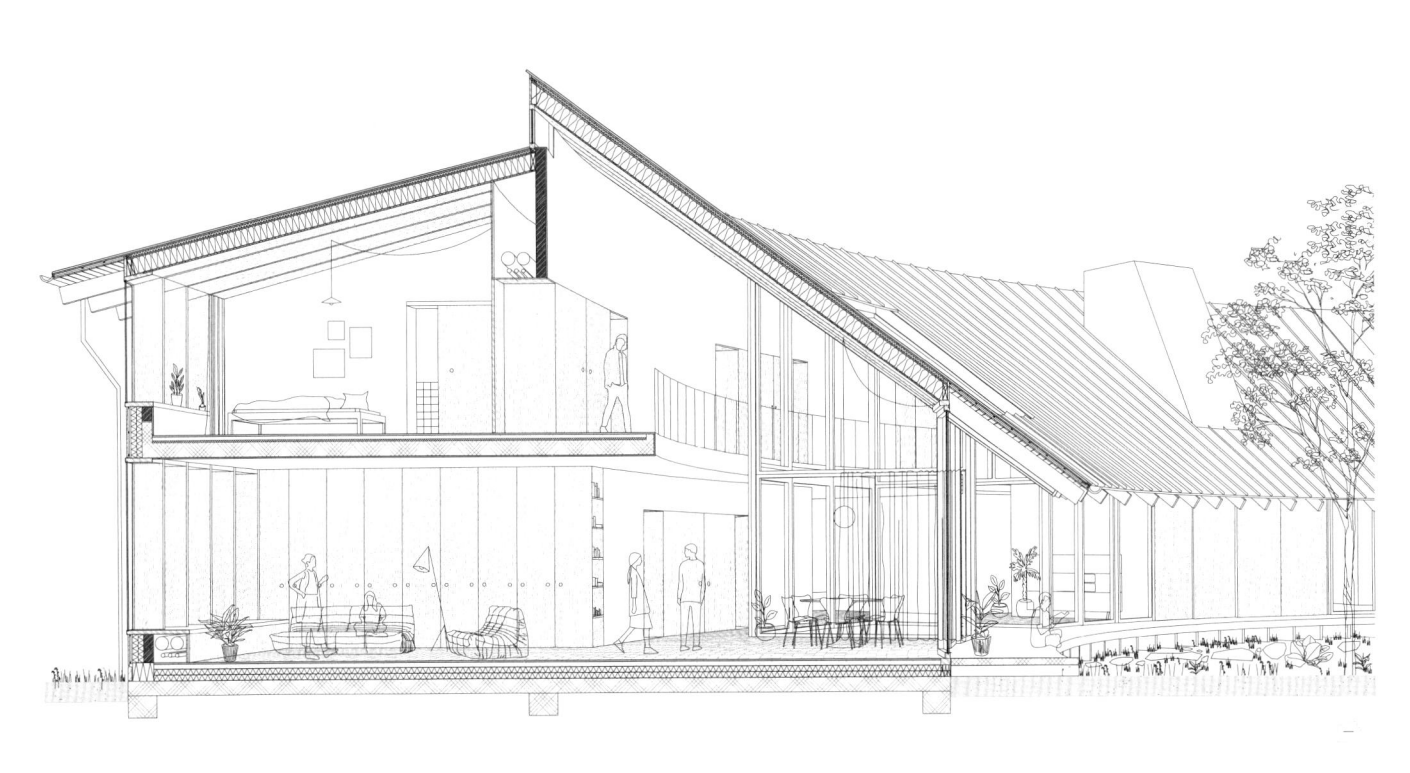

PROJECT   Duinhelm residential care centre   223

section Aa 0   1   5

project Duinhelm residential care centre **office** Raamwerk **design team** Freek Dendooven, Gijs De Cock,
Jon D'haenens, Louise Vanderlinden, Alice Sanders, Cis Vanlandschoot **website** www.raam-werk.com
address Zilverlaan 18, 8400 Ostend **client** Duinhelm vzw **design** February 2019
completion September 2023 **surface area** 1,520 m² **volume** 4.869 m³
total building cost (incl. layout surroundings) €3,560,000 excl. VAT
(excl. layout surroundings) €3,260,000 excl. VAT **total building cost per m²** €2,144 excl. VAT
main contractor Mevaco, Aalter **stability, engineering and EPB studies** Robuust ao, Ghent
landscape design Atelier Arne Deruyter, Machelen-aan-de-Leie **safety coordination** Kubiek, Bruges

text
Hülya Ertas
photography
01, 07-09 © Nick Moons
02-06 © Stijn Bollaert

PROJECT   **Raamwerk**

PROJECT Havana architectuur

Veldegem service centre, Zedelgem

The Veldegem service centre is a building complex with public functions such as municipal services and a library branch, conference and meeting rooms, as well as a cafeteria and housing units. It was realized following an initiative of the Public Centre for Social Welfare (OCMW) in Zedelgem and an Open Call in cooperation with the Flemish Government Architect. Veldegem is a village in West Flanders whose main road is the Koning Albertlaan. Two car parks, one in front of the church and the other between the shops, seem to be the only open spaces in the village centre. The lack of public space is a real problem. The design by Havana architectuur creates a diamond-shaped courtyard that brings all functions together: public on the ground floor and housing on the upper floors at the two ends of the square. Although the new paved courtyard forms a car-free public space, it has not remedied the lack of greenery in the village centre. The main reason for the paving of this square is the underground car park. Now that the complex is in use, a few potted trees and a pétanque court attempt to break up the monotonous, hard landscape.

The courtyard is accessed via a generous passageway above which housing is stacked. To the right is the cafeteria overlooking the main street, along with a number of counters for basic municipal services. The rest of the ground floor consists of a series of spaces of different sizes used or rented by the municipality, including a workshop space, meeting rooms and a music classroom. A library branch serves the community and at the back there is also a large reception room overlooking the vast landscape. The courtyard is open at both ends, providing a passageway from the centre to the open landscape (which is now, however, being filled with new constructions).

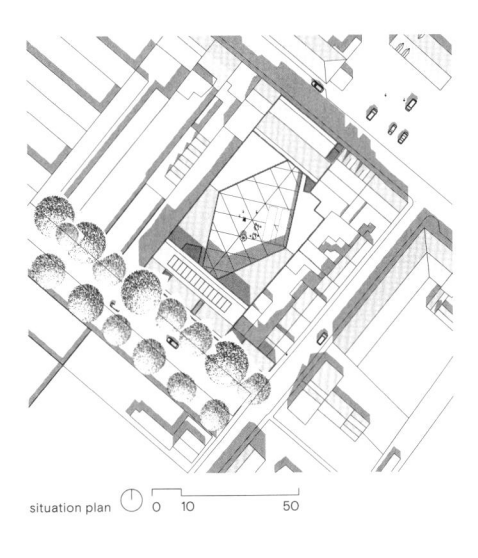

It is also on account of its ambition to create quality housing for the elderly that the project as a whole can serve as an example. The original plan was to reserve sixteen units for over-65s, who would thus enjoy easy access to the services on the ground floor. The architects broadened the scope of application by developing plans according to the social housing standards of the Flemish Social Housing Company (VMSW). Although the units were ultimately sold without any specific restrictions, most residents are senior citizens. The design with compact housing units also offers the possibility to combine, by adding a staircase, units on the first and second floor to form a duplex house. This flexible design means that in the future, homes for single households can be adapted to forms of intergenerational cohabitation if required.

PROJECT **Havana architectuur**

PROJECT **Havana architectuur**

PROJECT **Veldegem service centre** 230

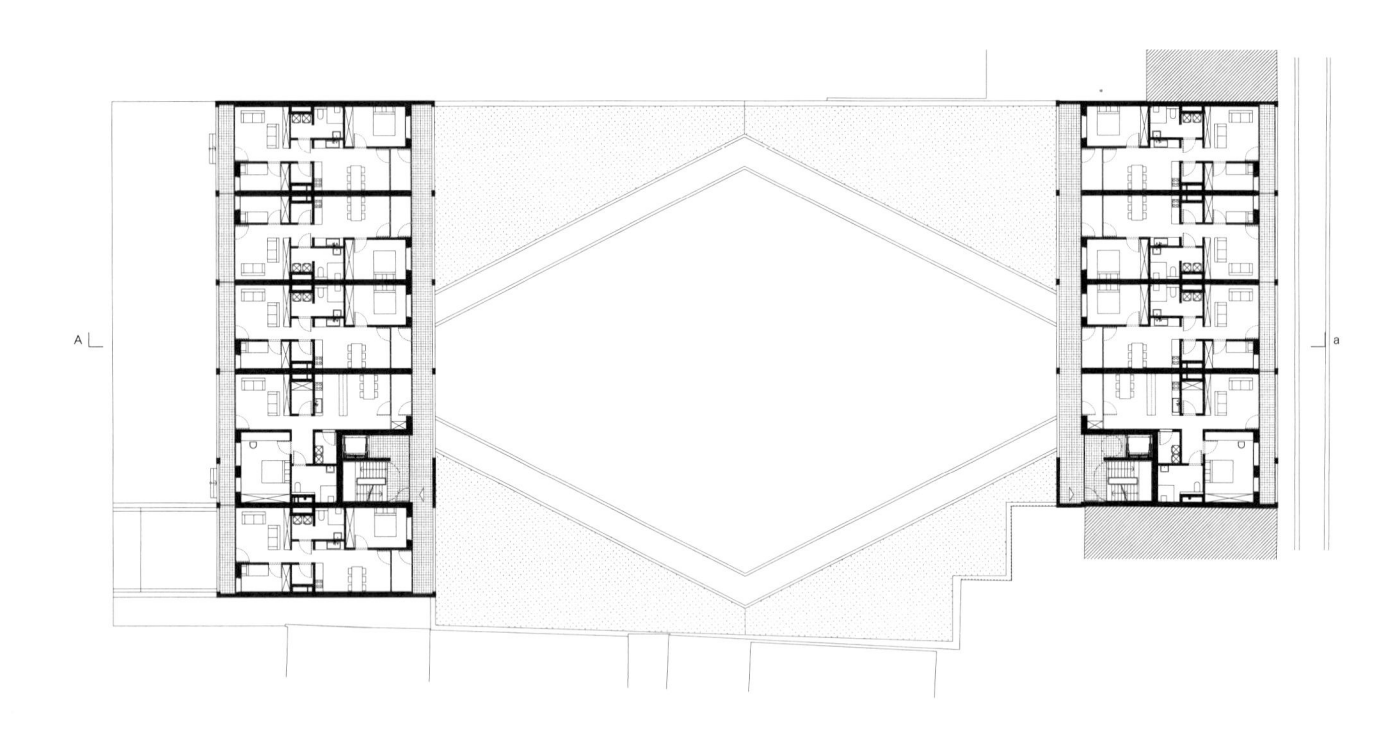

level 1

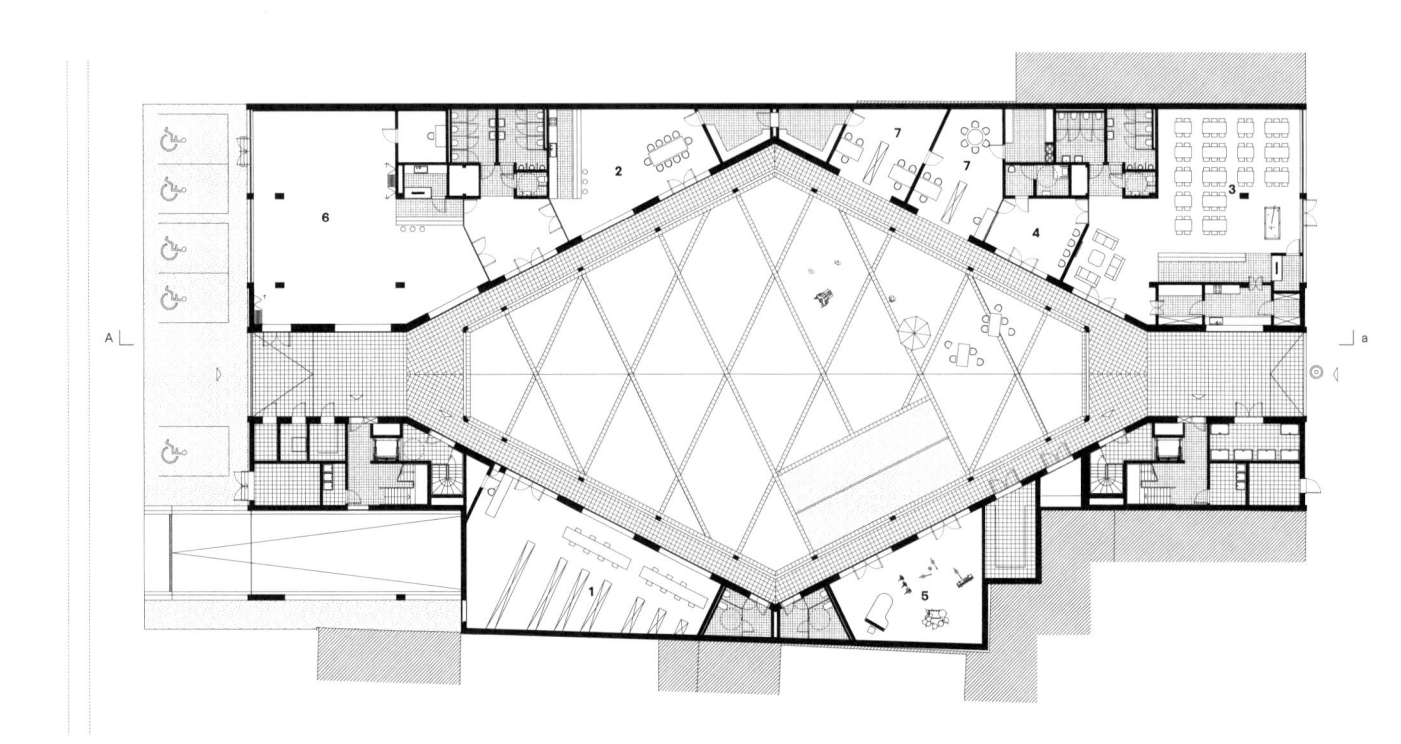

ground floor 0 2 10
1 library, **2** conference and meeting room, **3** cafeteria service centre, **4** reception, **5** workshop, **6** local music academy, **7** multipurpose hall, **8** office space

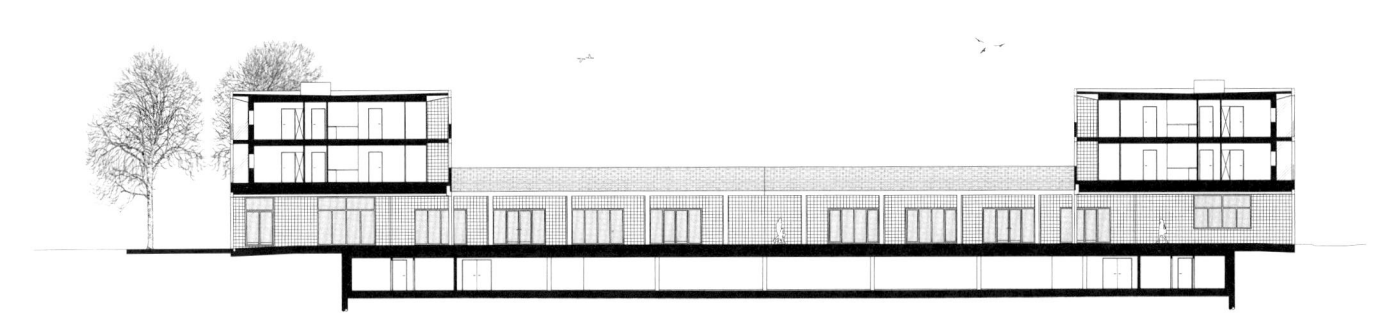

PROJECT **Veldegem service centre** 231

section Aa 0 2 10

text
Hülya Ertas
photography
01, 04, 07-09 © Farah Fervel
02-03, 05-06 © Stijn Bollaert

project Veldegem service centre **office** Havana architectuur
design team Tijl Vanmeirhaeghe, Servaas De Wandel **website** www.havana.be
address Koning Albertstraat 9-11, 8210 Zedelgem **client** OCMW Zedelgem **design** March 2014
completion April 2022 **surface area** (above ground) 3,070 m² (underground) 2,200 m²
volume 20,390 m³ **total building cost** €7,845,000 excl. VAT **total building cost per m²** €1,490 excl. VAT
main contractor Vuylsteke-Eiffage, Meulebeke **stability studies** Mouton, Ghent
engineering and EPB studies Boydens Engineering, Zedelgem
acoustics studies Bureau De Fonseca, Grimbergen **safety coordination** AC coördinatie, Roeselare

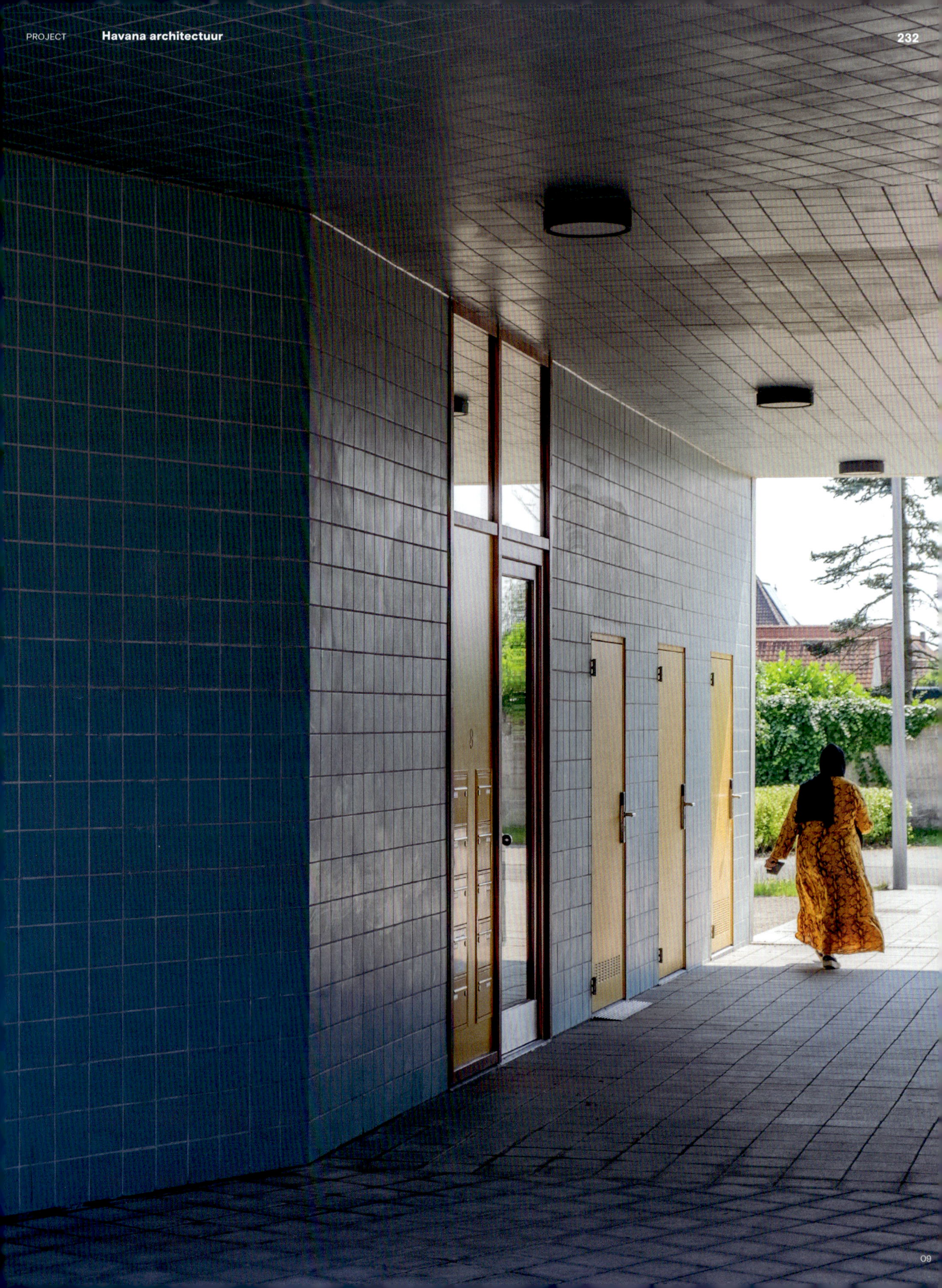

09

Housing Beyond the Spreadsheet

A Plea in Favour of a Holistic Vision of Housing as a Lever for Individual and Public Interest

Sofie De Caigny
Petrus Kemme

Alexander Dierendonck   'Social housing could be a lever, but it often amounts to stacking people in Excel spreadsheets.'

Individual ownership, private initiatives and the nuclear family have been the three pillars of Belgium's housing policy since the nineteenth century. The resulting dispersed housing model flourished in Flanders, especially during the post-war period. Climate change, the need for open space, the growing mobility crisis and greater awareness about the social cost of dispersed housing has pushed the model to the brink. Post-war housing forms are unsustainable: they devour space, energy and materials and do not lead to resilient social communities. Trying to make so many individual homes energy efficient is an impossible task. Even when money is not an issue, people often lack the knowledge or commitment to take the necessary steps.

    This is not a new observation. Housing has become a hot topic in recent years, both within the profession and in the media.[1] Yet architecture is conspicuously absent from the social debate. With the focus on affordability and efficiency, good design largely seems to slow things down – that, at least, is the perception. Housing and architecture are intimately intertwined, however. Housing as a social mission cannot exist without architecture, while architecture's primary objective is to provide shelter. Nevertheless, we note that the architectural profession is struggling with the contemporary housing assignment. In previous editions of the *Flanders Architectural Review*, Christoph Grafe (2018), Luce Beeckmans (2020) and Martino Tattara (2022) already pointed out, respectively, the dearth of innovative plan structure, the lack of diversity, and the market-oriented deployment of large urban developments that revolve around the production of quickly built and easily marketed housing.

For this edition of the *Review*, the editors also received numerous housing projects for potential inclusion. Collective housing developments can increasingly be divided into three main categories: (1) private, speculative housing developments; (2) social housing projects; and (3) alternative housing forms, especially co-housing projects. In the first category, architecture is instrumental to sales revenue, which is primarily generated upon completion. In social housing projects, building standards, long-term ownership and housing association management typically lead to a minimum quality standard which often comes with a lack of innovation or specificity. Progressive housing forms, by definition, allow greater scope for experimentation, but access to this model is reserved for those who can afford the time, money and commitment. Each collective housing form perpetuates its own objectives, serves its target audience and meets the attendant (architectural) expectations. The result, a tendency towards a triple enclave formation.

    In this essay, we contrast this collective-housing trend with the social issues in which housing is, or could be, central. The most obvious challenge is the so-called 'housing crisis', which manifests itself in long waiting lists at social housing companies, high rents and regulatory debates, and the perception that owning a home – still viewed as a key social-insurance policy – will soon become a pipe dream for many young people and lower- to middle-class families. Soaring demand has led to increasingly standardized housing at

---

[1] See, among others, *A+ 301 Affordable Housing* (April–May 2023); Pieter T'Jonck, ed., *Samen wonen ontwerpen* (2023); Hugo Beersmans, *Woonzaak* (2022); 'Wie kan nu nog een huis betalen, met al die regeltjes en extra kosten?', *De Standaard*, 31 May 2024; 'Zijn huizen echt onbetaalbaar geworden? En hoe is de woonsituatie in uw gemeente? 6 inzichten over wonen in Vlaanderen', De Morgen, 30 September 2022; the 'Pano' episode of *De wachtlijst* (5 March 2024); etc.

ESSAY   Sofie De Caigny, Petrus Kemme   234

01

ESSAY Sofie De Caigny, Petrus Kemme

a time of rapidly growing diversity and when living and working patterns are in flux, the population is ageing rapidly, the effects of climate change are ever more apparent, space is running out, etc. What is typically labelled 'collective housing' often amounts to the serial production of residential units, with a minimum of shared spaces and facilities, produced by private developers or social housing companies stuck in a structural catch-up mode. All too often, even co-housing projects turn out to be the sum of individual housing demands: the collective elements are mainly functional, and the schemes do little more than pay lip service to the public good. The housing landscape thus isolates itself from the overarching challenges for which it could, in fact, be a catalyst.

Oana Bogdan   'It is unfortunate that crises are needed to effect change. Open space wasn't important before the 2021 floods, and now it suddenly is.'

By looking at several recent housing projects, we hope to illustrate the point at which the untapped potential of socially beneficial housing becomes visible. In so doing, we deliberately alternate between scales, contexts and clients. With this essay in mind, we also organized a panel discussion with six experts: Oana Bogdan (&bogdan), Christine de Ruijter (awg architecten), Pascal De Decker (Prof. emeritus at KU Leuven), Alexander Dierendonck (Dierendonckblancke architecten), Anne Malliet (former member of Team Flemish Government Architect) and Luc Stijnen (former director of the social housing company De Zonnige Kempen). The conversation was not so much about the concrete realizations discussed in this essay as about the underlying fields of influence exposed by the current 'housing crisis'. Partially drawing on their insights, this text aims to appreciate the architectural dimension of the issue, at a time when fundamental decisions are looming.

Urban acupuncture

Small-scale collective housing plays into the urban fabric of individual dwellings. Compact housing projects, especially in the nineteenth-century city belt, nestle in the space created when a handful of individual plots are merged, or when a large shop or small industry disappears. The design challenge here is akin to that of the individual house next door: from an often small-scale housing programme and complex boundary conditions, a demand for customization arises. But any form of collective living, however small, requires an overarching view. This, by definition, differentiates it from the parcelled-out residential landscape on which it intervenes. Ideally, there is also an eye on the public interest, which, at least in theory, allows such housing projects to act as leverage for the neighbourhood. They are potential forms of urban acupuncture, which can serve different ambitions (such as opening up space in the urban fabric, densification, mobility, green outdoor space, etc.). The question, however, is who is at the source of the overarching vision, or perhaps even of what is in the best interest of society.

Luc Stijnen   'It is a good idea to look at vision rather than rules. Building and housing are so diverse, changing from place to place, that they don't conform to rules. You need a certain openness to grasp that.'

Urban development company AG Vespa saw an opportunity for urban acupuncture on the corner of Lange Beeldekensstraat and Greinstraat in Antwerp's Seefhoek district (see p. 201). After demolishing several 'dilapidated' terraced houses and erasing the mutual plot boundaries, space was created for a collective housing project of greater quality. The owner of the corner property couldn't be persuaded to sell, however, which posed a challenge for Dierendonckblancke architecten. Nevertheless, they managed to find the added value in collectivizing the remaining plots. The garden forms the starting point for a circuit of stairs and walkways within which each household also has its own outdoor space. The design thus offers, above all, a welcome area of respite between the bustle of the street and the domestic interiors. The rooms are structured by wooden walls, a material that also exemplifies the project's forward-thinking approach to the current sustainability requirements.[2] The project illustrates the scope for ambition – in terms of material use, depaving and layered use of space – that collective living makes possible, even on a small scale.

    At the same time, questions arise about the types of residents drawn to these projects and the demographic shifts they set in motion. Living in visibly sustainable shell flats around a collective outdoor space is considered 'exotic' in a densely populated residential area in Antwerp North. The same is true in Sint-Amandsberg (Ghent) for Jean co-housing by ectv architecten Els Claessens Tania Vandenbussche (see p. 257). This initiative was spearheaded by the urban development company sogent, which found a dozen like-minded middle-class households eager to realize their collective and sustainable housing dream on the site of a former mushroom farm. Aided by a good design, they made their idyllic residential oasis a reality in an area where gentrification is rampant. Such projects illustrate the precarious yet key position of urban development companies: they seem uniquely positioned to make the residential landscape more sustainable, with an eye for the local situation; in so doing, however, they quickly become complicit in gentrification as they respond to the capricious housing market. Indeed, even on the scale of small projects, municipal development agencies and co-housers compete with the clout of large developers, especially in terms of land acquisition.

    The same applies to social housing companies, where sales revenue is not a factor. From this perspective, it is logical to see the relatively large number of recent social housing projects as urban acupuncture. The search for affordable land has led housing companies towards 'more difficult' plots in the (peripheral) urban fabric. Modest social housing ensembles are springing up in these areas, united in their immaculate but strait-laced brick façades and clearly demarcated from the public domain. Building standards guarantee a minimum quality level for the housing units, and although the overall manicured appearance certainly has a place, this is usually where this level of quality ends. While small-scale developments should in principle integrate themselves into the residential fabric, these ensembles often seem to consolidate their place on the margins. The pressure to demarcate responsibilities (with fencing) gets in the way of any kind of dialogue with the neighbourhood. The surrounding, predominantly private, residential fabric equally signals boundaries towards the social housing (although more often with a hedge than a fence). Any kind of urban acupuncture would be more effective if the fabric were less paralysed, its cells not so isolated from each other.

Village dwelling

The relationship between the individualistic housing culture and the fabric is often more fragile in rural areas. The critical mass of 'non-residential' buildings is small, while houses continue to occupy space without too much resistance. This is the historical cause of excessive ribbon developments and parcelling, and what is principally expressed today – as we slowly realize that space is finite – in the so-called 'apartmentization' of villages. Individual housing dreams are stacked up in generic blocks of flats, usually without bringing any added value to the public domain nor to the collective interest of the village community. Taking a one-sided view of densification, it could be said that the carefully cultivated housing dream of the well-insulated nuclear family is now being ▸

2   The draft dates back to 2014.

ESSAY Sofie De Caigny, Petrus Kemme

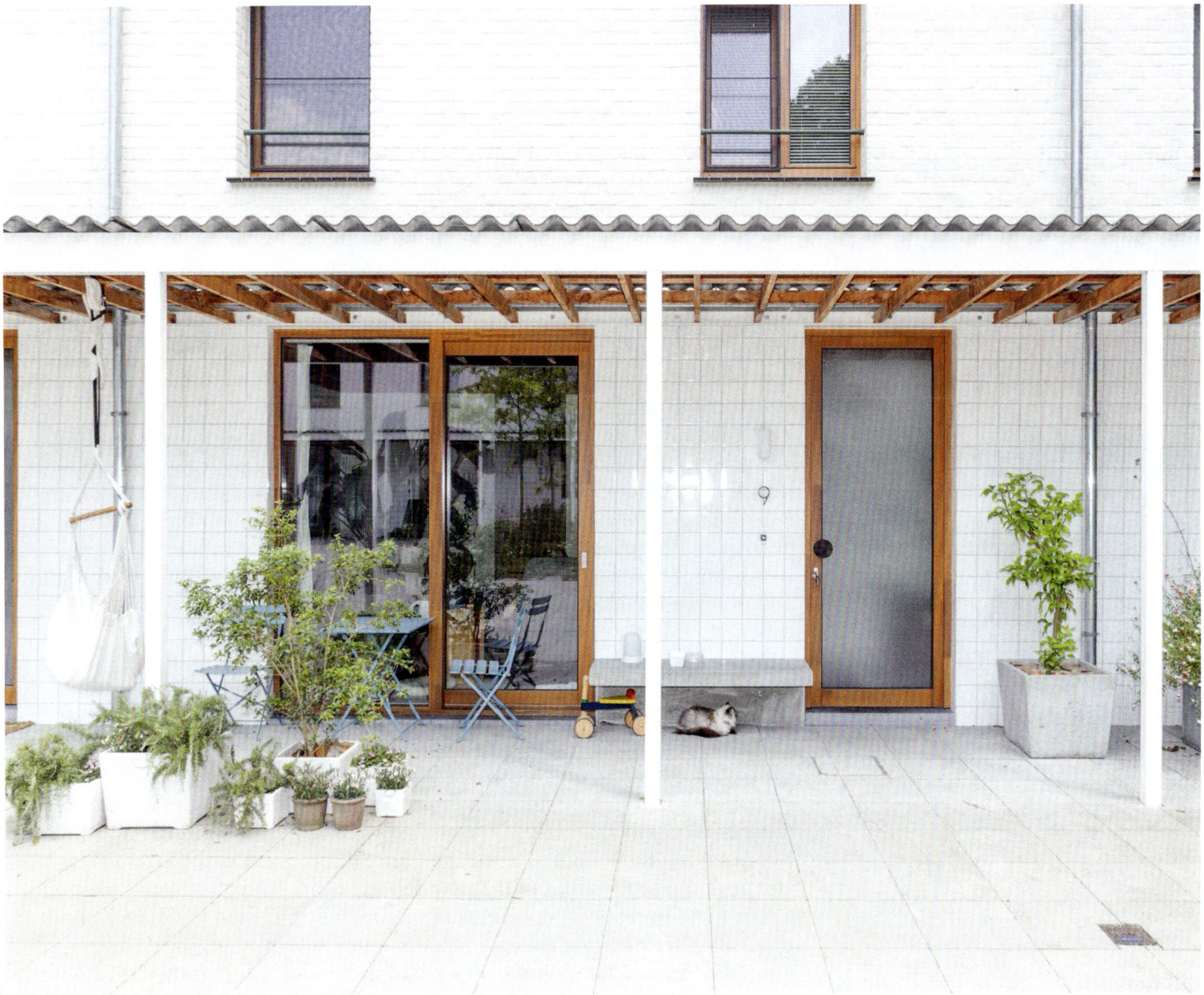

04

3   The units were originally earmarked as social housing, but were eventually put on the private market.
4   'OO2412 Zedelgem – Dienstencentrum', see www.vlaamsbouwmeester.be/nl/instrumenten/open-oproep/projecten/oo2412-zedelgem-dienstencentrum?f=opstart.
5   'Villageness' is a spearhead of Team Flemish Government Architect within Erik Wieërs' mandate: www.vlaamsbouwmeester.be/nl/subsite/dorpelijkheid.

sold in new packaging and in the biggest possible volumes. This quantitative approach has led to spatial impoverishment, which in turn has only increased the existing pressure on collective and public facilities in village centres.

Housing projects that make more meaningful injections into village centres offer a ray of hope. AIDarchitecten took full control of an initiative in the Kempen village of Malle. They purchased a plot of land diagonally opposite their office and, inspired by the British non-profit organization Abbeyfield, built a co-housing property exclusively for senior citizens. Their self-determined brief paved the way for some idiosyncratic architectural choices: the staircase and ceilings in carefully poured exposed concrete; thick walls to insulate by virtue of their mass; recessing the front façade by a metre to allow for streetside greenery. The average property developer would probably consider all this to be a waste of space, effort and money. At the same time, the project is conventional enough to remain highly marketable, occupying a position at the intersection of individual comfort, collective amenities and village tranquillity. The 'gatehouse', under which cars can pass, comprises two sets of four flats, one ground-floor unit serving as a shared living space with a guest room and laundry area. Besides the communal garden, the shared flat mainly complements the individual homes, which are comfortable enough for either singles or couples. The property equates to a gentle injection of collective living, one that is tailor-made to the village but fuelled by a distinct architectural vision and international references.

Anne Malliet   'The housing cooperatives in Zurich are led by groups of citizens, associations that realize they must take a collective approach to solving the housing problem. They are key players in affordable housing but are still somewhat lacking in Belgium.'

Dierendonckblancke architecten (see p. 181) built the group homes on the Jongensschoolpleintje in Zomergem. The project originated in a Design & Build (D&B) procedure in which creating housing in the village centre was as important as preserving the school as a 'village figure'. The fact that the local mayor was once the headmaster of the now defunct boys' school may have played a role, in addition to the headmaster's house being a listed building. But all this aside, the ambition set the umbrella municipality of Lievegem and intermunicipal association Veneco on a remarkable path towards the development of the school site. The D&B procedure placed the initial emphasis on finding a designer for the school first, after which a developer would be sought. The square's familiar perimeter was resurrected as a traffic-free, semi-public residential area, around which it is far more pleasant to live than in the jumbo farmhouse-style block of flats that could have been erected in its place. The project shows what is possible when local roots and procedural expertise meet at the regional level.

In the heart of a village to the south of Bruges, a small residential offering emerged in the wake of a public facilities project. Two floors of purpose-built flats for senior citizens were constructed above the Veldegem service centre (Havana architectuur, see p. 225), in which several services run by the fused municipality of Zedelgem were integrated on the ground floor.[3] On either side of a diamond-shaped courtyard, the residential volumes complete the terraced rows of the orthogonal street plan. The residential programme not only perpetuates the profile of the village street, but also helps to define a car-free village square in a place defined (more than elsewhere perhaps) by roads. Twelve years (!) after the launch of the Open Call,[4] the project remains a rare example of architecture that combines 'village'[5] housing and public functions. And this, at a time when the number of seemingly opportune shortcuts – for strengthening village cores, responsible densification and rendering them viable places to live in terms of space, mobility and access to services – has never been so great. Not just for senior citizens, and not just in Veldegem.

Housing is urban planning

Pascal De Decker 'We no longer build neighbourhoods. We build houses, we build numbers. But we should be building neighbourhoods, with good housing that doesn't necessarily include a garden, with adapted housing, and with an eye for care and affordability …'

Back in the metropolis, besides acupuncture, there is also a tradition of residential architecture with the capacity to 'make the city'. Collective housing ensembles formed the building blocks for whole new districts in Flanders and Brussels, particularly in the twentieth century. Although many of these buildings are now outdated (both structurally and in terms of energy efficiency), the spatial impression they make forms a solid basis for contemporary replacements or reinterpretations. In this instance, architectural quality is just as important as quantity, the number of housing units and occupants or the surface area. The former extends beyond the dwellings per se since it organizes the relationship between the public urban space and the urbanite's private domain.

An example of a 'city-making' housing development can be found in Kiel, to the south of Antwerp. BULK Architecten constructed a social housing block within the footprint of an older residential building. It thus adopts the grain size of the housing that defined the urban fabric of the surrounding streets in the second quarter of the twentieth century (and within which its demolished predecessor formed a relatively late, less valuable block).[6] Sand-yellow brick façades reference the previous constructions without obscuring the project's newness. Besides the building itself, the east façade (partially) defines a vibrant urban 'living room' for the area. The architects also provided the essential buffers between the public and private domains, however. For example, manageable numbers of neighbours share each of the stairwells, even in the stacked duplexes on the long side (where, for the lower units, a private front door would open too directly onto the square). Likewise, the ground-floor flats at the building ends are half a floor above street level. The logic of the paved courtyard was abandoned for a combination of modest urban gardens and roof terraces, as well as passages marked with round arches between the project's 'body' and two 'heads'. With the neat architecture of this figure, the building responds to the occasionally veiled qualities of the historic residential environment, but also demonstrates progressive insight in terms of its organization.

The two blocks of flats in central Antwerp known as the Fierenshoven were built, like the Kiel residential buildings, as social housing in the interwar period. Here, however, the outdated housing stock prompted a complete renovation of the existing building, for which AG Vespa awarded the design brief to Happel Cornelisse Verhoeven. In this instance, the urban development company managed to integrate the corner plot, which was not previously part of the housing project. Opposite the monumental Institute of Tropical Medicine, the old, lower corner building was replaced by a new volume. This new property echoes the modernist brick façades on either side and, by rising slightly above them, turns the project into a coherent ensemble. Inside, the cramped units of yesteryear have been merged horizontally or vertically into more spacious dwellings, retaining the original features wherever possible. The ground-floor commercial spaces were also given a complete overhaul, as a way of perpetuating the tradition of shopping within the historic urban fabric. The revaluation of this heritage proves that good architecture can also be economically valuable. Within the current frameworks, therefore, this kind of project is only possible via a payback model (admittedly in the 'affordable' category, but nevertheless). The 'sale' of a substantial number of social city-centre homes seems to be the bitter pill that must be swallowed in the process.

6 'Sociale woonblokken Hennig, Thiebaud en Eric Sasse', see inventaris.onroerenderfgoed.be/aanduidingsobjecten/97688.

ESSAY Sofie De Caigny, Petrus Kemme

ESSAY — Sofie De Caigny, Petrus Kemme

7 See Dennis Pohl's essay (p. 273).

'New' examples of city-making residential architecture also exist. Located next to Anderlecht station, NovaCity I (by &bogdan and DDS+, see also p. 265) combines an ambitious programme of housing and urban industry. Workshops make up the plinth while the floors above contain an innovative sequence of homes and individual and shared indoor and outdoor spaces. An initiative of citydev.brussels and the Brussels Bouwmeester Maître Architecte (BMA), the project also fits within the overall master plan by BUUR (Sweco). This visionary project links housing with urban functions, such as work and mobility, in a single concept, and this, on a scale befitting a city like Brussels. Unfortunately, it remains an exception.

&bogdan also designed a new urban district in Ghent, in the area around the Dampoort railway station. Bijgaardehof (see p. 249), a stone's throw from this transport link, elevates the concept of co-housing to an urban scale. The project is the brainchild of the Ghent city authorities and the urban development company sogent, which brought together three sizeable housing groups and the Sint-Amandsberg community health centre. During the design process, the residents had a far-reaching say in the layout of their personal unit (which on this scale admittedly tested the limits of workability). As (semi-)public bodies were involved in the development, it is no coincidence that the project connects directly to both the bicycle route along the railway line and the adjacent Bijgaarde park. It shows that individual, urban living comforts can indeed go hand in hand with public functions and vision.

Anne Malliet   'People don't see the links between the various policy areas, like aligning housing policy with public transport. But this means you can live affordably in those places, without a car. A win-win situation, but then regulations have to be adjusted accordingly, and the government has to take the initiative.'

The extent to which city-making housing developments align individual housing requirements with collective needs and public interests is a measure of their added value. The preconditions are a vital consideration. It is no coincidence that urban or regional development companies and those dedicated to social housing played a key role in the above projects. They respond to individual housing needs from, per definition, an overarching vision – at the least in terms of housing supply, ideally even more broadly. It is precisely these organizations, which could transform the housing issue from problem to leverage, that are under pressure today. A purely quantitative justification of their costs, benefits and units delivered often outweighs the singular qualities they (could) generate. The many societal challenges in which the residential landscape is a critical factor has created an unprecedented need for new answers on a scale that truly 'matters'.[7]

Room for vision(s)

In addition to the built residential projects, we also see many other initiatives that offer answers to housing challenges. Here, the architect moves in various contexts. To mention just some examples, *Stad van de menslievendheid* (City of philanthropy) is an unsolicited project by Sophia Holst, a young designer who moves between architectural, research and artistic practice. From such multi- or interdisciplinarity, she tries to offer a different perspective on social housing in Brussels, paying attention to the human lives that, all too often, are given in escalating numbers in architectural projects, policy plans and news reports. In the Kempen, architecture organization Ar-Tur developed a 'neighbourhood engine' for the renovation of residential areas and applied it to the modernist park district of Egelvennen in Mol. The inventors demonstrated the added value of a director with a vision, someone who could unite local interests and supra-local expertise. At Vrije Universiteit Brussel, Maker architecten worked within the framework of the Willy Van der Meeren Living Lab. For the renovation of the modernist student accommodation on the university's campus, they devised a range of approaches at the junction of architectural history, structural research and architectural design. Studio Tuin en Wereld, AgwA and Domus Mundi were commissioned by the city authorities and city architect of Ghent to draw up a concept study for future-proofing the so-called 'Scandinavia Blocks' on Afrikalaan. Their plan advocates an approach that not only explores the sustainability of the building in architectural or technological terms, but also via the different policy levels and the socio-economic aspects of liveability and ownership.

These are just a few examples of the broad-based awareness within the design field that an integrated vision of housing is needed, one that goes beyond building design. At the same time, we note a degree of fragmentation in this area as well. Architects work in project mode, including when employed in alternative offices, cultural organizations, academia or conducting research assignments linked to local policymaking. The modus operandi of the architectural world contains an inherent risk, namely, that structural challenges are tackled via project-based approaches, even when the urgency of the situation is universally recognized. In the wider scheme of things, the practices and organizations that are explicitly focused on the housing issue are still creating 'just' one project among a myriad of others. Hopeful initiatives are sprouting like mushrooms, but trees with deeper roots are needed to anchor a more sustainable vision of housing in Flanders and Brussels.

From residential property to regional development

The projects highlighted in this essay explicitly address the context and specific needs of residents within problematic landscapes, and therein lies their design intelligence. Constructed within tight economic and legal frameworks, they also seek to limit their ecological footprint. They encourage residents not only to carve out a place of their own but also to join a community. In so doing, the projects highlight the inherent weaknesses in Belgium's current housing policy. The projects illustrate that architects are almost wholly dependent on the courage of their clients when it comes to exploring boundaries and opportunities, or gaps and limitations, within a stringent regulatory framework, and in which the traditional family, plot and housing unit are invariably the starting points. Amid such fragmentation, even the most inspiring examples appear like sticking plasters on a gaping wound.

> Alexander Dierendonck 'We need people to develop a vision and try and change something at the administrative level. We experience that locally, at the level of municipal corporations, for example. They can impose things to effect change. They have to create the preconditions for social housing companies as well as private developers. The latter are risk-averse and, above all, just want to be able to keep building.'

Even today, the prevailing view in Flanders and Brussels is that housing models are static and specific. Yet housing needs are intrinsically dynamic. This applies to the life cycle of individual households as much as to the demographic level. The tension is no longer tenable, especially in the face of challenges like affordability, accessibility and climate resilience. Thinking about housing means thinking about the bigger picture. The measure of things must change, project development must make way for regional development and static visions of housing must be translated into flow models. Good architecture can respond to this, but the direction of a responsible and sustainable housing vision can never solely be in public hands. Land holdings are the crucial precondition. In well-connected places (near stations, for example), it is often still possible to densify in a way that connects housing to public functions in

07

ESSAY Sofie De Caigny, Petrus Kemme

a meaningful way. In such cases, housing construction can make a substantial contribution to solving mobility problems, improving the environment while also facilitating water management, fulfilling social and functional needs, etc. Social housing could – or should – be put in the driving seat, not sidelined as a compulsory item within an urban development scheme.

This type of approach demands the integration of different policy levels and domains. Thanks to its urban policy and city projects, Flanders is not inexperienced in this way of working. This approach could now be rolled out further as a task force for housing. But it will only succeed if the vision is sufficiently large-scale and if it tackles multiple spatial problems simultaneously. A comprehensive culture shift is unavoidable. It is senseless to discuss parking places and not mobility issues, housing deprivation and not social justice, homes as rolling capital and not housing as a basic human need, or renovation obligations and individual grants and not the long-term sustainability of the entire patrimony. An innovative and holistic approach, which will cost the community less in the long run, presupposes that we free ourselves from the existing conceptual frameworks. Today this may seem like a far-off dream. It requires a complete reversal of how Flanders, with its compartmentalized policy domains and levels, is structured. Greater vision and direction are needed, built on dialogue and cooperation. Dynamic, integrated models must replace master plans, which tend to be outdated already by the time they are implemented.

Christine de Ruijter 'Something we can learn from the Netherlands is that municipal project managers assist clients and designers. There are many more rules in the Netherlands, but the project managers also look at what rules produce. From there, they can engage in conversation with the designer and client, including about how to communicate with local residents to create the necessary support.'

And the architects? The majority feel powerless to make any kind of substantial contribution to a good living environment. From their front-row seats, they see all too clearly where the system is failing and who is profiting at the expense of the community. Unfortunately, the professional field is reacting in a scattershot way. The question is how architects can turn their social commitment into responsibility. In this context, it is fascinating to cast our minds back a hundred years. In the aftermath of World War I, housing shortages also dominated the public debate. Architects worked across borders to devise new models. When the economy allowed (from the 1950s onwards), these models were rolled out in large numbers. The specific architectural solutions of the time can certainly be debated, but the common vision that was developed remains inspiring. In this way, architects can regain a place in the debate, as publicly engaged intellectuals who communicate, in both words and images, to the public, governments and property owners. And within this process, architects can step outside their traditionally reactive position to become driving and guiding forces in the shift towards a different housing policy as a stepping stone towards a more just and sustainable society.

Oana Bogdan 'In an ideal world, we would submit planning applications for buildings, not individual functions. We should preserve structures for 300 years, design flexibly while also being specific, and be spatially generous. Such generosity already exists in buildings that originally were non-residential.'

photography
01, Lange Beeldekensstraat group housing, Antwerp – Dierendonckblancke architecten © Filip Dujardin
02, Jean co-housing, Ghent – ectv architecten Els Claessens Tania Vandenbussche © Kimberley Dhollander
03, 't Getouw co-housing, Malle – AIDarchitecten © Jochen Verghote (LUCID)
04, Jongensschool group housing, Lievegem – Dierendonckblancke architecten © Nick Moons
05, Social housing Eric Sasse, Antwerp – BULK Architecten © Nick Claeskens
06, Fierenshoven group housing, Antwerp – Happel Cornelisse Verhoeven with Molenaar & Co architecten © Karin Borghouts
07, NovaCity I group housing and SME zone, Anderlecht – &bogdan and DDS+ © Laurian Ghinitoiu
08, Bijgaardehof co-housing, Ghent – &bogdan © Laurian Ghinitoiu

PROJECT | &bogdan

Bijgaardehof co-housing, Ghent

The Bijgaardehof is a rather large housing complex of fifty-nine units newly built within the industrial railroad area of Gent-Dampoort, which separates the city centre from the Sint-Amandsberg neighbourhood to the east. Given its location and size, the Bijgaardehof is the most visible sign of the renewed interest in this area, which is undergoing a process of renovation and conversion with initiatives both public and private, big and small.

On this large plot of land, several industrial buildings have been demolished across time to make room for a park. A new path for bikes and pedestrians makes it possible to cross the tracks, connecting the two parts of the city. The negotiation between mineral and vegetal, industrial past and 'sustainable future' is also central to the Bijgaardehof project, which reaches a considerable height in an otherwise low district: densification enables wider outside areas for trees, vegetable gardens and recreation all around.

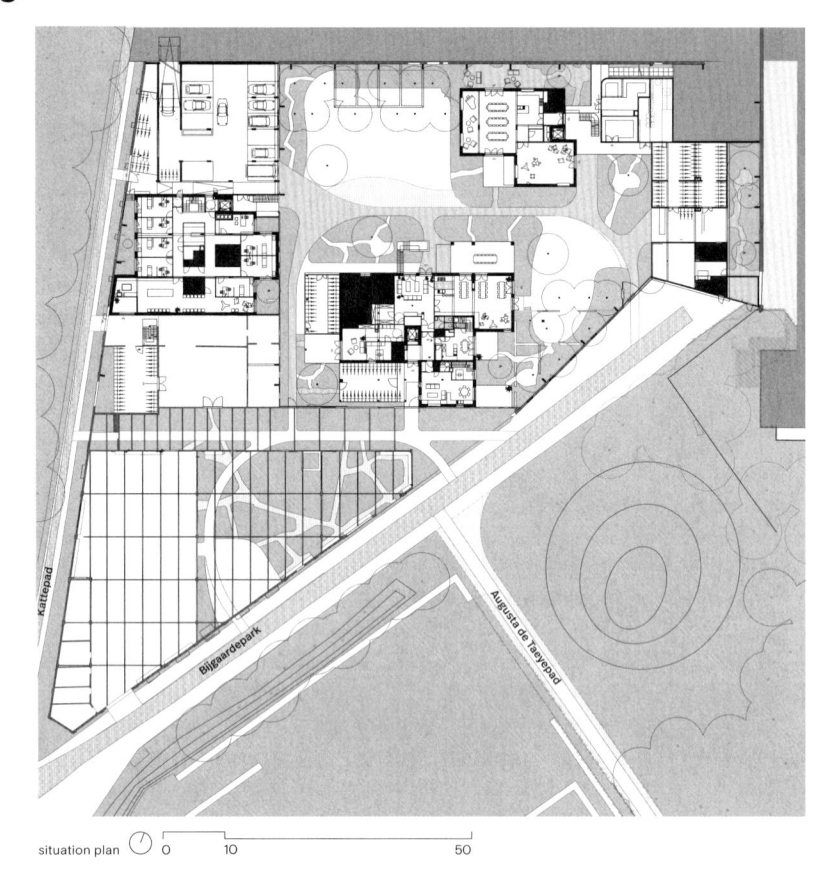

situation plan   0   10   50

The project stems from a district health centre and three co-housing collectives that joined and won a public bid to purchase the land and develop the project with a single architectural office, &bodgan. Public authorities (sogent and the municipality) were also stakeholders and financed the public areas. The three buildings form a coherent ensemble but present different

| PROJECT | **Bijgaardehof co-housing** |

spatial layouts, responding to the specific demands of each co-housing group and its members. An articulated communal area rests amid these buildings; it includes gardens, a playground and a co-working space. Other facilities extend the individual dwellings into different forms of sharing. Overall, large balconies, rooftops and external circulations animate the estate above the ground-floor level. Between the estate and the park, both connecting and keeping them apart, the vestiges of existing brick sheds have been treated as 'assisted ruins', with street art, plantations and new paths, functioning as outside rooms to play in. As residents wait for the new trees to grow into a lush garden, they constitute the anchor and memory of the place.

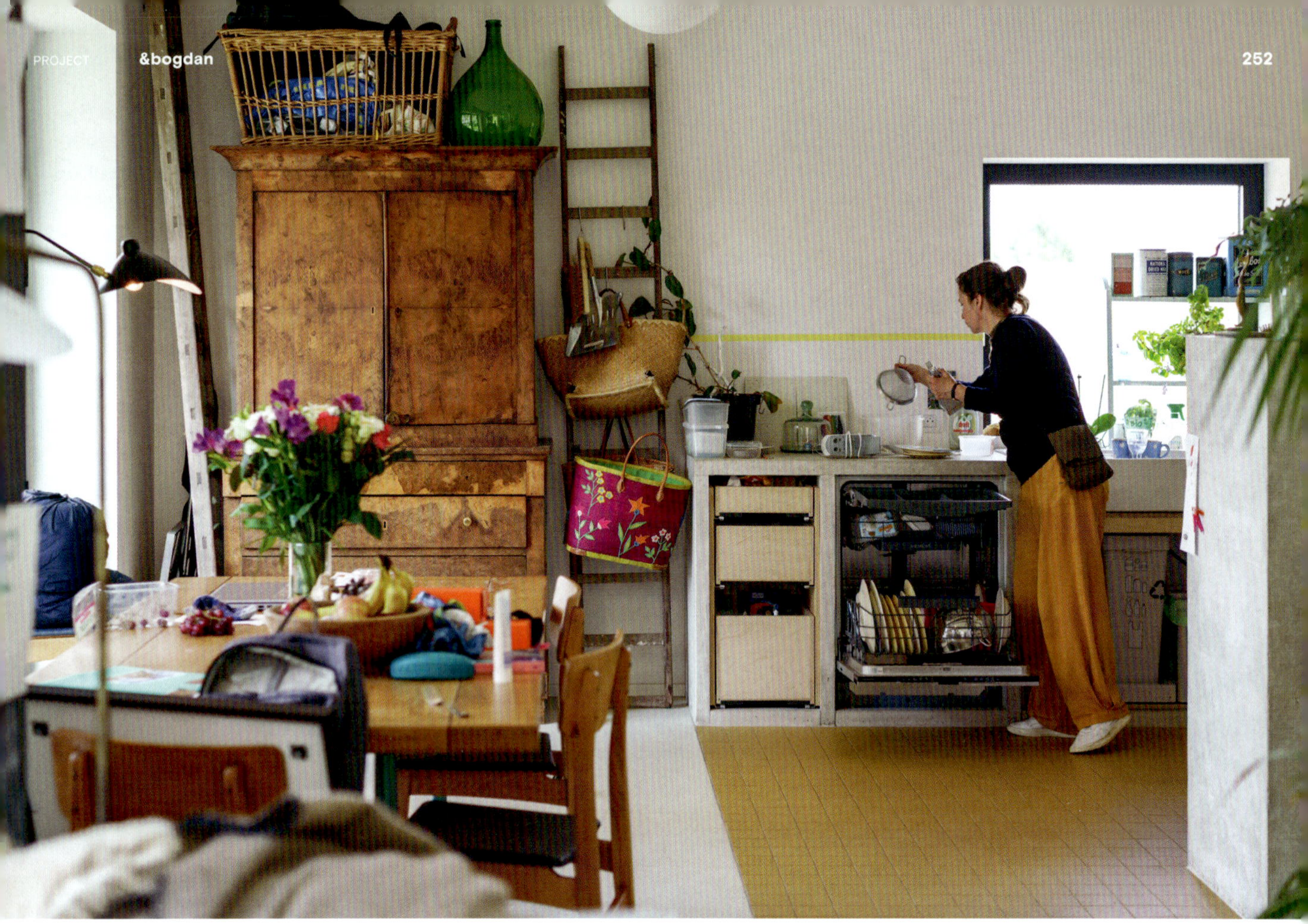

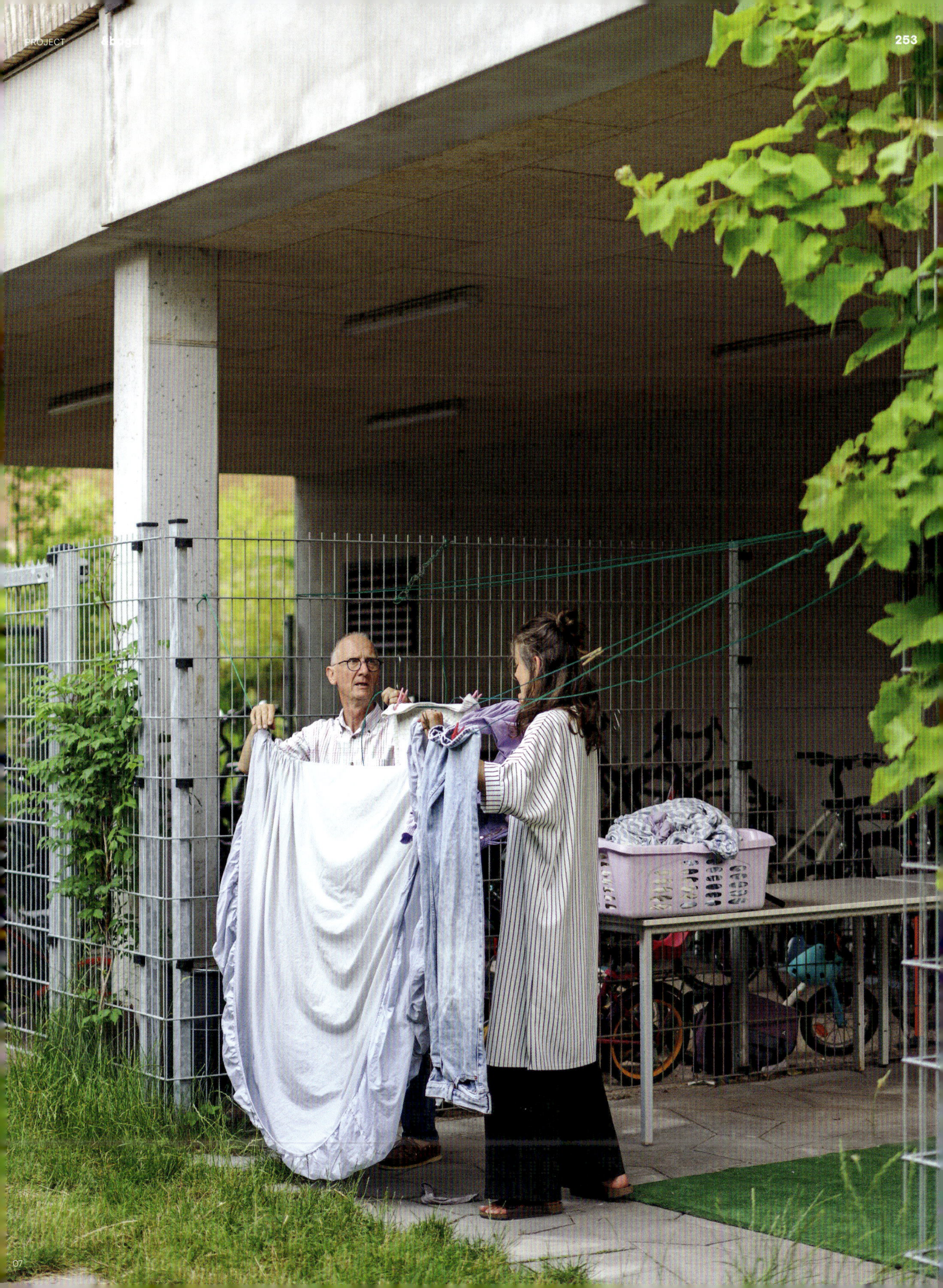

PROJECT **Bijgaardehof co-housing** 254

level 2
1 shared spaces Wijgaard living community

ground floor 0 5 25
1 car park, **2** health centre, **3** shared spaces De Spore housing group, **4** shared spaces Biotope housing group, **5** workshop, **6** central courtyard, **7** secret garden

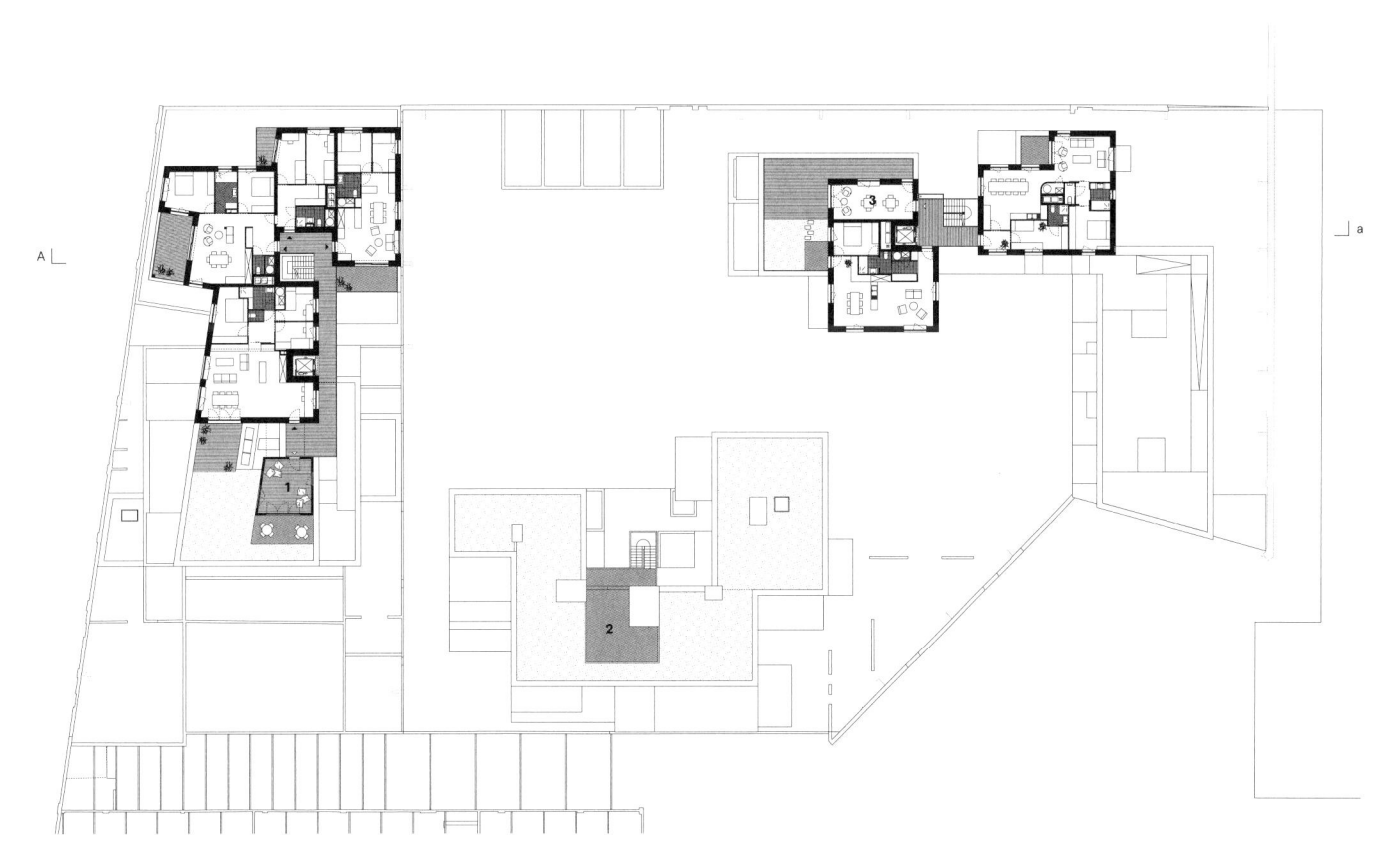

PROJECT **Bijgaardehof co-housing** 255

level 5
1 winter garden Wijgaard living group, **2** roof terrace De Spore residential group, **3** shared spaces Biotope housing group

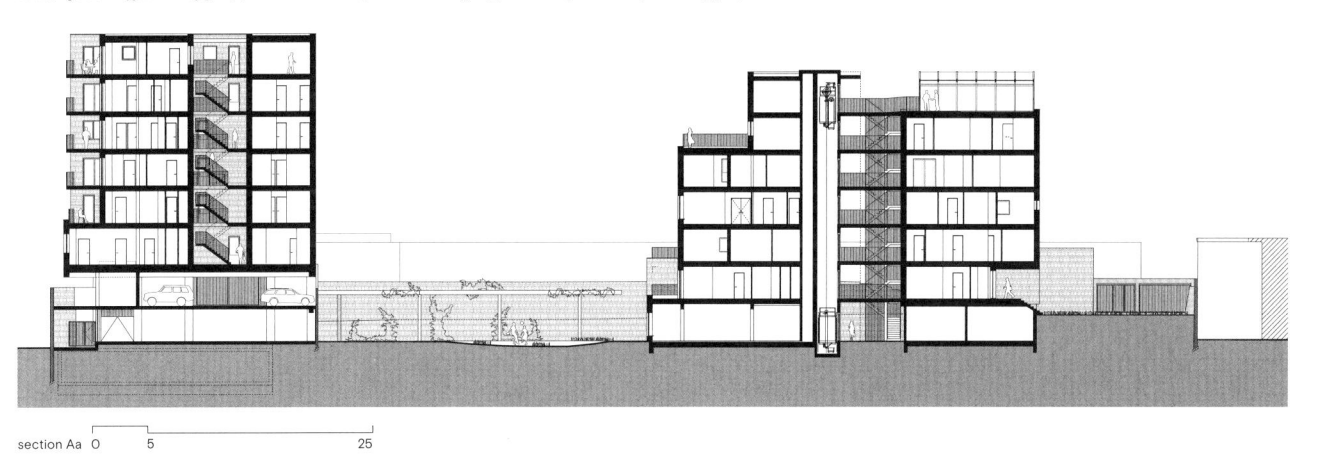

section Aa 0 5 25

project Bijgaardehof co-housing **office** &bogdan **design team** Oana Bogdan, Maxime Czvek, Valentin Ionescu, Marta Pawlowska, Sarah Poot, William Riche, Miguel Steel Lebre, Aron Sümeghy, Miguel Valério, Leo Van Broeck, Erik Vandenpoel, Simon Verstraete, Ken Vervaet, Thomas Willemse **website** www.bogdan.design **address** Sporewegel – Eliane Vogel-Polskypad – Deborah Lambillottepad, 9000 Ghent **client** Co-housing groups Biotope, De Spore and Wijgaard, Sint-Amandsberg district health centre, sogent **design** October 2009 **completion** December 2021 **surface area** (built-up area) 9,375 m² **volume** 27,438 m³ **total building cost** NA **total building cost per m²** NA **main contractor** Strabag, Antwerp **stability studies** Ney & Partners, Brussels & Engineers, Brussels **engineering and EPB studies** VK Architects **acoustics studies** Daidalos Peutz, Leuven **landscape design** LAND landschapsarchitecten, Antwerp **safety coordination** Prevebo, Veurne

text
Carlo Menon
photography
01, 06–08 © Kimberley Dhollander
02–05 © Laurian Ghinitoiu

PROJECT &bogdan 256

ectv architecten Els Claessens Tania Vandenbussche

PROJECT # Jean co-housing, Ghent

Ten families live in a green oasis with various swales located in an inner area in Sint-Amandsberg (Ghent). The site was once completely built up for a food company. sogent was able to sell it, with the aim of realizing a co-housing project. A residents' group of nine owners was selected who were willing to offer an additional rental home to a person with a disability. After a competition, the group chose the design by ectv architecten Els Claessens Tania Vandenbussche because of the pronounced equivalence between the residential units in their proposal.

Each unit is about 140 m² and has two stories with the night area on the top floor in each case. ectv positioned the units fairly compactly on one side of the garden. The row of units follows the height of the garden wall, creating a rhythm of two and three storeys that adds variety to the compact volume. Each unit relates to the communal outdoor space in a different but equivalent way. For half of the units, the living floor connects to the ground level; for the other half, external stairs lead from the communal outdoor space to the living quarters upstairs. Canopies play an important role in the mediation between indoor/outdoor and private/shared. They provide an informal threshold between the private and the collective. Sometimes they form a green roof, other times they feature an awning, and elsewhere still an open slat structure. In summer, they help against overheating and contribute to the site's overall energy neutrality.

PROJECT **Jean co-housing** 259

Besides the large garden, residents share an office, a laundry room, a lounge with spacious children's playroom, and a canteen.

These communal areas are perpendicular to the row of units, which means that the site is home to a loud play area and a quiet garden. The plot is at its narrowest on the street side. The fire department required a large access to the inner area. The designers used that requirement to create a covered outdoor courtyard that provides a view of the green housing site along the street side. This lends some relief to the streetscape and opens up the densely built residential area.

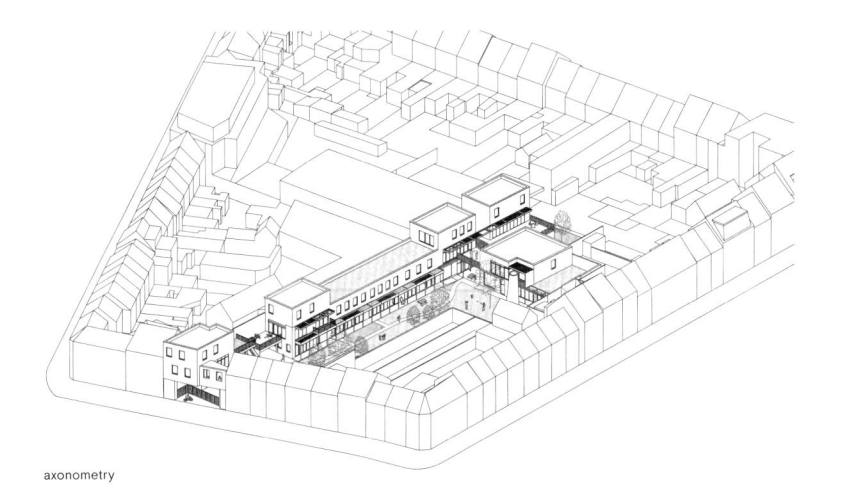

axonometry

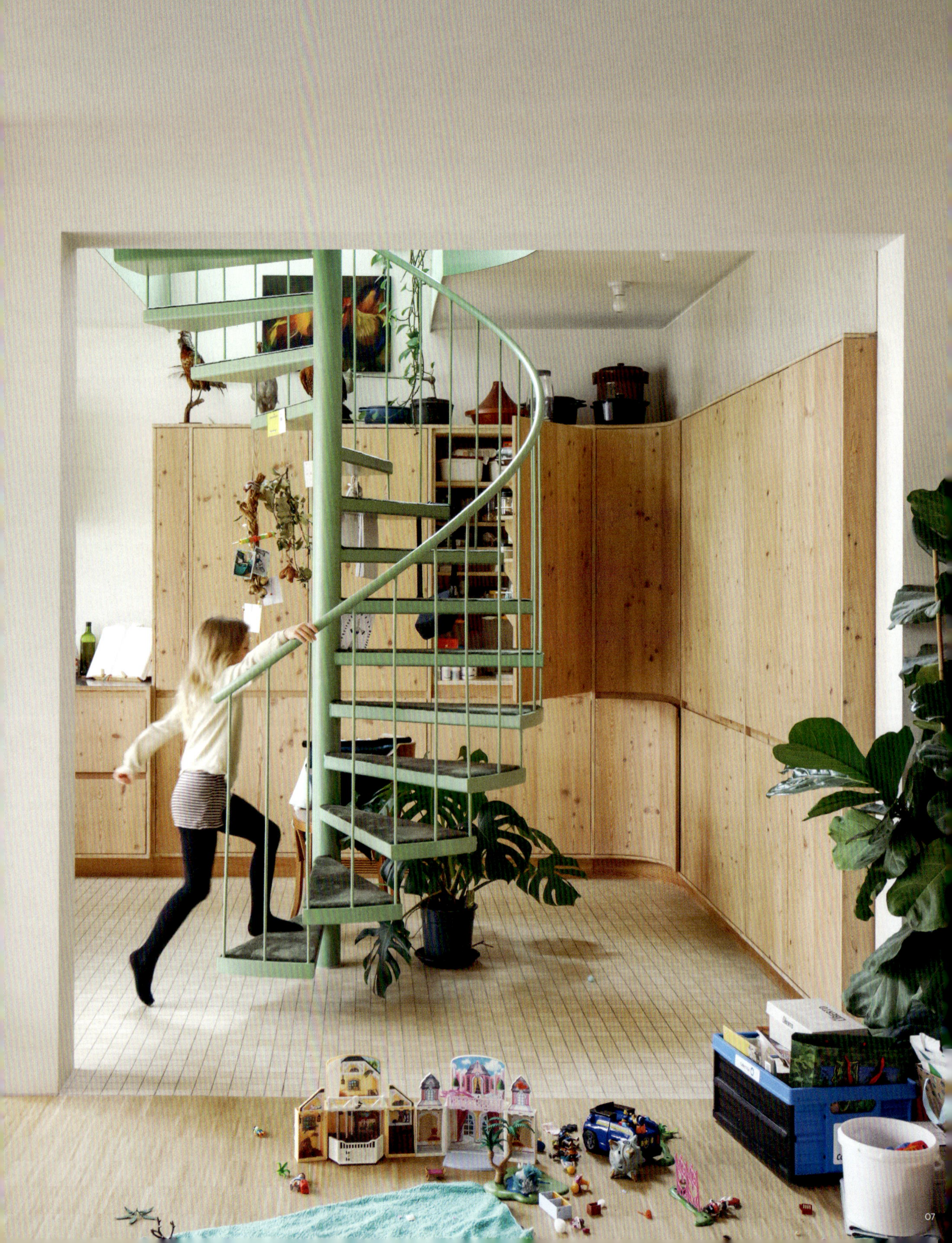

07

PROJECT | ectv architecten Els Claessens Tania Vandenbussche

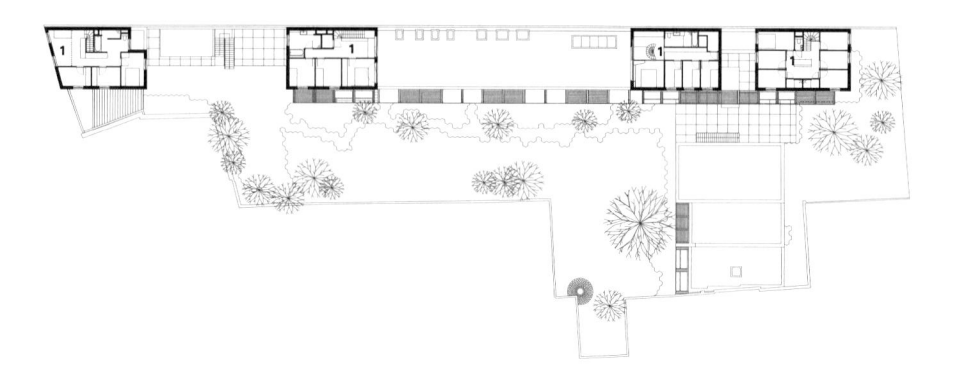

PROJECT **Jean co-housing** 262

level 2

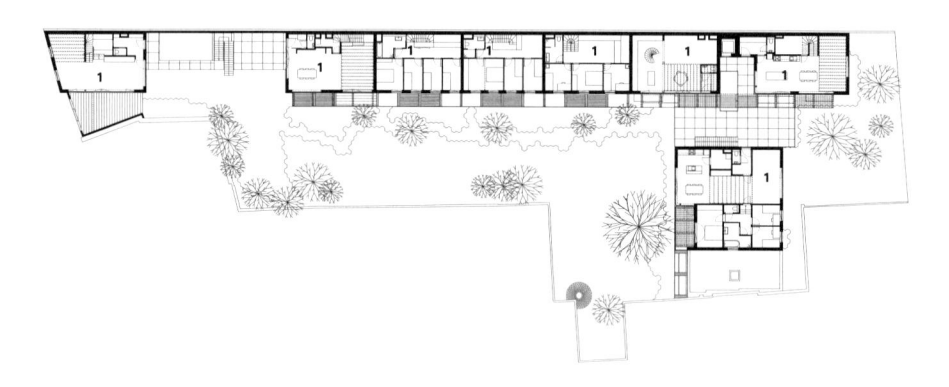

level 1

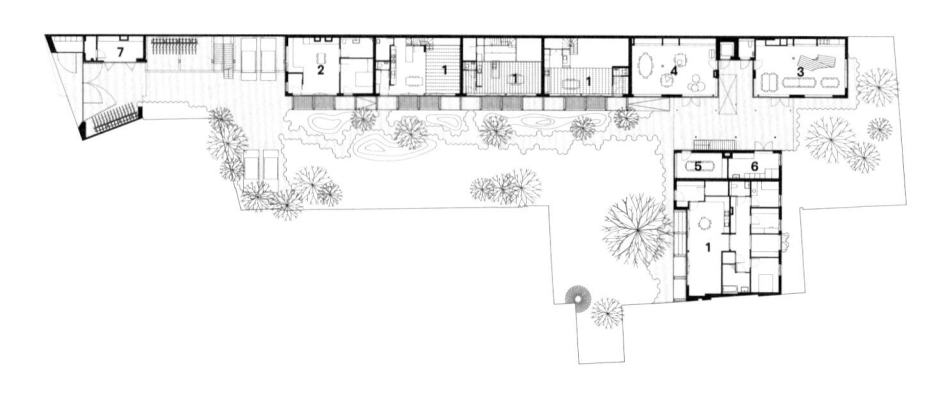

ground floor 0 5 25

1 family home, **2** accessible home, **3** shared dining area, **4** shared play area, **5** shared workspace, **6** laundry, **7** workshop and storage space

PROJECT **Jean co-housing** 263

09

text
Sofie De Caigny
photography
01, 07–08, 10 © Kimberley Dhollander
02–06, 09 © Filip Dujardin

project Jean co-housing **office** ectv architecten Els Claessens Tania Vandenbussche
design team Els Claessens, Tania Vandenbussche, Hong Wan Chan, Dries De Muynck
website www.ectv.be **address** Jean Béthunestraat 7–9, 9040 Ghent
client Cohousing Jean **design** September 2015 **completion** October 2022 **surface area** 1,774 m²
volume 5,969 m³ **total building cost** (incl. demolition and exterior layout) €3,809,426 excl. VAT
(excl. demolition and exterior layout) €3,430,282 excl. VAT **total building cost per m²** €1,933 excl. VAT
main contractor G-build, Lokeren **stability studies** Sileghem & Partners, Zwevegem
engineering studies emaze, Ghent **EPB studies** Egeon, Begijnendijk
acoustics studies Bureau De Fonseca, Waregem **landscape design** Geert Meysmans,
Antwerp & Koen Mennes, Kontich **safety coordination** Luk Verdegem, Markegem
interior design (image 07, 10) Johannes T'Hooft

PROJECT **ectv architecten Els Claessens Tania Vandenbussche**

PROJECT &bogdan, DDS+ 265

PROJECT **NovaCity I group housing and SME zone, Anderlecht**

NovaCity I by &bogdan and DDS+ is a landmark project born from a strategic partnership between citydev.brussels and the United Brussels Federation for Housing (BFUH-FéBUL). Launched under the 'Productive City' initiative of the Brussels Bouwmeester Maître Architecte (BMA), this mixed-use development includes approximately 7,500 m² of residential space and 7,600 m² of retail, office and workshop space. It aims to transform urban landscapes into sustainable ecosystems where production exists alongside daily life. By blending a diversity of spaces, NovaCity I fosters a cohesive and vibrant urban environment.

Strategically located in the Brussels municipality of Anderlecht, at the intersection of major roads, NovaCity I redefines the neighbourhood's urban fabric. The workshops, positioned to the south-east, act as a noise buffer against the adjacent train line. Housing volumes are oriented to include collective circulation areas and green roof spaces on top of the workshops, encouraging community interaction and transforming rooftops into shared social spaces.

Aesthetic and functional design features, such as corrugated steel panels painted in light green, provide an industrial look while mitigating noise. The building's plinth, made of precast concrete elements, offers flexible workshop spaces on the ground floor, enhancing adaptability.

Despite the innovative design, the outdoor workshop spaces currently lack communal areas, being dominated as they are by logistical circulation and a car park. However, tenants have creatively adapted their environments. Duplex Studio, for example, which designs objects from repurposed materials, has turned its entrance lobby into a multifunctional hybrid space serving as a kitchen, display area and photo studio.

Managed by citydev.brussels, the workshops have evolved into a self-sustaining community and a local ecosystem of exchange, highlighting the project's success in creating a new urban paradigm where production and living coexist harmoniously.

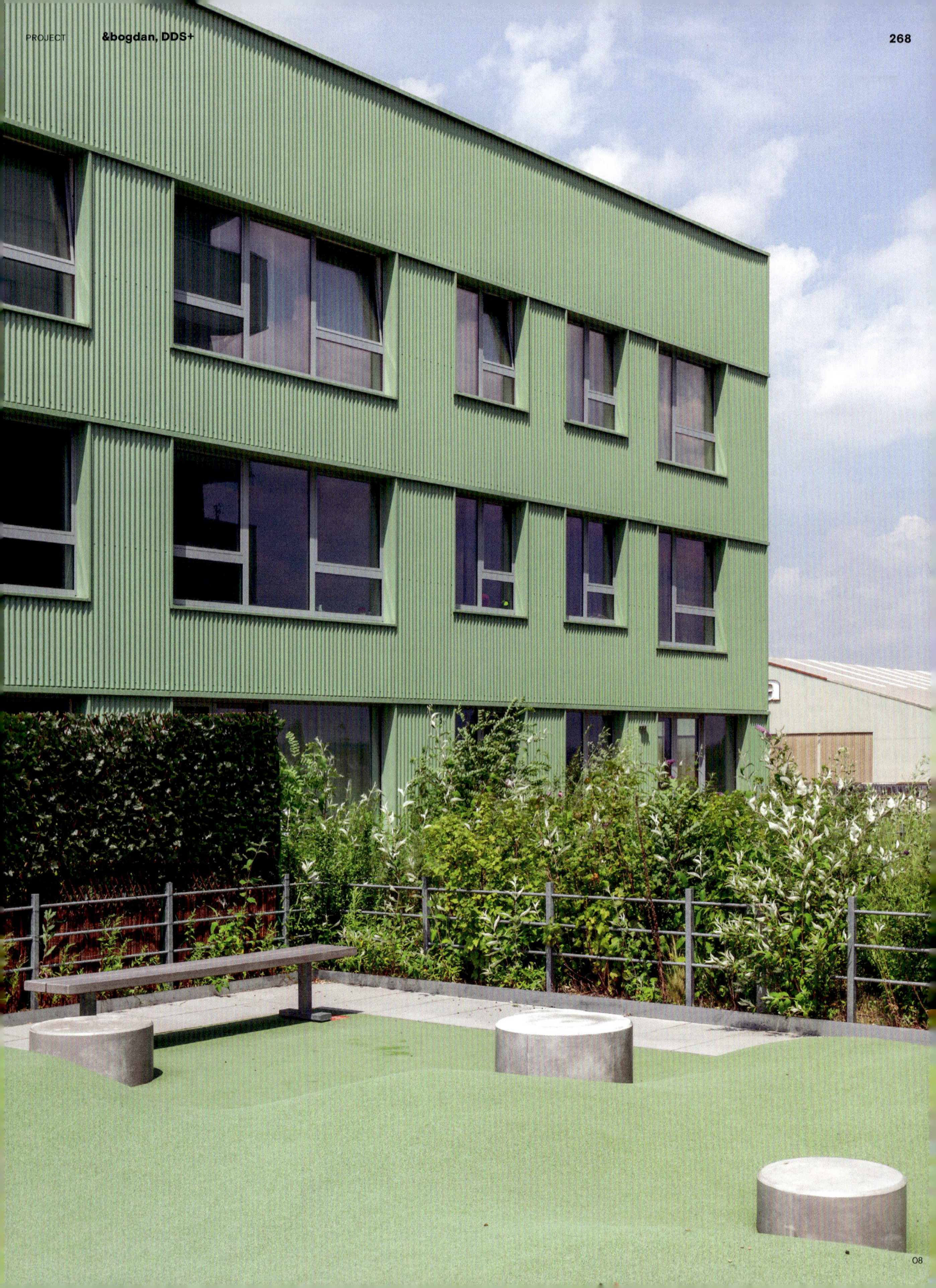

08

PROJECT &bogdan, DDS+

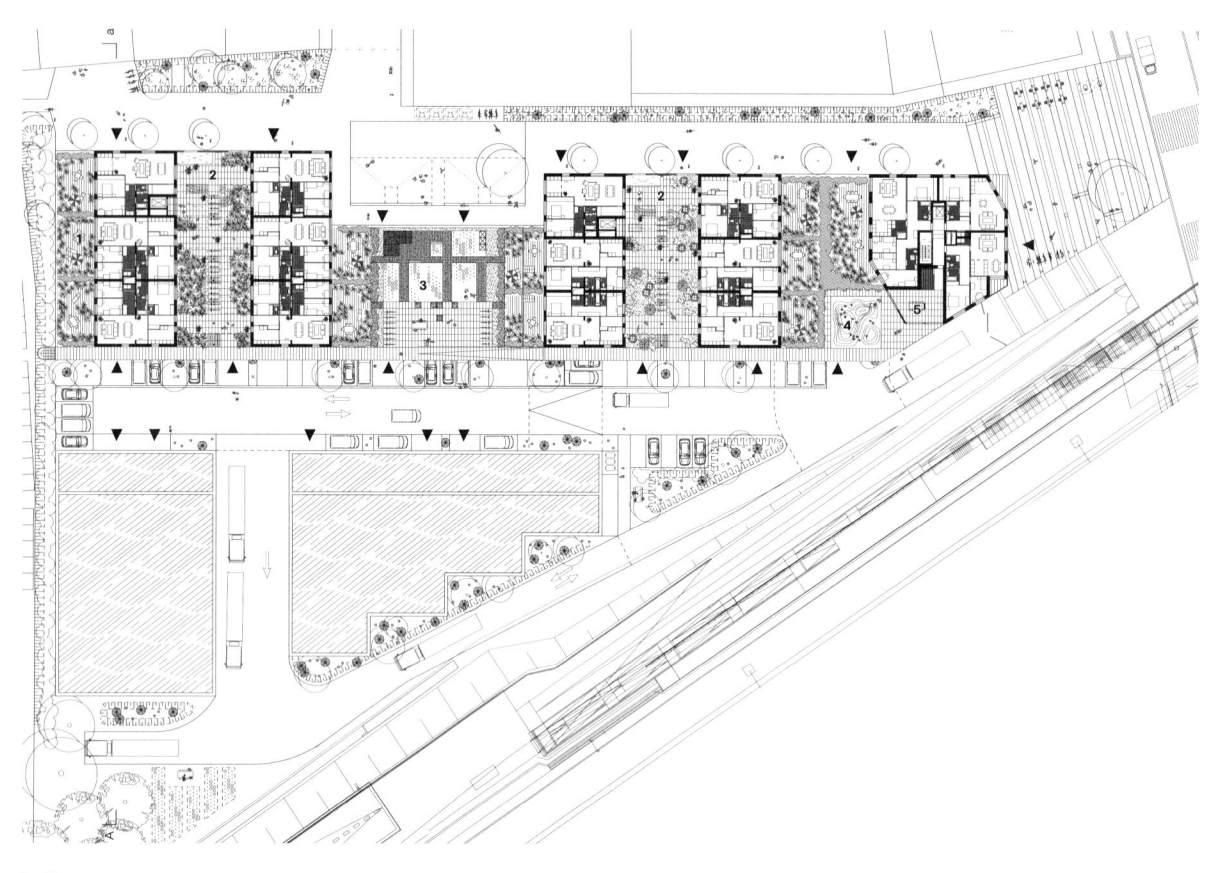

PROJECT **NovaCity I group housing and SME zone** 270

level 1
1 private garden, **2** patio, **3** communal garden, **4** playground, **5** multipurpose space

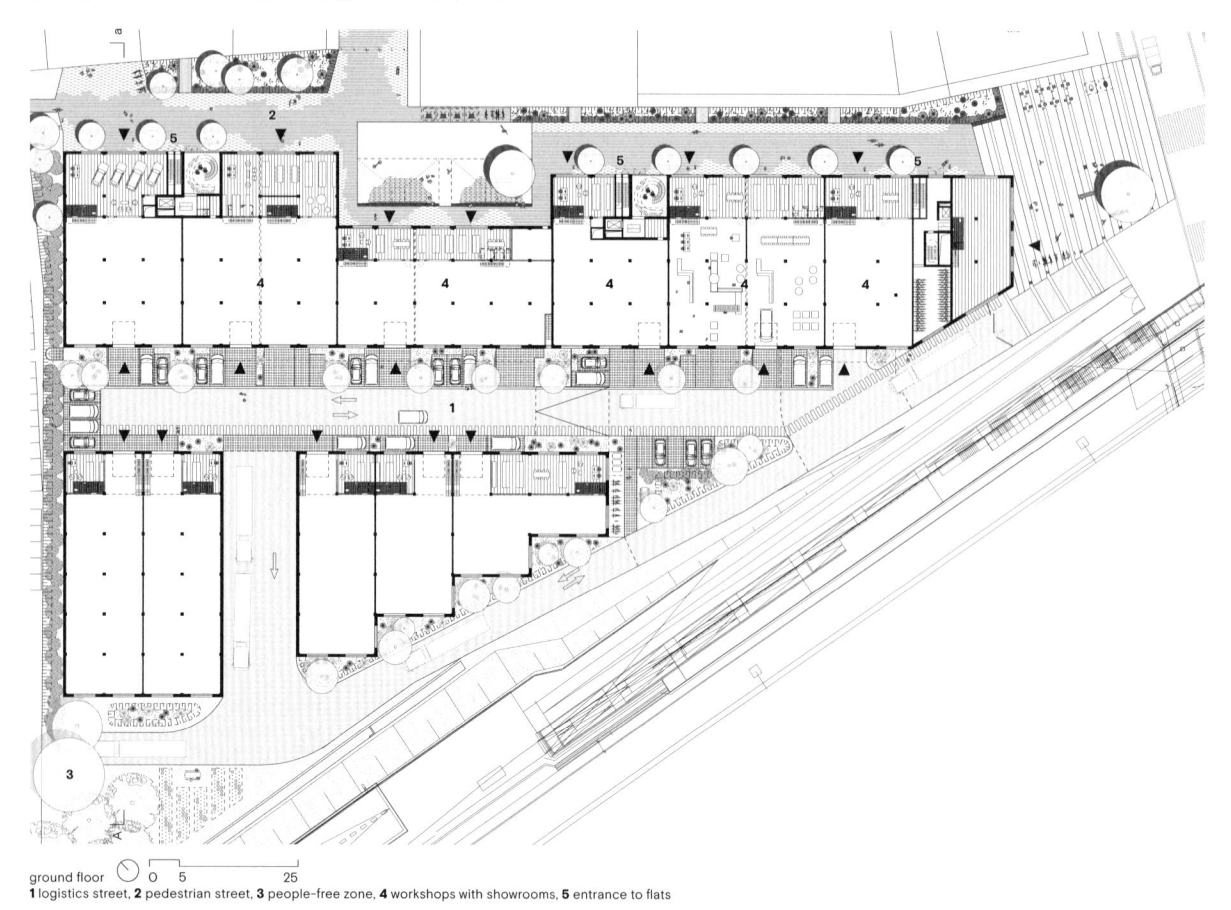

ground floor 0 5 25
1 logistics street, **2** pedestrian street, **3** people-free zone, **4** workshops with showrooms, **5** entrance to flats

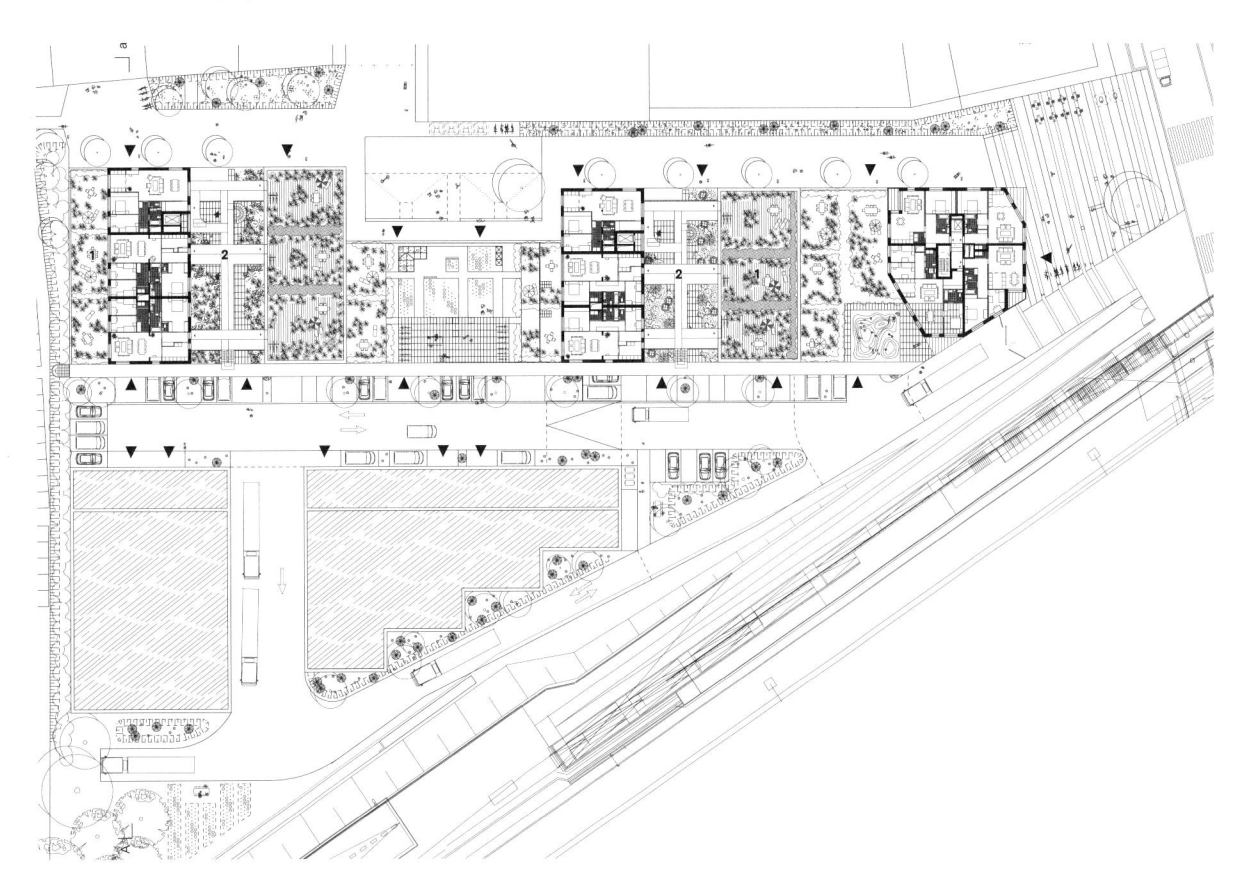

PROJECT | **NovaCity I group housing and SME zone** | 271

level 4
1 private garden, **2** patio

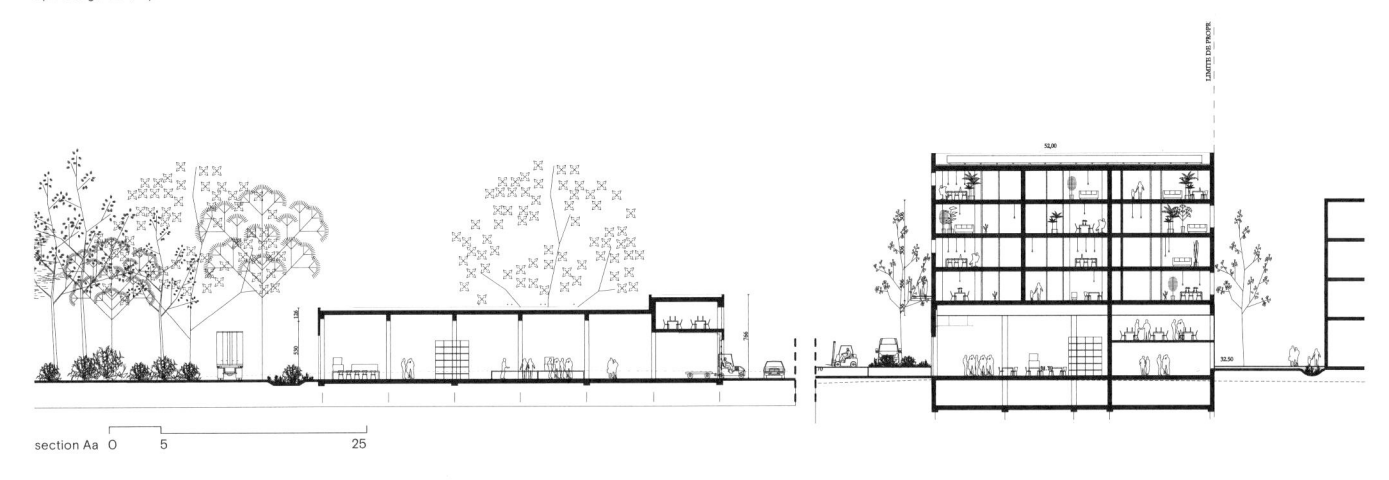

section Aa 0 5 25

text
Dennis Pohl
photography
01, 08-10 © Delphine Mathy
02-07 © Laurian Ghinitoiu

project NovaCity I group housing and SME zone **office** &bogdan and DDS+
design team (&bogdan) Oana Bogdan, Loïc Croegaert, Laura Janssens, Marta Pawlowska, Sarah Poot, Andreea Rădulescu, Leo Van Broeck (DDS+) Drik Bigaré, Geert Vanoverschelde, Catherine Paulissen, Renaud Scheffler, Nathalie Tavares Bastos, Eric Hennico **website** www.bogdan.design, www.dds.plus
address Marie Korèhoek – Klaverstraat – Monssesteenweg, 1000 Anderlecht
client Wolito/Kairos for citydev.brussels **design** July 2017 **completion** January 2023
surface area (SME space) 7,708 m² (housing space) 7,482 m² (public space) 3,648 m²
volume 51,458 m³ **total building cost** approx. €25,000,000 excl. VAT and fees
total building cost per m² NA **main contractor** BAM Interbuild/Galère, Antwerp
stability studies Establis, Roeselare **EPB and engineering studies** Boydens Engineering, Dilbeek
acoustics studies Venac, Brussels **landscape design** Atelier EOLE Paysagistes, Watermaal-Bosvoorde
safety coordination W4R, Drogenbos

PROJECT &bogdan, DDS+

Ecologies That Matter

The Importance of Scale in the Sustainability of Architecture

Dennis Pohl

[1] William McDonough and Michael Braungart, *Cradle to Cradle: Remaking the Way We Make Things* (New York: North Point Press, 2002).

[2] Lydia Kallipoliti, *Histories of Ecological Design: An Unfinished Cyclopedia* (New York: Actar, 2024).

[3] Bernard Rudofsky, *Architecture Without Architects: A Short Introduction to Non-pedigreed Architecture* (New York: Museum of Modern Art, 1969); Reyner Banham, *The Architecture of the Well-Tempered Environment* (London: Architectural Press, 1969).

Rammed earth, compressed earth mortar, algae-based compostable biopolymers, fermented mycelium, upcycled textile residues, cork and hemp insulation panels are all among the innovative materials now recognized for their infinite reusability and suitability for circular construction. In the evolving landscape of sustainable architecture, a shift towards bio- and earth-based materials has marked a significant step forward. This movement has inspired numerous experimental projects, especially across Flanders and Brussels, where the legacy of highly innovative practices such as BC Architects and Rotor DC is evident. These projects aim to drive systemic change in the construction industry through bioregional, low-tech, circular and inclusive design. Internationally renowned practices like the above specialize in the reuse and resale of building materials, fostering sustainable design through research, project design, exhibitions and the repurposing of reclaimed materials, and promoting a socially engaged approach to architecture and urban development.

While these initiatives are driven by a moral conviction that the 'right' choice of materials and techniques can guide architectural decisions, a critique arises from their bio-deterministic assumptions. Most of these current practices fail to reference the conceptual origins of their work. These can be traced back to the seminal writings of William McDonough and Michael Braungart, who introduced practical circularity in the built environment. Their cradle-to-cradle framework simplifies complex ecological and social interactions, often romanticizing nature and overlooking competitive aspects of evolution.[1] By likening human society to natural ecosystems, these models, both historic and contemporary, risk ignoring inherent conflicts and socio-cultural dimensions of urban life, potentially reducing sustainability to an overly idealistic and technocratic vision. This critique underscores the need for a more nuanced understanding of sustainability, acknowledging the complexities and relativism of culture, life, the economy and technology.

This leads to the fundamental question of whether sustainability is a matter of scale. Have the experiments advocating a circular approach reached their limits with small-scale projects, such as family homes clad with meticulously chosen, stored and reused materials from demolished buildings? Can recycled materials truly address societal issues when circularity has become common sense in architectural productions?

Proximity to nature vs synthetic replication

Reflecting on Lydia Kallipoliti's 'unfinished cyclopedia' of 'ecological design', a clear divide emerges between projects seeking proximity to nature and those driven by technoscientific ideals since the 1970s.[2] The former romanticizes vernacular building methods, translating them into modern society through small-scale interventions; by contrast, the latter integrates sustainability into capital-driven investments, aligning it with real-estate developments and urban gentrification. At the outer extremes, this alleged divide was backed by architecture history and theory with protagonists like Bernard Rudofsky emphasizing vernacular and craft integrity, while Reyner Banham advocated technologically advanced, 'well-tempered environments'.[3] This is not to say that Banham was unaware of ecological impacts, quite the contrary. Architecture's role in synthetic ecosystem recreation, fuelled by technological

ESSAY Dennis Pohl

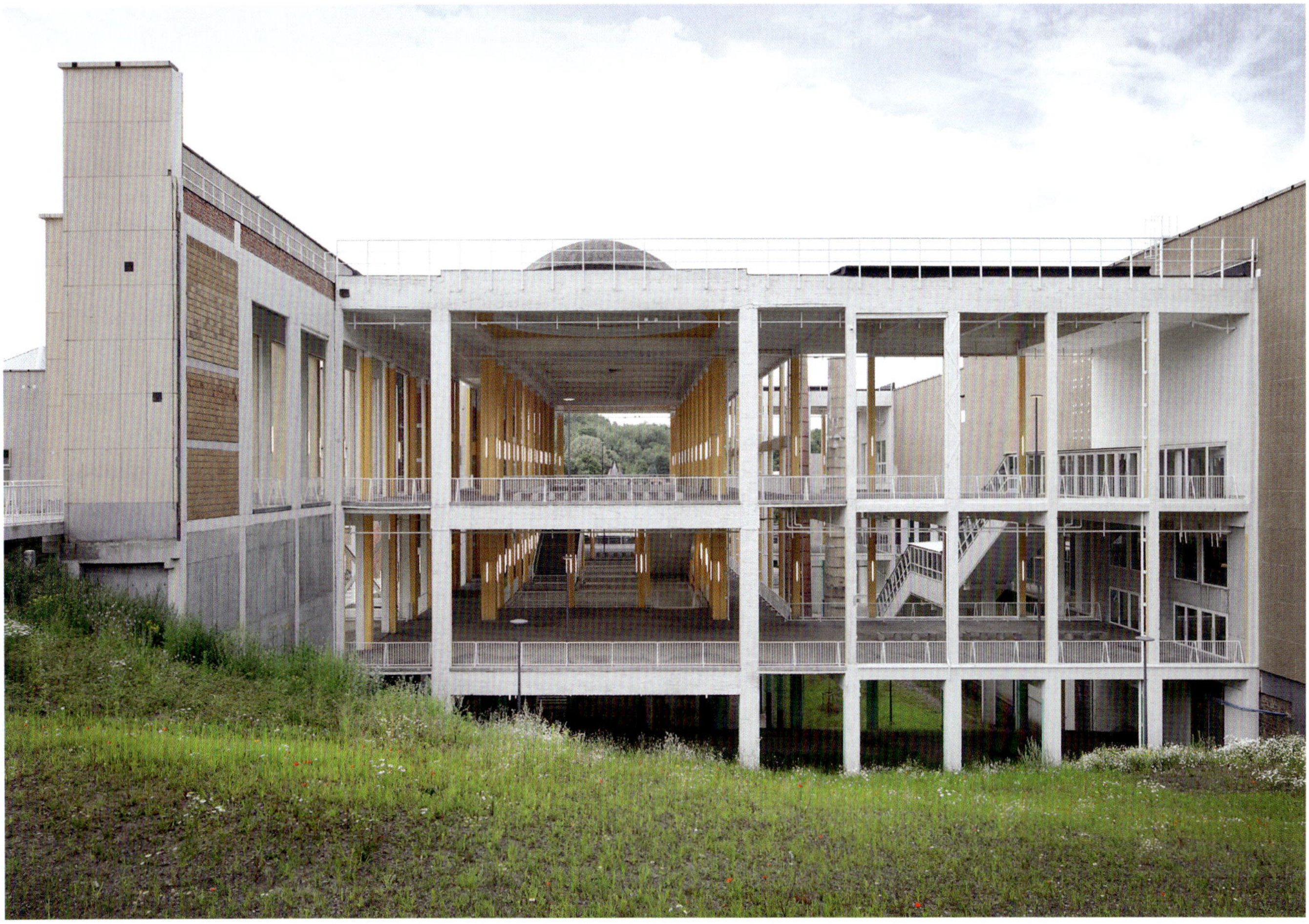

02

4 Nikos Katsikis, 'Two Approaches to "World Management": C. A. Doxiadis and R. B. Fuller', in *Implosions/Explosions: Towards a Study of Planetary Urbanization*, ed. Neil Brenner (Berlin: Jovis, 2013), 480–504.

5 Gro Harlem Brundtland and World Commission on Environment and Development, *Report of the World Commission on Environment and Development: Our Common Future* (New York: United Nations, 1987).

6 LEED (Leadership in Energy and Environmental Design) is the most widely used green building rating system set up by the US Green Building Council in 1998; BREEAM is a science-based suite of validation and certification systems for a more sustainable built environment developed by the British Building Research Establishment in 1990; Passivhaus is a standard introduced in Germany that defines the maximum heating requirement of a building to a maximum of 15 kWh/(m²a); an EPC label (energy performance certificate) indicates the energy efficiency of a building; a Building Energy Rating (BER) certifies the energy performance of a building on a scale from A to G.

7 Mimi Sheller, 'The Origins Of Global Carbon Form,' *Log* 47 (2019): 56–68.

8 Hülya Ertas, 'Designing from the Inside', in *Flanders Architecture Review N° 15* (Antwerp: Flanders Architecture Institute, 2022), 197–204.

progress, parallels the approaches of Constantinos Doxiadis and Buckminster Fuller in 'world management', Stewart Brand's *Whole Earth Catalog*, and the Biosphere 2 experiments.[4]

Despite originating in countercultural movements reacting to limited resources, these concerns were streamlined into mass capitalism around a decade later under the umbrella term of 'sustainability'. Most compellingly, the neologism was promoted in 'Our Common Future', the 1987 United Nations Brundtland Report that institutionalized sustainability policies.[5] This led to performance certification schemes like LEED, BREEAM and *Passivhaus* (Passive house), next to rating and labelling systems such as EPC norms and BERs.[6] No doubt that this carbon bureaucracy has spurred new revenues along the ethics of environmentalism, while fostering an industry of toxic insulation materials and increasingly complex and potentially harmful building materials. From asbestos-containing insulation to formaldehyde-based construction materials that trigger chemical sensitivities, the building industry has introduced new products as well as consumption, production, regulation and disposal methods that stealthily bring toxic substances into our living spaces while creating new experts that quantify, ensure and evaluate their fitting into a self-evolving system of sustainability standards.

But architecture is deeply embedded in an extractivist concept of carbon form, which perpetuates and conceals the socioecological exploitation foundational to modern energy cultures. Mimi Sheller elucidates that architecture, like vehicles and cities, is a temporary embodiment of grey energy, rooted in the raw material basis of energy, transport and communication infrastructures. Shaped by labour and capital investment, these infrastructures form geographies of social relations and cultural meanings, thereby embedding carbon form into our energy culture. This carbon form becomes naturalized, underpinning the 'structure of feeling' of modern life, obscuring the racialized extraction and exploitation that sustain it. Understanding architecture's role within this framework reveals its complicity in maintaining the socioecological inequalities intrinsic to the carbon form. This compels a critical reassessment of its role in contemporary energy transitions and sustainability efforts.[7]

In light of this, it was more than legitimate that the critical recognition of such a market-driven approach to sustainability led designers and thinkers to consider cradle-to-cradle methods as an answer towards new circular modes of design. Seeking proximity to nature, the idea of self-reliance romanticized for a long time the effects of circular design that have become their own ends if they are not fully embedded in today's mainstream discourse. While the abundant use and connotation of 'green' has been dominating urban developments, small-scale solutions and circular materials turned into the agents to solve societal problems through buildings. This shortcut nonetheless has reduced ecological design to the dimension of technics, not considering that ecology first and foremost causes and stems from social problems.

However, we need a model of sustainability that connects to habits, energy use and embodied carbon, extending from small-scale projects to large-scale urban developments.[8] It is evident that spatial and temporal density will be a core question of the coming decades.

Four decarbonizing forms

The following projects exemplify how these theoretical and conceptual frameworks translate into practical, innovative solutions, embodying ecological design principles that address both material and social dimensions of sustainability. By integrating spatial reduction, adaptive reuse and the preservation of cultural and carbon heritage, these projects showcase systematic large-scale approaches to redefining architectural practices for a carbon-conscious future.

ESSAY Ecologies That Matter

Chapex: Building back

The Chapex project in Charleroi illustrates how ecological design can be seamlessly integrated into the process of building back. The Palais des Expositions, a sprawling 60,000 m² exhibition hall dating from Charleroi's industrial past, symbolizes an era when coal was the region's seemingly unlimited resource. An open call by the Charleroi Bouwmeester resulted in the selection of the proposal by advvt and AgwA addressing the contemporary need for only 25,000 m² of exhibition space. This project proposes an innovative ecological design strategy focused on space reduction and repurposing.

Rather than prioritize performative or circular materials, the project transformed the central space into an outdoor, sheltered area by removing its façades. The creation of a 'Jardin Central' enhances connectivity between the upper and lower parts of the city, serving as both a communal space and a vital urban link that bridges Charleroi's fragmented landscape. The spatial quality is enhanced by milky light filtered through the gigantic glass stone domes on the roof and the open grid of columns painted in warm yellow and turquoise green.

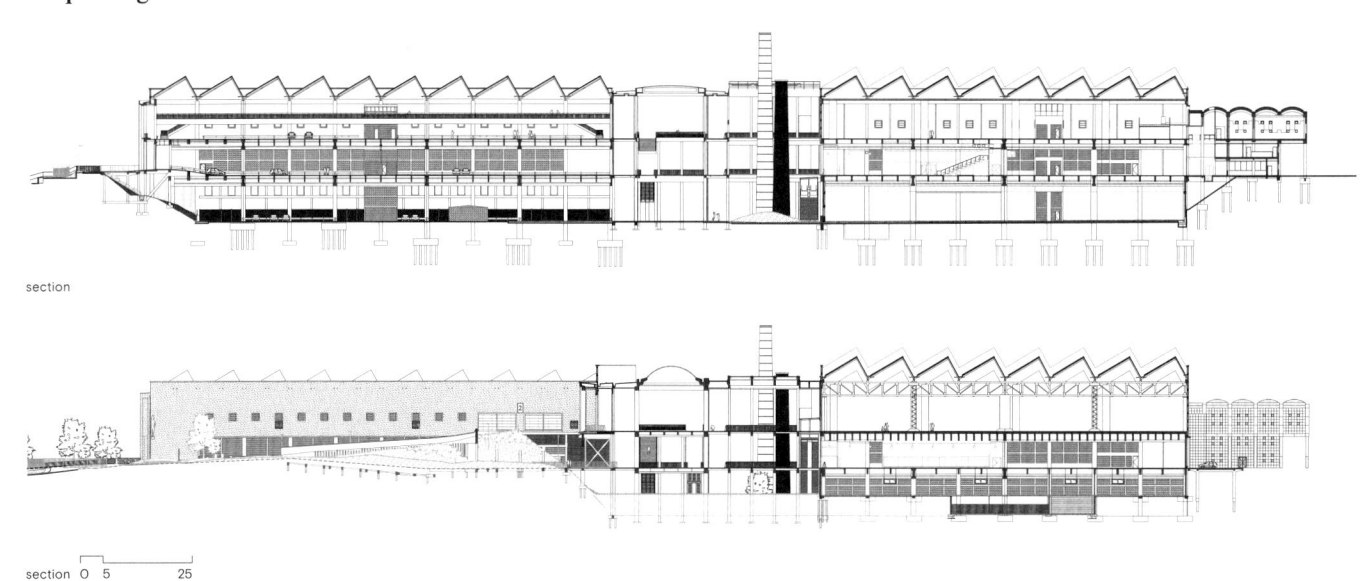

section

section 0 5   25

By maximizing the utility of the existing spaces, the retained halls are repurposed for multiple functions, with one group of three halls designated for parking and the other for core activities. This project exemplifies the pragmatic and innovative use of public funds, ensuring economic viability while preserving the cultural significance of the Palais des Expositions and adapting it to contemporary needs. However, it raises questions about whether designers should recalibrate their focus from material properties to the softer values of social change. Whether the project managed to generate social cohesion through cultural infrastructure is a long-term question that will only be answered in the coming years. ▶

project Chapex   **office** AjdvivgwA: TV architecten jan de vylder inge vinck – AgwA
design team Bureau Greisch, Doorzon Interieurarchitecten, Denis Dujardin, Delta GC, PROGRS, architectende vylder vinck tailllieu (2015–2019)   **website** www.architectenjdviv.be, www.agwa.be
address Avenue de l'Europe, Charleroi   **client** City of Charleroi c/o IGRETEC + Charleroi Bouwmeester
design 2015   **completion** ongoing – provisional delivery 2024
surface area 47,000 m² (landscape 29,500 m²)   **volume** 288,000 m³
total building cost (provisional budget) €46,500,000 excl. VAT
total building cost per m² (provisional budget) €989 excl. VAT
main contractor TV Eiffage+Bemat+Koeckelberg (Eiffage, Vélizy-Villacoublay, France) (Bemat sa, Charleroi) (Koeckelberg, Charleroi)   **stability and engineering studies** Bureau Greisch, Liège
acoustics studies PROGRS, Wépion   **landscape design** Denis Dujardin, Kortrijk
safety coordination Bureau PS2, Ecaussinnes   **interior design** Doorzon interieurarchitecten, Ghent

ESSAY **Dennis Pohl**

ESSAY   **Dennis Pohl**

9 Kiel Moe, *Unless: The Seagram Building Construction Ecology* (New York: Actar 2021).

10 51N4E, *How to Not Demolish a Building* (Berlin: Ruby Press, 2022).

From WTC to ZIN to carbon footprints

High-rise construction as an ecological design project may seem counterintuitive, especially as the devil of CO_2 footprints is often in the details. Undoubtedly, constructions from the 1970s onwards have brought about an entire generation of buildings that were considered by their designers as disposable objects. Their designs are literally written into what can be considered the geologies of the great acceleration during the Anthropocene. Aluminium, copper, brass: the sheer amount of rare metals used in postwar high-rise structures is embedded in a conundrum based on infinite energy resources and global capital streams.[9]

The result of this complex transition is the ZIN building in Brussels, designed by 51N4E together with the architectural firms l'AUC and Jaspers-Eyers Architects. The ZIN project involved the conversion of the existing towers into a sustainable mixed-use complex integrating offices, apartments and a hotel. Indoor spaces and the adjacent greenhouse host various plant species of mostly tropical origins that are technologically managed by climate control and irrigation systems – unfortunately missing out on the opportunity to integrate the self-regulation mechanisms and micro-climate impacts of these species into the design. Nonetheless, this project underscores the potential of adaptive reuse in high-rise buildings, aiming to significantly reduce the ecological footprint by repurposing existing structures rather than resorting to complete demolition and new construction. Such an approach aligns with the growing recognition of the need to rethink urban development practices in the context of climate change and resource depletion, paving the way for more sustainable and resilient cities.

It may seem even more counterintuitive to transform the World Trade Center (WTC) in Brussels – once a symbol of market deregulation and homeowner expropriation – into an ecological design model for large-scale preservation. This complex transition period, however, was anything but a smooth design process, affecting neighbourhood stakeholders and artist collectives, as documented by 51N4E in their publication *How to Not Demolish a Building*.[10] Despite only saving the concrete core of the two WTC towers from demolition, the spatial qualities of the design are exceptional. They are so because the Flemish Government, as a user, could afford double-height ceiling constructions, collective office spaces and various design choices private developers would usually not opt for due to profit margins.

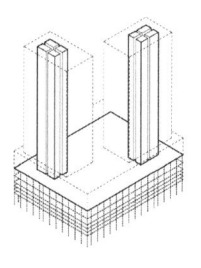

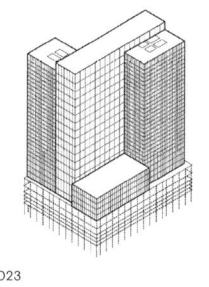

1972   2020   2023

This project was pivotal for both 51N4E and the Flemish Government, as it underscores the potential of heritage buildings for preserving grey energy embedded in constructions from the 1970s and 1980s. Consequently, the Flemish Government commissioned a feasibility and reuse study of twenty-one government buildings nearing the end of their engineered lifespan. If this study sparks debate on incentivizing renovation over demolition, it could have a significant impact. Potential policy changes include extending the 6-per-cent VAT charges (currently applied to private housing renovations) to companies and pushing the European Commission to include grey energy in their taxonomy. Such incentives could create new ecosystems of policies and design practices that address the energy loss of the past.

ESSAY   Ecologies That Matter   281

project ZIN   **office** 51N4E with l'AUC and Jaspers-Eyers
design team Johan Anrys, Freek Persyn, Olivier Cavens, Louise Vanderlinden, Guillem Pons, Charlotte Schmidt, Janik Beckers, Hunter Doyle, Matthias Salaets, Laura Villeret, Alba Tavares Vanhoutte, Ruben Janssens, Gianni Villa, Djamel Klouche, Alessandro Gess, Alice Loumeau, Noël Picaper, Guillaume Durand, Eva Lindsay, Alice Bondaty, Damien Nuyts-Roussel, Clara Fonder, Léa Noguès
Team Jaspers-Eyers: John Eyers, Jean-Michel Jaspers, Frank Theyssen, Loïk Eyers, Paul Puls, Willem Wouters, Bert Peeters, Toon Torfs, Jef Uyttendaele, Gilles Bollens, Tom Beckers, Lien Gysels, Tanja Van Hal, Dorien Sente, Valérie Deramée, Bart Lantmeeters, Kimberly Hamers, Alysse Knockaert, Jeroen Reynders, Mathilde Heilporn, Davide Cassanmagnago, Valentin Pascu, Jonathan Rothé, Bob Helsen, Nicolas Darge, Caroline Kasanda Kasonga, Mannfred Benditz, Christophe Beauvez, Aurea Bravo Martin, Mohammad Rujoub   **website** www.51n4e.com, www.laucparis.com, www.jaspers-eyers.com   **address** Koning Albert II Laan 28, 1000 Brussels   **client** Befimmo
design 2017–19   **completion** spring 2025   **surface area** 10,800 m²
volume 818,717 m³   **total building cost** €250,000.000 excl. VAT
total building cost per m² €1,750 excl. VAT   **main contractor** Open Minds – CFE, BPC, VMA and Van Laere
engineering studies Bureau Greisch, Liège   **EPB studies** Bureau Greisch, Liège & VK Architects & Engineers, Brussels   **art integration** Piet Coessens   **acoustics studies** Bureau De Fonseca, Waregem
landscape design Plant- en houtgoed, Overijse   **safety coordination** (façade) SECO Belgium, Diegem, VS-A Group, Lille, France, (circular building) Drees & Sommer Belgium, Brussels

Royale Belge and carbon heritage

Such a transition should not be motivated solely by economic considerations; it is also a cultural imperative to address the energy cultures of the past that revolved around peak oil and nuclear energy. If we consider that buildings are worth preserving not only for their symbolic cultural values but also for the energy values that enabled their construction, this perspective can lead to heritage innovation, transforming cultural heritage into carbon heritage. It is crucial to include energy as a factor in conservation policies, especially in an era when fossil fuel-driven growth has reached its limits.

07

The Royale Belge building is an example that qualifies on both counts. As a listed monument, it required a conscious and careful approach to reuse. Located in the green outskirts of Brussels, the building, originally constructed in the 1960s, stands as a significant architectural landmark with its striking modernist design characterized by large glass façades and innovative use of materials. Before initiating the renovation competition, the client engaged Bureau Bouwtechniek to conduct a reuse study. Undertaken in collaboration with the heritage administration, the study focused not on costs or feasibility, but on determining which parts of the building could be repurposed to comply with current fire safety and energy regulations as well as material standards. Based on this report, the recently transformed building has been adapted by Bovenbouw Architectuur, Caruso St John Architects and DDS+ for contemporary use while retaining its iconic features. The renovation involved updating the internal spaces to accommodate a mix of offices, leisure and retail functions, demonstrating how heritage buildings can be revitalized to meet current needs without compromising their historical and material significance. Hollowing out the central core and turning it into a round staircase void ▶

ESSAY   Dennis Pohl

ESSAY   **Dennis Pohl**

resulted in the perception of an unprecedented spatial quality. This project underscores the potential for adaptive reuse to conserve embodied energy, reduce environmental impact and preserve cultural heritage. As such, it sets a precedent for future conservation practices that integrate sustainability and historical preservation.

project Royale Belge **office** Bovenbouw Architectuur and Caruso St John Architects with DDS+
location Watermaal-Bosvoorde see p. 297

Urban density at NovaCity I

Many transformative projects result from the collaboration of multiple voices, often omitted from later reviews. These voices significantly influence how projects can reshape urban habits. Local policymakers, the Brussels Bouwmeester Maître Architecte (BMA), citydev.brussels, and the United Brussels Federation for Housing (BFUH-FéBUL) form the ecosystem that defines a project's ecology long before designers begin their work.

At NovaCity I, a housing project by &bogdan and DDS+ in the Brussels municipality of Anderlecht, a remarkable design ecology combines workshop ateliers with sixty-three social-housing units. This project densifies the urban landscape by integrating housing and reactivating former industrial zones with new forms of production, creating new urban synergies. Densification is crucial for energy efficiency and embodied carbon as it maximizes the use of existing urban infrastructure, reduces the use of energy and minimizes transport-related emissions. This demonstrates that new constructions can be environmentally responsible through thoughtful, integrated design strategies at the urban level.

In NovaCity I, form follows sound, from the urban scale down to the façade details. The workshops serve as a noise buffer to the adjacent train line in the south-east of the project, while the orientation of the newly designed housing volumes allows for a blend of collective circulation and green roof spaces on top of the lower workshop volume. The corrugated steel panels painted in light green used for cladding not only resonate aesthetically with industrial sites but also possess acoustic qualities that lower sound repercussions from the workshops and train lines. The plinth, made of precast concrete elements, offers flexible subdivision to accommodate workshops on the ground floor. Infrastructure facilities shared with the housing units on the upper floors reduce total building costs to less than €2,000 per m².

Companies like Duplex Studio, which produce design objects from waste, surplus and unused materials, have found their base at NovaCity I. Accepted by the site managers of citydev.brussels, they contribute to the local ecosystem, showcasing how architecture can serve a vibrant community. NovaCity I fosters the appropriation of shared spaces, making the 7,800 m² building an evolving project rather than a finished object.[11] More than that still, it illustrates the versatility and complementary agency of actors required to create large-scale urban ecosystems.

project NovaCity I group housing and SME zone **office** &bogdan and DDS+ **location** Anderlecht
see p. 265

Designing carbon cycles and relations

For future generations of architects, the imperative to integrate ecological consciousness into the decarbonization of our built environment cannot be overstated. Each historical energy epoch has influenced building techniques, norms and consumption standards.[12] Modernist and postmodernist habits have etched themselves into the fabric of our building culture with oversize concrete foundations, expansive glazed surfaces, toxic insulation materials, rare metals, unrecyclable façade panels and air-conditioned indoors.[13]

[11] Bruno Latour and Albena Yaneva, '"Give Me a Gun and I Will Make All Buildings Move": An ANT's View of Architecture', *Ardeth* 1 (2017): 103–11.

[12] Daniel Barber, *Modern Architecture and Climate: Design before Air Conditioning* (Princeton: University Press, 2020).

[13] Barnabas Calder, *Architecture: From Prehistory to Climate Emergency* (London: Pelican, 2022).

While other epochs offer inspiration through natural ventilation and materials serving as heat and cold storages, we must avoid the trap of relying solely on supposedly good material choices and small-scale solutions. This approach risks deferring responsibility to sustainability experts and engineers alone.

To truly embrace ecological awareness, we must transform our energy culture across all scales, from spatial habits and carbon footprints to urban densification. Adapting our spatial needs and moving away from the notion of comfort as a luxury commodity is crucial to addressing the social challenges associated with building for a net-zero future. By preserving the carbon heritage of our past, we can develop policy incentives for evidence-based reuse and retrofitting strategies. Changing our patterns of transport, commerce and industry will enable us to densify the use of space and time in our cities, thereby minimizing carbon emissions while fostering quality housing and work environments.

The four examples discussed above – Chapex, the transformation of the WTC into ZIN, the renovation of the Royale Belge, and the NovaCity I project – are not definitive solutions to the architectural challenges of a broken planet. They may not yet fully address the waste strategies needed for their own end-of-life scenarios. Instead, they serve as entry points to explore how to design ecosystems that link the interdependencies between human and non-human actors. These projects actively engage with new decarbonizing ecosystems, challenging conventional notions of sustainability and thereby opening up pathways for ecologies that matter at scale.

ESSAY   **Dennis Pohl**

ESSAY **Dennis Pohl**

ESSAY **Ecologies That Matter** 288

photography
01-02, Chapex, Charleroi – AjdvivgwA: TV architecten jan de vylder inge vinck – AgwA © Filip Dujardin
03, ZIN, Brussels – 51N4E with l'AUC and Jaspers-Eyers © Filip Dujardin
04, ZIN, Brussels – 51N4E with l'AUC and Jaspers-Eyers © Maxime Delvaux
05, Royale Belge, Watermaal-Bosvoorde – Bovenbouw Architectuur and Caruso St John Architects with DDS+ © Benjamin Wells
06-07, Royale Belge, Watermaal-Bosvoorde – Bovenbouw Architectuur and Caruso St John Architects with DDS+ © Illias Teirlinck
08-09, NovaCity I group housing and SME zone, Anderlecht – &bogdan and DDS+ © Delphine Mathy

murmuur architecten, Robbrecht en Daem architecten, Callebaut Architecten

PROJECT # City shop and archives, Sint-Niklaas

It is on the largest market square in Flanders that the city of Sint-Niklaas built a new wing to the neo-Gothic town hall. The ground floor houses a city shop with reception desk and counters. Large windows with warm wooden accents welcome citizens and merge seamlessly with the reception rooms of the city archive, which is housed in three concrete volumes resting on sturdy legs that vertically break through the double-height space. The floating volumes give a sense of security and demarcate underlying spaces, creating some distance and privacy without impeding accessibility.

Dirk Zoete's art integration adds colour and a sense of play to the welcoming atmosphere of the urban foyer. The interactivity of the artworks reinforces the harmony between the human scale of the visitor and the superhuman scale of the urban apparatus. A lift and staircase link the new wing to the neo-Gothic town hall, the public services on the ground floor to the archives, offices and a multipurpose hall on the floor above.

The construction of the new wing involved the pitting of the city block to provide a green courtyard. The wings of the complex were grafted onto this, restoring direct daylight to the workplaces.

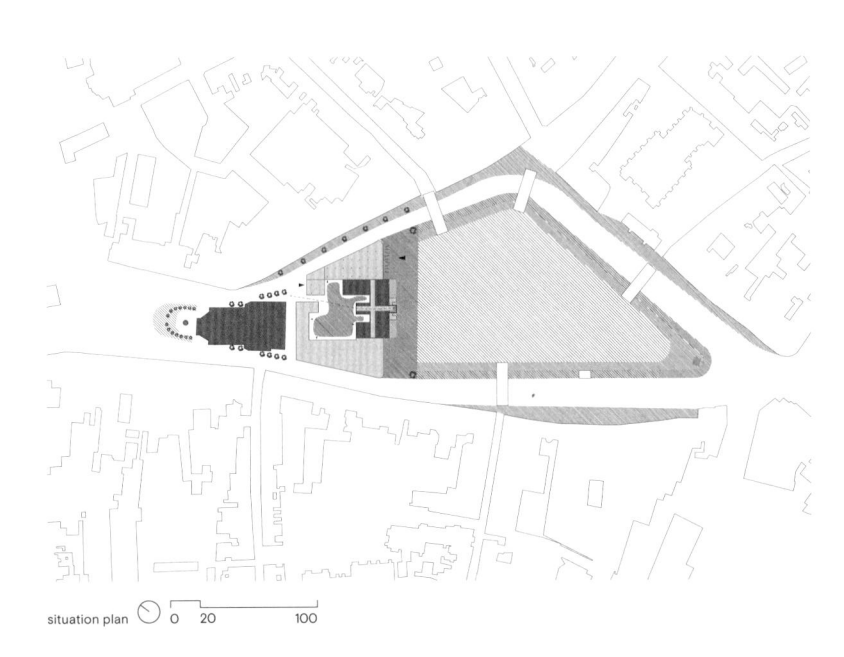

situation plan   0   20   100

PROJECT **City shop and archives** 291

The redevelopment of the block faced heritage challenges, but also focused on historical elements precisely such as the central underpass.

The new wing contrasts with the ceremonial character of the neo-Gothic town hall in the middle, and certainly also with the more banal wing on the left, which still houses many services. The new wing on the right has created a vibrant urban space, but behind the scenes of the administration, work is certainly not yet done. The overarching project illustrates the challenge of seeking harmony between old and new, prioritizing different project phases and caring for both citizens and civil servants.

PROJECT   murmuur architecten, Robbrecht en Daem architecten, Callebaut Architecten

PROJECT   murmuur architecten, Robbrecht en Daem architecten, Callebaut Architecten

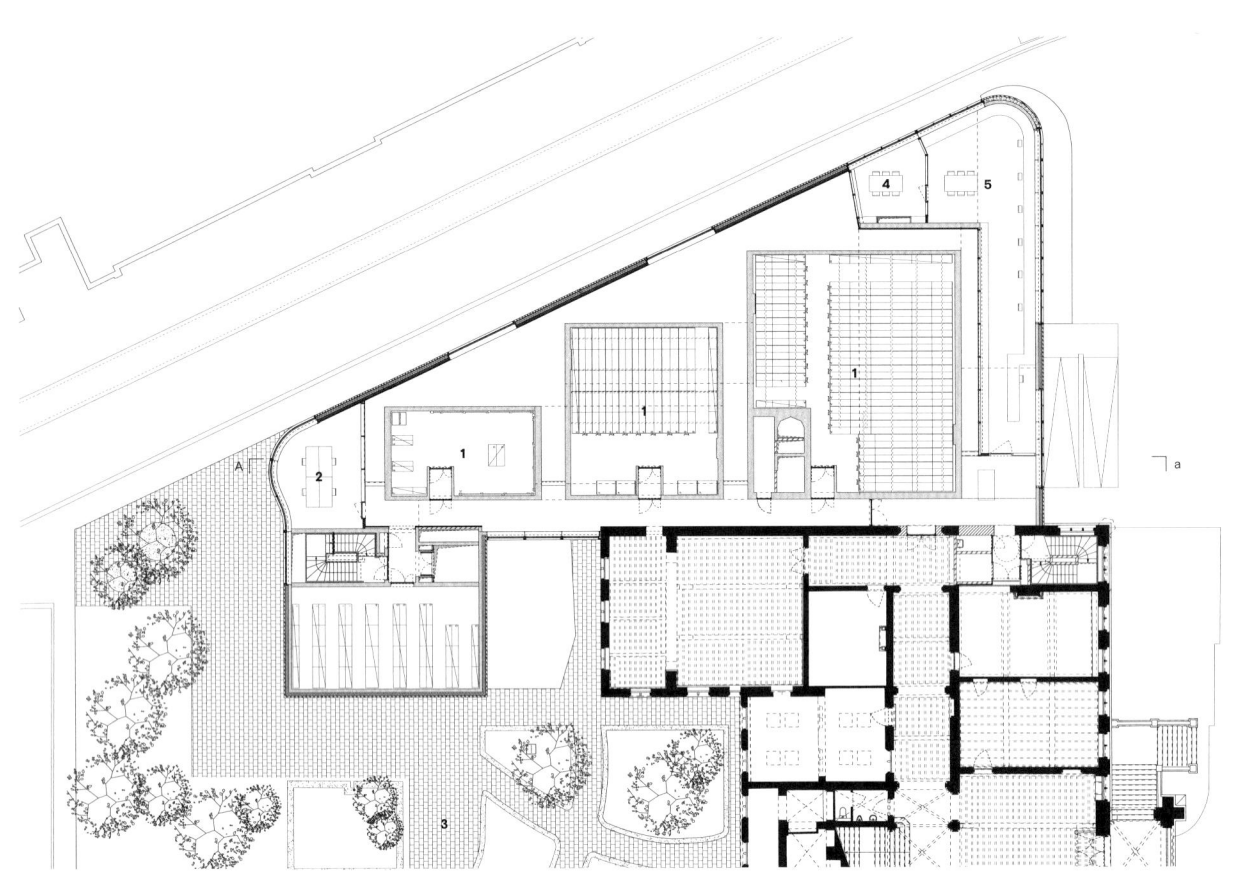

PROJECT **City shop and archives**

level 1
1 repository, **2** office space, **3** courtyard, **4** meeting room, **5** reading room

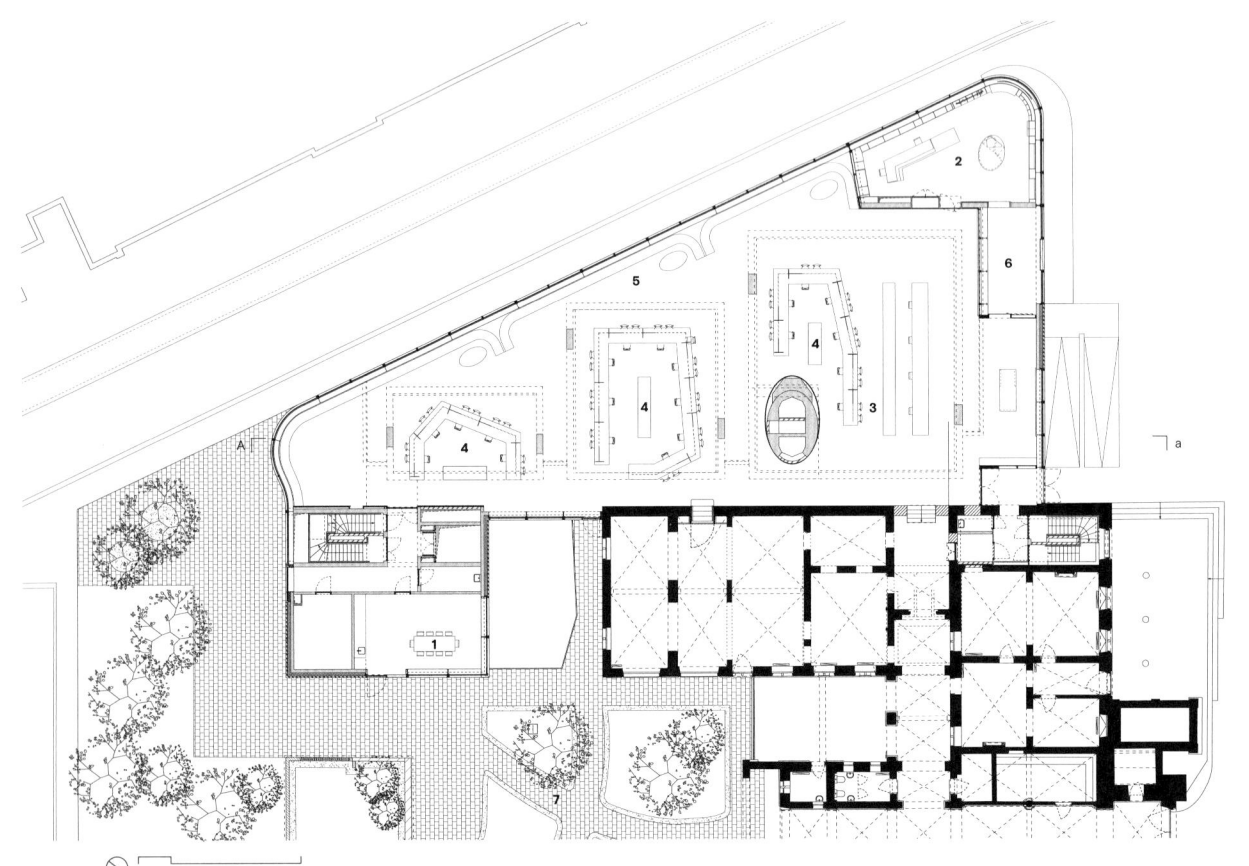

ground floor 0 2 10
1 staff room, **2** city shop, **3** reception counter, **4** counter, **5** waiting room, **6** vestibule, **7** courtyard

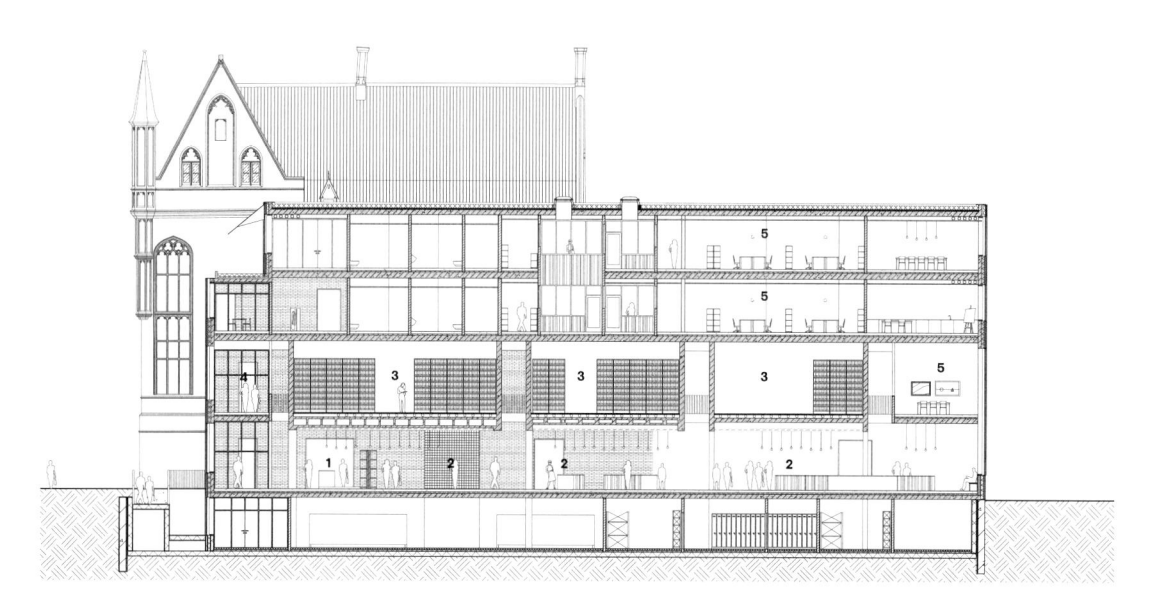

PROJECT **City shop and archives** 295

section Aa 0 2 10
1 reception counter, **2** counter, **3** repository, **4** reading room, **5** office space

project City shop and archives   **office** murmuur architecten with Robbrecht en Daem architecten and Callebaut Architecten   **design team** (murmuur) Emanuel Verstraete, Stephanie D'hondt, Sara Vandelanotte, Sharon Bauwens, Loes Lonneville, Aurike Quintelier, Hannah Bohez, Tinne Verwerft (Robbrecht en Daem) Tom De Moor, Luc Beckstedde, Lara Kinds, Valerie De Ketelaere, Paul Robbrecht, Hilde Daem en Johannes Robbrecht (Callebaut) Nicholas Matthijs, Wouter Callebaut
website www.murmuur.eu,   www.robbrechtendaem.com,   www.callebaut-architecten.be
address Grote Markt 1, 9100 Sint-Niklaas   **client** Stad Sint-Niklaas   **design** February 2016
completion June 2022   **surface area** 4,721 m²   **volume** 20,016 m³
total building cost €9,121,461 excl. VAT   **total building cost per m²** €1,932 excl. VAT
main contractor Strabag, Antwerp   **art integration** Dirk Zoete, Ghent
stability studies UTIL Struktuurstudies, Brussels   **engineering and EPB studies** HP Engineering, Oudenaarde
acoustics studies Daidalos Peutz, Leuven   **safety coordination** Ab-Solid, Ghent

text Sophie Bresseleers
photography 01, 07-09 © Farah Fervel   02-06 © Michiel De Cleene

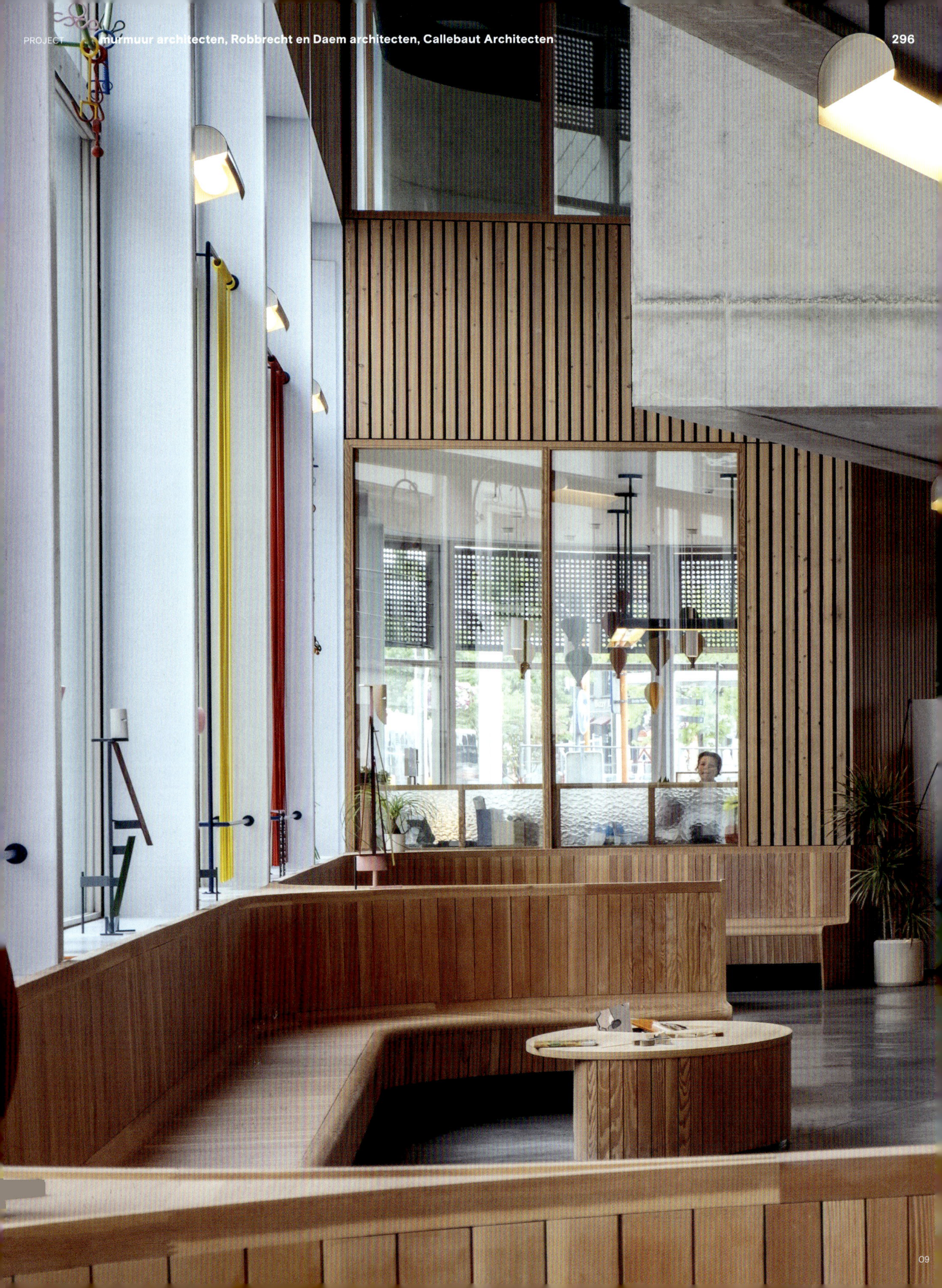

Bovenbouw Architectuur, Caruso St John Architects, DDS+

PROJECT
Royale Belge, Watermaal-Bosvoorde
298

The Royale Belge building, a listed monument in the Brussels municipality of Watermaal-Bosvoorde, exemplifies adaptive reuse. Originally constructed in the 1960s, its modernist design features large glass façades and innovative materials. Recently renovated by Bovenbouw Architectuur, Caruso St John Architects and DDS+, the building has been updated for contemporary use while preserving its iconic features, demonstrating how heritage buildings can be revitalized without compromising their historical significance.

Designed by architects René Stapels and Pierre Dufau between 1967 and 1970, the building served for nearly fifty years as the headquarters of one of Belgium's largest insurance companies. It boasts a striking façade of Corten steel and bronze-tinted glass, set against a park designed by Jean Delogne and Claude Rebold. The building includes a grand lobby, conference rooms, a restaurant and extensive parking facilities.

After the building was vacated in 2017, an investor reimagined it as a mixed-use development, including a hotel, restaurant, conference centre, fitness club and spa.

Awarded through an architectural competition organized in 2019 by the Brussels Bouwmeester Maître Architecte (BMA), the renovation aimed to modernize the building while retaining its original character. The entire steel structure of the curtain façade was preserved, and the glass panels were replaced to improve energy efficiency. Internally, the grand lobby with marble walls and brass accents was reconfigured to enhance functionality and accessibility.

A significant transformation involved creating a central, 21-metre-wide circular hall connecting the hotel, fitness club and offices. This three-storey-high space features sweeping

02

location plan 0 10 50

PROJECT **Royale Belge**

03

06

04

05

staircases and cross-shaped concrete supports that echo the original design. The removal of suspended ceilings exposed the robust concrete framework, and a new glazed ceiling allows daylight to reach the lower levels. The adaptive reuse of the Royale Belge building underscores the potential for conserving embodied energy, reducing the environmental impact, and preserving cultural heritage, setting a precedent for future sustainable architectural conservation practices.

PROJECT   Bovenbouw Architectuur, Caruso St John Architects, DDS+

PROJECT   Bovenbouw Architectuur, Caruso St John Architects, DDS+

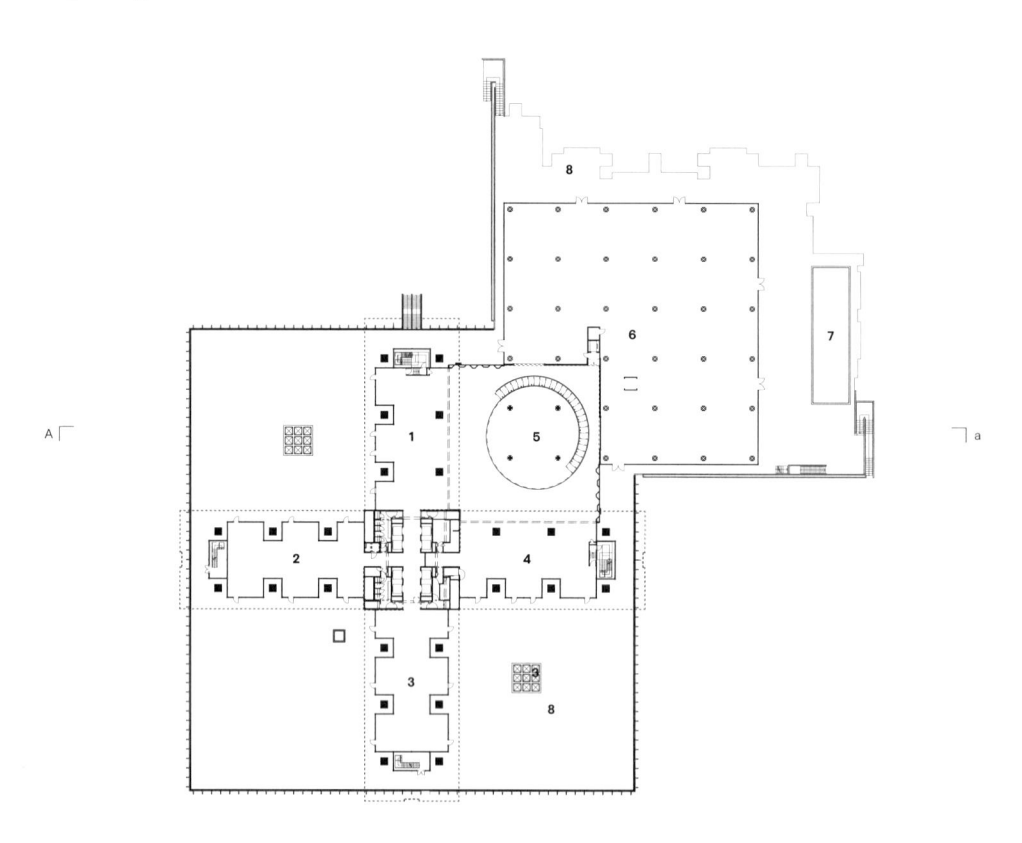

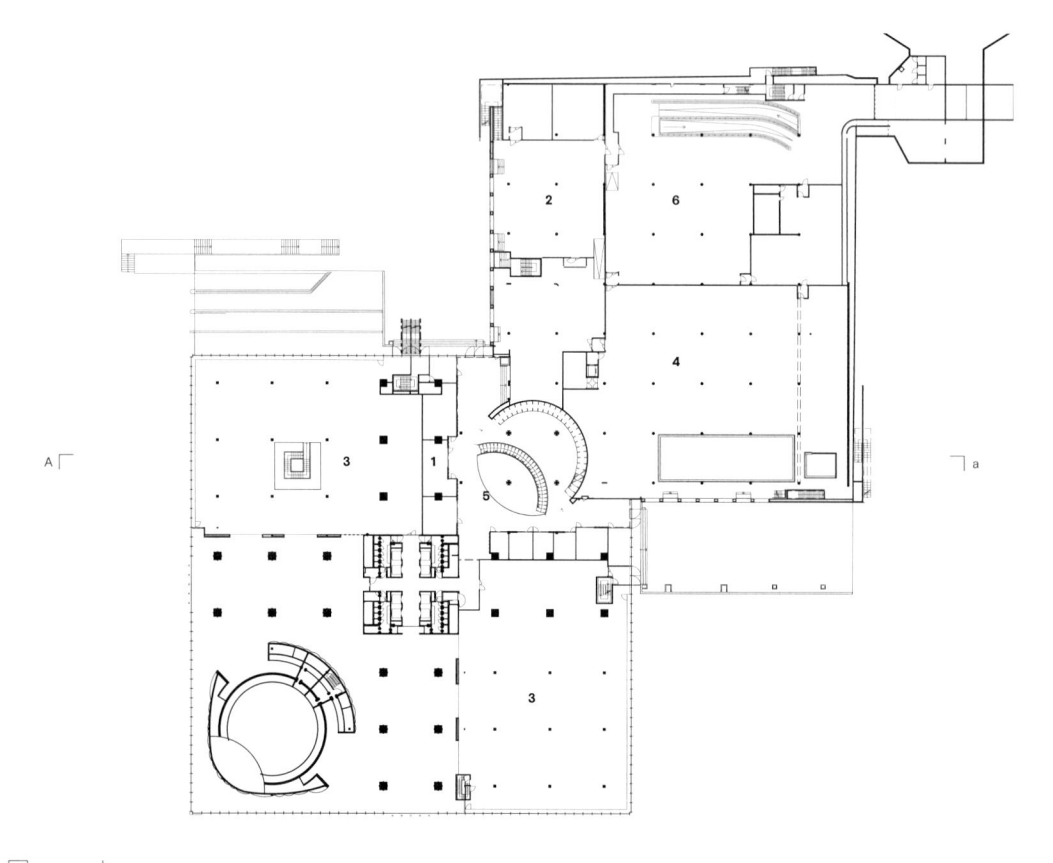

PROJECT **Royale Belge** 302

level 2
1 meeting room, **2** co-working, **3** restaurant, **4** bar, **5** atrium, **6** fitness, **7** pool, **8** terrace

level 1 0 2 10
1 meeting room, **2** conference room, **3** office space, **4** wellness, **5** atrium, **6** parking

PROJECT **Royale Belge** 303

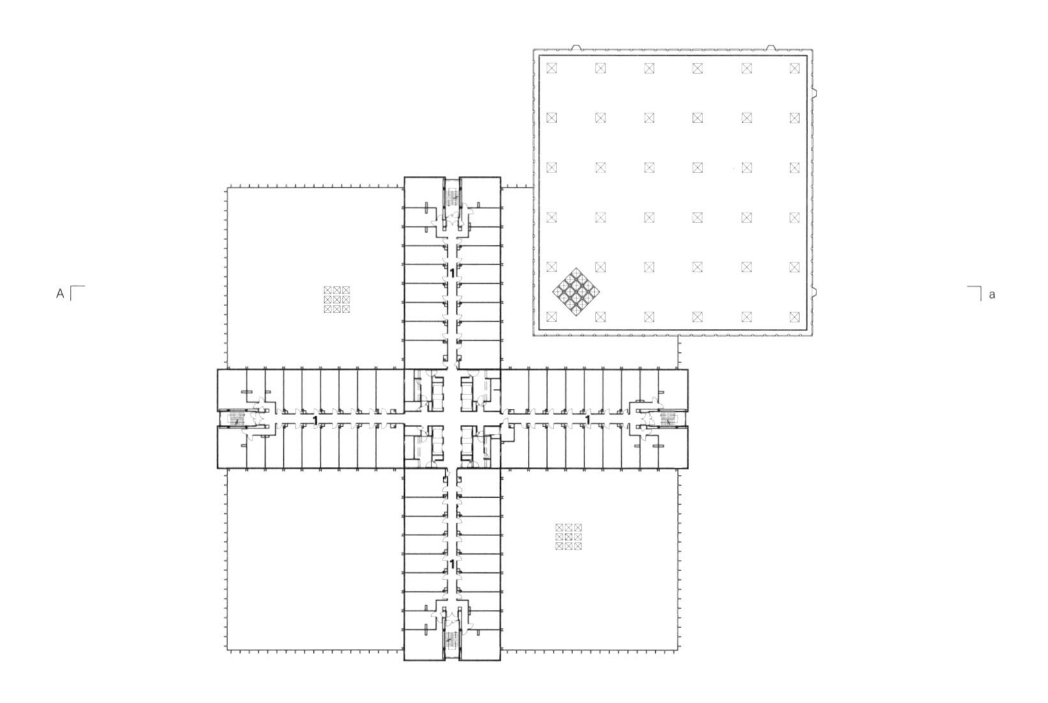

level 4
1 hotel

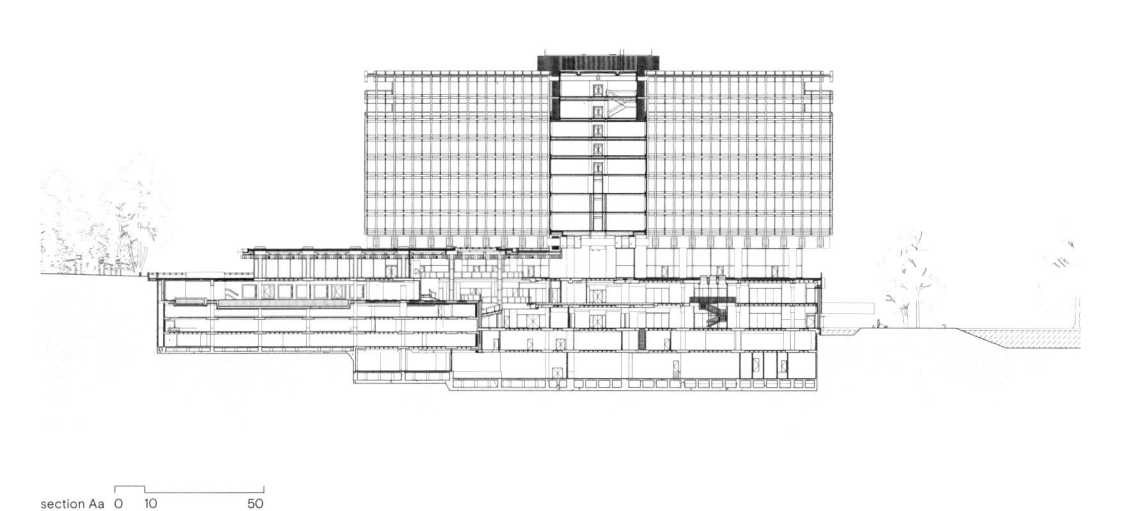

section Aa 0 10 50

text
Dennis Pohl
photography
01, 07–09 © Illias Teirlinck
02, 04–05 © Filip Dujardin
03, 06 © Stijn Bollaert

project Royale Belge   **office** Bovenbouw Architectuur and Caruso St John Architects with DDS+
design team Dirk Somers, Wim Boesten, Jakub Srnka, Joris Willems, Casper Pasveer, Alex Turner, Tobias Puhlmann, Sjoerd Bosch, David Schönen and Fabian De Vriendt
website www.bovenbouw.be,   www.carusostjohn.com,   www.dds.plus
address Vorstlaan 25, 1170 Watermaal-Bosvoorde   **client** Souverain 25 SA
design November 2019   **completion** August 2023   **surface area** 80,000 m²   **volume** 160,000 m³
total building cost €75,000,000 excl. VAT   **total building cost per m²** €940 excl. VAT
main contractor CIT Blaton, Brussels   **stability studies** Lemaire Ingénieurs, Brussels
engineering studies RVR Van Reeth Studiebureau, Kontich   **EPB studies** Bureau Bouwtechniek, Antwerp
acoustics studies Macobo-Stabo, Tessenderlo   **landscape design** Atelier EOLE Paysagistes, Watermaal-Bosvoorde   **safety coordination** VETO & Partners, Oosterzele

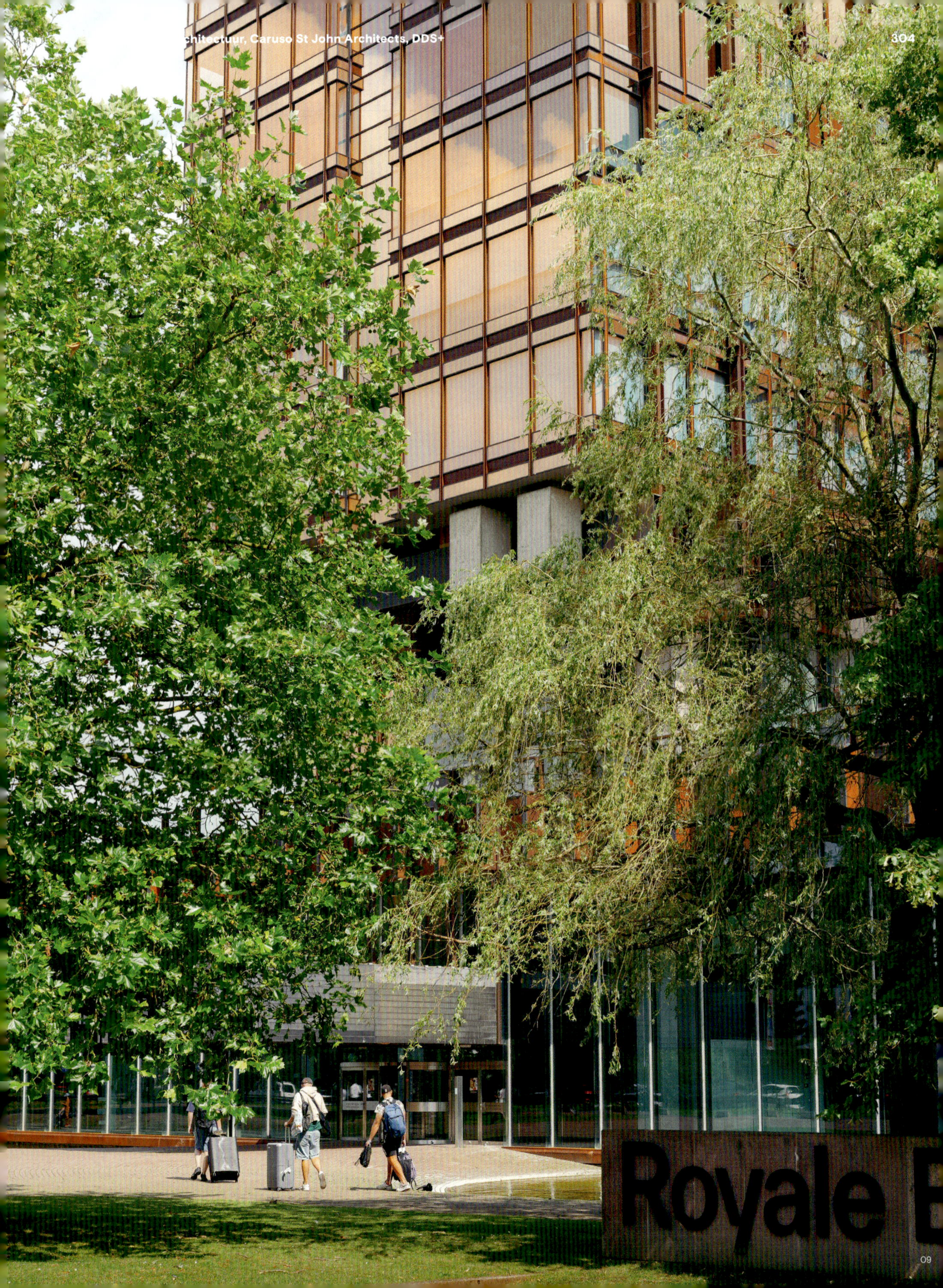
Royale

How Dare They?

Reflections on the Power(lessness) of Architecture and the Importance of Daring

Hülya Ertas

In the documentary/fiction *WTC A Love Story*,[1] there is a scene in which a politician, a developer and the Brussels Bouwmeester Maître Architecte (BMA) explain that they are not the ones with power. The BMA, Kristiaan Borret, identifies architects as the main actors from whom, together with users, 'concrete spatial solutions mostly come'. On the other hand, we keep hearing in architectural circles that many urban or regulatory decisions have already been made, that the programme and brief have already been determined, and that architects themselves have very little to contribute – and yet they stay in the process and try to deliver the best possible design within the given framework. Ultimately, it is as if no one claims responsibility over a built project: neither the owner nor the city, neither the developer nor the architect, neither the policymaker nor the mediator … As the list of actors involved in the decision-making process of the built environment grows longer, one would expect to have a better outcome. Sadly, however, this is not always the case.

The agency of architects and the limits of their responsibility have been discussed again and again since Alberti 'invented' the profession of architect in the fifteenth century. The source of today's ambiguity regarding the duties of the architect can be found there, according to Tim Anstey.[2] Alberti believed the architect would enjoy all the fame but would also be the one to blame if things went wrong. Being neither a mason nor a carpenter, the architect was not expected to perform or even appear in 'the theatre of building'. The responsibility for the poor application of details must lie with the craftspeople, while King Solomon – who today can be considered the equivalent of the client – should be praised for choosing the right architect to realize his ideals. By walking a thin line between claiming agency and refusing responsibility, the figure of the architect 'will turn increasingly to rhetoric both to do all that can be done to exercise influence without authority and to lay claim to a vicarious authority through which he or she can exercise their own judgement (and although this authority stems from outside themselves, architects will claim personal glory from the actions taken according to it)'.[3]

    Two acclaimed critics on the Flanders architecture scene recently wrote about the Beurs, the newly repurposed stock exchange building in the heart of Brussels. Both Pieter T'Jonck[4] and Marc Dubois[5] praised the intervention by Robbrecht en Daem architecten, Bureau d'Études en Architectures Urbaines (BEAU), and Popoff architectes, while regretting that the building was programmed by the city as a beer museum, a new tourist attraction. With their discourse, they rip the form of the building from its content: the architects did a great job, but the project brief was wrong. And yet one wonders whether 'elegant' brass gates and 'pretty and playful little brass "stock baskets"'[6] actually get their colours from the shiny golden colour of beer, or from the gilded ornaments of the original nineteenth-century building. Or whether, instead of the building being 'given back to the citizens', the public connections on the ground floor contribute to, perhaps even facilitate, the flow of tourists from the Grand-Place to Anspachlaan, the pedestrianized street lined with restaurants and shops.[7] Yet the question remains: Can architects provide the right answer to the wrong question? Where do their responsibilities lie? In fulfilling the requirements of the brief and delivering a high-quality spatial design only? Can the architects claim success by ▸

---

1 The documentary *WTC A Love Story* (2020) by Lietje Bauwens and Wouter De Raeve uses fiction to understand the decision-making mechanisms and the actors involved in and excluded from these processes during the transformation of the WTC Tower in the Northern Quarter of Brussels. A follow-up documentary by the same directors, *WTC A Never-Ending Love Story* (2023), focuses on local actors and the possibility of a unified social contract for the future of the neighbourhood.

2 Tim Anstey, 'The Ambiguities of *Disegno*', *The Journal of Architecture* 10, no. 3 (2005): 295–306.

3 Anstey, 'The Ambiguities'.

4 Pieter T'Jonck, 'Bruxelles chantait, Bruxelles bruxellait', *A+ Architecture in Belgium* 306 (January–February 2024): 20–24.

5 Marc Dubois, 'Van stedelijk fort tot publiek gebouw: Beurs van Brussel door Robbrecht en Daem', accessed 6 September 2024, harmtilman.nl/blog/van-stedelijk-fort-tot-publiek-gebouw-beurs-van-brussel-door-robbrecht-en-daem.

6 T'Jonck, 'Bruxelles chantait'.

7 Robbrecht en Daem architecten, 'BeursBourse, Brussels, Belgium', see robbrechtendaem.com/projects/beursbourse.

ESSAY Hülya Ertas

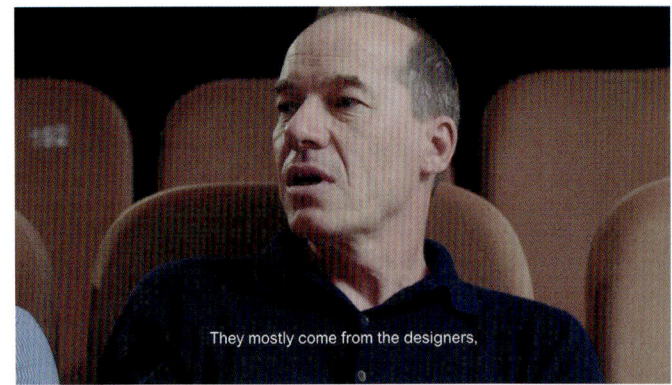

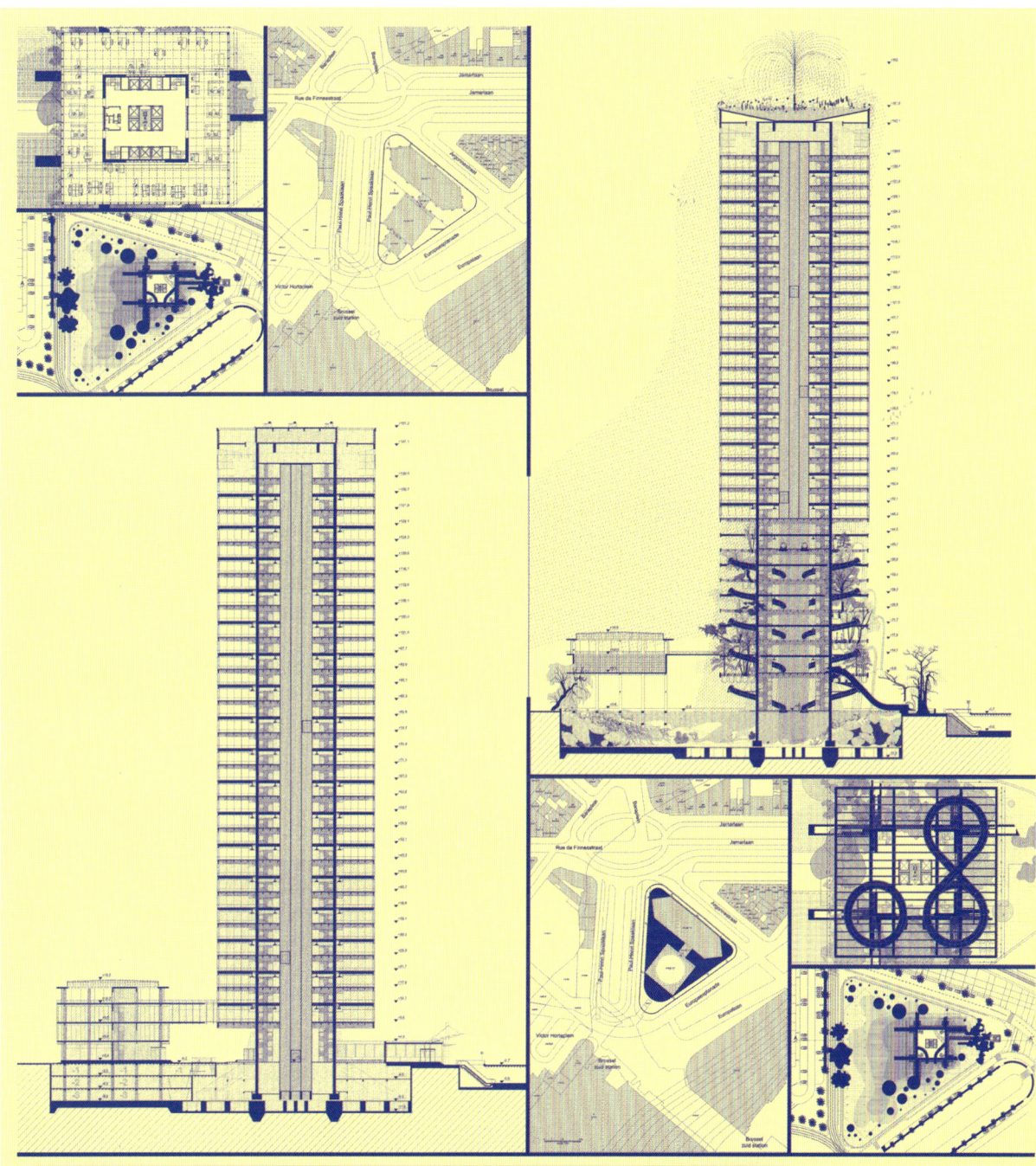

OCEANS PARK

AFBRAAK ZONDER HEROPBOUW EN WIJZIGING BODEMRELIËF

Afbraak zonder heropbouw en wijziging bodemreliëf

Locatie: 2-4 Avenue Paul-Henri Spaak, 1000 Brussel

Van zodra je uit het station Brussel-Zuid komt bots je op de Zuidertoren, een spiegelende glasgevel van 150 meter hoog, het hoogste kantoorgebouw van België. De Zuidertoren / La Tour du Midi werd voltooid in 1967 en wordt vandaag de dag vooral ingenomen door kantoren van de pensioendienst van de Federale Overheid, vandaar ook de bijnaam 'Pensioentoren'. Naast de anonieme toren staat een viertal kleiner volume dat de ingang vormt, en een veelhoekig gebouw met vier bouwlagen. Deze wordt net de toren verbonden door een privaat loopbrug op hoogte. Hoewel het geheel opgeteld tot een indrukwekkende 375.000 m² nuttig volume, wordt de oppervlakte van de Zuidertoren onderbenut en schrijft zich zo in een Brusselse trend waar een veelvoud van kantoorgebouwen en industriële panden onderbenut worden of leegstaan.

OCEANS PARK stelt voor de overmaat van ruimte te supprimeren en en te bouwen tot een natuurlijke, verwilderde bron van verkoeling voor de stad Brussel en zijn inwoners. De gedeeltelijke leegstand en het water hebben de potentie voor een waterpark. OCEANS PARK is het grootste natuurlijke waterpark van Europa. De oude funderingen worden omringd door een wonderlijk onderwaterbos, bevolkt door scholen zoetwatervissen, wieren en andere condities. De bovenste verdiepingen blijven in gebruik door de pensioendienst. Wie naar de Zuidertoren komt de te werken staat in werkpak naast de badgast in zwembroek in de lift.

De vloeren en gevels van de onderste 10 verdiepingen worden gestript en op de naakte schoonheid van de bijzondere structuur van de toren. Met de billen bloot wordt de toren op de structuur gestoeld en plaats te maken voor een omvangrijke en natuurlijke wereld. De bomen en planten zijn aangestuit aan de natte condities.

De gebouwen die het massaalst bezetten worden samen met de ondergrondse verdiepen in op de structuur gestoeld en plaats te maken voor een omvangrijke en natuurlijke wereld. De bomen en planten zijn aangestuit aan de natte condities. De bovenste verdiepingen blijven in gebruik door de pensioendienst. Vlak boven de waterspiegel komt men via een pad van roostering de monumentale inkomhal binnen. Links slapen kinderen onder een waterval, rechts slapen de schildpadden in de zon. Boven de bezoekers begint een hangende tuin van 40 meter hoog.

De kern van de toren wordt ontsloten van overbodige dienstruimtes. Zes glazen liften staan centraal in de toren, en brengen badgasten of kantoorui samen. Een passarelle leidt naar het verhoogde Olympische zwembad. Vanaf deze hoogte start een druipende hangende tuin de ontmantelde structuur hangen grote jute zakken, gevuld met allerhande klim- en hangplanten. Op het dak van de toren wordt een waterbak geïnstalleerd dat zorgt voor actieve koeling van de kantoren. Een fontein spuit het opgepompte water de lucht in, waterdruppels verstuiven de omgevende verharding. Het vallende water ligt doorheen de plantzakken en de kanaaltjes een zuiverende weg af naar de vijver beneden. Op de betonnen structuur vormen zich stalactieten en stalagmieten. Het geheel voelt aan als een vervaren grot met uitzicht op Brussel, gehuld in groen en constant gedruip.

Bovenaan het hangende park wacht de keuze verder te stijgen of terug af te dalen. Wie hogerop naar kantoor wil gaan identificeert zich langs toegangspoortes. De daler start voor het grootste spektakel. Een cirkelende waterglijbaan, de hoogte ter wereld, neemt hem terug helemaal mee naar beneden, recht naar de natuurlijker met spelende kinderen en zonnende schildpadden.

Welk de wijkende en vandaag realiseert anders om te gaan met kwalitatieve open en benut leegstaande volumes voorgangen. De ongebruikte potentie zit al in de bestaande structuur vergaderde leegstand zit al in ogen bijkomende toename brouwijzende reverzien.

- De context en de bestaande toestand.
- Functionele inspaarbaarheid.
- De ingenieuze structuur A. Lipski wordt als erfgoedwaarde behouden.
- Impact op ontharding.
- De ontwikkeling van een bijzonder ecosysteem met een indrukwekkende biomassa.
- Een sloop- en vegetatiewijziging wordt aangevraagd.
- Het water is een circulair systeem van koeling en verkoeling en geeft kansen aan een bijzonder ecosysteem gebruiksgoed en veiligheid in het hart van de stad.

8 Christophe Van Gerrewey, 'An Architecture of Distraction', *OASE* 81 (2010): 111–16.

9 See Douglas Spencer, *The Architecture of Neoliberalism* (London: Bloomsbury, 2016); Space Caviar, ed., *Non-Extractive Architecture*, Vol. 1, *On Designing Without Depletion* (London: Sternberg Press, 2021); Dana Cuff, *Architectures of Spatial Justice* (Cambridge, MA: MIT Press, 2023).

10 Gabriela Vasilescu, 'Return of the Same with a Difference: A Brief History of Mediocrity from Antiquity to Modernity', *Word and Text: A Journal of Literary Studies and Linguistics* 3, no. 1 (June 2013): 53–64.

facilitating public access to the Beurs while the overall design is the outcome of a touristification plan? Christophe Van Gerrewey's argument for Museum aan de Stroom (MAS) in Antwerp also holds for the Beurs in Brussels: 'It simply makes this unavoidable situation – to which it owes everything, of course – into a visible reality.'[8]

It has been proven time and again how architectural production is complicit in socioeconomic motivations and political projects, how it reflects and/or amplifies social injustices, natural extraction and suppression.[9] And yet, what can architects do with this information? The main ethical dilemma seems to rest in this unknown. The architect as the driver of change for a better world and the heroic stance of the genius fell from grace along with the promises of modernism. What was left in the post-political turn was the architect as service provider. Waving the white flag to the existing world order, many architects moved along the market line, which was now supposed to be freer. The market needed maximum profit, which in turn proved not so efficient with regard to the recent, ongoing crises (climate, migration, social injustice, etc.). For a sustainable future, every actor acknowledges today that something has to change, yet steering the big ship of business towards that future seems difficult if not impossible. In this environment, the challenge for architects today is to reposition themselves in a society facing many challenges. Of course, all eras have faced their own challenges – in that regard, today is not so specific – yet the struggle to self-define their political stance, to claim responsibility for the built environment are some of the particularities that architects are searching for today.

What is particular about the agency of architects in Brussels and Flanders today? Despite all the collaborative processes in place that involve quality chambers, government architects, consultants, heritage agencies, sustainability managers and more, the outcome is still not guaranteed to be outstanding. We are still witnessing mediocre architectural production, not bad in terms of spatial quality and material choices nor in terms of context. But not good either. When none of the actors involved dares to make a statement or take up a position, we experience 'the return of the same with a difference'.[10] It is at the same time an expression of indifference to the existing challenges. Mediocrity can also be related to the inertia of people who see themselves individually as part of society but who refuse to take part in its formation. On the other hand, a daring move can break the limits of mediocrity. It is with unexpected behaviour, the risky move, that a change in rhetoric or in action can happen.

In their *Bouwaanvraag* (Building application) projects, Laura Muyldermans, LDSRa and Olivier Goethals mention 'the common good' as their client. Their research on public spaces has resulted in a series of unsolicited projects. This is the moment when architects define the issue, make up their own briefs and come up with a design that meets their fabricated briefs. It is a fictive, speculative design that takes its motivation seriously. As building applications, these projects are not only a critical reflection on our approach to public space but also legal documents submitted to the urban planning departments of Brussels and Ghent. Through this act, they trigger our imaginations as to what can happen in vacant buildings or in the royal gardens. Moreover, they push the boundaries of possibilities in these planning agencies. In this type of practice, the limits of today's city-making practice, its regulations and emphasis on property and ownership are left aside. In doing so, the architects dream of a different materialization of the culture of co-living. Here, it is the programme that activates spatial configurations. And they offer simple functions: a beech forest in the Urbis complex which is used as a shopping centre in Ghent today, an open-air natural swimming pool and the world's highest water slide at the first ten floors of the South Tower in Brussels, and a promenade across six unique biotopes in the royal gardens. Urbis Beech

Forest, Oceans Park and Safari Royal are not merely provocations, they dare to remind us how our public spaces lack imagination and thus fail to become spaces of collective use and action. The architects propose the unproposable, and in doing so they expand the 'distribution of the sensible'.[11] Our culture is shaped by the limits of the sensible, yet what is defined as sensible is where the change happens. What is deemed impossible today might become the norm in the near or far future, as the evolution of culture over the centuries shows. By generating this tension between now and tomorrow, and by triggering our imagination for a divergent use of spaces for the common good, these projects invite us to rethink our culture of city-making.

 Yet the daring act of the architect does not always have to follow a lonely path. In some cases, the stars can align. Once in a while, societal needs, political atmosphere, spatial configuration and management of the space can line up. Veldegem service centre by Havana architectuur (see p. 225) is one of these exceptions, but certainly no accident. The Public Centre for Social Welfare (OCMW) in Zedelgem issued an open call in 2013 with a programme for a community centre and homes for people over 65. The brief was rooted in their insightful reading of the demographic change in the small town of Veldegem, West Flanders. The population is growing older and their existing conventional living arrangements, namely detached villas, were not practical for their age and new daily routines: they were too big, required the use of cars to reach shops and services, included stairs, etc. At the same time, the town, with its single axis, lacked quality public space, free from cars. Thus, the thoughtful brief of the city brought together a community centre and housing. In a village environment in which people are very much used to living in their detached houses, drawing up a brief for a denser style of living is a bold ambition. At the end of the decade-long project process, the housing units were sold without specific limits, yet still they are mostly bought and inhabited by elders. Havana's plan locates these homes at the two ends of the courtyard, as living spaces hovering over the social ones. At the centre of the project, the courtyard is put forward as a new public space, devoid of cars, connecting the main axis of the town to the back, towards the new developments – a free space for organizing activities, passing through or hanging out.

 The importance of this diamond-shaped courtyard is accentuated with the use scenario. Across the church square (which rather looks like a car park), people can be seen, behind a grandiose glass façade, sitting around large tables, reading their newspapers and exchanging with others at the table. To enter the café, however, you have to go through the courtyard. First, you need to discover this new public space, then greet the receptionists of the municipality and finally enter the café. The spatial design enriches social interaction on the level of both plan and visual connection. This is where architects have dared not only to make this generous space for the public, but also to emphasize its presence. The community centre coordinator tells us that she spent the past couple of days delivering brochures to the nearby, newly completed housing block, inviting residents over for a mug of soup in the café. Around the diamond-shaped courtyard, a series of rooms of varying sizes are spread out: a music class, workshop rooms (either rented out or used by the municipality services, for example to teach the elderly how to use messaging applications on smartphones), meeting rooms, municipal offices, a reception hall, a proxy library (you can order books from the main library to be delivered to you here). Neither shops nor services so as not to compete with the town's existing social structure, but rooms in which to gather and get to know each other. The hard surface of the courtyard is due to the parking space underground, yet today some trees in pots and a pétanque court together with some street furniture break the feeling of harshness. From the open call to its completion, the project took almost a decade. Along with the insightful architectural design, the visionary brief and skilful management of the centre,

11 Jacques Rancière, 'The Aesthetic Revolution and Its Outcomes', *New Left Review* 14 (March–April 2002): 133–51.

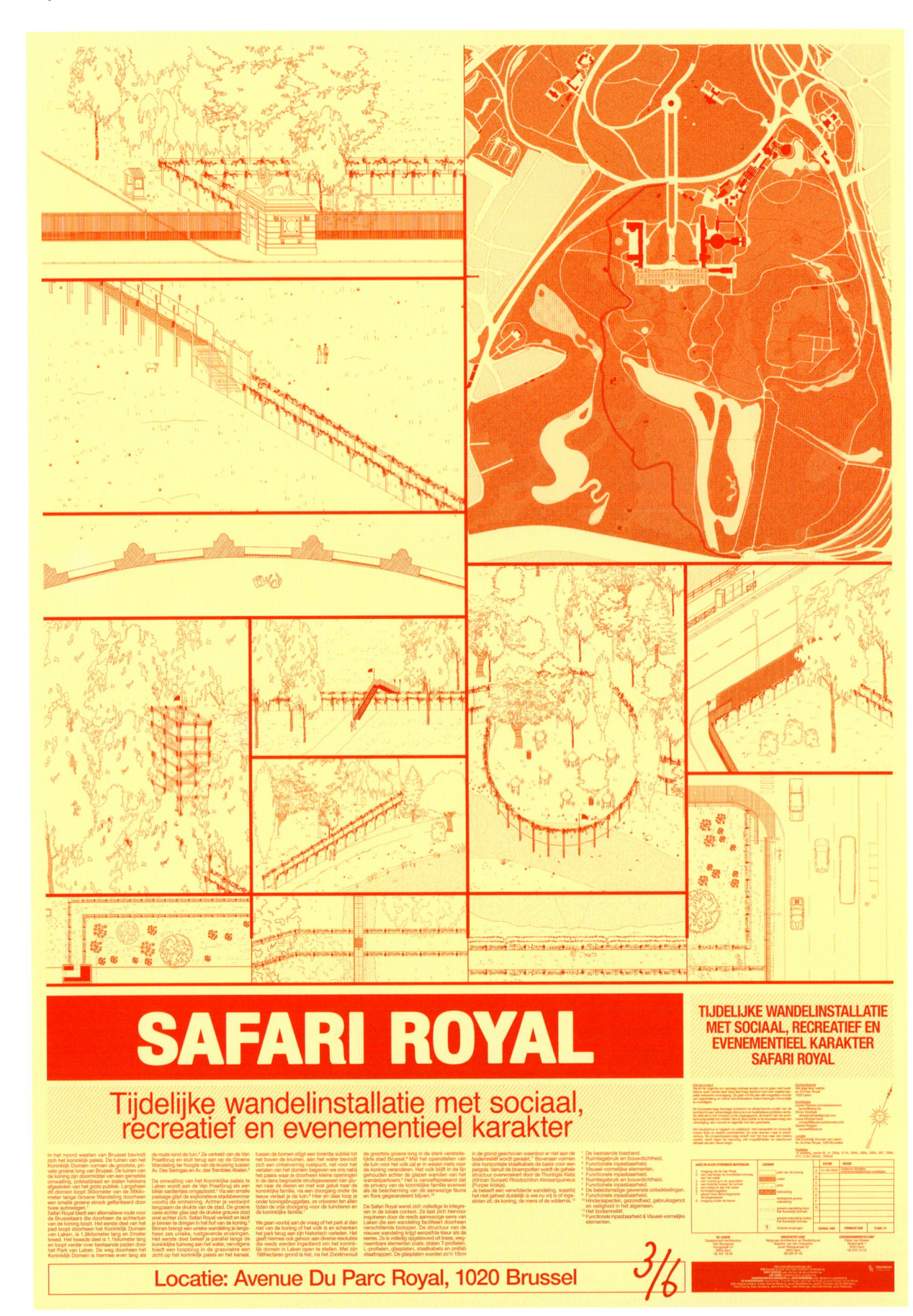

ESSAY   Hülya Ertas

SAFARI ROYAL
Tijdelijke wandelinstallatie met sociaal, recreatief en evenementieel karakter

Locatie: Avenue Du Parc Royal, 1020 Brussel

URBIS BEUKENBOS
Sloop– en Vegetatiewijziging

Locatie: Woodrow Wilsonplein 4, 9000 Gent

12   Byung-Chul Han, *What Is Power?* (Medford, MA: Polity, 2018), 2.
13   Hannah Arendt, *The Human Condition* (New York: Doubleday Anchor Books, 1959), 157–58.

it is the persistence of all the actors involved that made this project what it is. Here the daring act lies mostly in this persistence, in the city's insistence on a new type of social life, the architects' spatial scenario to welcome people in the courtyard, and the board's implementation of these in daily use.

To dare is to manifest power. It is with that risky move that one tries to convince others of what they are capable. 'Power is thus a phenomenon pertaining to form. How an action is motivated is crucial. Not "I have to anyhow" but "I want to" expresses the presence of a superior power.'[12] When talking about architecture gaining more ground, especially in decision-making processes, we cannot ignore its preconditions for power. With its uncanny and hazy presence, agency in architecture still occupies us. It manifests itself in various forms: in buildings, research projects, reflective practices while we seek the daring actor behind them. We long for the bold, uncompromising decisions that show us other possibilities for designing our built environment. We want to be happily surprised by the unexpected. 'The fact that man is capable of action means that the unexpected can be expected of him, that he is able to perform what is infinitely improbable.'[13]

photography
01, stills from *WTC A Love Story* (2020), by Lietje Bauwens and Wouter De Raeve, production company Video Power
02–04, *Bouwaanvraag* (Building application) – Laura Muyldermans, LDSRa and Olivier Goethals

Biographies

Sofie De Caigny is a curator, writer and lecturer. She teaches Architectural Criticism and Architectural Developments at the University of Antwerp and Cultural Studies at Hasselt University. In 2024 she was made an Honorary Fellow of RIBA. She chairs the Committee on Environmental Quality and Cultural Heritage of the city of Rotterdam. She was secretary general of ICAM (International Confederation of Architectural Museums) from 2014 to 2022 and director of the Flanders Architecture Institute from 2018 to 2024. In the latter capacity, she curated several exhibitions and published on contemporary architecture and architectural heritage in Flanders and Brussels. In 2021 she commissioned *Composite Presence*, the Belgian contribution to the Venice Architecture Biennale.

Barbara De Coninck is a Belgian author, independent curator and friend of artists. She currently oversees publications at the Flanders Architecture Institute. She publishes frequently on the visual arts and is a contributor to the *Pompidou* programme on the classical radio station Klara (VRT). Her texts have been published by Gallimard, Mercatorfonds, SKIRA, Silvana Editoriale and Templon, among others. She is an editorial board member of the Brussels art magazine *GLEAN*. Barbara De Coninck is also a passionate birdwatcher.

Kimberley Dhollander is one half of the Evenbeeld duo, who specialize in architectural, interior and documentary photography. She discovered her passion for photography during her studies, when she learned to capture moments in an authentic and nuanced way. She works for cultural institutions and editorial clients, applying her creative vision. In her free time, she enjoys photographing colourful and vibrant street scenes during her walks. Her work is a harmonious mix of professional assignments and personal discoveries, constantly enriching and inspiring her creative journey.

Hülya Ertas is the coordinator of exhibitions and publications at the Flanders Architecture Institute. She graduated from Istanbul Technical University (Department of Architecture) in 2005, completing her master's degree in architecture at the same school in 2011. From 2004 to 2020 she worked at the monthly *XXI Architecture and Design Magazine*, becoming its editor-in-chief in 2013. She completed her PhD at the KU Leuven Faculty of Architecture, Sint-Lucas Brussels Campus in 2024. She curates exhibitions, edits books, writes articles and does research. Her main focus is on architecture's societal and political role and the critical reading of socio-spatial practices.

Franco-Burundian photographer **Farah Fervel** was first drawn to street photography. While studying architecture, she developed an interest in and eventually studied architectural photography. Today, she mixes the two styles to capture interactions between people and the built environment. Her photographs place people and their appropriation of space on an equal footing with materiality, light and spatial elements. This approach allows her to create images that are not only visually appealing, but also reflect architecture's primary mission of creating living spaces.

Graphic designers Arthur Haegeman and Jonas Temmerman started collaborating as **atelier Haegeman Temmerman** in 2019. Arthur graduated from KASK & Conservatorium in Ghent in 2014 and Jonas from Sint-Lucas Ghent in 2011. In their practice, design runs parallel to production. Through a systematic approach, choices are made based on medium, content and necessity. They focus on both analogue and digital media, mainly in the field of art and architecture. Alongside their atelier, they are both involved at KASK & Conservatorium in Ghent, where Jonas works as a designer and Arthur teaches and runs the print workshop in the Graphic Design department.

Klaske Havik is Professor of Methods of Analysis and Imagination at Delft University of Technology and Chair of the European COST Research Network Writing Urban Places. Her work relates architectural and urban questions such as the use, experience and imagination of place to literary language. Her publications include *Urban Literacy: Reading and Writing Architecture* (2014). She initiated both the platform Writingplace, with which she published the volume *Writingplace: Investigations in Architecture and Literature* (2016), and the *Writingplace Journal for Architecture and Literature*. Earlier, she was editor of *OASE* and the Dutch architectural review *de Architect*. Havik's literary work has appeared in Dutch literary magazines. Recently her collection *Way and Further* (2021) was released in English by RightAngle Publishing.

Petrus Kemme obtained a master's degree in engineering science and architecture from Ghent University. He worked at the Copyright Art and Architecture Bookshop in Ghent before becoming a project manager for publications, lectures and symposia at the Flanders Architecture Institute in 2018. He has since been the project coordinator and editor of the *Flanders Architectural Review*. He is also the curator of *Table Setting*, an exhibition series for young architects on the square in front of De Singel.

Patrick Lennon has been a full-time freelance translator from Dutch and French to English and English copy editor since 2010. He specializes in arts and culture, particularly architecture, visual arts, music, dance, literature and performing arts. He lives in Brussels and works with artists, publishers and institutions.

Delphine Mathy is a Brussels photographer who graduated from the École Supérieure des Arts de l'Image 'Le 75'. She began her career by exploring various fields, including stage set and fashion photography. Today, she devotes most of her time to architectural photography and documentary reportage. She works with architecture offices in Belgium and France, covering private and public projects from site to finished work. She also leads workshops at photography and architecture schools. Delphine has developed a long-term collaboration with the Zinneke organization, where she has captured the highlights of their projects and events. At the same time, she has carried out extensive photographic work documenting the transformation of their headquarters, which have undergone major renovation work in recent years. Her work reflects a particular sensitivity to urban spaces and human interaction, and is marked by a unique narrative depth.

Saar Meganck combines in a hybrid way three trajectories within the architectural field. Together with David Dhooge, she heads the team Dhooge & Meganck architecten. In this architecture practice, the focus is on the field of tension between the unknown and the formulation of a design response by challenging the design process and thought pattern without remaining in the world of ideas. The portfolio highlights a diversity of projects: the repurposing of churches and a mustard factory, new interventions on a monumental castle, housing, a theatre auditorium, etc. Their work has been exhibited in Flanders and abroad (including the Lisbon Architecture Triennale, the Deutsches Architekturmuseum Frankfurt, the Venice Architecture Biennale 2021 and M KHA Antwerp). She is also Head of Theory at the Architectuur Academie Maastricht (AAM), where she teaches and, together with students and lecturers, makes up a 'research cell'. She has started a PhD at the AAM and KU Leuven on the topic 'The animated wall: On materiality, patina, texture and chroma composition in architecture'. This research draws on the archives of Wim van Hooff (polychromer, teacher, painter and colour adviser, namely within the Bossche School of architects).

Carlo Menon is an architect and researcher in history and theory, with degrees from La Cambre, Brussels (bachelor's, 2006) and The Bartlett, London (master's, 2013, and PhD, 2023). His collaborative practice, mostly with partner Sophie Dars, interweaves architectural thinking with publications (frequently), exhibitions (occasionally) and education (continuously). In particular he has developed writing and editorial skills, his outputs appearing mostly in the magazine *Accattone*, which Dars and Menon co-founded. He currently teaches architectural design at the La Cambre Horta Faculty of Architecture (ULB Brussels) and representation in the MA Civic Design (PBSA Düsseldorf).

Nick Moons is a photographer who walks the path between documentary and conceptual art, looking through an autobiographical lens. His work is not only a personal representation of the world around him, but also a reflection on his own experiences and memories. Impermanence and death are among the recurrent themes in Nick's work. And yet he imbues his photographs with a playful sense of humour and often leaves viewers with an uneasy feeling. Nick invites viewers to join him on a journey of self-discovery and introspection. He looks for beauty in everyday absurdity and tries to find satisfaction in life's challenges.

Architect and urban planner **Els Nulens** trained in Antwerp and Barcelona. In 2013 she founded Blauwdruk Stedenbouw. With her firm, she has been involved in various urban and rural densification and renewal projects. Between 2014 and 2019, she sat on and chaired the Winvorm Quality Chamber. Since 2018, she has chaired the Mechelen Quality Chamber and since 2020 the Antwerp Integral Quality Chamber. She has been teaching at the architecture school in Antwerp since 2020. Over the course of her twenty-six-year career, she has sat on many sides of the table. This overlap bolstered her expertise with regard to design practice in architecture, urban planning, landscape and spatial planning policy as well as public commissioning. Over the years, her interest has explicitly broadened from buildings *an sich* and the public domain to the interplay of buildings, open space and infrastructure.

Evelien Pieters is the initiator of PAF (Platform for Architecture & Feminism), with which she is working towards a community for a more equal and just architecture practice. She trained as an architectural engineer at Eindhoven University of Technology and took a course in cultural management at the Management School of the University of Antwerp. After her studies, she founded Buro Evelien Pieters in 2007, a practice for researching, editing and coordinating projects on architecture (culture) and urban development. Evelien coordinates, moderates, writes and advises. In doing so, she combines knowledge of the Dutch and Flemish architecture sectors. From her practice in Antwerp, she works for clients in the Netherlands and Belgium, such as the Flanders Architecture Institute, the Netherlands Architecture Institute, *de Architect, A+ Architecture in Belgium*, the Province of Antwerp and VITO. From 2013 to 2023 Evelien was business manager and project manager at AR-TUR. She is an assessor in grant committees for the Flemish Arts Decree and the Creative Industries Fund NL. ▶

Dennis Pohl is the director of the Flanders Architecture Institute. As a postdoctoral researcher, he was a member of the Design, Data and Society group at Delft University of Technology (TU Delft) and worked as a research coordinator at The New Open. He frequently publishes on the relations between energy, politics and architecture in the post-war era. His recent book *Building Carbon Europe* (Sternberg Press, 2023) analyses how architectural design influenced political planning in post-war Europe. Dennis was a research fellow at the DFG research group 'Knowledge in the Arts' at the Berlin University of the Arts (2015–18) and a DAAD Fellow at the Graduate School of Architecture, Planning and Preservation at Columbia University in New York (2018). He also received a fellowship for the LOEWE project 'Architectures of Order' at Goethe University Frankfurt (2022).

Eva Pot studied art history at Ghent University. After her studies, she worked for the nomadic and cultural platform Gouvernement in Ghent. Since 2019, she has been working as a production manager at the Flanders Architecture Institute. Additionally, Eva is an avid home baker and runner.

Maxime Schouppe studied Romance philology at Ghent University and journalism at the École supérieure de journalisme de Lille. His journalistic career path began in the Indian Ocean and continued at the The Hague office of Agence France Presse. Later, he was a communications adviser for ING Group in Amsterdam and an information officer at the International Court of Human Rights in The Hague. For over a decade now, he has been active in Brussels as a copywriter and translator for the cultural sector. He previously collaborated on the *Flanders Architectural Review N°15* (2022) and on the reissue of *Juliaan Lampens 1950–1991* (2020).

Helen Simpson studied ancient history and Egyptology at University College London before completing a master's degree in museum studies at the University of Leicester. She worked in the UK as a museum registrar before specializing in the organization of large-scale exhibitions, including for the Hayward Gallery in London. After moving to Belgium in 1994, she worked for the Museum of Fine Arts Ghent before embarking on a freelance career as a translator and editor in 2012.

Vjera Sleutel currently works as an architect-researcher-artist. In 2017 she obtained her master's in architecture from KU Leuven, Faculty of Architecture, Ghent. Since then, she has gained extensive experience as a researcher at BAVO within diverse projects on healthcare architecture, especially mental healthcare. She has worked at several architecture firms. She also developed her own art practice with VROOMM.collectif. She has collaborated on several publications, including *Unless Ever People* (VAi, 2018), *Architectural Culture in Flanders* (VAi, 2019) and *Living in Monnikenheide: Care, Inclusion and Architecture* (VAi, 2023). She writes for various platforms, including *Psyche* and *Archined*. Since 2021 she has acted as a Lab-O teaching assistant at the KU Leuven Faculty of Architecture.

Illias Teirlinck is a Brussels-based documentary photographer who loves to escape pigeonholes. It would not be unusual for Illias to spend his day first making portraits at the public library, then switching to photographing stills for a theatre production, before finally, in the evening, observing demolition work with the same keen eye. A constant theme in his work is the authentic connection with the people he photographs – never staged, always with genuine interest. Whether up close or from a distance, his images convey an intimate proximity to his subjects.

Koen Van Caekenberghe was a permanent staff member of the communication and marketing departments of cultural institutions such as the Koninklijke Muntschouwburg (1993–2002), the Ghent Handelsbeurs (2002–05) and NTGent (2005–18). As a freelancer he is mainly active in the cultural sector as a copywriter/editor, also providing translations from French, English, German and Italian of cultural-historical, musicological and literary texts. He specializes in opera, music, theatre, dance, visual arts and architecture. In the field of architecture, he recently worked for CIVA (exhibitions on Simone Guillissen-Hoa, Jules Buyssens, Le Logis-Floréal, Superstudio Migrazioni, etc.), UCL/LOCI (*Institutions and the City*) and the Flanders Architecture Institute (*As Found*), among others.

Laura Vleugels studied psychology in Antwerp and photography at KASK, Ghent. The bridge between these two fields is the common thread running through her photographic work. She works mainly for magazines, combining this with her own documentary work. Her camera is like a pass that allows her to enter and get to know worlds that are otherwise unfamiliar to her. She always tries to remain aware of her role as a photographer in an environment. She also always sees the making of a personal portrait as a collaboration and interaction between the photographer and the person portrayed.

Flanders Architecture Institute at work

Who We Are and What We Do
The Flanders Architecture Institute (VAi) is the main centre for information about architecture from Flanders and Brussels. It creates a platform for everyone who wants to make, share and experience architecture.

What We Share
In 2024-26, the VAi will focus on shared spaces where people live and gather together. Architectural design and urban planning can enable and enrich social interaction between people and propose new forms of co-existence in the built environment involving both other people and other living beings. What we share are more than spaces, but also histories, cultures and everyday habits. With this theme, we aim to highlight the intricate tapestry of collective spaces, examining their impact on the social patterns, cultural narratives and natural landscapes of our communities.

© Dogma

The theme shapes the programme of the VAi in a range of formats, such as exhibitions, workshop series, publications and film screenings, and also in various perspectives, from collective housing to participatory design, urban nature to spaces of assembly. One of the first productions in this theme is *Dogma: Urban Villa*, an exhibition (4 October 2024-9 February 2025, De Singel) and book (co-published with Black Square). With this, Brussels-based architecture office Dogma explores the potential of the urban villa typology for contemporary collective living arrangements. At the same time, in the fall of 2024, the VAi will hold a series of workshops, titled 'Participation for Real', to develop a critical reflection on the participatory design processes that exist today in Flanders and Brussels, in collaboration with Timelab, Ghent. Over the years, the theme of *What We Share* will outline a first exhibition on the history of green spaces and daily urban living, and another on architecture's engagement in generating and enriching social interactions among diverse groups of people.

Public Mediation
Since 2024, the VAi has had a Public Mediation team. With this, we are building on experience gathered from earlier projects such as the Festival of architecture (F/a). We are committed to inclusion, a plurality of voices, and accessibility. How do we make sure everyone feels welcome? Who gets a voice and whose voice are we not hearing? As an organization, are we easy to find? Are we accessible and does everyone understand what we are saying? Over the next few years, we will explore new ways of thinking about architecture, dreaming about it, looking at it and working on it ourselves.

© Dries Luyten

In 2023, for instance, we launched Children's Island, an installation at DE SINGEL where children can discover architecture. For us, architecture is about space, people, materials and the memory of places. This vision takes different forms in our exhibitions. From school buildings to green spaces in the city and even an artist who walked and filmed more than two thousand kilometres. Our exhibitions are the perfect opportunity to talk to children about their surroundings. But where do you start? With books, quotes and questions, we help children and adults get going. A tailor-made visitor's guide accompanies them through the expo. On the Children's Island, they can sit and talk, draw and build. With the Children's Island, we encourage intergenerational contact in an accessible way.

Collection
The collection managed by the Flanders Architecture Institute is an invaluable resource for anyone interested in the history of architecture, urban planning and construction engineering in Flanders. The extensive collection of more than five thousand running metres contains some two hundred archives. More than 36,000 boxes full of plans, photos, correspondence and specifications texts as well as an extensive library of books and magazines from Belgium and abroad, drawers with treasures of colourful plans, a floor brimming with mock-ups, prototypes and models are carefully preserved in the archive house in Antwerp's Parochiaanstraat.

© Vlaams Architectuurinstituut

The VAi makes information accessible on all aspects of architecture and design practice, from urban planning policy and design visions to technical project details. The often invisible and time-consuming tasks of appraising and preserving this heritage collection are crucial for future generations. As a leading sector institute, the VAi combines public engagement with consistent collection management and provides expert and empathetic services to a broad field of relevant parties. This forward-thinking approach enables the VAi to transcend the traditional heritage framework and emphasize the enduring social significance of architecture in the past, present and future.

VAi Knowledge Centre
The VAi Knowledge Centre works around cultural heritage from chair to city. This includes the disciplines of architecture, urban planning, construction and design. As an organization with a national service-providing role, it supports designers, researchers, heritage professionals and other actors. We do this by centrally registering archives and collections, providing support and gathering knowledge through thematic projects.

© Dieter Daniëls

In 2023 the VAi launched the Archive Hub, a new research database with data on people, organizations and events. The Knowledge Centre subsequently also carried out a field analysis on cultural heritage from chair to city. This report gives an overview of the state of this heritage and maps out gaps and trends.

With Wiki Women Design (2021), we gave women designers and architects a place in history by means of Wikipedia pages. Countless resources have now been sustainably transformed into the Women* in Architecture and Design knowledge file. The year 2023 saw the launch of the pilot project around the legacy of graphic designer Lucien De Roeck. The Knowledge Centre provides support for the inventorying and digitizing of the archive. In the exhibition series *Unfolding the Archives* (UTA), contemporary themes on societal challenges are fed with archive material. The most recent UTA exhibition focused on Marcel Raeymakers, a pioneer in circular construction. In the fall of 2024, the Knowledge Centre will organize a three-part course on archive management for designers and companies. In the spring of 2025 we will publish the *Bronnengids Interieurontwerp in België, 1945-2000* (Source guide to interior design in Belgium, 1945-2000). This guide explores the sources essential for understanding the evolution of interior design as an independent discipline in Belgium and offers, for the first time, in-depth insights into the field.

International
The VAi is an active player in international networks like ICAM (International Confederation of Architectural Museums) and represents Flanders at prestigious events like the Venice Architecture Biennale. The VAi's exhibitions and publications are highly praised, both by the public and in the press, and draw international attention. The *As Found* exhibition, for instance, delved into the evolving relationship between contemporary design and heritage, showcasing experimental projects. In collaboration with the Delegation of Flanders (Embassy of Belgium) and the European Parliament Liaison Office in the United Kingdom, the VAi presented eight innovative projects by Flemish and Brussels architects at 12 Star Gallery in London in the spring of 2024. This exhibition helped to put architectural reuse projects on the international agenda.

Complementing the *As Found* exhibition, the VAi organized a panel discussion titled 'Carbon Heritage', focusing on the environmental impact of architecture. This event featured architects from Flanders and the UK who discussed reuse principles and heritage conservation strategies with a view to inspire policymakers to implement strategies to reduce carbon emissions.

The VAi's international engagement also extends to academic research. With participating practices in the *As Found* exhibition, the VAi organized, in collaboration with TU Wien, a round-table discussion in March 2024. Moreover, the VAi was part of 'Communities of Tacit Knowledge: Architecture and its Ways of Knowing', a Marie Skłodowska-Curie Actions initiative under the European Union Framework Programme 'Horizon 2020'. This innovative training network involved thirteen international partner organizations and trained young researchers to understand the specific knowledge architects apply in designing buildings and cities. The VAi continues to play a leading role in the international debate on architecture museums, as demonstrated by its participation in the ICAM conference in Hong Kong in December 2024.

© Dieter Daniëls

This engagement also contributes to making the VAi a stage for international debate in Flanders. The institute frequently hosts renowned international guests for lectures, such as Anne Lacaton (Lacaton & Vassal, Paris), Matthew Gandy (University of Cambridge), Emily Wickham (Assemble, London) and Lydia Kallipoliti (Cooper Union, New York), further solidifying its commitment to advancing architectural discourse globally.

Looking ahead, the 19th Venice Architecture Biennale in May 2025 will feature the *Building Biospheres* exhibition at the Belgian Pavilion, curated by Bas Smets, Valerie Trouet and Stefano Mancuso. This project envisions buildings as artificial microclimates where plants play a crucial role in air purification and cooling, with a view to creating more liveable and sustainable urban environments.

Publications
With its publications, the Flanders Architecture Institute seeks to foster and stimulate social debate on what architecture is and can be, including through its role as publisher. Next to the biennial *Flanders Architectural Review*, the VAi produces books accompanying exhibitions, research, architectural oeuvres and topical themes. Recent publications include the volumes *Living in Monnikenheide: Care, Inclusion and Architecture* (Gideon Boie, ed.), *Malgorzata Maria Olchowska: Waiting Rooms of Architecture and As Found: Experiments in Preservation* (Sofie De Caigny, Hülya Ertas and Bie Plevoets, eds.). Upcoming titles include *ENDEAVOUR: Making Space Together* (2025), *FELT: Scenography as an Architectural Commission* (2025) and the catalogue accompanying the Flemish submission for the Venice Architecture Biennale 2025.

Royale Belge, Brussels – Bovenbouw Architectuur, Caruso St John Architects and DDS+
© Stijn Bollaert

Building with Concrete

FEBELCEM, the Belgian Cement Association
- documentation and in-house publications
- communication and events
- technical assistance

FEBELCEM

Kunstlaan 20 – 1000 Brussels | www.febelcem.be | info@febelcem.be | +32 (0)2 645 52 11

JEWELLERY FOR WALLS

Niko Rocker and Niko Toggle
Belgian flair and craftsmanship

niko.eu/rockertoggle

niko

Meaningful
Design to Inspire
People's Lives

COSENTINO

COSENTINO CITY ANTWERPEN
Kloosterstraat 96
2000 Antwerpen, Belgium
+32 2 789 70 05

silestone   silestone XM   DEKTON   SENSA

Terrazzo   since
Natural   *1923*
Ceramics

ZNA CADIX
Robbrecht & Daem Architecten
XXL_1329 Verde Alpi

STONE Olsene
Grote Steenweg 13, 9870 Olsene
T. +32 (0)9 388 91 11
info@stone.be

www.stone.be

STONE

Wasserstrich Special, characterful elegance

BK ARCHITECTEN, OUDENAARDE - PHOTOGRAPHER LAURENT BRANDAJS

360ARCHITECTEN, GENT

The slim Waterstruck Special exudes rough elegance. The weathered, slightly abraded look gives your façade extra character. The Waterstruck Special is longer than the average facing brick. This enables you to create horizontal lines in your architecture. These bricks are also available in the Eco-brick format that leaves more room for insulation or creates more living space.

Eco-brick
- ☑ Narrow facing bricks
- ☑ More room for insulation
- ☑ Sustainable choice

Discover the Waterstruck Special collection in our 'World of Façades' brochure, via **www.wienerberger-world.com**.

Wienerberger

Bulo
Timeless design since 1963

CELEBRATING 30 YEARS OF H2O

BULO.COM

Gyproc® & Isover® launch their second Purpose Report

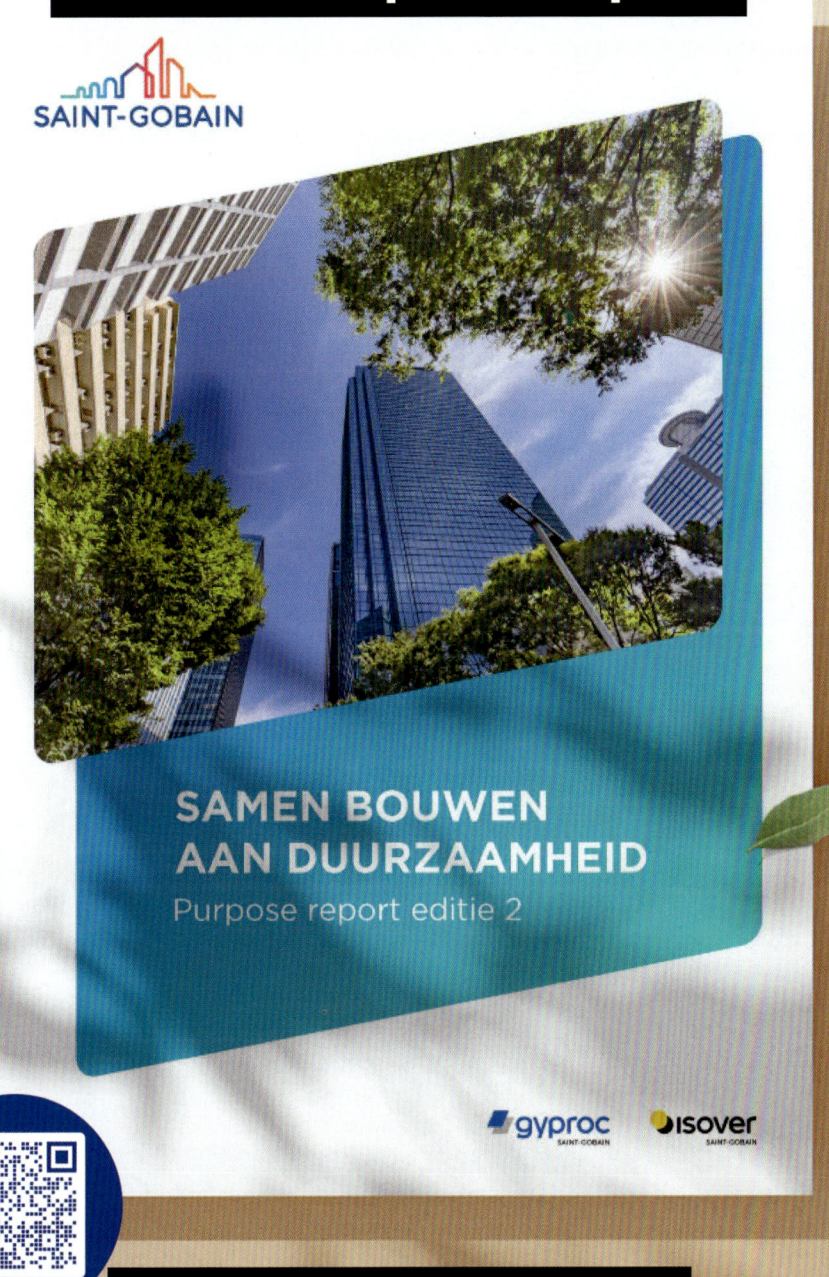

SAMEN BOUWEN AAN DUURZAAMHEID

Purpose report editie 2

Scan the QR-code or go to: isover.gyproc.be/purpose-report/2023

Collaborating in enduring beauty

True beauty is something you'd rather not let go of. That is why your projects are not only about aesthetics, but also about sustainability. This way your customers can enjoy your realisations for a lifetime. Together with Reynaers Aluminium you can give your project that timeless touch. Our high-quality aluminium solutions will inspire you in countless ways and will effortlessly stand the test of time. So your creations will provide long-lasting living pleasure.

Get inspired by our realisations.
Get your free reference book projects at
www.reynaers.be/gratis-inspiratieboek-projecten

R Reynaers Aluminium

Windows | Doors | Curtain Walls

A+ Architecture in Belgium reviews and curates to amaze, inspire, confuse, surprise, reflect, and fascinate.

Magazines 2024

- A+306 **Building for Culture**
- A+307 **Mixing & Stacking**
- A+308 **Textile & Texture**
- A+309 **Identity & Iconism**
- A+310 **Material Flows**
  guest edited by Rotor

Subscribe or Buy

A+ Issue
€ 25 paper / € 15 digital

A+ Classic
€ 99 5 paper issues

A+ Student
€ 59 5 paper issues

More options and details: a-plus.be or abonnement@a-plus.be

INDEX

&bogdan
Bijgaardehof co-housing, Ghent p. 244, 249

&bogdan and DDS+
NovaCity I group housing and SME zone, Anderlecht p. 244, 265, 284

51N4E with l'AUC and Jaspers-Eyers
ZIN, Brussels p. 280

ae architecten
Robust housing, Ghent p. 201

AIDarchitecten
't Getouw co-housing, Malle p. 240

Architecten De Bruyn
Corner building on Peperstraat, Aalst p. 64

AjdvivgwA: TV architecten jan de vylder inge vinck - AgwA
Chapex, Charleroi p. 277

ATAMA
Deelfabriek, Kortrijk p. 9, 28

Atelier Kempe Thill i.s.m. aNNo (architect-concept designer), Baro Architectuur with SumProject (architect)
Winter Circus, Ghent p. 121

B-ILD
Dagpauwoog kindergarten and primary school, Koninkshooikt p. 197

Bovenbouw Architectuur and Caruso St John Architects with DDS+
Royale Belge, Watermaal-Bosvoorde p. 281, 297

Bruno Spaas Architectuur
Anapneusis community house p. 29, 45

BULK Architecten
Social housing Eric Sasse, Antwerp p. 241

Büro Juliane Greb, Summacumfemmer and ARCH+
Open for Maintenance - German pavilion, Architecture Biennale 2023, Venice p. 136

Carton123 architecten, atelier Starzak Strebicki and Natural Born Architects
Begijnenborre kindergarten and playground, Dilbeek p. 205

De Gouden Liniaal Architecten
De Helix school campus, Maasmechelen p. 189

De Smet Vermeulen architecten
Repurposing of the Sacred Heart Church, Ghent p. 101, 169
Repurposing of the Cordonnier factory, Wetteren p. 96

Dierendonckblancke architecten
Jongensschool group housing, Lievegem p. 173, 181, 240
Lange Beeldekensstraat group housing, Antwerp p. 201, 236

DMOA architecten
St Anne's Chapel redevelopment, Dentergem p. 68

DMOA architecten, Maggie Program vzw
Maggie goes to Leuven, Leuven p. 69

ectv architecten Els Claessens Tania Vandenbussche
Jean co-housing, Ghent p. 237, 257

FELT architecture & design
Household practice, Ghent p. 64

fijn architectuur atelier
De Plas swimming pavilion, Rotselaar p. 109

Happel Cornelisse Verhoeven with Molenaar & Co architecten
Fierenshoven group housing, Antwerp p. 241

Havana architectuur
Veldegem service centre, Zedelgem p. 200, 225, 240

import.export Architecture
Klavertjevier primary school (Balschool), Antwerp p. 112
Renovation of a retail space on Koxplein, Antwerp p. 65

Laura Muyldermans, LDSRa and Olivier Goethals
Bouwaanvraag (Building application) p. 308

Lietje Bauwens and Wouter De Raeve
WTC A Love Story (2020) p. 305

MADE architects and Karuur Architecten
Erasmus primary school, Zelzate p. 153

murmuur architecten
De Ringelwikke primary school, Ronse p. 17, 32

murmuur architecten with Mattias Deboutte
Verwerft carpentry workshop, Herentals p. 81

murmuur architecten, Robbrecht en Daem architecten and Callebaut Architecten
City shop and archives, Sint-Niklaas p. 289

NERO
Letters & Co bookshop and group housing, Deinze p. 61

NU architectuuratelier with Archipelago
Botanic Garden greenhouses, Meise p. 92

OFFICE Kersten Geers David Van Severen
Brussels Beer Project Brewery, Anderlecht p. 73

ono architectuur with Philip Aguirre y Otegui, Ludovic Devriendt and Universal Design Studio
M127 office building with public plinth, Antwerp p. 32, 53

Ouest Architecture, Rotor and Zinneke
Zinneke, Brussels p. 161, 176

Poot Architectuur
Groenhout secondary school, Antwerp p. 113

Raamwerk
Duinhelm residential care centre, Ostend p. 217

Studio Paola Viganò and vvv architecture urbanisme
Marie Jansonplein, Sint-Gillis p. 112

URA Yves Malysse Kiki Verbeeck
De Telescoop kindergarten and primary school, Laken p. 200, 209

urbain architectencollectief
Church of St Cornelius and community centre, Aalbeke p. 25, 37, 197